JAVA
2D API | Graphics

SUN MICROSYSTEMS PRESS
A PRENTICE HALL TITLE

VINCENT J. HARDY

Two of the lighting filters in the Lights example on page 493 use the Caviar gray scale texture included on the Photoshop 4.0 CD-ROM. It is used with permission from Adobe.

Portions of this book were included in articles by the author and were published in 1999 in *Java Report*, a SIGS publication.

The publisher offers discounts on this book when ordered in bulk quantities.
For more information, contact: Corporate Sales Department, Phone: 800-382-3419;
Fax: 201-236-7141; E-mail: corpsales@prenhall.com; or write: Prentice Hall PTR,
Corp. Sales Dept., One Lake Street, Upper Saddle River, NJ 07458.

Editorial/production supervision: *Patti Guerrieri*
Acquisitions editor: *Gregory G. Doench*
Editorial assistant: *Mary Treacy*
Manufacturing manager: *Alexis R. Heydt*
Cover design director: *Jerry Votta*
Cover designer: *Anthony Gemmellaro*
Cover illustration: *Bruno Mallart*
Marketing manager: *Bryan Gambrel*
Interior designer: *Gail Cocker-Bogusz*
Sun Microsystems Press:
Marketing manager: *Michael Llwyd Alread*
Publisher: *Rachel Borden*

10 9 8 7 6 5 4 3 2

ISBN 0-13-014266-2

Sun Microsystems Press
A Prentice Hall Title

A mon épouse, Anne

CONTENTS

LIST OF FIGURES

ACKNOWLEDGMENTS

Writing a book is a long journey and an author does not make this journey alone. Rather, many people make this journey possible in many different and critical ways. I want to acknowledge the individuals and companies who have been involved in the creation of this book.

Putting the Book Together

Rachel Borden and Michael Alread of Sun Microsystems Press, with Greg Doench, Patti Guerrieri, Gail Cocker-Bogusz and Mary Treacy of Prentice Hall, have made special efforts for this book. While part of the Java Series, this book has a unique design created to fit the content matter. Furthermore, as the first color book in the series, it has required a lot of additional work from the whole team: thank you for taking all the extra steps to complete this book!

No matter how hard you try, inaccuracies, typos, and unclear content always creep into what you write. This is why reviewers are so key to the creation of a book: they provide constructive comments, point out problems of all kinds, and help make the book better. I am in debt to all the technical reviewers: Kevin Bourgault of Corel, Paul Byrne of Sun Microsystems, Heloise Doucet of Corel, Cameron Gregory of olabs.com, Arnaud Guerrand of Nortel Networks, Justin Hill of Eaton Corporation, Howard Katz of Fatdog Software, Raoul Mallart of Philips, Paula Patel of Sun Microsystems, and Peter Sanders of the ESSI university in Nice, France.

In addition to the technical review, Mary Lou Nohr, the book's editor, has done an incredibly thorough review of the manuscript and made this book more enjoyable to read.

This book is the result of a long-lasting effort, and I thank my director at Sun Microsystems, Raj Dosaj. I want to extend special thanks to Jan Russak, my manager, for supporting my work with enthusiasm, for providing expert and encouraging comments, and reviewing early drafts of this book.

Working with the Java 2D API has always been enjoyable, and my recognition goes to the Java 2D team for crafting such a beautiful design. I also want to thank the team members for finding time to answer my questions and reviewing the parts of this book corresponding to their respective areas of expertise.

The Graphic Layers Framework software (GLF, created for the purpose of this book) has been available on Sun Microsystem's web site since June of 1999 (http://java.sun.com), thanks to the efforts of Jerry Evans from the Java 2D team and Michael Bundschuh of Sun Microsystems. The web site has allowed GLF to be reviewed by many programmers before this book became available, and I want thank all those who have emailed me their comments.

The CMYK color profile used in the first part and included on the CD-ROM was kindly provided by Dawn Wallner from the Java Advanced Imaging team at Sun Microsystems.

Many of my colleagues kindly offered comments and reviewed numerous drafts of different chapters. My gratitude goes to Brian Brown's team at Sun Microsystems: Jean-Christophe Collet, Gary Ellison, Stepan Sokolov, and Thierry Violleau.

This book's cover was created by an illustrator, Bruno Mallart, whom I thank for the beautiful work he has done and for working within our constraining requirements. The cover illustrates the different features of the Java 2D API and has the colorful joy that reflects the fun that working with the API brings!

The software that comes with this book was double-checked by the reviewers but also by Ari Shapiro, who ran a final check on the software provided on the CD-ROM.

Finally, I want to thank my family for their loving support, understanding, and patience.

Credits

The different examples in this book use various images and fonts. Several companies have allowed us to use these images and fonts in the book and include them on the CD-ROM that comes with this book. Thanks to them, you can run all the book examples and get the same results as shown in this book.

Images and fonts are critical to make graphical compositions appealing. Following are the names of the companies that have provided those critical resources and corresponding ordering information.

Backgrounds

Most of the background images used in this book come from the Syberia Volume 1 CD-ROM. The CD-ROM can be ordered at 800-992-0607.

Object Images

Images of objects (such as telephones or microphones) come from the Classic PIO Partners CD-ROMs (http://www.classicpartners.com). You can order them at: Classic PIO Partners, 87 E. Green St. Suite 309, Pasadena, CA 91105, Tel: 818-564-8106.

Paintings

The image that is used repeatedly throughout the first part is the Van Gogh self-portrait, used by permission of Wood River Gallery. The gallery in the last chapter of Part III also uses images from the "Da Vinci & the Italian Renaissance" CD-ROM. You can order those CD-ROMs through EyeWire at: http://www.eyewire.com or from Wood River directly at: Wood River Gallery, 1099 D Street, Penthouse A, San Rafael, CA 94901-2843, Tel: 1-415-256-9300.

Fonts

Using legible fonts makes any product or art work look more professional. A clean, readable font on screen will ensure that your message is understood and remembered by the reader.

Besides the fonts that are part of the Java 2™ platform, this book uses fancier and more elaborate fonts in the various examples. Those fonts are included on the accompanying CD and are provided by Monotype Typography. Monotype specializes in producing highly legible fonts and multilingual font solutions for developers.

You can order fonts from Monotype Typography at: http://www.monotype.com.

PREFACE

The Java 2D API provides the underlying support for graphics in the Java platform (see Figure P.1). Other APIs that need graphic support, such as the Abstract Window Toolkit (AWT) or Swing, rely on the Java 2D API for all drawing operations.

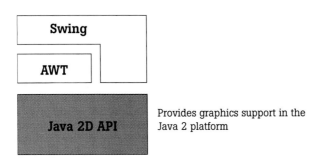

Provides graphics support in the Java 2 platform

Figure P.1 ■
The Java 2D API in the Java platform

The Java 2D API became available to programmers in its beta form during the second half of 1997 when the first early-access releases of the Java 2 platform (JDK 1.2) became available. The specification had been out for some time before that, and I (although not working at Sun at the time), along with many, had great expectations. Why?

The Java 2D API: An Amazing Addition to the Java Platform

If you had a look at the specification back then, you soon realized that Java graphics were about to change dramatically. The announced feature set was impressive:

■ Transparency support
■ Generalized geometry support
■ Output device resolution independence

- Improved font support
- Sophisticated fills such as gradient fills
- New, simplified, and powerful imaging model
- and a lot more

Expectations ran high, and when the API finally became available, many programmers started using all these promising features. Anybody who went through this experience soon noticed a number of key points about the Java 2D API.

1. *The Java 2D API is a sophisticated API.* It is easy to program, but it is not simple. Similar to Swing in that regard, the Java 2D API has an extremely powerful and extensible design, but it is not simple. It is important to understand this design well. Then, the API becomes easy to program.
2. *The Java 2D API is a rich, generic, and low-level API.* The API covers a broad portion of computer graphics (but not 3D graphics), and it is designed to serve all kinds of graphics needs. As a consequence, it is feature rich and has a generalized model that fits the largest possible range of requirements: it is generic and low level.

Purpose of This Book

The Java 2D API delivers a wealth of features, but it may not be obvious how they can or should be used. Actually, it depends on the type of application; the way features are used or the reason for which they are used depends on whether you are, for example, writing a satellite image processing program or a web animation.

This book looks at how the Java 2D API features can be used, combined, and extended.

When we say the API is feature rich, we really mean that there has been a huge feature improvement from earlier versions of the JDK. To use a musical analogy, earlier versions of the Java platform provided a flute. The Java 2D API gives us an orchestra. With a flute, a music score is useful to play the proper sounds. This is even more true for a symphonic orchestra: guidance is needed to have all the instruments and musicians play in harmony and produce a pleasing result. The goal of this book is to provide guidance so that programmers can write beautiful partitions with the Java 2D API.

For example, the images in Table P.1 are completely created with the Java 2D API and the Graphic Layers Framework (GLF) provided in this book. These examples show the type of visual output the Java 2D API can create; this book explains how to obtain this type of result and provides all the related software.

Table P.1 ■ Example Rendering Effects; Examples from Part III

Book Structure

We said this book explains how to use, combine, and extend the Java 2D API features. The book structure reflects this purpose; it has three parts.

Part I contains a detailed overview of the Java 2D API. It starts with an introduction to the API rendering model (Chapter 1) and a summary of its features (Chapter 2). Chapters 3, 4, and 5 study the different parts of the API in greater detail.

Part II introduces the Graphic Layers Framework (GLF) that builds on the Java 2D API and provides a higher-level programming model to create and compose rendering effects. I developed the Graphic Layers Framework for this book: it provides an advanced example of how the Java 2D API can be used and extended.

GLF contains the following:

1. A layer framework that allows programmers to create visual compositions by stacking up simple layers and specifying how each layer should combine with the other ones.
2. A set of extensions to the Java 2D API. GLF offers custom types of fills, brushes, filters, and more that build on the Java 2D API's extensible design.
3. A set of tools and utilities. They help configure, save, and restore graphical compositions in the form of Java beans. The tools make it easier to deal with the large and sometimes overwhelming number of parameters the API contains. These tools let us change parameters dynamically and view the effect of the change.

The different GLF packages are the foundation for the rendering effects in Part III. That part is about combining features; it demonstrates how sophisticated the graphics support of the Java platform now is. This part shows how to create effects such as shadowing, lighting, and carving. The final chapter of Part III contains a gallery of images that further illustrates the sophistication of the Java 2D API and shows GLF at work.

How to Read This Book

This book can be read in different ways. It can be read linearly, from start to end. This is the recommended way if you are not familiar with the Java 2D API or with computer graphics. This approach will give you an in-depth understanding of the Java 2D API and how this book uses it to create rendering effects.

However, you might decide that you are not interested in the inner workings of the Java 2D API or of the Graphic Layers Framework. In that case, you can start with Part II directly; Chapters 6 and 8 provide enough information about GLF to enable you to use it with no need to understand its implementation or the underlying Java 2D concepts. You will learn how to use the GLF capabilities to create rendering effects. The "Hello Layers" example (Chapter 6) can get you started with GLF quickly. You can then proceed to Part III and start experimenting with advanced rendering effects. If you choose that route, you will likely need to refer back to Parts I and II, where you will find explanations for issues that might seem obscure.

No matter how you read this book, you will find that it contains many code samples (there are about ninety examples, in addition to the Graphic Layers Framework itself). We usually chose to first show the code and then to explain it. This approach gives you a chance to read the code in its entirety first and then to read explanations. So, don't be discouraged if some point seems difficult while you are reading the code: it usually is the point that the following explanation details.

Notational Conventions

Code segments

The following font style is used for code segments and to refer to class names or variables:

```
Graphics2D g; // g provides access to the Java 2D API features.
```

Note that some concepts, such as fonts or images, are sometimes used with the code font, sometimes not, depending on whether we refer to a class name or to the more general underlying concept. For example, Font refers to the java.awt.Font class and "font" refers to the typographic concept.

Coding conventions

Table P.2 shows the conventions we use in this book.

Table P.2 ■ Coding Conventions

CONVENTION	EXAMPLE
Class names start with an uppercase letter. Each word in the name also starts with an uppercase letter.	`public class LayerComposition`
Class member variable names start with a lowercase letter. Each word in the name starts with an uppercase letter.	`private Layer[] layers;` `private Color backgroundColor;`
Class method names start with a lowercase letter. Each word in the name starts with an uppercase letter.	`public Layer[] getLayers()` `public Color getBackgroundColor()`
Constants (static final variables) are all upper case; each word is separated by an underscore	`static final int ANCHOR_BOTTOM`

Installing the Book Software

The CD-ROM that comes with this book contains two files:

- readme.txt
- glfall.jar

Please refer to the readme file for instructions on how to install the Graphic Layers Framework and the book code examples on your computer.

Running the Code Samples

Throughout the book, you will see code examples and references to the source code on the CD-ROM. For example, on page 238, you can see that the code example is **AnchorPlacementTransform.java**. We use the name of the corresponding class to refer to the example name, for example, `AnchorPlacement-Transform`.

There are two ways to run the examples provided in this book.[1] One way is to use a tool with a user interface. The other one is to use a script. The former lets you browse through the book's examples. The latter lets you run a specific code example directly.

Using demorunner

At the command prompt, type:

```
cd <installDir>
demorunner
```

---

1. In the following, we use the notation `<installDir>` to refer to the directory where you have installed the Graphic Layers Framework software.

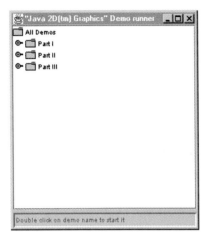

Figure P.2 ■
demorunner startup window

This last commands summons a window, as shown in Figure P.2. The window contains folders for each part of the book. Each folder can be expanded into the different chapter folders, and each chapter folder can in turn be expanded to show its code samples, as illustrated in Figure P.3.

Double-click on an example name to start it. The status bar, at the bottom of the window, shows a message reading *Starting <ExampleName> in separate VM. Please wait.* For example, in Figure P.4, we double-clicked on the Anchor-PlacementTransform example. The example starts after a couple of seconds.[1]

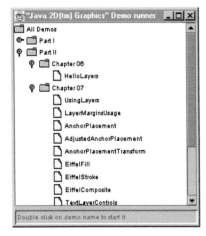

Figure P.3 ■
Expanding demorunner's code example tree

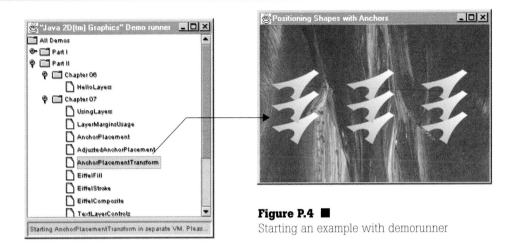

Figure P.4 ■
Starting an example with demorunner

Using the runsnippet script

An alternate way to run a specific example directly is to use the runsnippet script. At the command line, type the following:

```
cd <installDir>
runsnippet <exampleName>
```

For example:

```
runsnippet AnchorPlacementTransform
```

---

1. The example may take several seconds to start because it runs in a separate Java virtual machine. The time it takes to start the demo depends on the code example you run, the operating system you are using, and the type of hardware you have.

JAVA 2D API OVERVIEW

1

THE JAVA 2D API RENDERING MODEL

This first part introduces the Java 2D API and provides an in-depth tour of the Java 2D API by focusing on its design. This part's chapters explain how classes interoperate and support various features, from advanced text support, to transparency, to image filtering, and more.

Readers not familiar with the Java 2D API can read this part linearly; others can use it as a reference. Part I supports both Parts II and III of this book: the 2D API provides the foundation for the Graphic Layers Framework (GLF), which builds both on the API features and its extensibility. At times, you might want to refer back to this part to clarify how an underlying feature of GLF actually works.

The Java 2D API brings a new set of features, and the book introduction discussed how it enhances the core Java graphics and is central to all kinds of graphics, from standard AWT components to Swing. This central role played by the API is built around a simple rendering model that has extended that of earlier versions of the Java platform.

The Java 2D API Rendering Model

Rendering is a name used to describe the process of drawing graphics on an output device such as a screen or a printer. The Java 2D API allows the developer to do advanced graphics rendering. At the center of the API is the `java.awt.Graphics2D` class. This class is the interface between the program and the output device where rendering operations (such as filling a rectangle with a given color or drawing a string of characters) are carried out. Earlier versions of the Java platform used the `java.awt.Graphics` class. The new `Graphics2D` class extends the `Graphics` class and provides

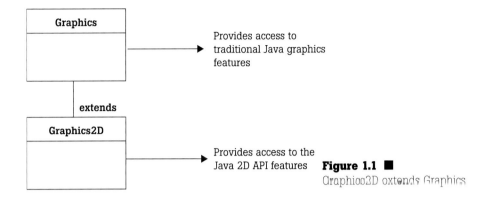

Figure 1.1 ■

Graphics2D extends Graphics

access to the additional features Java 2D brings. Because `Graphics2D` implements all the features of the `Graphics` class and more, Java 2 (the version of the Java platform where Java 2D first appeared) is backward compatible with code written for earlier versions of the Java platform. In the remainder of this book, we refer to `Graphics2D` methods that implicitly include methods of the `Graphics` class that `Graphics2D` inherits. Figure 1.1 illustrates the relation between the `Graphics2D` class and the `Graphics` class.

Let us see how a program uses the Java 2D API rendering model.

Before rendering to an output device, the program acquires a corresponding `Graphics2D` object. The API defines how to get a `Graphics2D` object for different kinds of output devices (see Figure 1.2).

Once a `Graphics2D` object is obtained, rendering can occur. The first step consists in setting the attributes that control the `Graphics2D` rendering operation. Collectively, those attributes, such as the `Font` attribute used for drawing text, are referred to as the ***graphic context***. This first step, referred to as step A, is shown in Figure 1.3. Subsequent rendering operations use the attribute values in the rendering context at the time they are invoked. The different graphic context attributes are explained later.

Once the context is set up as desired, the second step is to select the graphic object to render. The API can render three kinds of objects: geometrical forms (defined by a `java.awt.Shape` implementation, equivalent to line art), text, and images. This second step, referred to as step B, is shown in Figure 1.4.

The last step in the rendering model is to invoke a specific rendering operation on the selected graphic object. Figure 1.5 shows an example where the `Graphics2D` object is requested to render a string of character for this last step, step C. `Graphics2D.drawString` is the rendering method. The text string is the graphic object that will be rendered and the different settings for the graphic context determine how the string will look on the output: the `Font` attribute

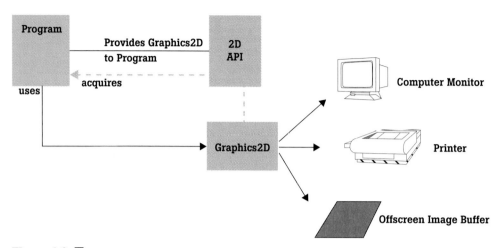

Figure 1.2 ■
Accessing a Graphics2D object

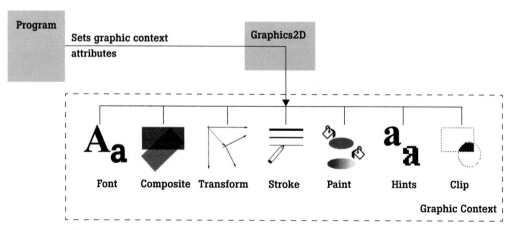

Figure 1.3 ■
Rendering Model. Step A: Setting the graphic context attributes

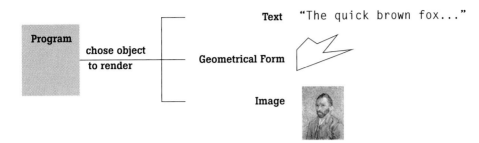

Figure 1.4 ■
Rendering Model. Step B: Selecting a graphic object to render

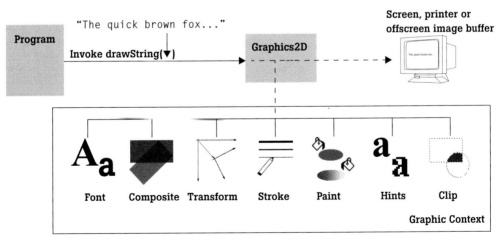

Figure 1.5 ■
Rendering Model. Step C: Invoking a rendering operation (e.g., drawString)

defines the style of the individual characters, the `Paint` attribute defines the color of the pixels used to draw the string, the `Composite` attribute defines how the drawn string blends with the background, and so forth.

Except for the method used to acquire a `Graphics2D` object for a specific type of output device, the API provides a device-independent rendering framework. `Graphics2D` has the same operation mode regardless of the type of device it renders to and is illustrated in Table 1.1 on page 7. The rendering steps are always the same:

1. Set the rendering context:
   ```
   // Black will be used to render text and Shapes
   g.setPaint(Color.black);

   // The "Curlz MT" font will be used to render text
   g.setFont(new Font("Curlz MT", Font.PLAIN, 60));

   // A special technique will be used, if available,
   // to render text and Shapes so that they appear smoother.
   g.setRenderingHint(RenderingHints.KEY_ANTIALIASING,
                       RenderingHints.VALUE_ANTIALIAS_ON);
   ```
   This is step A illustrated in Figure 1.3.

2. Select the object to render. In our example, we simply render a `String` of text:
   ```
   String text = "Hello Rendering Model";
   ```
   This is step B illustrated in Figure 1.4.

3. Invoke a rendering method, here `drawString`, on the `Graphics2D` object:
   ```
   g.drawString(text, 40, 80);
   ```

This completes our first example of the Java 2D API. It demonstrated the rendering model the API works with. This model is called the **immediate mode rendering model** because rendering happens immediately as rendering methods are invoked. We have also illustrated a few of the API characteristics:

- Enhanced font support. We used a platform-specific font (but loaded in a platform-independent way). Earlier versions of Java graphics were limited to only six so-called **logical** fonts (still supported for backward compatibility).
- Rendering quality control. The antialiasing hint allowed us to control the rendering quality. Earlier versions allowed no control over the API rendering process.

Table 1.1 ■ Hello Rendering Model

HELLORENDERINGMODEL.JAVA

Output

```
private void render(Graphics2D g){
    // Step A:
    // Prepare rendering context

    // Black will be used to
    // render text and Shapes
    g.setPaint(Color.black);

    // The "Curlz MT" Font will be used to render text
    g.setFont(new Font("Curlz MT", Font.PLAIN, 60));

    // A special technique will be used to render text and Shapes to
    // make them appear smoother.
    g.setRenderingHint(RenderingHints.KEY_ANTIALIASING,
                       RenderingHints.VALUE_ANTIALIAS_ON);

    // Step B: Prepare graphic object to render

    // Select graphic object to render: a string of character.
    String text = "Hello Rendering Model";

    // Step C: Invoke rendering method.
    g.drawString(text, 40, 80);
}
```

There are more features in the Java 2D API than these two. The following sections examine each one.

The Java 2D API Features

The Java 2D API is feature rich. There are over twice as many classes in the Java 2 `java.awt` package and child packages (for example, `java.awt.font`, `java.awt.image`) than there were in earlier versions of the Java platform. All these classes support new features that are best categorized around the rendering model we just presented:

- Output device independence
- Renderable graphic objects
- Graphic context attributes

Output device independence

The `Graphics2D` class provides device and output resolution independence. This means that a program can render to a screen with the same drawing primitives it uses to render to a printer or an offscreen buffer, regardless of their resolution.[1]

Renderable graphic objects

A `Graphics2D` object can render three types of objects: geometrical forms (described by `java.awt.Shape` implementations, as we will see), text, and images. Each object type provides many capabilities. The API now allows any 2D form to be rendered. Text support has been brought to a new level with extended internationalization features, built-in instrumentation for text editing, and complex text layout. Finally, a new imaging model, built around the `java.awt.image.BufferedImage` class, offers a more immediate and flexible imaging solution.

---

1. An output device's resolution is defined by its spatial resolution (i.e., the number of controllable discrete elements per inch) and by the color resolution each element can represent (e.g., some screens have pixels that can display over 16 million colors, but a laser printer dot can only represent 2 colors: black or white). Devices with low color resolutions, such as printers, usually use a technique called dithering, which uses an aggregation of pixels to simulate a higher color resolution, at the cost of the spatial resolution.

Graphic context attributes

We illustrated that there are seven attributes in the graphic context (see Figure 1.3 on page 4). Together, they control the rendering process, and each one of them characterizes a new feature or set of features in the API.

- **Font**. The API now supports several font formats, and more fonts can be used (as in our example). This book makes extensive use of that feature.
- **Paint**. In earlier versions of the Java platform, the rendering of geometrical forms was limited to drawing or filling them with a solid color (using the java.awt.Color rendering context attribute). Now, the more flexible Paint interface allows different kinds of pixel patterns to be used to fill geometrical forms and text. While Color still provides a way to fill shapes with a solid pixel pattern (that is, pixels of the same color), new implementations such as java.awt.GradientPaint and java.awt.TexturePaint offer more sophisticated alternatives.
- **Stroke**. In earlier versions of the Java platform, drawing a geometrical form was limited to a one-pixel-wide solid outline. The new java.awt.Stroke interface enables any kind of **pen** to be used to draw a Shape's outline, and the java.awt.BasicStroke implementation provides for pens of different width and also supports dash patterns.
- **Compositing**. The java.awt.Composite interface controls how to blend the source (for example, an image) with the destination (for example, the screen pixels) in all rendering operations (for example, Graphics2D.draw-Image). The java.awt.AlphaComposite implementation provides transparency composition (for example, you can draw an image so that it looks translucent).
- **Rendering Hints**. As we saw in our example, java.awt.RenderingHints can be used to influence the rendering process. Other hints allow programmers to specify their quality/speed trade-off preferences.
- **Clipping**. The clip area defines the limits wherein rendering operations have an effect. This feature has been extended so that any geometrical form (defined by a Shape object) can now be used as a clipping area.
- **Transform**. The java.awt.geom.AffineTransform class provides a generic way to transform coordinates from one coordinate system (or space) to another coordinate system. Transforms are used for many different purposes in the API and allow, for example, Shape objects to be rotated, sheared, or scaled.

Chapter 2 illustrates each of these features and provides a first-level overview of what the Java 2D API is about. Subsequent chapters provide a more in-depth introduction to each specific topic. Table 1.2 summarizes the content and purpose of each chapter.

Table 1.2 ■ Part I chapter contents and purpose

CHAPTER	PURPOSE	CONTENT
Chapter 2	Overview of the Java 2D API features	Provides short examples and illustrations of device-independent Graphics2D manipulation, graphic context attributes, text, Shape, and BufferedImage.
Chapter 3	Detail device-independent rendering capability.	Illustrates how to acquire a Graphics2D object to render to the screen, printer, or offscreen image. Discusses how resolution independence is achieved.
Chapter 4	Detail each type of graphic object: Shape, text, and BufferedImage.	Explains how and where the API uses each type of graphic object.
Chapter 5	Detail each of the rendering context attributes.	Explains where and how each of the rendering context attributes is used and outlines its influence on the rendering process.

Before we move on to the Java 2D API overview, note that one of the strengths of the API is its extensibility. Almost every single feature can be extended because the API is built around interfaces. For example, the graphic context attribute controlling the actual pixel pattern used to render shapes or text is defined by an interface, `java.awt.Paint`, which makes it possible to create additional `Paint` implementations and use them with the API. The API follows an important design principle, the ***Open-Closed*** principle: it is open to extensions because it allows new features to be added through the use of interfaces. However, to be available, those extensions do not require the Java 2D code to be modified: the API is closed to changes.

This principle is very powerful and we illustrate it at length in the second and third parts of this book.

2

JAVA 2D API OVERVIEW

This chapter presents an overview of the different parts of the API. It goes one level deeper than our introduction of the rendering model. The overview is followed by chapters that focus on a single part of the API. We recommend that you read the overview first, especially if you are not familiar with computer graphics concepts.

We explained in our introduction that the Java 2D rendering model consists of:

1. Acquiring a `Graphics2D` object for the desired output device, such as a screen or a printer
2. Selecting a graphic object to render (that is, text, a `Shape`, or an `Image`) and invoking one of the `Graphics2D` rendering methods to draw the object to the output
3. Setting the `Graphics2D` context attributes that control the rendering process, such as the `Paint` or the `Composite` (those are explained later)

This chapter expands on each of these tasks in greater detail.

Acquiring a Graphics2D Object

Rendering can happen on different kinds of output. They are:

- Screen. The result of rendering operations appears on a screen. For example, AWT (`java.awt`) and Swing (`javax.swing`) components have a `paint` method that the framework invokes. This method takes a `Graphics` object as an input parameter. That object provides an interface to render to the screen.
- Printer. The result of rendering operations appears on a printer. Objects that support printing implement the `java.print.Printable` interface, which is used by a

`java.print.PrinterJob` object. The `paint` method in the `java.print.Printable` interface takes a `Graphics` object as its input parameter.

■ Offscreen buffer. The result of rendering operations appears in an offscreen buffer, that is, in a set of pixel values, kept in memory, which may not have any visual representation. Creating a `Graphics` object from an image is simple: the `Image` class contains a `getGraphics` method that returns a `Graphics` object. This `Graphics` object can then be used to paint into the image. The `java.awt.image.BufferedImage` class (which is introduced later) also contains a `createGraphics` method that directly returns a `Graphics2D` object.

Table 2.1 lists methods and classes for accessing these output devices.

Table 2.1 ■ Relevant classes and methods for accessing Graphics for different output devices

OUTPUT TYPE	CLASSES AND METHODS
Screen	`java.awt.Component.paint(Graphics g)`, `java.awt.Component.getGraphics()`
Printer	`java.awt.print.PrinterJob`, `java.awt.print.Printable.print(...)`
Offscreen Buffer	`java.awt.Image.getGraphics()`, `java.awt.image.BufferedImage.createGraphics()`

Note that no matter which method is used to acquire a `Graphics2D` object, that object is used the same way, regardless of the underlying output device. This is what makes the Java 2D API device independent: rendering is done the same way, independently of the actual output device.

Coordinate spaces

`Graphics2D` provides output device independence. But how do rendered objects (text, shapes and images) end up being drawn at the "right place" on the output device? To answer this, we need to understand that the Java 2D API works with two different coordinate spaces: the *user space* and the *device space*.

▼ **User space** The programmer using the 2D API works in a coordinate space known as the *user space*. In that coordinate system, x coordinates

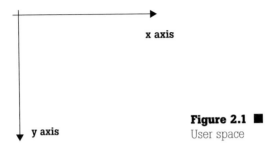

Figure 2.1 ■
User space

increase to the right and y coordinates increase downward, with the origin in the upper-left corner, as shown in Figure 2.1. All the methods in the `Graphics2D` class that involve coordinates (all rendering methods do, directly or indirectly), refer to the *user space*.

▼ **Device space** The coordinate space definition for different devices may vary. For example, the orientation of the x and y axis as well as the physical size of one unit differs widely from a screen to a printer.

▼ **Reconciling user space and device space** Back to our initial question: how do rendered objects end up being rendered at the right place? The answer lies in the role of the default `AffineTransform` attribute in the `Graphics2D` graphics context. We detail that class later on, but it is important to remember that the default value of the `AffineTransform` attribute is such that the device space and the user space correspond in a reasonable way.

By default, the default transform is such that the device space will appear to be the same as that of the user space: x and y axis will have the same orientation, and the origin will be at the same place (the upper-left corner, for a screen). As a consequence, rendering a yellow rectangle the size of the screen with its origin in (0, 0) in the user space will fill the screen with yellow.

As we discuss later, it is possible to modify the `AffineTransform` attribute to define the spatial transformation applied to a graphic object before it is rendered to the output device. This is discussed in greater detail in "Graphic Context Attributes" on page 34 and in "AffineTransform" on page 133.

It is also important to note that the default mapping between the user space and the device space is such that 72 units have a size of about an inch. On typical screens, which work at a 72 dpi resolution (dpi = dots per inch), this means that a pixel "size" is equal to a unit.[1] So, a line that is 3 units long will be drawn by 4 pixels on the screen.[2] On a printer using a higher resolution, the same line will appear as many more consecutive "dots." However, the physical size of the line will be the same on the screen and on a printed page (see Figure 2.2 for an example of the same object rendered at different resolutions).

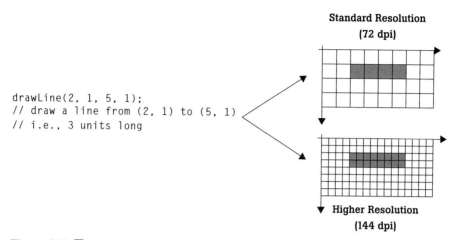

```
drawLine(2, 1, 5, 1);
// draw a line from (2, 1) to (5, 1)
// i.e., 3 units long
```

Figure 2.2 ■
Resolution independence

Therefore, Java 2D is not only device independent, it is also resolution independent, meaning it can work equally well on high-resolution and low-resolution devices. This is further discussed in Chapter 3 (see "" on page 54).

Graphic Objects and Rendering Methods

As illustrated in Figure 1.4 on page 5, Graphics2D can render three types of objects:

■ Shapes, that is, geometrical forms of any kind, such as rectangles, ellipses, or arbitrary forms
■ Text, in different font and with complex style attributes
■ Images, whose content can be replicated on the output

This section describes each type of graphic object and the related Graphics2D methods that render them.

---

1. The choice of 1/72 inch as the default unit size has two advantages. One, it is backward compatible with earlier versions of the Java platform where pixels were the unit of drawing primitives. Second, it is compatible with PostScript® (see [Adobe98] p151) and about the same size, but not exactly, as a point, a unit used in the printing industry (e.g., used for font sizes).
2. The line is 3 units long and is represented by an extra point due to the default Stroke used to draw the line. That default Stroke is one unit wide and adds half a point at each extremity of the line it strokes, which explains the extra unit on the output device.

Rendering shapes

Shape is an interface in the java.awt package. Its methods let an implementation describe any geometrical form that can be rendered as a combination of lines and second- or third–order Bezier curve. Bezier curves (see [Foley96]) are a mathematical model that can be used to approximate almost any type of curve. Bezier curves have a polynomial form, and those of second and third order are precise enough to accurately represent most curves of interest in 2D graphics.

The java.awt and java.awt.geom packages contain many implementations of the Shape interface, from Rectangle, which describes a simple rectangular area, to the more complex GeneralPath class, which can be used to describe any arbitrary geometrical form.

There are two ways to render a Shape object:

1. Fill. A Shape can be filled with the Graphics2D.fill method or other equivalent methods (for example, fillRect). Among other attributes, the fill method uses the current Paint attribute to determine the pixel pattern it uses to render a Shape on the output. For example:

    ```
    // Set up rendering context attributes
    g.setPaint(Color.orange); // Set solid orange as the
                              // current Paint

    // Prepare graphic object to render : a Shape
    Shape shape = ...;         // Create Shape

    // Invoke rendering method
    g.fill(shape);
    ```

2. Draw. A Shape can be drawn with the Graphics2D.draw method or other equivalent methods (for example, drawRect). Drawing a Shape means that its outline is painted to the output. Among other attributes, the draw method uses the current Paint attribute to define the pixel pattern used to render the outline (that is, the color of the pixels on the outline) and the current Stroke attribute to define the type of the outline (for example, thickness or dash pattern).

    ```
    // Setup rendering context attributes
    g.setStroke(new BasicStroke(10));// Set a 10 points wide³
                                    // thick stroke
    ```

---

3. "10 points wide" refers to user space units.

```
g.setPaint(new Color(128, 0, 0));// Set a dark red as the
                                 // current Paint attribute

// Prepare graphic object to render : a Shape
Shape shape = ...;              // Create Shape

// Invoke rendering method
g.draw(shape);
```

Table 2.2 shows an example that invokes both `fill` and `draw`, but with different settings for the graphic context's `Paint` attribute (different `Color` instances). Note how the coordinate system orientation is with the origin in the upper-left corner of the output, with x-coordinate values increasing to the right and y-coordinates increasing downward.

Table 2.2 ■ Rendering a rectangle Shape

SHAPERENDERING.JAVA

```
// Prepare graphic object to
// render : a Shape
Shape shape
  = new Rectangle(40, 40, 200, 100);

// Setup rendering context attributes
g.setPaint(Color.orange);

// Invoke rendering method
g.fill(shape);

// Setup rendering context attributes
// Set a thick stroke
g.setStroke(new BasicStroke(10));

// Set a dark red as the current Paint
g.setPaint(new Color(128, 0, 0));

// Invoke rendering methods
g.draw(shape);
```

Output

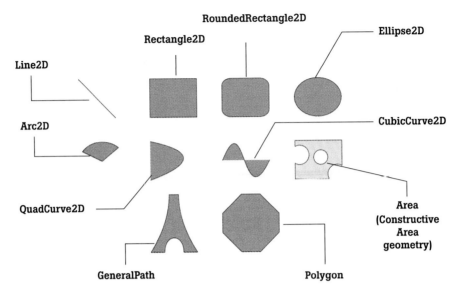

Figure 2.3 ■
Visualization of the different Shape classes

Figure 2.3 shows the visual representation of the different `Shape` implementations available in the API. These classes are mostly defined in the `java.awt.geom` package (some, such as `Polygon` and `Rectangle`, are defined in the `java.awt` package). We further detail the `Shape` interface, its use in the API, and its various implementations in Chapter 4 (see "Shapes" on page 58).

Rendering text

Text is one of the three types of graphic object that `Graphics2D` can render. The Java 2D API provides extended text support so that complex text manipulation becomes possible. As we will see, it is possible to render text in any language, which includes different alphabets and display logic (for example, some foreign scripts read from right to left).

However, text support follows the Java philosophy: simple things are easy, complex things are possible. In order of increasing complexity, the API enables us to perform the following:

1. *Simple text string rendering.*
2. *Styled text rendering.* The API allows us to draw text with varying style attributes (that is, different fonts, color, etc.).

3. *Advanced text manipulation*. This covers the capabilities needed to support international text display, text editing instrumentation, and more.
4. *Custom glyph layout*. Glyphs are the visual representation of text characters. The API allows manipulation of individual glyphs, making it possible to implement custom layout algorithms (that is, custom ways of aligning characters).

▼ **Simple text rendering**   The `Graphics2D.drawString` methods that take a `java.lang.String` argument draw a string of text at a requested position. Table 2.3 illustrates how the position defines the origin of the baseline. The baseline, discussed in further detail in Chapter 5 (see "Font" on page 156), defines the imaginary line about which characters align visually. Some characters go below (for example, the "g" glyph) but most rest on the baseline. When you draw a string at coordinate (x, y), the text's leftmost side starts about the x coordinate on the x-axis with its baseline at the y y-axis elevation. The displayed glyphs will have the correct ordering: left to right for English text, right to left for other languages such as Hebrew and Arabic.

The current `Font` and `Paint` attributes in the graphics context are used to render the text; simple text rendering follows the standard rendering process:

1. Set the graphic context attributes
2. Select an object to render. Here, we use a simple `String` object.
3. Invoke rendering method: `drawString`.

This text drawing method is simple, but it is limited: all glyphs have the same style. They are all created from the same `Font` object (the one in the rendering context at the time `drawString` is invoked), and they are all filled using the same `Paint` object: the rendering context's current `Paint` attribute (`Color.gray` in our example). The API provides richer style support than this.

▼ **Styled text rendering**   The `java.text.AttributedString` class describes text with varying style attributes. An `AttributedString` encapsulates both a string of text and the set of attributes that apply to subparts of the string, called *runs*. The `java.awt.font.TextAttribute` class contains the definitions of different style attributes that can be applied to an `Attributed-String`. For example, it contains the `TextAttribute.FONT` constant used to set the `Font` attribute and the `TextAttribute.BACKGROUND` attribute used to set the text background `Paint` attribute (a detailed list of the different `TextAttributes` is given in Chapter 4 on page 109).

One of the `Graphics2D.drawString` method renders stylized text. However, it does not render an `AttributedString` directly. Instead, it takes a `java.text.AttributedCharacterIterator` as an input parameter. Such an

Table 2.3 ■ Simple Text Rendering

SIMPLETEXTRENDERING.JAVA

Output

```
// Set rendering context attributes:
// Font and Paint
Font font = new Font("serif",
                     Font.PLAIN, 30);
Paint paint = Color.gray;
g.setFont(font);
g.setPaint(paint);

// Select object to render
String text = "B";

// Invoke rendering method
g.drawString(text, 5, 35);
```

x = 5

y = 35

(x, y)

Baseline

iterator allows `Graphics2D` to iterate over an `AttributedString`'s content and attribute information.[4] The `AttributedString`'s `getIterator` method returns an `AttributedCharacterIterator` that `Graphics2D` uses to render the styled text.

To summarize the process for rendering an `AttributedString`:

1. Build an `AttributedString`.
2. Set the newly built `AttributedString`'s style attributes, such as the font, foreground and background.
3. Create an `AttributedCharacterIterator` from the `AttributedString` object.
4. Invoke `Graphics2D.drawString` to render the styled text at the desired position.

Note how this is different from the simple rendering process. In the simple rendering process, all the attributes controlling the way text is rendered are part of the graphics context. When an `AttributedString` is rendered, the attributes controlling the text rendering are provided by an `AttributedCharacterIterator`. For example, the `Paint` instance used to fill the glyphs can be provided by the iterator, not the current graphics context `Paint`[5] attribute.

---

4. The iterator abstracts away the storage of style and text information. Programmers can implement their own storage models if they desire.
5. However, if an attribute is not specified, the `Graphics2D`'s `Paint` attribute is used.

Attributed Strings are

Figure 2.4 ■
Rendering styled text

See "Text Manipulation" on page 109 in Chapter 4 for an example showing how to render the styled text in Figure 2.4.

▼ **Advanced text manipulation** The Java 2D API offers more support for text than just the two rendering methods we discussed so far: simple text rendering and styled text rendering.

TextLayout

The TextLayout class, in the java.awt.font package, provides the following key features:

- ■ *Bidirectional text support.* Some languages, such as Arabic and Hebrew, read right to left and not left to right as in English. TextLayout can render both and mix the two types.
- ■ *Text editing support.* TextLayout includes hit testing, cursor positioning, highlighting, etc.

Note that rendering international text is supported by drawString: simple and styled text rendering are both based on the Unicode character set, which can represent most of the world's written languages.[6]

Tied to the various ways of laying out text is the support for text editing. TextLayout provides a wealth of methods to support text selection, selection highlighting, cursor positioning and other text editing-related features.

In addition, TextLayout provides metrics information (such as ascent, descent, leading—see "Font metrics" on page 167) and offers an alternate and convenient way to perform text rendering. That is, you can use TextLayout to render text instead of using Graphics2D.

TextLayout is feature rich, but it also provides a concise and convenient solution for drawing text, as illustrated in Table 2.4. Note that the draw method is invoked on the layout object, not on the Graphics2D object. Again, as for AttributedString, the model for rendering a TextLayout departs from the

---

6. See [Flanagan 1997] p205 for a short introduction to the Unicode character set and its use in the Java platform.

default rendering model. This is just a difference in the programming model, and the underlying implementation relies on the rendering model that we discussed in our introduction.

Table 2.4 ■ TextLayout rendering

```
SIMPLETEXTLAYOUTRENDERING.JAVA
```

Output

Simple TextLayout usage

```
Graphics2D g = ...;

// Width : for example, window width
int w = ...;

Font font = new Font("serif", Font.PLAIN, 60);

TextLayout layout = new TextLayout("Simple TextLayout usage",
                            font, g.getFontRenderContext());

// Horizontally center the text, using the layout metrics.
layout.draw(g,
        (w - layout.getAdvance())/2, // x-axis position: leftmost point
        layout.getAscent());         // y-axis position: baseline
                                     // elevation
```

As we will see in Chapter 4 (see "Advanced text rendering with TextLayout and LineBreakMeasurer" on page 118), TextLayout can be used in conjunction with AttributedStrings and AttributedCharacterIterator to render styled text as well. Another class often used in conjunction with TextLayout is the java.awt.font.LineBreakMeasurer class.

LineBreakMeasurer

All the text support features we discussed so far deal with single text lines. The LineBreakMeasurer class breaks a paragraph of text into lines that fit within a given wrapping width. This capability allows us to break text into pieces that fit into a specific paragraph layout, even if the text has multiple styles or multiple script directions.

Figure 2.5 shows the output of a program that uses a LineBreakMeasurer to break down a text string, read from a file, into lines that fit within the display area.

See Chapter 4 ("Creating a text paragraph" on page 121) for details on the use of the LineBreakMeasurer class.

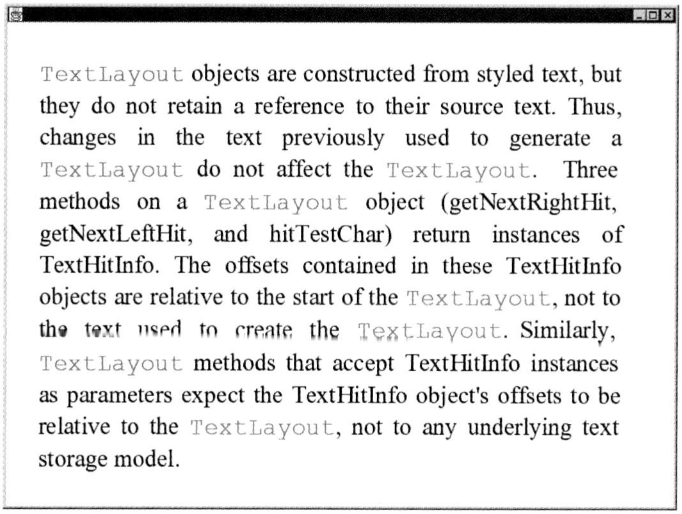

> TextLayout objects are constructed from styled text, but they do not retain a reference to their source text. Thus, changes in the text previously used to generate a TextLayout do not affect the TextLayout. Three methods on a TextLayout object (getNextRightHit, getNextLeftHit, and hitTestChar) return instances of TextHitInfo. The offsets contained in these TextHitInfo objects are relative to the start of the TextLayout, not to the text used to create the TextLayout. Similarly, TextLayout methods that accept TextHitInfo instances as parameters expect the TextHitInfo object's offsets to be relative to the TextLayout, not to any underlying text storage model.

Figure 2.5 ■
Text block layout with LineBreakMeasurer

▼ **Custom glyph layouts** All the text rendering and manipulation we have discussed so far use a default glyph layout method. Glyphs are aligned along the baseline and spaced according to information from the font file. This layout logic can be overridden, and the java.awt.font.GlyphVector class provides a way to override how individual glyphs are arranged for display.

Implementing a custom layout algorithm involves the following steps:

1. Select the Font object used for a given set of glyphs.
2. Invoke Font.createGlyphVector method to generate a GlyphVector object.
3. Invoke GlyphVector.setGlyphPosition or setGlyphTransform[7] to modify the default glyph placement.
4. Invoke Graphics2D.drawGlyphVector to render the modified GlyphVector object.

Figure 2.6 shows the output of a program that modifies individual glyph positions as we just described. The code for that program is detailed in Chapter 4 (see "Custom glyph layout" on page 127).

---

7. This method was not implemented at the time of this writing.

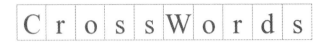

Figure 2.6 ∎
Changing glyph layout with GlyphVector

Text rendering is a highly complex topic, especially when international text support is targeted. As we discussed, the API provides several levels of text management:

1. Simple text rendering. This is done through the `Graphics2D.drawString` method, which uses the current `Font` attribute to create the glyph representing characters and the current `Paint` attribute to fill the glyphs.

2. Styled text rendering. Both `Graphics2D` and `TextLayout` can render styled text. The `AttributedString` class supports the definition of text with attached style attributes. Attributes are defined by `TextAttribute`/value pairs, and `AttributedCharacterIterator` lets `Graphics2D` and `TextLayout` iterate through the style and content of an `AttributedString`.

3. Advanced international text support and text editing. The `TextLayout` class provides very sophisticated international text and text editing support: bidirectional text, cursor management, text highlights, hit testing, and more. It is also a "one stop shopping" class for text rendering because it can handle both simple and styled text, provide text metrics (see "Font metrics" on page 167), and can render text. The `LineBreakMeasurer` class, used in conjunction with `TextLayout`, allows rendering of multiple lines of text by wrapping.

4. Custom glyph layout. The `GlyphVector` class allows us to modify the default method used for spacing glyphs.

These features are listed in order of complexity. This is also the order of "common use." That is, simple text rendering is the most commonly used feature and custom glyph layout is the least commonly used. However, the API supports all of them, making the JDK a very sophisticated platform for text rendering.

Note that for common GUI development, AWT components, such as `java.awt.TextArea` or `javax.swing.JTextField`, provide adequate common text display and text editing support.

Rendering images

With shapes and text, images are the other type of graphic objects `Graphics2D` can render. In earlier versions of the Java platform, there was a single type of image object, embodied by the `java.awt.Image` abstract class. Java 2 has introduced new types of image objects; the one central to the Java 2D API is the `java.awt.image.BufferedImage` class.

Drawing an image is simple and is performed by several `drawImage` methods in `Graphics2D`. The simplest `drawImage` replicates the image onto the output device at a given location. Other variations support the following features.

- *Replicate a portion of an image onto the output.* `drawImage` methods that enable this feature take arguments that specify the rectangle to be replicated in the image and the rectangle where the image should be copied. If the two do not have the same dimensions, the image is scaled to fit the destination size.
- *Scale an image.* In addition of the location where the image should be replicated, some `drawImage` methods let you specify the dimension of the rectangle where the image should be drawn. If the destination has a different dimension than the source, then the image is scaled (that is, shrunk or blown up) to fit into the destination.
- *Transform an image.* This is a generalization of the scaling capabilities of some `drawImage` methods. It is possible to apply an `AffineTransformation` (for example, a rotation) to the image before it is drawn to the output.
- *Replace transparent pixels.* For images that have transparent pixels, specify the color that should be used in place of transparent values.
- *Filter an image before it is drawn.* As described later, it is possible to filter images for different purposes. One `drawImage` method lets you filter a `BufferedImage` before it is drawn to the output device.

Table 2.5 illustrates those different features.

Table 2.5 ■ Features of the `drawImage` methods

FEATURE	ILLUSTRATION
Original image	
Plain Draws an image at a specified location. The parameters control the location where the image is drawn.	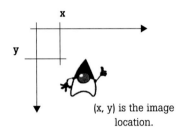 (x, y) is the image location.
Partial image paint Some `drawImage` methods specify which portion of the input image should be drawn to the output. Here, only half of the source image is drawn.	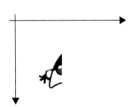
Scale `drawImage` fits the input image in a specified rectangle and scales the input image if necessary.	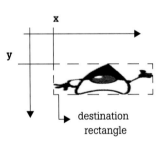 destination rectangle
Transform `drawImage` transforms the input image before drawing it. For example, a rotation can be applied.	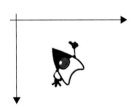

Table 2.5 ■ Features of the `drawImage` methods (Continued)

FEATURE	ILLUSTRATION
Transparent pixel replacement `drawImage` replaces transparent pixels with a specific color when rendering the input image. Here, a dark red was used.	
Filter `drawImage` filters the input image before drawing it. Here, the image was blurred before it was rendered.	

We mentioned that Java 2 has introduced new types of images. They support different imaging models, and there are now three imaging models in Java.

1. *Push model.* This is the imaging model available in the Java 1 platform. Images are loaded by the `java.awt.Toolkit` class, and data is pushed to an `ImageConsumer` as it is loaded (presumably over the Internet). This model works really well for applets and Web applications that need to address the problem of loading images over networks with latency. However, the push model is a little cumbersome to use. This model is described in detail in books about the Java programming language and AWT graphics (see [Geary1998]). This is not the core model of the Java 2D API, and it is not described in this book.

2. *Immediate mode model.* In this mode, image data is made immediately available, and the user can access the internal arrays storing pixel values. The `java.awt.image.BufferedImage` class is at the center of this imaging model. `BufferedImage` is much easier to program with and provides greater programmatic control than does `Image` in the push model. This is the model the Java 2D API uses and the one we discuss at length in this book.

3. *Pull model.* For high-end graphic applications (for example, very high quality, very high resolution image processing for some professional photography or medical applications), the immediate mode presents drawbacks because it requires all the image data to be loaded in memory, among other things. A much more sophisticated mode (also more complex programmatically) was created to allow optimization of the image processing pipeline. This mode is implemented by the *Java Advanced Imaging API* and is compatible with the Java 2D core imaging classes in the `java.awt.image` package. This model, like the push model, falls outside the scope of this book. More information about the Java Advanced Imaging API (JAI) can be found on Sun's Web site, under the Java Media umbrella.[8]

As we will see, the immediate mode model of `BufferedImage` provides a very convenient programming model. Its internal structure is flexible and accommodates different strategies for organizing pixel information. Finally, the API provides many filters to manipulate `BufferedImage` objects.

▼ **BufferedImage** Images are made of pixels. Pixels represent the color value of the different points in the image. The `BufferedImage` class provides for the storage and interpretation of pixel values (see Figure 2.7). This design is sufficiently general to allow any type of storage and color representation to be supported in the API.

For example, if we decide to represent pixel values by their red, green, and blue components, we could do one of the following:

■ Create a `Raster` that stores integer values, where each integer represents one pixel value (packing three sample values into each integer, one sample for red, one for green, and one for blue). We can use a `ColorModel` that will interpret the three sample values as three color components when necessary.
■ Create a `Raster` that stores byte values, where each byte represents one pixel value. We can use a `ColorModel` that will map each pixel value to an index in a color map, thus turning the pixel value into its color components.

▼ **Creating a BufferedImage and loading images** The `BufferedImage` class contains a number of constructors that make it easy to aggregate a `BufferedImage` with the proper `Raster` type and `ColorModel` for common cases. ARGB (Alpha-RGB) and RGB are common types of color spaces used in `ColorModel`. They represent color values with red, green, and blue compo-

---

8. Java Advanced Imaging information can be found at: http://java.sun.com/products/java-media/jai/

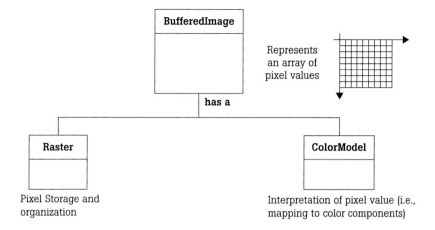

Figure 2.7 ■
BufferedImage structure

nents with or without transparency information. Creating this type of `Buff-eredImage` is straightforward:

```
BufferedImage opaqueImage
        = new BufferedImage(width, height, BufferedImage.TYPE_INT_RGB);
BufferedImage transparentImage
        = new BufferedImage(width, height, BufferedImage.TYPE_INT_ARGB);
```

In each case, the constructor takes care of building an appropriate `Raster` to store pixels as integers, as well as an appropriate `ColorModel` (more on this in "ColorModels" on page 86 in Chapter 4).

Loading an image from the file system can be done with the `java.awt.Toolkit` and `java.awt.MediaTracker` classes. Those classes automatically recognize the format of the image file and load it with the appropriate encoder. For JPEG images, an alternate solution is provided by the `com.sun.image.codec.jpeg` package, which contains JPEG format image coder and decoder. This package is not part of the Java 2 Platform core classes, even though it is included in the Sun Microsystems Java platform implementation. However, it is handy because it handles `BufferedImage` directly (that is, the coders and decoders work in the immediate mode model), whereas `Toolkit` and `MediaTracker` use the push model.

The following code segment shows how to load a JPEG image, both with the traditional `MediaTracker` class and with `JPEGDecoder` (the code is available in the **ImageLoad.java** file on the CD-ROM). The `imageName` variable holds the name of the JPEG file to load.

```
public class ImageLoad extends JComponent {
.....

  //
  // Traditional method to load images: MediaTracker
  //
  MediaTracker tracker = new MediaTracker(this);
  Image defaultLoadImage
      = Toolkit.getDefaultToolkit().getImage(imageName);
  tracker.addImage(defaultLoadImage, 0);
  try{
    tracker.waitForAll();
  }catch(InterruptedException e){
    throw new Error("Could not load " + imageName
                    + " with MediaTracker");
  }

  //
  // Alternate method for JPEG Images: JPEGImageDecoder
  //
  try{
    InputStream in = new FileInputStream(imageName);
    JPEGImageDecoder decoder = JPEGCodec.createJPEGDecoder(in);
    BufferedImage jpegLoadImage = decoder.decodeAsBufferedImage();
  }catch(IOException e){
    e.printStackTrace();
    throw new Error("Could not load " + imageName
                    + " with JPEGImageDecoder");
  }
....
}
```

Note how the two are different. `MediaTracker` first builds an `Image` object (through the `Toolkit.getImage` factory method) that may not have all its data loaded. It is merely a reference to an image source. `MediaTracker` then loads the image data (this is what happens during the `waitForAll` call). Only then is it guaranteed that the image data has been loaded.[9]

The `JPEGDecoder` class operates in the spirit of `BufferedImage`: the image is loaded and decoded during the `decodeAsBufferedImage` call. Having the image returned as a `BufferedImage` is more convenient for later manipulations with the new Java 2D filters. The `Toolbox` class, in the `com.sun.glf.util` package, contains several methods to load images and return them in the `BufferedImage` form. It uses `JPEGImageDecoder` for JPEG images. For other images (for example, gif), it uses `MediaTracker` but then copies the `Image` content into a `BufferedImage`.

---

9. Actually, you should use the `MediaTracker`'s `isErrorAny` or one of its `getErrors` methods to truly validate that the image data was loaded properly after `waitForAll` returns.

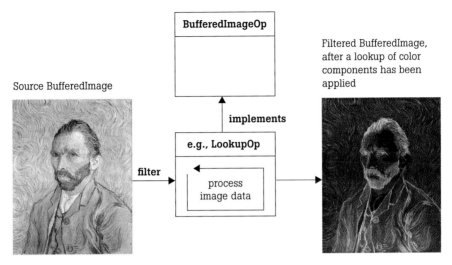

Figure 2.8 ■
Filtering BufferedImages

▼ **Filtering images**　The API supports a simple model for filtering a `Buff-eredImage`: single source, single destination. `BufferedImage` filters must implement the `BufferedImageOp` interface in the `java.awt.image` package[10] (see Figure 2.8).

Translated into code, a filtering operation is expressed as:

```
// Create or load source image.
BufferedImage sourceImage = ...;

// Create a lookup filter to invert image
BufferedImageOp invertFilter = new LookupOp(...);

// Filter image
BufferedImage filteredImage = invertFilter.filter(sourceImage, null);
```

_____

10. There are image filters that work with the push imaging model. `BufferedImageOp` implementations can be made to work with that model using the `BufferedImageFilter` wrapper that conforms to the push model `ImageFilter` uses. This allows new filters to be used with applications written using the push model.

Note how simple this is. Filtering occurs on the last line. Note that the second parameter is the destination BufferedImage, that is, the place where the result of the filtering operation should be stored. Here, a null parameter is given, which requests that the filter create a destination BufferedImage for the caller.

BufferedImageOp is an interface, so it is possible to create custom filters and use them in the same manner as any of the default implementations in the API. Some custom filters are defined in Chapter 9 (see "Custom BufferedImageOps and RasterOps" on page 336). However, there are many implementations built into the API that support a wide range of needs, as summarized in Table 2.6.

Table 2.6 ■ BufferedImageOp implementations

CLASS NAME AND PURPOSE	EXAMPLE
AffineTransformOp Performs a spatial transformation of pixels from the source into the destination. For example, an image can be rotated, skewed, or flipped.	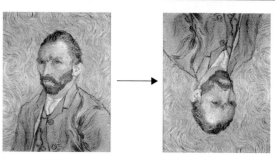 AffineTransformOp using a rotation about the image center
ColorConvertOp Performs color conversion of image pixels to the model of the destination image.	 ColorConvertOp from standard RGB to gray scale

Table 2.6 ■ BufferedImageOp implementations (Continued)

CLASS NAME AND PURPOSE	EXAMPLE
ConvolveOp Computes destination pixel values by combining the value of pixels around the source pixel at the same location. This class can be used for blurring an image, sharpening it, or doing edge detection.	 ConvolveOp used for edge detection
LookupOp Performs lookup operations on color components. This class can be used for operations such as inverting color components or thresholding (i.e., increasing pixel differences to visually enhance color variations).	 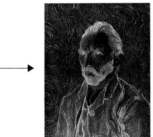 LookupOp used to invert color components
RescaleOp Rescales the color component values. This class can be used to adjust an image brightness or color balance.	 RescaleOp used to brighten image

Table 2.6 ■ BufferedImageOp implementations (Continued)

CLASS NAME AND PURPOSE	EXAMPLE
BandCombineOp[a] Performs a linear combination of the different bands of a Raster. A band stores one sample (e.g., the red component) of each pixel value (see "BufferedImage internals" on page 79 for more details on bands, elements, etc.).	 BandCombineOp used to adjust colors in image

a. All these filtering operations except BandCombineOp have semantics related to color components. BandCombineOp is different from other filters in that it only applies to Raster objects, and not to BufferedImage objects. All the other filters apply to both.

We explained how Graphics2D renders text, shapes, or images, and we have just had a closer look at each of those. The rendering process for each is influenced by the attributes in the graphic context, and our last paragraphs illustrate each of the seven graphic context attributes.

Graphic Context Attributes

Figure 2.9 shows the seven attributes that control the Graphics2D rendering operation.

These control attributes are referred to as the *graphic context*. To render shapes, text and images, the attributes are set before rendering methods such as drawString or fillRect are called.

The graphic context attributes are described below; their setting and output are illustrated.

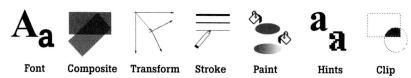

Font   Composite   Transform   Stroke   Paint   Hints   Clip

Figure 2.9 ■
The seven graphic context attributes

■ Font attribute. Through the setFont method, it is possible to set the Font object that should be used for the subsequent text rendering, that is, until another Font attribute is set.[11] See Table 2.7.

Table 2.7 ■ Setting the Font rendering attribute

FONTATTRIBUTE.JAVA

Output

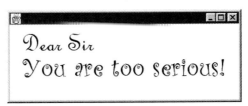

```
Graphics2D g = ...;
Font scriptFont = new Font("French Script MT", Font.PLAIN, 40);
Font funFont = new Font("Curlz MT", Font.PLAIN, 40);
g.setFont(scriptFont);
g.drawString("Dear Sir", 20, 40);
g.setFont(funFont);
g.drawString("You are too serious!", 20, 80);
```

■ Composite. The Composite object defines how a rendering operation should "blend" with the existing output. For example, imagine a blue rectangle is filled on top of an image. If a fully opaque composition rule is used, it will completely replace the image. If a 50% transparent composition rule is used, the resulting output will be 50% the value of the output (containing the image) and 50% the blue rectangle, giving a viewer the illusion of seeing through the blue rectangle. See Table 2.8.

■ AffineTransform. The AffineTransform attribute transforms coordinates from one coordinate system to another. The user of the Graphics2D object manipulates objects in a coordinate system referred to as the *user space*. The output device has a coordinate system known as the *device space*. The AffineTransform attribute defines how the two coordinate systems should relate: it transforms coordinates from their value in the user space to their value in the device space. For example, if the AffineTransform attribute is set to identity (that is, no transform is applied to coordinates), then the user space and the device space match. If the AffineTransform attribute is a

11. As we discuss in Chapter 4 (see "Text Manipulation" on page 109), some advanced text rendering operations do not use the graphic context Font attribute.

Table 2.8 ■ Setting the Composite attribute

COMPOSITEATTRIBUTE.JAVA

Output

```
Graphics2D g = ...;
Image image = ...;

// First, drawImage
g.drawImage(image, x, y, null);

// Set Composite context attribute
g.setComposite(AlphaComposite.getInstance(AlphaComposite.SRC_OVER, 0.5f));

// Set Paint attribute
g.setPaint(Color.blue);

// Fill rectangle with blue Paint. See how the blue paint blends with
// the background Image
g.fillRect(x-10, y-10,
        image.getWidth(null)/2 + 10,
        image.getHeight(null) + 20);
```

translation of 100 pixels along each axis, then the user space's origin is 100 pixels down and to the right of the device space's origin. See Table 2.9.

■ Stroke. Graphics2D can either fill or draw a Shape. Drawing a Shape consists of rendering its outline. The way the outline is drawn is controlled by the Stroke attribute, which is equivalent to a pen, or marker. See Table 2.10.

Table 2.9 ■ Setting the AffineTransform attribute

AFFINETRANSFORMATTRIBUTE.JAVA

```
Graphics2D g = ...;
Image image = ...; // Load image code.

// No Transform : device space and
// user space overlap.
g.drawImage(image, 0, 0, null);
```

User space and device space match.
Here, only the user space is shown (in green)

```
Graphics2D g = ...;
Image image = ...; // Load image code.


// Translation : the user space is
// offset compared to the device space
AffineTransform t =
AffineTransform.getTranslateInstance(100
                              ,100);
g.transform(t);

// The following drawImage requests
// the image to be drawn in (0, 0) in
// user space. Because the
// Graphics2D transform has been set
// to a (100, 100) translation, the
// image is effectively drawn in
// (100, 100) in the device space.
g.drawImage(image, 0, 0, null);
```

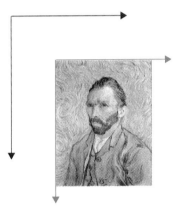

User space and device space do not match:
user space is translated

■ Paint. When drawing or filling text or shapes, Graphics2D uses a Paint object to define what actual pixel pattern should be used on the output. For example, the Color implementation of the Paint interface defines a simple pattern where all pixels have the same value. The GradientPaint implementation defines a more sophisticated pattern where pixels progressively change from one color to another color. See Table 2.11.

Table 2.10 ■ Setting the Stroke attribute

STROKEATTRIBUTE.JAVA

```
Graphics2D g = ...;

// Create an Eiffel tower Shape
GeneralPath eiffel = ...; // See Page 62.

// Draw the Shape with the default stroke
g.setPaint(new Color(60, 60, 80));
g.draw(eiffel);

// Create a border rectangle from the shape's bounds
Rectangle border = eiffel.getBounds();
border.x -= 10;
border.y -= 10;
border.width += 20;
border.height += 20;

// Draw the border with a dash Stroke
Stroke dashStroke = new BasicStroke(3f,            // Width
                            BasicStroke.CAP_ROUND,  // Cap deco
                            BasicStroke.JOIN_ROUND, // Join style
                            0f,                     // Mitter limit
                            float[]{0, 5}, 0);      // Dash pattern
g.setStroke(dashStroke);

// This actually fills the 'dots' with blue
g.draw(border);
```

Output

- RenderingHints. There are many options from which a rendering engine can choose. For example, a common option is antialiasing. Aliasing is the jagged or staircase effect that occurs when diagonal lines, text, or curves are rendered on a raster device.[12] The antialiasing technique can be used to attenuate this effect and make the output look much smoother. As the following example illustrates, the RenderingHints class contains an attribute that defines whether or not this technique should be used. There are many other hints, and their goal is to give control over speed and quality trade-offs. For example, turning antialiasing on increases the output quality but slows down rendering. See Table 2.12.
- Clip. This last attribute in the rendering context defines the limit of the area where the rendering operations apply. That is, a Shape object defines the

---

12. "Raster device" is the name given to devices that use a discrete array of points to produce a visual result, as opposed to continuous, analog systems. Raster device examples are a screen or a laser printer.

Table 2.11 ■ Setting the Paint attribute

PAINTATTRIBUTE.JAVA

```
Graphics2D g = ...;

// Fill background with GradientPaint
GradientPaint bkgPaint
  = new GradientPaint(0, 0, Color.black,
                      0, 20, Color.blue);
g.setPaint(bkgPaint);
g.fillRect(0, 0, w, h);

// Create two triangular shapes .
// one pointing up containing a smaller
// one pointing down.
GeneralPath upTriangle
  = new GeneralPath();
upTriangle.moveTo(10, 0);
upTriangle.lineTo(20, 20);
upTriangle.lineTo(0, 20);
upTriangle.closePath();

GeneralPath downTriangle = new GeneralPath();
downTriangle.moveTo(5, 10);
downTriangle.lineTo(15, 10);
downTriangle.lineTo(10, 20);
downTriangle.closePath();

// Create two Gradient Paints
GradientPaint blueToBlack = new GradientPaint(0, 0, blue,
                                              0, 20, Color.black);
GradientPaint blackToBlue = new GradientPaint(0, 10, Color.black,
                                              0, 20, blue);
// Paint big triangle
g.setPaint(blueToBlack);
g.fill(upTriangle);

// Paint small triangle
g.setPaint(blackToBlue);
g.fill(downTriangle);
```

Output

clip area, and any part of the output lying outside the clipping region is left unmodified by all rendering operations. The short code examples show how the same rendering method call (`Graphics2D.fill`) produces different results depending on the clip. Note that the clip is defined as a `Shape`, which means that any geometrical form can be used as a clip area. See Table 2.13.

Table 2.12 ■ Setting the RenderingHints

CODE (RENDERINGHINTSATTRIBUTE.JAVA)

```
Graphics2D g = ...;

Font scriptFont
    = new Font("French Script MT", Font.PLAIN, 40);
g.setFont(scriptFont);

g.setRenderingHint(RenderingHints.KEY_ANTIALIASING,

RenderingHints.VALUE_ANTIALIAS_OFF);

g.drawString("L", 20, 40);
```

No antialiasing
Fast rendering

```
Graphics2D g = ...;

Font scriptFont
    = new Font("French Script MT", Font.PLAIN, 40);
g.setFont(scriptFont);

g.setRenderingHint(RenderingHints.KEY_ANTIALIASING,
                   RenderingHints.VALUE_ANTIALIAS_ON);

g.drawString("L", 20, 40);
```

Antialiasing on
Better quality

Table 2.13 ■ Setting the clip

CLIPATTRIBUTE.JAVA

```
// No clip set:
Rectangle rect
    = new Rectangle(20, 20, 200, 100);
g.setPaint(Color.red);
g.fill(rect);
```

Simple Rectangle is filled with red.

Table 2.13 ■ Setting the clip (Continued)

CLIPATTRIBUTE.JAVA

```
// Clip set to an Ellipse2D which
// partially intersects with
// rendered rect:

Rectangle rect
  = new Rectangle(20, 20, 200, 100);

Ellipse2D clip
  = new Ellipse2D.Float(120, 70,
                        100, 100);
g.clip(clip);

g.setPaint(Color.red);
g.fill(rect);
```

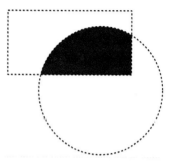

Dashed lines are drawn to show the `rect` and `clip` Shapes. They do not appear on the output: only the red area does.

Chapter 5 describes in detail each of the graphic context attributes we just briefly introduced here. For now, it is important to remember which ones exist and how they influence the rendering process. The `Font` attribute modifies the style of glyphs used to represent text characters. The `Composite` attribute controls how a given rendered object (for example, a blue rectangle) blends with an existing background. The transform attribute controls where and how text, shapes and images are drawn on the output device. The `Stroke` attribute defines the nature of the pen used to draw a `Shape`'s outline, and the `Paint` attribute defines the pixel pattern used to fill glyphs and `Shapes`. The `RenderingHints` attribute lets us specify rendering speed and quality trade-offs; and the clipping attribute, the region to which rendering is limited.

Conclusion

After this first introduction to the Java 2D features and some code examples, we have seen the major parts of the API. Figure 2.10 summarizes the Java 2D rendering pipeline and shows the different types of graphic objects that can be rendered on the left, the output devices where rendering happens on the right, and, at the bottom, the set of graphic context attributes that influence the rendering process.

Table 2.14 summarizes what we have seen from the package perspective, linking the features we have discussed to the package containing the relevant classes.

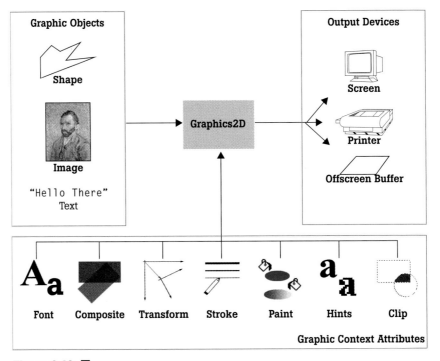

Figure 2.10 ■
The Java 2D API Rendering Pipeline

Table 2.14 ■ Feature-to-package map

FEATURE	PACKAGES
Graphics2D device independence	java.awt. The java.awt.print package contains all the classes needed to support the printing process.
Shape	java.awt and java.awt.geom. The Shape interface is part of java.awt, but most implementations are part of java.awt.geom.
Text support	java.awt (includes the Font class), java.awt.font (TextLayout, GlyphVector, etc.) and java.text (AttributedString).
Immediate mode imaging model	java.awt.image and java.awt.color.
AffineTransform	java.awt.geom
Font, Composite, Stroke, Paint, RenderingHints, clip	java.awt

The next chapters provide further details about the different areas we have introduced here, starting with a discussion on how to acquire a Graphics2D for a given output device.

3

RENDERING TO AN OUTPUT DEVICE: SCREEN, PRINTER, AND IMAGES

The Java 2D designers have been careful to make the API independent of any output device. For example, shapes are described in a user space that is independent of the actual output device and its resolution. Shapes are pure geometric abstractions and can be blown up or shrunk without restriction. However, the output device needs to render those geometrical forms with discrete pixels (on a screen), ink dots (on a printer), or memory elements (for an offscreen buffer). The term pixel (picture element) is often used to designate one discrete element on printers and images as well. Collectively, devices that represent image information with pixels are called raster devices. The process of converting graphic objects to pixels is called scan conversion and depends on attributes specific to the output device, such as its color support and its resolution.

None of these differences are visible to the programmer because the `Graphics2D` class offers the same interface whatever the underlying conventions needed to render on a raster output are. However, gaining access to a `Graphics2D` object depends on the type of output.

A `Graphics2D` object can give access to three types of outputs:[1]

■ Screen
■ Printer
■ Image

---

1. This does not mean that the same `Graphics2D` object can render to those three device types. Different extensions of the `Graphics2D` class provide access to the different outputs. Those different subclasses are accessed as described in the next pages.

For each output, the method for acquiring a related `Graphics2D` object is different. However, the `Graphics2D` methods are always the same. In the following paragraphs, we will reuse the same class for all `Graphics2D` rendering. The class is called `SimplePainter`, and it paints an image in its center after filling the background with a gradient paint, as detailed in Table 3.1.

The code relies only on the `Graphics2D` abstract class, and `SimplePainter` returns the dimension of the area it paints *in user space* through its `getSize` method. Now, let's see how to use `SimplePainter` to render to different output devices.

Drawing to the Screen

To render to the screen, we use one of the `java.awt` classes. The simplest way to do it is:

1. Derive from the `java.awt.Component` class.
2. Override the `paint` method. The input parameter is of type `Graphics`.
3. Cast the `paint` method's `Graphics` parameter into a `Graphics2D` object.
4. Use the `Graphics2D` object for rendering.

Table 3.2 shows the code for a program, available on the CD-ROM, that does just that.

Because the default size of a user space unit is 1/72 of an inch, which is also the common size of a screen pixel, the `ScreenRendering Component` will have the same pixel size as `painter`'s size in user space:

```
Dimension getPreferredSize(){
    return painter.getSize();
}
```

We can achieve the same screen result by using the more sophisticated Swing framework.[2] However, in Swing, double buffering can be turned on or off, which means that the `Graphics` object passed to a `Component`'s `paint` method may actually be an interface either to the screen (if double buffering is turned off) or to an offscreen buffer (if double buffering is turned on). In double buffer-

---

2. Note that the examples in the overview and in the remainder of this part all use the Swing framework for screen rendering. See any of the examples on the CD-ROM. The design is similar: derive from the `JComponent` instead of a `Component` and use a `JFrame` instead of a `Frame`. The essential difference is that Swing uses the lightweight `Component` framework instead of the default, platform-specific, `ComponentPeer` AWT architecture. Refer to [Geary 1998] for details on those issues.

Table 3.1 ■ The SimplePainter class

SIMPLEPAINTER.JAVA

```java
public class SimplePainter {
  // Image drawn in render method
  private BufferedImage image;

  // Margin size
  private static int MARGIN = 10;

  // Size of the area drawn by this class (in user space)
  private Dimension size;

  // Background is first filled with GradientPaint
  private Paint gradientPaint;

  // Constructor
  public SimplePainter(String imageName){
    // Load image
    image = ...; // See Page 28 for image loading

    // Size is based on image size plus margin
    int w = image.getWidth() + 2*MARGIN;
    int h = image.getHeight() + 2*MARGIN;
    size = new Dimension(w, h);

    // Create GradientPaint for border
    Color darkBlue = new Color(63, 64, 124);
    Color lighBlur = new Color(112, 128, 154);
    gradientPaint = new GradientPaint(0, 0, darkBlue,
                                      0, h, lightBlue);
  }

  // Dimension, in user space, that the SimplePainter paints,
  // starting from (0, 0)
  public Dimension getSize(){
    return size;
  }

  public void render(Graphics2D g){
    // First, fill background with gradientPaint
    g.setPaint(gradientPaint);
    g.fillRect(0, 0, size.width, size.height);

    // Now, paint image
    g.drawImage(image, MARGIN, MARGIN, null);
  }
}
```

Table 3.2 ■ Rendering to a screen

CODE (SCREENRENDERING.JAVA)

```
public class ScreenRendering extends Component {
                                    // 1. Derive from Component
  // Use a SimplePainter to do the rendering
  private SimplePainter painter;                        Output

  public ScreenRendering(String imageName){
    painter = new SimplePainter(imageName);
  }

  public Dimension getMinimumSize(){
    return painter.getSize();
  }

  public Dimension getPreferredSize(){
    return painter.getSize();
  }


public void paint(Graphics _g){      // 2. Override paint
    Graphics2D g = (Graphics2D)_g;   // 3. Cast to Graphics2D to get
                                     // access to Java 2D features

    painter.render(g);               // 4. Use Graphics2D for rendering
  }

public static final String USAGE
      = "java com.sun.glf.snippets.ScreenRendering <imageFileName>";

public static void main(String args[]){
    // Check input arguments
    if(args.length<1){
      System.out.println(USAGE);
      System.exit(0);
    }

    // Create a new Frame object that will appear on the screen
    // as any other Frame of the window manager.
    Frame frame = new Frame();

    // Add a ScreenRendering component to the Frame, and fit to content.
    frame.add(new ScreenRendering(args[0]));
    frame.pack();


    // Show the frame
    frame.setVisible(true);
```

Table 3.2 ■ Rendering to a screen (Continued)

CODE (SCREENRENDERING.JAVA)

```
// The following WindowListener will close the frame
// when closing the frame from its system menu.
frame.addWindowListener(new WindowAdapter(){
  public void windowClosing(WindowEvent evt){
    System.exit(0);
  }
});
  }
}
```

ing, all the rendering operations are done in an offscreen buffer and the offscreen buffer is then copied to the screen once all the rendering is complete. This technique is often used to avoid flickering.

Drawing to the Printer

To render to the printer, we use the `java.awt.print` package classes:

1. Implement the `Printable` interface.
2. Write the `print` method. One of the input parameters is of type `Graphics`.
3. Cast the `print` method's `Graphics` parameter into a `Graphics2D` object.
4. Use the `Graphics2D` object for rendering.
5. Create a `PrinterJob` from the `PrinterJob.getPrinterJob` method.
6. Set the `PageFormat` and printer options either manually or through dialog boxes (`PrinterJob.pageDialog` and `Printer-Job.printDialog`).
7. Call `PrinterJob.setPrintable` with the `Printable` implementation that we created. `PrinterJob` will use this `Printable` to `paint` the printed pages.
8. Call `PrinterJob.print`. This will automatically call the `Printable` implementation's `print` method for the different pages.

In essence, the `Printable` object that implements the rendering logic is called back by the printing engine. Note that the `print` method may be called several times for the same page because pages are actually printed band by band.

Table 3.3 shows how `SimplePainter` is used in a different context to render to a printer.

Table 3.3 ■ Rendering to a printer

```
PRINTERRENDERING.JAVA
public class PrinterRendering implements Printable{
                         // 1. Implement the Printable interface
  // Delegates rendering to a SimplePainter
  private SimplePainter painter;

  // @param imageName image the painter should render
  public PrinterRendering(String imageFileName){
    painter = new SimplePainter(imageFileName);
  }

  public int print(Graphics _g, PageFormat pageFormat, int pageIndex){
                         // 2. Write print method
    if(pageIndex == 0){
      Graphics2D g = (Graphics2D)_g;
                         // 3. Cast to Graphics2D to access
                         // Java 2D features
      // Modify user space to device space transform so that
      // output is centered
      double xMargin = (pageFormat.getImageableWidth()
                     - painter.getSize().width)/2;
      double yMargin = (pageFormat.getImageableHeight()
                     - painter.getSize().height)/2;
      g.translate(pageFormat.getImageableX() + xMargin,
               pageFormat.getImageableY() + yMargin);

      painter.render(g);        // 4. Use Graphics2D for rendering

      // Return status indicated that we did paint a page
      return PAGE_EXISTS;
    }
    else
      return NO_SUCH_PAGE;
  }

  public static String USAGE
    = "java com.sun.glf.snippets.PrinterRendering <imageFileName>";

  public static void main(String args[]) throws Exception{
    // Check input arguments
    if(args.length<1){
      System.out.println(USAGE);
      System.exit(0);
    }
```

Table 3.3 ■ Rendering to a printer (Continued)

PRINTERRENDERING.JAVA

```
PrinterJob printerJob              // 5. Create a PrinterJob object
    = PrinterJob.getPrinterJob();

PageFormat pageFormat              // 6. Set PageFormat and printer options
    = printerJob.defaultPage();

  if(printerJob.pageDialog(pageFormat) != pageFormat){
    // User has okayed his settings
    // Let the user select the print options
    if(printerJob.printDialog()){
      printerJob.setPrintable(new PrinterRendering(args[0]));
                              // 7. Set Printable object

      printerJob.print();   // 8. Print now
    }
    else
      System.out.println("PrintDialog was cancelled");
  }
 }
}
```

An interesting point to note is that, with the default graphic context transform, the origin of the device space is at the upper-left corner of the page, where no rendering can happen because printers usually have minimal margins they need to guide the page they print. The page format dialog (`PrinterJob.pageDialog` makes the dialog box in Figure 3.1 pop up) specifies the margins of the page.

As Figure 3.1 shows, the part of the page that can be rendered, the imageable area, is smaller than the page. Its metrics are provided by the `PageFormat get-ImageableXXX` methods (`getImageableX`, `getImageableY`, `getImageable-Width`, and `getImageableHeight`). In our example, we used that information to center our rendering onto the page.

```
double xMargin
    = (pageFormat.getImageableWidth() - painter.getSize().width)/2;

double yMargin
    = (pageFormat.getImageableHeight() - painter.getSize().height)/2;

g.translate(pageFormat.getImageableX() + xMargin,
            pageFormat.getImageableY() + yMargin);
```

Finally, it is important to understand that the default transform makes the dimensions of the user space and the device space match. In other words, 72 units in user space will appear as an inch in device space, that is, an inch on the printed paper. For example, the image we used in our example (that is, to pro-

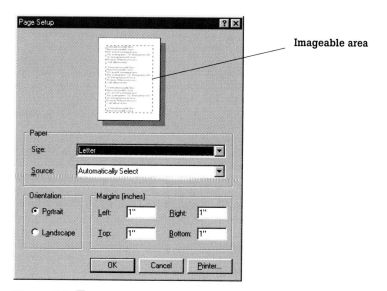

Imageable area

Figure 3.1 ■
The page setup dialog

duce the output shown in Table 3.4 on page 52) is 384 by 485 pixels. In user space, its physical dimensions are: 384 x 1/72 = 5.333 inches by 485 x 1/72 = 6.736 inches. Because, by default, the device space and the user space match, this is the dimension of the image when we print it.

On a high-resolution printer, pixels on the output device have a smaller dimension than 1/72 by 1/72 inch. As a result, when we print our Image, one pixel in the source image is mapped to several pixels on the output device. As we explain in Chapter 4 (see "AffineTransformOp" on page 95), there is a process of pixel interpolation that does this mapping. One of the interpolation methods (known as the nearest neighbor method), can create blotchy results and give the impression of low image resolution.

To print an image at a different printer resolution, we need to modify the graphic context's AffineTransform attribute. For example, if we modify the code as follows—

```
double xScale = 1/2.0;
double yScale = 1/2.0;

// Modify user space to device space transform so that output is
// centered
double xMargin = (pageFormat.getImageableWidth()
                        -
                painter.getSize().width*xScale)/2;
```

```
double yMargin = (pageFormat.getImageableHeight()

                  painter.getSize().height*yScale)/2;

g.translate(pageFormat.getImageableX() + xMargin,
            pageFormat.getImageableY() + yMargin);

g.scale(xScale, yScale);

// Delegate rendering to painter
painter.render(g);
```

—the image is printed at a higher resolution (that is, an image pixel maps to fewer printer dots). Table 3.4 shows the printed page for different scale values.

Table 3.4 ■ Printing at high resolution

DEFAULT	DOUBLE	QUADRUPLE
xSCALE=1	xSCALE=1/2	xSCALE=1/4
ySCALE=1	ySCALE=1/2	ySCALE=1/4

Another way to look at this resolution issue is to determine the desired output resolution. In that case, the scale factor would be:

```
scaleFactor = 72.0/resolution;
```

Important note: about resolution

There are two different aspects to what we call resolution: color resolution and spatial resolution. Different devices have different capacities. On a raster device, the color resolution is the number of colors that an individually addressable element (pixel) can display. The spatial resolution is the number of pixels or dots per unit of space, typically per inch.

For example, a screen typically has a high or very high color resolution (from 256 to several millions) and a fairly low spatial resolution (typically 72 dpi). A printer can have a very high spatial resolution (600, 1200, 2400), but each pixel dot usually has a low color resolution. For most desktop printers (for example, a black-and-white laser printer), each pixel can represent only two color values: ink or no ink (for example, black or white). To achieve higher color resolutions, printers use a process, called dithering, that increases the number of colors the printer can represent but also decreases its spatial resolution.

Images present a special challenge as far as resolution goes. They do store pixel values, so they have a color resolution. However, their pixels have no physical size. When an image is displayed on a screen, it is often displayed using the screen resolution: an image pixel is mapped to a screen pixel. This is how images are displayed in a Web browser. For printing, it is common to associate a resolution to an image: this is a way to determine the physical size of the image on the final printout. The higher the printing resolution, the smaller the image on the output because more pixels will be used to fill one unit of space, as we have seen in our example.

Rendering to an Offscreen Buffer

To render to an offscreen buffer, we use the `java.awt.image` package classes:

1. Create a `BufferedImage`.
2. Create a `Graphics2D` object to render into the newly built `BufferedImage` using the `createGraphics` method.
3. Use the `Graphics2D` object for rendering.

Table 3.5 shows a program that loads an input image, creates an offscreen gray scale `BufferedImage` for rendering output, uses our `SimplePainter` for rendering, and finally saves the result in a JPEG file.

Note that we could have used a regular RGB image by simply creating a different `BufferedImage`:

```
// 1. Create a BufferedImage
BufferedImage image
    = new BufferedImage(painter.getSize().width,
                        painter.getSize().height,
                        BufferedImage.TYPE_BYTE_RGB);
```

The result is illustrated in Figure 3.2.

Table 3.5 ■ Rendering to an offscreen buffer

OFFSCREENBUFFERRENDERING.JAVA

```java
public class OffscreenBufferRendering{
  static String USAGE
    = "java com.sun.glf.snippets.OffscreenBuffereRendering "
    + "<inputFileName> <outputFileName>";

  public static void main(String args[])
      throws Exception{

    if(args.length<2){
      System.out.println(USAGE);
      System.exit(0);
    }

    // First, create a SimplePainter
    SimplePainter painter
      = new SimplePainter(args[0]);

    // 1. Create a BufferedImage
    int imageWidth = painter.getSize().width;
    int imageHeight = painter.getSize().height;
    BufferedImage image
      = new BufferedImage(imageWidth,
                          imageHeight,
                          BufferedImage.TYPE_BYTE_GRAY);
    // 2. Create a Graphics2D object
    Graphics2D g = image.createGraphics();

    // 3. Use Graphics2D object for rendering
    painter.render(g);

    //
    // Save result as a JPEG image into outputImageFileName
    //
    FileOutputStream out
      = new FileOutputStream(args[1]);   // The second arguments contains
                                         // the output file name.

    JPEGEncodeParam param = JPEGCodec.getDefaultJPEGEncodeParam(image);
    param.setQuality(1, false);          // Use maximum JPEG quality

    JPEGImageEncoder encoder = JPEGCodec.createJPEGEncoder(out, param);
    encoder.encode(image);
    out.close();
  }
```

Output

Figure 3.2 ■
Color BufferedImage rendering

Resolution Independence

We said in the introduction that Shape objects are resolution independent and that they are turned into pixels by a process called scan conversion at rendering time. Figure 3.3 illustrates how the same geometrical form (a line from (2, 1) to (5, 1) is rendered on two different output devices. The two devices use a different number of pixels to draw the same line.

```
drawLine(2, 1, 5, 1);
// draw a line from (2, 1) to (5, 1)
// i.e., 3 units long
```

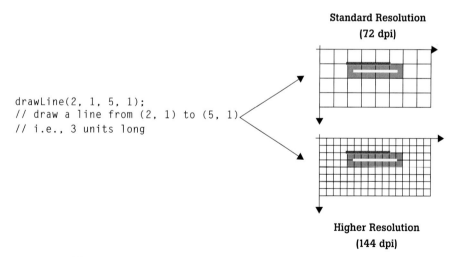

Figure 3.3 ■
Resolution independence

Our illustration assumes that we are using a one-point-wide stroke and the default transform. The grids represent the output device raster grids (that is, arrays of addressable pixels). Note that the output coordinates fall between pixels: (0, 0) is the upper-left corner of the first pixel, (1, 0) the upper-left corner of the second one, and so forth.

The red lines represent the "logical" line, and the gray rectangles represent how it is rendered on the output. The yellow lines represent the line after a default (.5, .5) translation has been applied by BasicStroke. That default translation, downward and to the right, maintains a consistent behavior with earlier versions of the API where the only pen (there was no Stroke interface at the time) was one pixel wide with a bias below and to the right of the stroked Shape. This also provides consistent behavior with regard to the anti-aliasing hint.[3]

Conclusion

Acquiring a Graphics2D object for a specific device is the only required device-specific operation in Java 2D,[4] and it has to be. Depending on the nature of the application you develop, it might be interesting to organize your rendering code in a way that is output device independent. For example, it might not be a good idea to write all the rendering code inside a java.awt.Component's paint method. Even though it is true that this method can be called with a Graphics2D object other than one for the screen, it requires that a UI Component be created for the rendering logic to be available, and this may not be acceptable (and it is overkill anyway).

Isolating the rendering code from the output context is what we have done with the SimplePainter class; as we will see in Part II, the Graphic Layers Framework, which deals with the creation of graphical compositions, also renders in separate objects (com.sun.glf.Composition implementations) that can be used to render on screen, on a printer, or in an offscreen buffer. This design choice was driven by the framework's requirements (be able to batch process compositions or generate image files, for example).

---

3. The javadoc documentation for Graphics2D articulates the reasons driving this behavior.
4. Note that there are ways to access device information. See the GraphicsDevice, GraphicsConfiguration, and GraphicsEnvironment classes in the java.awt package.

The important point to remember is to carefully evaluate *where* you write your rendering code: the fine line is that the rendering code itself is device independent, but the place where it is written might not be. If the code may be used for different kinds of output, then it is a good idea to isolate the rendering logic as we just explained. Otherwise, there is no reason to do so.

In the following chapters, most code samples ignore the way `Graphics2D` objects are acquired, and code segments start with:

```
Graphics2D g = ...; // Specific to the output
```

This notation is an implicit reference to this chapter and means that the subsequent code can be used from a `java.awt.Component`'s `paint` method or from a `java.awt.print.Printable`'s `print` method, or that g is returned by a `BufferedImage`'s `createGraphics`.

chapter **4**

MANIPULATING AND RENDERING SHAPES, IMAGES, AND TEXT

The rendering model is similar for shapes, text, and images. However, each of them covers a complete area of computer graphics. Shapes *are resolution independent and provide a generic way to represent geometrical forms.* BufferedImage *provides advanced pixel storage, manipulation, and filtering capabilities. Finally, text support addresses the complex issues of proper international text support, rendering, and editing.*

In this chapter, we discuss each of these areas in turn.

Shapes

What is a Shape? According to the JDK API documentation, a Shape is:

"The interface for objects which represent some form of geometric shape. The shape is described by a PathIterator object which can express the outline of the shape as well as a rule for determining how the outline divides the 2D plane into interior and exterior points. Each Shape object provides callbacks to get the bounding box of the geometry, to determine whether points or rectangles lie partly or entirely within the interior of the shape, and to retrieve a PathIterator object to describe the trajectory path of the outline of the shape."

Let's reword this definition. A java.awt.Shape implementation describes a geometric form that can:

■ Determine whether or not a point or rectangle lies inside it or outside it
■ Describe itself though a PathIterator
■ Return its bounds

The Shape interface provides flexibility to the API because it can manipulate *any* geometric form that conforms to the interface. Therefore, the API is extensible, and we can easily comply with the `Shape` interface if we need a new geometrical type not already provided. We will present the different `Shape` implementations, such as `Rectangle` or `Area`, but let us first look at how `Graphics2D` relies on `Shape` features so that shapes can be:

- Drawn
- Filled
- Transformed
- Used for clipping
- Used for hit detection

Different uses of Shape

Table 4.1 shows the output of a program that illustrates each of the above points by showing an arbitrary `Shape` drawn, filled, transformed, and used for clipping. One characteristic of this program that does not show with a screen shot is that a short message is printed when the mouse is clicked over the left-most Eiffel tower.

Table 4.1 ■ Different uses of Shape

SHAPEUSAGE.JAVA

```
public class ShapeUsage extends JComponent { // Extends Swing JComponent
    ...
    GeneralPath eiffel=null;
    ...

    // First, build an Eiffel Tower like Shape
    eiffel.moveTo(20.0f, 0.0f);
    eiffel.lineTo(30.0f, 0.0f);
    eiffel.quadTo(30.0f, 30.0f, 50.0f, 60.0f);
    eiffel.lineTo(35.0f, 60.0f);
    eiffel.curveTo(35.0f, 40.0f, 15.0f, 40.0f, 15.0f, 60.0f);
    eiffel.lineTo(0.0f, 60.0f);
    eiffel.quadTo(20.0f, 30.0f, 20.0f, 0.0f);

    // Add hit detector to check on first eiffel tower hits
    addMouseListener(new MouseAdapter(){
        Rectangle hitRect = new Rectangle(0, 0, 3, 3);
        public void mouseClicked(MouseEvent evt){
            hitRect.x = evt.getX()-1;
            hitRect.y = evt.getY()-1;
            Graphics2D g
                = (Graphics2D)getGraphics();  // Returns Graphics2D object used
                                              // to render in this JComponent.
```

Table 4.1 ■ Different uses of Shape (Continued)

SHAPEUSAGE.JAVA

```
            g.scale(scale, scale);
            g.translate(margin, margin);
            g.setStroke(dashStroke);
            if(g.hit(hitRect, eiffel, true))
              System.out.println("Rotated eiffel was hit");
        }
      });

    ...
}
```

Output

```
Graphics2D g = ...;

// The eiffel bounds rectangle is used to compute the translations
// used for each rendered eiffel instance.
Rectangle bounds = eiffel.getBounds();

// Move to the initial rendering position
g.translate(margin, margin);

// Set Stroke for first eiffel drawing
g.setStroke(dashStroke);

// Invoke rendering method: draw.
g.draw(eiffel);

// Move to the next rendering position
g.translate(bounds.width + margin, 0);

// Set Paint for filling Shape
Color blue = new Color(100, 100, 200);
Color black = Color.black;
Paint gradientPaint
    = new GradientPaint(0, bounds.y, blue,
                        0, bounds.y + bounds.height, black);
g.setPaint(gradientPaint);
```

Table 4.1 ■ Different uses of Shape (Continued)

SHAPEUSAGE.JAVA

```java
// Invoke rendering method: fill
g.fill(eiffel);

// Move to the next rendering position
g.translate(bounds.width + margin, 0);

// Create a rotated eiffel from an AffineTransform

// Rotation of PI/4 about the Eiffel Shape center.
AffineTransform rotation
    = AffineTransform.getRotateInstance(Math.PI/4.f,
                bounds.x + bounds.width/2,   // x axis rotation center
                bounds.y + bounds.height/2); // y axis rotation center

Shape rotatedEiffel = rotation.createTransformedShape(eiffel);

// Render rotated Shape
g.fill(rotatedEiffel);

// Clipping

g.translate(margin + bounds.width, 0);
g.setClip(eiffel);
g.fill(bounds);


// Restore clip
g.setClip(defaultClip);

// AffineTransform usage: Alternate solution:
// set the rendering context transform instead of
// creating a transformed Shape.

// Move to rendering position
g.translate(bounds.width + margin, 0);

// Concatenate rotation
g.transform(rotation);

// Fill eiffel
g.fill(eiffel);
```

Note that each Eiffel tower is rendered differently. The first one is stroked (stroking is the process of drawing a Shape's outline),[1] the second one is filled with GradientPaint, the third one as well, but it is also rotated and the last but one is rendered by using the Eiffel tower as a clip. The rightmost Eiffel tower illustrates an alternative method for rendering the third, rotated Eiffel tower. Let us look at the code.

▼ **Creating an arbitrary shape**   Before any rendering happens, we create a Shape object. The sample Shape implementation we use is GeneralPath, from the java.awt.geom package. It is the most flexible Shape class and it can define almost any geometrical form we can imagine (as long as it can be described in terms of lines and cubic or quadratic Bezier curves, as we explain later). Our code creates an Eiffel Tower Shape by specifying the successive lines and curves that compose it, starting at the tower's top left, in a clockwise direction (Figure 4.1).

Once the Eiffel tower Shape has been created as we just explained, it can be used, as would any other Shape implementation, with the various Graphics2D features that rely on the Shape interface.

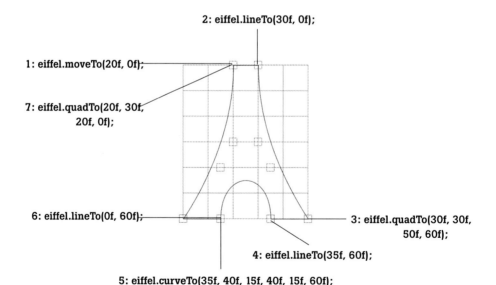

Figure 4.1 ■
Using GeneralPath to define an Eiffel tower Shape

---

1. See "Strokes" on page 140 in Chapter 5 for complete description of this process.

▼ **Drawing shapes**   Drawing a `Shape` is simple:

```
graphics.draw(eiffel);
```

This code draws the input `Shape` parameter, whatever it is, using the current `Stroke` attribute in the graphic context. The `Stroke` interface defines the pen or brush characteristics: line width, solid or dashed, etc. Chapter 5 (see "Strokes" on page 140) describes the `Stroke` at length. In our example, we use the `BasicStroke` implementation with a dash pattern and a width of one. The dash pattern made of a 4 point dash followed by a 4 point gap.

```
Stroke dashStroke = new BasicStroke(1, BasicStroke.CAP_ROUND,
                              BasicStroke.JOIN_ROUND, 10f,
                              new float[]{4f, 4f}, 0f);
...
g.setStroke(dashStroke);
```

The result of the draw is the first dashed outline Eiffel tower (Table 4.1 on page 59). Remember that any invocation of the `Graphics2D`'s draw rendering method uses the current `Stroke` attribute in the graphic context. The `Stroke` implementation is responsible for defining the outline resulting from stroking a `Shape`, again as a `Shape`, through its `createStrokedShape` method (we describe this method in greater detail in the next chapter).

The process of drawing a `Shape`'s outline amounts to requesting the current `Stroke` attribute to create the stroked `Shape` object defining the `Shape`'s outline and then filling that outline `Shape` with the current `Paint` in the graphic context. So, drawing a `Shape` is technically equivalent to filling a `Shape`, except that the `fill` is done on a different `Shape` (the `Shape` object's outline, as defined by the `Stroke` attribute, as opposed to the `Shape` object itself).

▼ **Filling shapes**   Filling a `Shape` is similar to drawing:

```
g.fill(eiffel);
```

This code fills the input `Shape` by using the current graphic context `Paint` attribute. The `Paint` defines how a `Shape` is filled: solid color (the `Color` class implements the `Paint` interface), `GradientPaint`, `TexturePaint`, or any other implementation of the `Paint` interface.[2] We use a linear blue-to-black `GradientPaint` from the top of the tower (0, bounds.y) to its bottom (0, bounds.y + bounds.width):

```
Paint gradientPaint
   = new GradientPaint(0, bounds.y, blue,
                       0, bounds.y + bounds.width, black);
...
g.setPaint(gradientPaint);
g.fill(eiffel);
```

---

2.   See "Paints" on page 148 in Chapter 5 for more details

The result of the `fill` is the second Eiffel tower from the left, with a blue tip; see Table 4.1 on page 59. For now, the important thing to remember is that the graphic context `Paint` attribute is set with the `setPaint` method and that it is used both for filling shapes (`Graphics2D.fill`) and drawing their outlines (`Graphics2D.draw`).

▼ **Transforming shapes**   We have already introduced `AffineTransform` and described how it is one of the graphic context attributes.[3] Table 4.2 provides a formal definition of `AffineTransform`'s mathematical foundation: the mathematical matrix it embodies is what `AffineTransform` uses to transform coordinates between coordinate spaces.

Table 4.2 ■ AffineTransform definition

An affine transformation is a geometrical transformation of coordinates and has the following form:

```
x' = a.x + b.y + tx
y' = c.x + d.y + ty
```

where (x,y) are the coordinates of the point to be transformed and (x', y') are the coordinates of the transformed point. An affine transformation is easily described as a matrix:

```
    a b tx
M = c d ty
    0 0 1
```

and we have : `P' = M.P` with `P(x, y, 1)` and the transformed point `P'(x', y', 1)`.

A two-dimensional affine transform can be expressed as the composition of five types of transformations: translation, rotation, scaling, reflection, and shear.

See [Hearn1997] for more details.

A `Graphics2D` object renders shapes after applying an `AffineTransform`. The Eiffel tower `Shape` is defined in *user space*. If we were doing nothing before drawing or filling it, the `Graphics2D` object would assume that it should render the `Shape` object on the device at the same device coordinates, because by default the API makes the user space and the device space match.[4]

---

3. See "Graphic Context Attributes" on page 34 in Java 2D API Overview.
4. The coordinate systems match in the sense that they have the origin in the upper-left corner of the display area, the x-axis running to the right, the y-axis running downward, and 72 units in user space match an inch in device space. See our discussion in Chapter 2 ("Acquiring a Graphics2D Object" on page 12).

In our example, the Eiffel tower has its upper-left corner at (0, 0) in the user space. If we did not modify the `AffineTransform` attribute, each Eiffel tower we render would appear at (0, 0) on the screen (if we use a screen as our output device). To render the shapes side by side and add some margin, our code actually modifies the `AffineTransform` attribute to render the Eiffel tower at the proper location:

```
// Leave some margins up and left
g.translate(margin, margin);

// ... Draw first eiffel, as we have seen

// Move to next position, leaving a margin between the two Shapes
g.translate(bounds.width + margin, 0);

// ... Fill second eiffel as we have seen, etc...
```

With this approach, the same `Shape` object can be reused over and over again and rendered at different locations. An alternate method consists in creating a transformed `Shape`. That is, create a `Shape`, still in the user space, from an `AffineTransform`. In our example, we use a rotation about the Eiffel tower's center and create a rotated version of that `Shape` object:

```
AffineTransform rotation
  = AffineTransform.getRotateInstance(Math.PI/4.f,
                      bounds.x + bounds.width/2,
                      // x axis rotation center
                      bounds.y + bounds.height/2)
                      // y axis rotation center

Shape rotatedEiffel = rotation.createTransformedShape(eiffel);

// Render rotated Shape
g.fill(rotatedEiffel);
```

Note how this is different: the context's `AffineTransform` attribute is not modified. The equivalent, using the previous method, is:

```
// Concatenate current context transform with a rotation about the
// Eiffel tower's center.
g.rotate( Math.PI/4.f,
          bounds.x + bounds.width/2,  // x axis rotation center
          bounds.y + bounds.height/2) // y axis rotation center

// Render Shape
g.fill(eiffel);
```

This alternative method is the one used to render the rightmost Eiffel tower in our example. The key thing to remember is that shapes are defined in the user space and are transformed by the current graphic context's `AffineTransform` attribute before they are rendered to the output. Consequently, there are two ways to render a given `Shape` at a specific location (or with any transformation) onto the output device. One way is to set the graphic context's `AffineTransform` attribute. The other is to leave the context's `AffineTransform` unmodified and create a new `Shape` object in the user space that is at the desired location (using `AffineTransform.createTransformedShape`). The right method really depends on the type of application. For example, in an animation where a `Shape` needs to traverse a screen, it is wiser to modify the context's transform to avoid creating a large number of `Shape` instances, one for each position.

Another important point to remember is that, to set the current transform, we can either use `Graphics2D.setTransform`, or use `Graphics2D` methods to modify the current transform (for example, `translate`, `rotate`), or use both approaches, as we did in our example. The right method depends on what is most convenient.

We discuss `AffineTransform` at length in Chapter 5 (see "AffineTransform" on page 133). That chapter details important issues such as transform concatenation.

▼ **Clipping**   Another feature that employs the `Shape` interface is clipping. The clip area is the area where rendering operations take effect. Everything lying outside this area is unaffected. The clip area can be any `Shape` object, thanks to the `Graphics2D.setClip` and the `Graphics2D.clip` methods. The first method sets the clip to a given `Shape`, and the second intersects the current clip area with a new `Shape`. In our example, we first set the clip area and then fill the Eiffel tower bounding rectangle with the same `GradientPaint` as before.

```
g.setClip(newClip);
// Remember we did : g.setPaint(gradientPaint);
g.fill(bounds);
```

The output is the second-last `Shape` to the right in Table 4.1 on page 59: not all the rectangular `Shape` is rendered: only the part that falls into the clipping region is, which explains why rendering a `Rectangle` shows as an Eiffel tower again.

▼ **Hit detection**   The last feature that relies on the `Shape` interface is hit detection. In our example, the `MouseListener` object we create checks for hits on the leftmost Eiffel tower. Hit detection is an extremely powerful feature because it takes the rendering attributes into account. For example, the transform we set on the graphics object is used for hit detection. Similarly, the `Stroke` attribute is used, which is useful to properly detect hits on a `Shape`'s perimeter, especially if it has been drawn with a thick stroke: its thickness and dashes are taken into account.

The hit detection code is as follows:

```
addMouseListener(new MouseAdapter(){ // Will detect mouse clicked events
    Rectangle hitRect
        = new Rectangle(0, 0, 3, 3);     // Whenever a rectangle centered
                                         // on the mouse click intersects
                                         // the Shape, the click is
                                         // considered a hit.

    public void mouseClicked(MouseEvent evt){
        hitRect.x = evt.getX()-1;        // Center hitRect about the mouse
        hitRect.y = evt.getY()-1;        // click location.

        Graphics2D g = (Graphics2D)getGraphics();⁵
        g.scale(scale, scale);           // Restore the same graphic context
        g.translate(margin, margin);     // attributes before using the hit
        g.setStroke(dashStroke);         // method.
        if(g.hit(hitRect, eiffel, true)) // true for outline hit detection
            System.out.println("Rotated eiffel was hit");
    }
});
```

To understand how this works, we can write the following pseudocode for
Graphics2D's hit method:

```
public boolean hit(Rectangle rect, Shape shape, boolean onStroke){
    if(onStroke){ // Hit only on dashes
        // Get geometrical description of outline, if we are hit
        // testing on outline
        Shape strokedPath = currentStroke.createStrokedShape(shape);

        // Take user space to device space transform into account:
        // transform strokedShape to device space.
        strokedPath
            = currentTransform.createTransformedShape(strokedPath);

        // Use the Shape interface to do define whether or not the Shape
        // outline was hit
        return strokedPath.intersects(rect);
    }
    else{
        // Take user space to device space transform into account.
        Shape deviceShape
            = currentTransform.createTransformedShape(shape);

        // Use the Shape interface to define whether or not
        // the Shape was hit
        return deviceShape.intersects(rect);
    }
}
```

---

5. getGraphics() is invoked on the java.awt.Component where this anonymous Java class
   is declared (i.e., the MouseAdapter extension).

The pseudocode explains how it is possible to determine whether or not a hit was in between dashes for a dashed Stroke. Because createStrokedShape returns a Shape that encompasses only the dashes and none of the spaces, the following intersects call only returns true if the hit is on a dash, not on a gap.

Different types of shapes

Our first example uses GeneralPath to create an arbitrary Shape. The API comes with enough predefined Shape implementations to create pretty much any geometrical form.

Figure 2.3 on page 18 shows the visual representation of all the available Shape implementations (the **ShapeClasses.java** program on the CD-ROM produces this output). Table 4.3 demonstrates each of those implementations and visually relates the code used to create Shapes with their corresponding control parameters.

Table 4.3 ■ Shape implementations (ShapeClasses.java on CD-ROM)

SHAPE CONTROL AND CORRESPONDING CODE

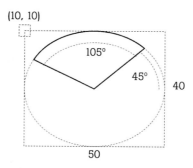

```
Arc2D arc = new Arc2D.Float(10f, 10f, 50f, 40f, 45f, 105f, Arc2D.PIE);
// PIE adds line segments from the center of the controlling ellipse to the
// to the arc start and end points.
```

Table 4.3 ■ Shape implementations (ShapeClasses.java on CD–ROM) (Continued)

SHAPE CONTROL AND CORRESPONDING CODE

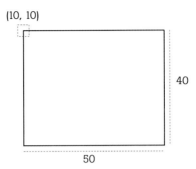

```
Rectangle rect = new Rectangle(10, 10, 50, 40);
```

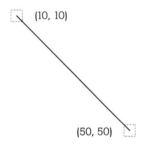

```
Line2D line = new Line2D.Double(10.0, 10.0, 50.0, 50.0);
```

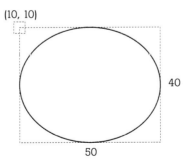

```
Ellipse2D ellipse = new Ellipse2D.Double(10.0, 10.0, 50.0, 40.0);
```

Table 4.3 ■ Shape implementations (ShapeClasses.java on CD-ROM) (Continued)

SHAPE CONTROL AND CORRESPONDING CODE

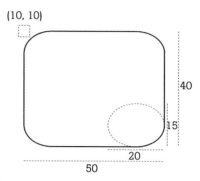

```
RoundRectangle2D rect2
    = new RoundRectangle2D.Double(10.0, 10.0,
                                  50.0, 40.0,
                                  20.0, 15.0);
```

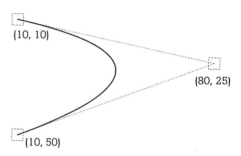

```
QuadCurve2D quad = new QuadCurve2D.Double(10.0, 10.0,
                                          80.0, 25.0,
                                          10.0, 50.0);
```

Table 4.3 ■ Shape implementations (ShapeClasses.java on CD–ROM) (Continued)

SHAPE CONTROL AND CORRESPONDING CODE

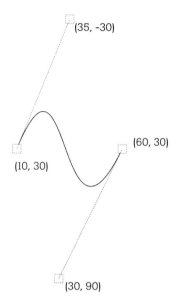

```
CubicCurve2D wave = new CubicCurve2D.Double(10.0, 30.0,
                                            35.0, -30.0,
                                            30.0, 90.0,
                                            60.0, 30.0);
```

Table 4.3 ■ Shape implementations (ShapeClasses.java on CD–ROM) (Continued)

SHAPE CONTROL AND CORRESPONDING CODE

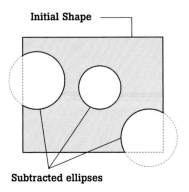

Initial Shape

Subtracted ellipses

```
Area cheese = new Area(rect);
cheese.subtract(new Area(new Ellipse2D.Double(5.0, 15.0, 20.0, 20.0)));
cheese.subtract(new Area(new Ellipse2D.Double(30.0, 20.0, 15.0, 15.0)));
cheese.subtract(new Area(new Ellipse2D.Double(45.0, 35.0, 20.0, 20.0)));
```

```
GeneralPath eiffel = new GeneralPath();
eiffel.moveTo(20f, 0f);
eiffel.lineTo(30f, 0f);
eiffel.quadTo(30f, 30f, 50f, 60f);
eiffel.lineTo(35f, 60f);
eiffel.curveTo(35f, 40f, 15f,
               40f, 15f, 60f);
eiffel.lineTo(0f, 60f);
eiffel.quadTo(20f, 30f, 20f, 0f);
```

moveTo   lineTo

quadTo   quadTo

lineTo curveTo lineTo

```
Polygon polygon = new Polygon();
polygon.addPoint(20, 0);
polygon.addPoint(40, 0);
polygon.addPoint(60, 20);
polygon.addPoint(60, 40);
polygon.addPoint(40, 60);
polygon.addPoint(20, 60);
polygon.addPoint(0, 40);
polygon.addPoint(0, 20);
polygon.addPoint(20, 0);
```

first point

addPoint
order

`Arc2D`, `Line2D`, `Rectangle2D`, and `Ellipse2D` are straightforward.

`QuadCurve2D` and `CubicCurve2D` are *Bezier* curves. They let us approximate any kind of curve. If we cannot properly approximate a curve with one `CubicCurve2D`, we are usually able to obtain the desired result by concatenating several. For more details on Bezier curves and their mathematical foundations, see Chapter 10 of [Hearn97]. The important thing to remember is that Bezier curves allow us to create curves of all types.

We use an `Area` to create a cheese-like `Shape` (Swiss cheese). It is very convenient and powerful for combining shapes of different kinds, as it provides instrumentation for adding, subtracting, or intersecting one `Shape` to/from/with another and even to perform exclusive addition (that is, there is an `exclusiveOr` member that will add the areas that do not intersect and subtract those that do).

Finally, `GeneralPath` provides means to create arbitrary shapes, as shown in our Eiffel tower example. We create this `GeneralPath` object by iterating through its path in terms of lines, quadratic curves, and cubic curves. In earlier versions of the AWT, the `Polygon` class provided a simpler way to create arbitrary forms but was limited to straight lines.

`GeneralPath` helps understand how the `Shape` interface really works. How can various `Shape` implementations be manipulated uniformly? Well, just as the `GeneralPath` lets you define a `Shape` in terms of lines, quadratic curves, and cubic curves, all `Shape` implementations are required to provide a `PathIterator` that describes their geometry in terms of lines, quadratic curves, and cubic curves. We will use `PathIterator` for our custom `Stroke` implementations in Chapter 9 (see "Custom Strokes" on page 316).

How do we know which `Shape` implementation to use or combine to create a given geometry? For simple cases, we can use `Arc2D`, `Line2D`, or `Ellipse2D`. When a shape is the composition of several geometrical forms, we can either use `Area` or `GeneralPath`, because they both let us aggregate shapes through their respective `add` and `append` methods. If we need to perform more sophisticated shape compositions, such as subtracting one shape from another, then `Area` is the right answer. Note that `Area` implements all the logic for constructive area geometry and is more sophisticated and of heavier weight than the `GeneralPath.append` method. That last method simply appends a `Shape` object's set of segments, as returned by its `PathIterator`, to the `GeneralPath` object content.

Finally, when the outline of a shape does not resolve to any of the default implementations, we can also use `GeneralPath`. We can think of the quadratic curve as a "single turn" curve and a cubic curve as a "two turn" curve, and we need to divide the outline of the geometry into segments that are either lines, quadratic curves, or cubic curves. Once this division is done, we use the `Gen`-

eralPath methods (such as lineTo and curveTo) to describe each of the outline segments, as we did for the Eiffel tower Shape in our first example.

A last note about the different java.awt.geom package Shapes: at a minimum, they are provided in two versions: single precision (for example, Rectangle2D.Float) and double precision (for example, Rectangle2D.Double) so that we can get the kind of precision fitting the requirements of any particular application. In our example, we used both kinds.

As an illustration of the flexibility the Shape interface provides, the code in Table 4.4 (**DukeShapeDemo.java** on the CD-ROM) shows how various Shapes can be combined to create the Duke™ logo, the mascot of the Java programming language. Of course, this is an exercise of style, but it does demonstrate that the Java 2D API handles sophisticated geometry.

Table 4.4 ■ The Duke Logo Shape

DUKESHAPEDEMO.JAVA

```
// Nose is an Ellipse2D.
public Shape getNose(){
 return new Ellipse2D.Double(70, 75,
                             60, 50);
}

// Nose shine is an Ellipse2D
public Shape getNoseShine(){
   AffineTransform t
      = new AffineTransform();
   t.setToTranslation(90, 90);
   t.rotate(-Math.PI/10);
   return t.createTransformedShape(
     new Ellipse2D.Double(-12, -9,
                          24, 18) );
}

// Arms are the concatenation of two cubic curves
// in a GeneralPath
public Shape getArms(){
   CubicCurve2D leftArm = new CubicCurve2D.Double(138, 100, 170, 135,
                                    180, 120, 150, 140);
   CubicCurve2D rightArm = new CubicCurve2D.Double(63, 100, 33, 135,
                                    23, 120, 53, 140);
   GeneralPath a = new GeneralPath(leftArm);
   a.append(rightArm, false);
   return a;
}
```

Table 4.4 ■ The Duke Logo Shape (Continued)

DUKESHAPEDEMO.JAVA

```java
// Body is composed of 4 cubic curves.
public Shape getBody(){
  GeneralPath s = new GeneralPath();
  s.moveTo(100, 25);
  s.curveTo(140, 60, 170, 200, 140, 200);
  s.curveTo(130, 200, 120, 175, 90, 175);
  s.curveTo(70, 175, 70, 200, 60, 200);
  s.curveTo(40, 200, 60, 60, 100, 25);
  return s;
}

// Head = Body - Nose - Ellipse2D
// The ellipse part clipping out the body bottom
public Shape getHead(){
  Area h = new Area(getBody());
  h.subtract(new Area(getNose()));
  h.subtract(new Area(new Ellipse2D.Double(-50, 100, 300, 250)));
  return h;
}
```

We take real advantage of the `Shape` interface when we combine it with other features (especially transforms), as the Duke logo example illustrates. Here, we use `AffineTransform` to scale down and shear the Duke logo and create a drop shadow. The Duke `Shape` itself is made of Bezier curves combined in `GeneralPath` and `Area` objects.

Summary

We have seen that `Shape` is an interface in the `java.awt package` and that it has most of its implementations, such as `Rectangle2D` and `GeneralPath` in the `java.awt.geom` package. We discussed how shapes are used by `Graphics2D` for rendering (the `fill(Shape shape)` and `draw(Shape shape)` methods), how their coordinates are transformed by the graphic context's `AffineTransform` during rendering and how they can be used both to define the clip area and to detect hits.

We have mentioned how various graphic context attributes influence `Shape` rendering: the `Paint` attribute defines how shapes and their outlines are filled, the `Stroke` attribute defines the outline form of a `Shape`, the `AffineTransform` attribute defines how `Shape` coordinates (defined in user space) map to device coordinates. In addition, the clipping limits the part of a `Shape` that is actually rendered: only the portion that falls within the clip boundaries will show. The

Font attribute has no influence on Shape rendering. However, the other two attributes, the Composite and the RenderingHints do, and this is further discussed in Chapter 5.

Shapes, in general, can be compared to line art and fall into the category of vector graphics: the visual elements are defined by sets of coordinates and are thus resolution independent. Images, which we discuss next, are made of discrete elements, pixels, and fall into the imaging category where pixels are manipulated, transformed, and filtered.

Table 4.5 lists the key classes used with shapes.

Table 4.5 ■ Key Shape rendering classes

CLASS	PURPOSE
Graphics2D	Provides Shape rendering support. Its draw methods renders the outline of a Shape to the output, using the current graphic context Paint and Stroke. Its fill method and the like (e.g., fillRect) fill a Shape with the current Paint attribute.
Shape	Interface expected from any geometric form that Graphics2D can render. Any Shape has to be able to describe itself in terms of lines, quadratic and cubic Bezier curves through a PathIterator object.

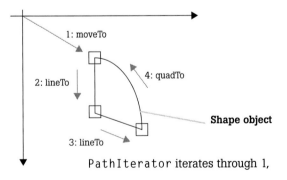

PathIterator iterates through 1,

Table 4.5 ■ Key Shape rendering classes (Continued)

CLASS	PURPOSE
PathIterator	Returned by the Shape.getPathIterator method. It allows a Graphics2D or other object to iterate along any geometrical form.
Stroke, Paint, and other graphic context attributes	They are part of the graphic context and define how Graphics2D actually fills or draws a Shape. For example, if the Paint attribute is set to Color.blue, a call to draw will paint the outline of the input Shape parameter in blue.

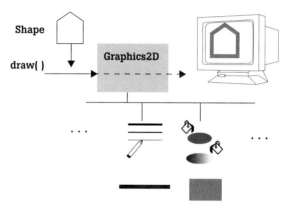

Note that Paint and Stroke are not the only rendering attributes that affect the way a Shape is rendered. Composite, AffineTransform, the clip and RenderingHints also control the rendering process.

Rendering Images: BufferedImages

As we saw in our overview of the Java 2D API, BufferedImage adds a new imaging model to the Java 2 platform graphics. This model is called the immediate mode model, because once a BufferedImage has been created, all its pixels are available, immediately. This mode is simpler to program than the push model that was used in earlier versions of the Java platform.

Rendering a BufferedImage

Our overview of the API presented the different variations of the Graphics2D drawImage methods that can be used to render an image onto an output device. Note that `BufferedImage` extends the abstract `Image` class and can therefore be drawn with all the `Graphics2D drawImage` methods that take an `Image` as an input parameter. Refer to Chapter 2 (see Table 2.5 on page 26) for the features supported by the different `drawImage` methods.

Those methods are very straightforward in their use, except one, which takes an `AffineTransform` as an input parameter:

```
drawImage(Image img, AffineTransform xform, ImageObserver obs);
```

Why is there such a special `drawImage` method? The graphic context already has `AffineTransform` among its attributes, so why an additional transform? The reason is that, strictly speaking, an image is defined in its own coordinate space, called the *image space*. In that space, an image has its upper-left corner in (0, 0) and extends along the positive side of the x and y axis, to the right and downwards. The `AffineTransform` input parameter which `drawImage` takes specifies the transform between the *image space* and the *user space*, whereas the `Graphics2D`'s `AffineTransform` graphic context attribute defines the transform between the *user space* and the *device space*. It may prove useful to control these transforms separately, which explains why this version of `draw-Image` was provided

In Figure 4.2, the red coordinate system is that of the image space, the black one the one of the user space, and the blue one is the one of the device space. The leftmost image is shown drawn in the image space. The second image is shown when drawing with a rotation as the transform between the image

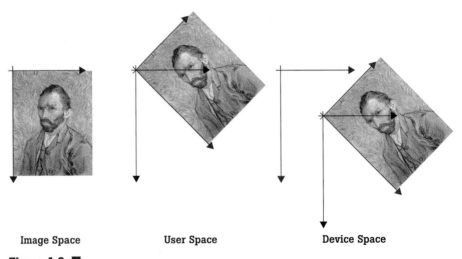

Image Space   User Space   Device Space

Figure 4.2 ■
The Image space

space and the user space. Finally, the rightmost image shows the device output, when the user-to-device space transform is set to a translation.

The following code segment creates the results shown in the rightmost image.

```
//
// This concatenates the User Space to Device Space
// transform with a translation.
//
float tx = ...;                    // x-axis translation
float ty = ...;                    // y-axis translation
g.translate(tx, ty);

//
// Create the Image Space to Device Space transform:
// a rotation of -Math.PI/4 radians
//
AffineTransform rotation = new AffineTransform();
rotation.rotate(-Math.PI/4);

//
// Draw Image: the Image first rotates about the
// origin in the user space. Then it translates into
// the device space.
//
g.drawImage(image, rotation, null);
```

Now that we know exactly how to render an image with the different `Graphics2D` `drawImage` members, let us discuss the `BufferedImage` class, its structure and how it can be manipulated through filters.

BufferedImage internals

In this book, we are interested by rendering effects. Filtering operations that apply to `BufferedImage`[6] object are key to creating appealing rendering effects. The internal structure of `BufferedImage` would not matter much if it were not important to understand it well in order to understand how filters work. It is actually easier to understand filters once the concerns that `BufferedImage` deals with are made clear.

▼ **Concerns addressed by BufferedImage** An image is a two-dimensional array of pixel values that represent color information. This is simple enough, but the number of variables is large:

■ ***Data storage strategy.*** Pixels are stored, but what format should be used? What elementary types are best suited for storage?

6. See "Filtering images" on page 31 in Chapter 2 for a list of such filters. They are also further described later in this chapter

- **Pixel organization**. Once a given type of data storage has been chosen, there might be different strategies for storing pixels, or different organizations. For example, if a two-color image is stored using a byte array, one byte could store one pixel value. Another, more efficient approach would be to pack pixels into a single byte. Given a storage, there are many ways to organize pixel values into that storage.
- **Pixel interpretation**. We said that pixels represent color information, but there are many ways to represent color information. A common way is to have a pixel value contain three color components, one for red, one for green, one for blue. But pixels may also contain information not directly related to color information: pixel values could simply be an index to a color map.

Figure 4.3 further details the `BufferedImage` design that we presented in Chapter 2 (see "Rendering images" on page 25).

Before looking at the role of each of these classes, we need the help of a glossary, as it is important to understand several different concepts.

The concepts in this glossary (Table 4.6 on page 81) are used in the following explanation, and we will gain a deeper understanding of where and how they are used as we progress through the internal structure of the `BufferedImage` class.

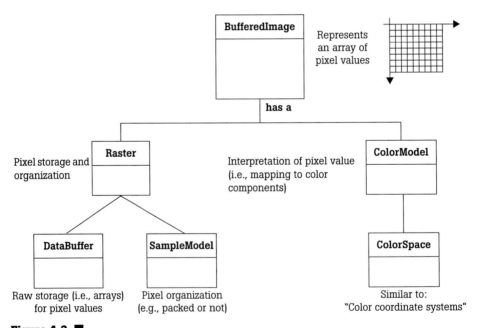

Figure 4.3 ■
BufferedImage internals

Table 4.6 ■ BufferedImage Glossary

TERM	DEFINITION
bank	Array of primitive type used to store pixel data. A `DataBuffer` contains one or more banks.
data element	One entry in a bank. If the bank is an array of integers, then a data element is an integer. bank = array of data elements One data element
pixel	Value of one element in an image that can be mapped to a color value and a transparency value.
sample	A pixel is made of distinct samples. Sometimes, they represent color components in a given color model. For example, cyan, magenta, yellow, and black can be samples. But samples may also represent non color values, such as transparency values or even an index into a color map. A sample is one entry in a band. Pixel Sample A pixel is made of one or more samples CMYK Pixel *Example* RGB Pixel *Example*
band	Group of pixel samples of the same kind. For example, all the red samples in an RGB image. The figure below shows the red, green, and blue bands in an RGB image. 

Table 4.6 ■ BufferedImage Glossary (Continued)

TERM	DEFINITION
component	A color value is represented by several color components, which are typically defined relative to primary colors. For example, in an RGB representation, the color components are relative to red, green, and blue primaries. Each component represents the amount of each primary color found in a given color. In the 2D API, pixels have a color value (defined by its components) plus an optional transparency value, known as the *alpha value*.
primaries	Set of elementary colors used to represent all other colors in a given color representation. For example, in the CMYK representation, the primaries are Cyan, Magenta, Yellow, and Black. For RGB, they are Red, Green, and Blue.

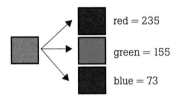

red = 235

green = 155

blue = 73

▼ DataBuffer   The DataBuffer class provides for the raw data storage in a Raster. Data is stored into one or more primitive types arrays known as *banks*, as mentioned in the glossary. Figure 4.4 illustrates the operation of the class: it provides members to get and set individual elements in its banks. Note that the different banks do not have to be different arrays: each bank can be a subset of the same array.

Four implementations of the DataBuffer class use different data types for the bank arrays or with a different intent (signed or unsigned values): DataBufferInt, DataBufferByte, DataBufferShort, and DataBuffer-UShort. Creating a DataBuffer is straightforward. For example, the following line of code creates a DataBufferInt with four banks of 128 integer values:

```
DataBufferInt buffer = new DataBufferInt(128, 4);
```

Most often, we do not create DataBuffer objects directly. Rather, they are created as by-products of creating Raster objects (and BufferedImage objects, because they contain a Raster).

DataBuffer is rarely used directly because it defines a generic interface that accommodates different primary types. Using it works, in the sense that it produces correct results, but is not very efficient. Typically, a DataBuffer instance

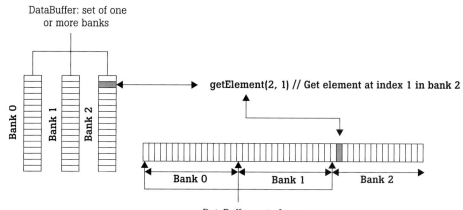

Figure 4.4 ■
DataBuffer operation

is cast to one of its implementations to improve performance when accessing data elements.

▼ **SampleModel** SampleModel subclasses extract pixel values from DataBuffer objects. Another way to look at it is to say that SampleModel extensions organize pixels into storage. Table 4.7 illustrates the different SampleModel extensions and their strategies for storing pixel values. Again, note that we use color components as sample examples (red, green, blue, and gray). Those are just examples: remember that samples do not necessarily represent color information (a component can also be an index in a color map, for example).

Table 4.7 ■ SampleModel subclasses

CLASS	PIXEL LAYOUT STRATEGY
ComponentSampleModel	Stores pixel samples in separate data elements. For example, if DataBufferInt is used, each sample is stored in a separate integer. There are various ways to do this, and the two extensions of the ComponentSampleModel class, BandedSampleModel and PixelInterleavedSampleModel, implement two possible options: either a single bank of data is used for all samples (PixelInterleavedSampleModel), or several banks are used (BandedSampleModel).

Table 4.7 ■ SampleModel subclasses (Continued)

CLASS	PIXEL LAYOUT STRATEGY
BandedSampleModel	Like ComponentSampleModel, which it extends, BandedSampleModel stores pixel samples in separate data elements.

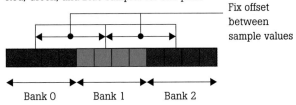

Red, Green, and Blue samples for one pixel

Fix offset between sample values

Bank 0   Bank 1   Bank 2

It does so in separate data banks of its DataBuffer. If the banks are created so that they are into the same array but consecutive, then bands are interleaved, meaning that fixed offsets separate different sample values for the same pixel.

PixelInterleaved-SampleModel	Like ComponentSampleModel, which it extends, PixelInterleavedSampleModel stores pixel samples in separate data elements. It does so in a

Red, Green and Blue samples for one pixel

Pixel Boundary

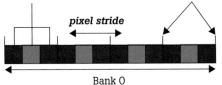

pixel stride

Bank 0

single data bank. Pixels are interleaved, which means that consecutive samples of the same band are not at consecutive array elements. Rather, a fixed offset, called the *pixel stride*, separates them.

Table 4.7 ■ SampleModel subclasses (Continued)

CLASS	PIXEL LAYOUT STRATEGY
MultiPixelPacked-SampleModel	This model can be used for images that use a single sample per pixel (for example, gray scale images). For example, if 4 bits are enough to represent a gray scale value, then 8 pixels can be packed into a single data element of a DataBufferInt (32 bits).

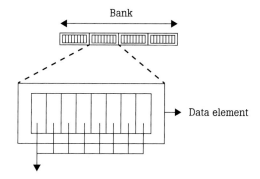

8 samples, one per pixel:
8 pixels packed in one element

CLASS	PIXEL LAYOUT STRATEGY
SinglePixelPacked-SampleModel	This model packs all the samples that make one pixel into a single data element in a DataBuffer. For example, if DataBufferInt is used, all the samples are packed into a single integer. Each element stores the samples for only one pixel.

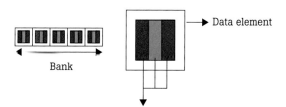

The three samples for one pixel are
packed in one data element.

The important thing to remember is that `SampleModel` defines how the pixel samples are stored into a `DataBuffer`. It provides methods for accessing pixel values, that is, given an index coordinates in a `Raster`, it will return the samples that compose that pixel. Creating a `SampleModel` is simpler than the above descriptions may lead you to believe. The following code creates a `SinglePixelPackedSampleModel` that packs the pixel samples in integer values:

```
SampleModel model
    = new SinglePixelPackedSampleModel(DataBuffer.TYPE_INT,
                          width,  // Width of the pixel area
                                  // in Raster
                          height, // Height of the pixel area
                                  // in Raster
                          new int[] { 0x00ff0000,    // red mask
                                      0x0000ff00,    // green mask
                                      0x000000ff}); // blue mask
```

To pack the samples into an integer, the integer is used as an array of four bytes. The samples are stored as illustrated: the first sample, in byte 2, the second sample in byte 1, and the last sample is the first byte.

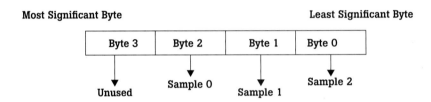

The ability to support many different storage formats is key to the 2D API because it covers a broad range of needs (for example, color formats, color resolution).

▼ **ColorModels** `ColorModel` extensions are responsible for interpreting sample values and turning them into color components. In our illustrations of the different `SampleModel` extensions, we used RGB and gray scale meaning for samples. This is arbitrary, and in fact, `SampleModel` extensions work without attaching any color semantics to sample values. They are just considered mathematical quantities. For example, a `ComponentSampleModel` would deal with a four-sample pixel exactly the same way whether the four samples represent Alpha, Red, Green, and Blue values or whether they represent Cyan, Magenta, Yellow, and Black values. `SampleModel` extensions are "color blind."

Interpreting samples is the role of `ColorModel` extensions: they translate pixel values into color components plus alpha. The alpha value defines the opacity of a pixel. For images that do not support alpha, the opacity is assumed to be 1, which means fully opaque.

A way to understand what `ColorModel` does is to look at `ComponentColorModel`. With that `ColorModel`, pixel samples and color components have a one-to-one correspondence. For example, if we create a `ComponentColorModel` with an RGB `ColorSpace`, which has three color components for each pixel, pixel samples will represent the red, green, and blue components of the pixel color. If the `ComponentColorModel` object is created with a CMYK `ColorSpace`, which has four color components, pixel samples will represent the cyan, magenta, yellow, and black components of the pixel color. To create an analogy with geometry, we can think of `DataBuffer`, `SampleModel`, and `ColorModel` as doing the following with coordinates (which are the equivalent of image pixels in our analogy):

- `DataBuffer` provides raw storage for coordinates.
- `SampleModel` organizes coordinates into storage by packing them into integers, for example, or storing each coordinate in a separate array element.
- `ColorModel` provides the definition of the coordinates space necessary to understand the coordinates semantics: is it a two- or three-dimensional space, what is the size of a unit, and similar questions.

Without `ColorModel`, pixel data is meaningless because it is impossible to know what the data refers to.

Why is there a difference between samples and components? Because they do not always map one to one, as is the case when indexing is used. With `Index-ColorModel`, the single pixel sample represents an index in a color map the `IndexColorModel` holds. Therefore, the pixel sample does not map directly to a color component and is truly a different concept. Again, `ColorModel` is responsible for interpreting the sample meaning.

Table 4.8 illustrates the different `ColorModel` implementations supported by the API. A `ColorSpace` that is always associated with a `ColorModel` provides the definition context for the color components, that is, the coordinate system where they are defined (for example, RGB, ARGB, CMYK, HSV), as well as support for translating colors to well-known color spaces.

Table 4.8 ■ ColorModel subclasses

CLASS	DESCRIPTION
`ComponentColorModel`	Represents color components and alpha value as separate samples that are stored in separate data elements (i.e., it is compatible with `PixelInterleavedSampleModel`).
`IndexColorModel`	Represents color components and alpha value as a single sample that is an index into a color map defined in the sRGB `ColorSpace` (this is the default `ColorSpace` in the Java 2D API).

Table 4.8 ■ ColorModel subclasses (Continued)

CLASS	DESCRIPTION
PackedColorModel	Represents color components and alpha value as separate samples that are packed into a single data element (i.e., it is compatible with SinglePixelPackedSampleModel).
DirectColorModel	This is the default ColorModel on the Java platform, i.e., the model returned by ColorModel.getRGBDefault(). This model extends PackedColorModel and represents RGB values with an optional alpha component.

▼ **ColorSpace**   The ColorSpace class is responsible for precise color definition. What is that about?

To understand the issues related to color, it is important to realize that what we take for a simple and obvious thing—color—is extraordinarily complex. Here are a few of our challenges:

1.   There are many ways to represent colors. For example, representing colors by their red, green, and blue components is appropriate for computer monitors, but cyan, magenta, yellow and black are more appropriate for printing because these are the inks most color printers use. These ways of representing colors are called color spaces, and it is hard to compare them: each has its purpose and each is more appropriate in some context (for example, printing) and less in others (for example, monitor display).
2.   Gamut. Most color spaces are not able to represent all the visible colors.[7] The range of colors they are able to represent is called the gamut. Not being able to reach all colors is not an issue for most applications, but it is for some. The other issue with gamut is that different color spaces have different gamuts. Therefore, when a color is converted from one space to another, it may not be representable in the destination space. In that case, it has to be approximated, resulting in a color shift.
3.   Color definition. Saying that color is represented with its red, green, and blue primaries does not mean much unless the exact related color definitions are provided, usually by reference to a

7.   Common color spaces such as RGB and CMYK use a set of primary colors (Red, Green, and Blue or Cyan, Magenta, Yellow, and Black) that are mixed to produce a full range of colors. However, the number of visible colors that can be reached that way is limited. See [Foley 1997] for details on gamut differences between color spaces.

standard (for example, sRGB). Without this reference to a common and strict standard color definition, different devices may use a similar system but produce different colors. Thus, RGB is really a *type* of color space: there are many RGB spaces.

The `ColorSpace` class addresses these challenges by:

- ▓ Representing a system for measuring color, usually in reference to some international standard.
- ▓ Converting colors in its color space to and from two reference color spaces: the sRGB (standard RGB) and the CIEXYZ color spaces. The CIEXYZ color space is a high-precision color space standard that we will discuss later.

Therefore, the 2D API can be used with any color representation, provided that the corresponding `ColorSpace` implementation can be found or developed. The second point enables the API to convert a color defined in any color space to any other color space (see Figure 4.5).

The single subclass of the abstract `ColorSpace` class, the `ICC_ColorSpace` class, uses an `ICC_Profile`. ICC stands for International Color Consortium. That organization has defined a standard profile format for specifying color conversions between an input space and a connection space. This concept is similar to that of `ColorSpace` and is used by Color Management Systems (CMS) to convert colors. The `ICC_Profile` class is the Java representation of color profiles and is used by the `ICC_ColorSpace` to provide a generic `ColorSpace` implementation, based on standard color profiles.

Figure 4.5 shows how a CMYK color value is accurately converted from the CMYK `ColorSpace` to a gray scale color space. The code for this conversion follows the figure.

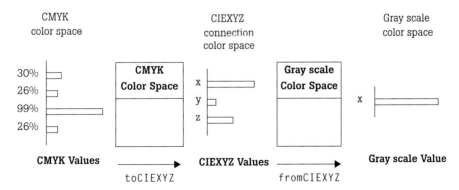

Figure 4.5 ■
ColorSpace color conversion

```
// Get the two ColorSpaces
ICC_Profile cmykProfile
  = ICC_Profile.getInstance(new FileInputStream(cymkProfileFileName));
ColorSpace cmykCS = new ICC_ColorSpace(cmykProfile);

// Gray Scale
ICC_Profile grayScaleProfile =
ICC_Profile.getInstance(ColorSpace.CS_GRAY);
ColorSpace grayScaleCS = new ICC_ColorSpace(grayScaleProfile);

// Define the Color components in the CMYK Space
float cmykComponents[] = { 0.3f, 0.26f, 0.99f, 0.26f };

// Convert to CIEXYZ
float ciexyzComponents[] = cmykCS.toCIEXYZ(cmykComponents);
for(int i=0; i<ciexyzComponents.length; i++)
  System.out.println("ciexyzComponents[" + i + "] = "
                   + ciexyzComponents[i]);

// Convert to Gray Scale
float grayComponents[] = grayScaleCS.fromCIEXYZ(ciexyzComponents);
for(int i=0; i<grayComponents.length; i++)
  System.out.println("grayComponents[" + i + "] = "
                   + grayComponents[i]);
```

This code illustrates how the API is able to manipulate colors defined in any space.

Another example of the use of color conversion is the `java.awt.Color` class constructor. One of the constructors lets us define the color components in any color space:

```
Color(ColorSpace cspace, float components[], float alpha)
```

So, we could define a color in CMYK or gray scale. If we have a look at the implementation of that constructor,[8] we find that the color components are converted to standard RGB:

```
srgbvalue = cspace.toRGB(components);
```

The ability to convert between color spaces allows color matching. Because the Java 2D platform can use the underlying Color Management System to find the best color profiles for the device it uses, the platform can ensure appropriate color reproduction to the output device. For example, given a color in sRGB to print, the Java 2D API can translate it properly so that it matches the printer characteristics (if the platform CMS, Color Management System, makes the profile information available).

---

8. The source code for all the core platform classes can be downloaded from the Sun Microsystems web site: http://java.sun.com

Note about CIE XYZ

The CIE XYZ color model defines all colors as the combination of three other primary colors. There is no set of real colors that allows the definition of all other colors, so the primary colors are not "real" colors. However, this space's gamut covers all visible colors and provides an ideal solution for converting colors: no loss happens because of the conversion to CIE XYZ because it can represent more colors than the input and output spaces. However, there might still be shifts in color when converting between color spaces because of the difference in gamut. A common problem happens when converting RGB colors to CMYK because those two spaces have different gamuts: the conversion results in color shift that can be very visible. This explains why you sometimes get surprises when doing color printing: WYSI*N*WYG (What You See is ***Not*** What You Get!).

▼ **Putting it all together again**   `BufferedImage` internals may seem complicated because there are many classes and concepts to deal with. While it is true that there are many ways to combine the different classes, using them does not have to be complicated. Here are several ways to easily create `BufferedImage` objects.

1. `BufferedImage` constructors. There is a constructor that only takes the image size and image type as an input and creates the necessary `Raster` and `ColorModel` objects. There are type constants in the `BufferedImage` class (such as `TYPE_INT_RGB`, `TYPE_BYTE_GRAY`) that are really shortcuts to specify pixel storage organization and color meaning.
2. `ColorModel` factory methods: `createCompatibleSampleModel` and `createCompatibleWritableRaster`. The `ColorModel` class contains these methods which automatically create the appropriate support classes that can be used to put together a `BufferedImage`.
3. `Raster` factory methods: `createXXRaster` (for example, `createBandedRaster`). Several factory methods create `Raster` objects with coherent `DataBuffer` and `SampleModel`. Furthermore, the `createCompatibleRaster` method provides a generic way to create `Raster` objects that can later be combined (for example, using `RasterOp`–`Raster` filters which require compatible `Raster` objects).

To see the power of the `BufferedImage` class design, consider the two code segments in Table 4.9.

Those two very similar programs differ by only one line: the `BufferedImage` constructor. But the result is widely different: the two images have different ways of storing pixels (one uses integers, the other bytes), of organizing them (one packs them in data elements, the other does not) and different representa-

Table 4.9 ■ Color model and pixel storage independence

CODE A

```
// Load image from disk
Image image = ...;

int imageType = BufferedImage.TYPE_INT_RGB;
BufferedImage buf = new BufferedImage(30, 30, imageType);

Graphics2D g = buf.createGraphics();
g.drawImage(image, 0, 0, null);
```

CODE B

```
// Load image from disk
Image image = ...;

int imageType = BufferedImage.TYPE_BYTE_GRAY;
BufferedImage buf = new BufferedImage(30, 30, imageType);

Graphics2D g = buf.createGraphics();
g.drawImage(image, 0, 0, null);
```

---

tions for color information. Still, they are used the same way: it is equally easy to draw an image into one or the other. The framework takes care of converting color, packing and unpacking values, and so forth.

To illustrate the inner working of the `BufferedImage` class and how it can be used, the **CMYKSave.java** program, on the CD-ROM, shows how to load an RGB JPEG image and save it in the CMYK format. This example uses the `ICC_Profile`, `ICC_ColorSpace`, `ColorModel`, and `WritableRaster` classes.

▼ **Saving a JPEG file in CMYK**   The first thing `CMYKSave` does is load an input RGB JPEG.[9] The image is loaded into a `BufferedImage`, `rgbImage`.

The next step consists in converting the `rgbImage` into CMYK format, using a `ColorConvertOp` filter. That class is detailed in Chapter 4 (see "BufferedImageOp" on page 94). The two things `ColorConvertOp` needs are the source and destination `ColorSpace` objects and a `WritableRaster` in which to store the result of the conversion. The source color space can be retrieved from the `rgbImage`:

```
ColorSpace rgbCS = rgbImage.getColorModel().getColorSpace();
```

---

9. "Creating a BufferedImage and loading images" on page 28 in Chapter 2 explains how to load a JPEG image.

There is no default support for a CMYK `ColorSpace` in the API, but it is easy to add provided you have the CMYK ICC profile you want.[10] The `ICC_Profile` class can load our ICC profile—

```
ICC_Profile p
  = ICC_Profile.getInstance(new FileInputStream(cmykProfile));
```

—which we can then use to build a CMYK `ColorSpace`:

```
ColorSpace cmykCS = new ICC_ColorSpace(p);
```

To create an appropriate `WritableRaster` that will store our CMYK pixels, we create a `ComponentColorModel` by using our newly created `cmykCS`:

```
ColorModel cmykModel
  = new ComponentColorModel(cmykCS,      // ColorSpace
            new int[] { 8, 8, 8, 8 },// 8 bits for each C, M, Y, K
            false,                   // No alpha,
            true,                    // alpha premultiplied (ignored)
            Transparency.OPAQUE,     // Only opaque values  in model
            DataBuffer.TYPE_BYTE);   // Type used to represent
                                     // pixel values
```

Remember that a `ComponentColorModel` works with a `PixelInterleaved-SampleModel`. We can then rely on the `cmykModel` to provide an appropriate `WritableRaster`, which has the same size as the input `rgbImage`:

```
WritableRaster cmykRaster
    = cmykModel.createCompatibleWritableRaster(rgbImage.getWidth(),
                                               rgbImage.getHeight());
```

With the `ColorSpace` objects and output `WritableRaster` ready, we convert `rgbImage` to CMYK:

```
ColorConvertOp rgbToCmyk = new ColorConvertOp(rgbCS, cmykCS, null);
rgbToCmyk.filter(rgbImage.getRaster(), cmykRaster);
```

At this point, the `cmykRaster` contains the CMYK values for all the `rgbImage` pixels. We then use the `JPEGEncoder` to save the `cmykImage`:[11]

---

10. The appropriate CMYK profile depends on the output. The CD-ROM includes a sample CMYK profile, but this is only an example, as CMYK values represent ink coverage for the different primaries and are tightly dependent on the output device (typically, a printer). If you use the example with the provided profile and open the file in an image processing tool, you will see a very obvious color shift because the CMYK values are meant for a specific printer, not for display.

11. Some image processing applications actually invert the CMYK components when saving in CMYK JPEG. The `CMYKSave` program takes a parameter that defines whether components should be inverted before the image is saved. Inverting the components relies on the `LookupOp` `BufferedImageOp` described in the following section.

```
OutputStream out = new FileOutputStream(cmykJPEGFile);
JPEGImageEncoder encoder = JPEGCodec.createJPEGEncoder(out);
JPEGEncodeParam param
    = encoder.getDefaultJPEGEncodeParam(cmykRaster,
                                        JPEGDecodeParam.COLOR_ID_CMYK);
param.setQuality(1, false);  // Maximum quality
encoder.encode(cmykRaster, param);
```

The `ColorConvertOp` class we used in our example is one of the `Buffered-ImageOp` implementations that we cover next in more detail.

BufferedImageOp

In the immediate mode model, we can filter `BufferedImage` objects; the requirements for filters are defined by the `BufferedImageOp` interface,[12] which specifies:

■ Filters have a single source and single destination. This means that the filter should only process the pixels of a single source to create the destination pixel values. Among other things, this means that the destination image pixel values should not be used in the process.
■ Filters can operate "in place," that is, they can place their output into the source, but this is not a requirement. It is left to the filter implementation to specify whether or not this is supported.

Filtering a `BufferedImage` is simple:

```
BufferedImageOp filter = ...; // Create filter
BufferedImage source = ...;   // Acquire or build source image

// null means that the filter is requested to create the
// destination image.
BufferedImage destination = filter.filter(source, null);
```

In the remainder of this section, we describe how each of the `BufferedImageOp` filters operates. In all these examples, we use the same input image (Figure 4.6). All the filters are used as we just described, and the **ImageFilter.java** program (on the CD-ROM) can apply each of the filters presented here to an image defined by the program's input parameter.

---

12. As we will see later, there is another interface for filtering `Rasters`. This is the interface we used to color convert to CMYK in our previous example.

Figure 4.6 ■
Image used for illustrating the different filters

In the remainder of our `BufferedImage` filters discussion, only the output of the filtering operation is shown, to avoid redundancy.

▼ **AffineTransformOp**   This filter implementation of `BufferedImageOp` performs a spatial transformation of the input `BufferedImage` pixels. That is, it transforms pixels in the input `BufferedImage` space to pixels in the destination `BufferedImage`'s space (Figure 4.7).

Table 4.10 shows an example where a flip is used.

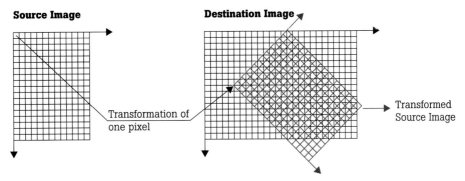

Figure 4.7 ■
AffineTransforOp operation

Table 4.10 ■ AffineTransformOp

<table>
<tr>
<td>

```
// Create AffineTransform to rotate the image about
// its center
AffineTransform rotation = new AffineTransform();
rotation.rotate(Math.PI, source.getWidth()/2,
                          source.getHeight()/2);

// Create BufferedImage to hold the destination
BufferedImage destination
  = new BufferedImage(source.geWidth(),
                      source.getHeight(),
                      source.getType());*



// Create AffineTransformOp with rotation
AffineTransformOp rotator
   = new AffineTransformOp(rotation, AffineTransformOp.TYPE_BILINEAR);

// Filter happens here
rotator.filter(source, destination);
```

</td>
<td>

Output

</td>
</tr>
</table>

*This construction assumes that the source type is one of the predefined `BufferedImage` types. If the type of the source image is `BufferedImage.TYPE_CUSTOM`, another, more sophisticated, constructor should be used. Refer to the API documentation.

There are two important things to note in the above code segment:

1. The source and destination have the same size, that is, the transformed bounding rectangle of the input image is the same as that of the destination image. Usually, it is more appropriate to let the filter figure out the size required for the destination image, as in the code—

```
AffineTransform shear = new AffineTransform();
shear.shear(.2, 0);  // Shears the image horizontally because we add
                     // 20% of the y coordinate value to the
                     // x coordinate:
                     // the higher the y value (i.e. further down),
                     // the more shifted to the right the x
                     // coordinate value, resulting in the
                     // shear effect.

AffineTransformOp skewer
  = new AffineTransformOp(shear, AffineTransformOp.TYPE_BILINEAR);
BufferedImage filteredImage = skewer.filter(source, null);
```

—which produces the following image:

If we had used a `BufferedImage` the same size as the source, the result would have been:

2. The interpolation strategy is set by the second constructor argument, `AffineTransformOp.TYPE_BILINEAR`. Many spatial transformation require that pixels be interpolated because there is not a one-to-one correspondence between pixels in the source and destination. For example, in Figure 4.7 on page 95, we see that pixels from the source do not exactly overlap pixels in the destination. What should the destination pixel values be? This is what interpolating pixel value does: estimate those values. There are different methods for interpolating pixels, and `Affine-TransformOp` offers two alternatives (also available through the `RenderingHints` class): nearest neighbor and bilinear. The nearest neighbor algorithm is simpler and faster, but it is also less effective (the artifacts are clearly visible, pixelation appears on the blown-up image). The bilinear algorithm delivers much better results but is less efficient. As for other rendering hints, the right alternative depends on the objectives: quality or speed.

▼ **ColorConvertOp** This filter provides an easy way to convert between different color spaces. We used that filter for our JPEG CMYK example on Page 92. `ColorConvertOp` takes care of all the details of `ColorModel`, `SampleModel`, and `DataBuffer` we discussed: the filter performs the conversion according to the definitions of the source and destination color spaces, as illustrated in our example in Table 4.11.

Using a `ColorConvertOp` on a `BufferedImage` amounts to "translating" the color components for each pixel from the source `ColorSpace` to the destination `ColorSpace` and storing the resulting value into the destination `BufferedImage`.[13]

Table 4.11 ■ ColorConvertOp

```
// Create a gray scale image which has the same
// size as the source.
int imageType = BufferedImage.TYPE_BYTE_GRAY;
BufferedImage destination
    = new BufferedImage(source.getWidth(),
                        source.getHeight(),
                        imageType);

// Get source and destination ColorSpaces.
ColorSpace sourceSpace
    = source.getColorModel().getColorSpace();

ColorSpace destSpace
    = destination.getColorModel().getColorSpace();

// Build a ColorConvertOp from the source and destination
// ColorSpaces.
ColorConvertOp convert
    = new ColorConvertOp(sourceSpace,
                         destSpace, null);

// Color conversion happens here.
convert.filter(source, destination);
```

Output

▼ **ConvolveOp** Convolution is the term used to describe the process of combining pixels with its neighbors in the source image to compute the value of the pixel at the same location in the destination image. There are many useful things that convolutions can do: blurring, detecting edges, embossing, etc.

---

13. In our JPEG CMYK example on Page 92, we actually used `ColorConvertOp` to filter a `Raster`. As we explain later in this section, `ColorConvertOp`, as most other filters, is both a `BufferedImageOp` and a `RasterOp`.

The `java.awt.image.Kernel` class contains a matrix (called the convolution kernel) that defines exactly how pixels should be combined. Each element of the matrix is the weight given to the surrounding pixels. That weight is used to combine neighboring pixels in the source image and compute the output pixel. The origin of the `Kernel` object is the matrix center and defines the pixel position for which the output value is processed (see Figure 4.8).

The convolution process consists of sliding the convolution window shown in Figure 4.8 over each pixel in the source image to get the values of the pixels to convolve. For each pixel, the values in the convolution window are used as input to the convolution kernel to compute a weighted sum, which produces the pixel value for the output pixel.[14]

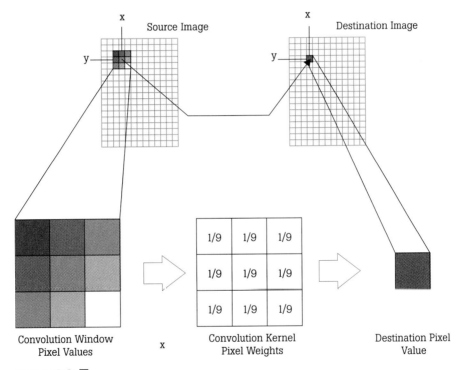

Figure 4.8 ■

The convolution process

---

14. Note that the matrix is conceptually rotated $180°$ about its center before it is used. See [Pratt 1997] for details.

Table 4.12 shows a simple example that gives the same weight to all pixels (we also used the same value for all weights in Figure 4.8). Because all pixels in the destination will tend to have values closer to those of their neighbors after the filtering, the image appears blurred.

Table 4.12 ■ ConvolveOp: blur

```
// Matrix that will be used to build kernel
float k[] = { 1/9f, 1/9f, 1/9f,
              1/9f, 1/9f, 1/9f,
              1/9f, 1/9f, 1/9f };

// Build a 3 by 3 Kernel from matrix
Kernel kernel = new Kernel(3, 3, k);

// Construct a ConvolveOp with the blur Kernel
// and filter source image.
ConvolveOp blur = new ConvolveOp(kernel);
blur.filter(source, null);
```

Output

As we said, there are many uses for the `ConvolveOp`. The process is always the same as for the blur:

- Build a convolution matrix into an array.
- Build a `Kernel` object from the convolution matrix.
- Build a `ConvolveOp` from the `Kernel` object.

All the effort goes into creating the right convolution matrix. Table 4.13 illustrates some of the most commonly used convolutions with their related matrices.

Before we move on to those common convolution kernels, note the following important points:

1. In our sliding window analogy in Figure 4.8, what happens on the edges? As shown in our illustration, there is no input pixel to

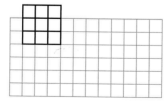

process for the upper row of the convolution window. This means that pixel values in the destination `BufferedImage` cannot be computed as are the other ones from the source `BufferelImage` pixels. The API offers two options: either fill the edges with zero values (`ConvolveOp.EDGE_ZERO_FILL`) or reproduce the source pixels (`ConvolveOp.EDGE_NO_OP`). `ConvolveOp` uses the zero fill by default,[15] but one of the constructors lets us decide on our strategy. The advantage of the two edge-condition options is that they are fast. However, there might be situations where the result is not satisfying. Alternate strategies for dealing with edges are discussed in Chapter 3 of [Crane1997] and can be used with the API with a little extra work.

2. The source and destination cannot be the same `BufferedImage`. If this were allowed, the output would not contain the desired values because an input pixel is used to process the output value for itself, but also for its neighbors.

3. Convolution is a computation-intensive process, and the processing load grows exponentially with the kernel size.

4. To preserve pixel intensity, the sum of the convolution kernel weights should be 1. Otherwise, there might be cases of pixel overflow producing undesired results. However, this is not necessarily a desired constraint, and it is not wanted for some types of convolutions, like edge detection, where coefficients do not add up to 1.

5. `ConvolveOp` operates on the input `BufferedImage`'s color components. This means that the semantics of the filter are applied to each of the color components. For example, edge detection is the process of finding intensity variations in a `BufferedImage`. When applied to an RGB `BufferedImage`, the red, green, and blue channels are convolved separately, so the resulting image is actually the sum of edge detection done in the red, green, and blue bands of the `BufferedImage`.[16]

---

15. This explains the black border in Table 4.12.
16. The notion of edge is sometimes argued about. In the mathematical sense used by the Java 2D API, it means sharp variations in the color components. However, it is interesting to remember that the eye is more sensitive to variations in intensity than it is to hue variations. Therefore, for some uses, it may be more appropriate to convert a `BufferedImage` to HSB (Hue Saturation and Brightness) and run edge detection on the Brightness component only.

Table 4.13 ■ Common convolution matrices

CONVOLUTION MATRIX

Edge Detection

An edge is defined by a variation in intensity. There are several ways to perform edge detection, and many different matrices can be used (see [Crane 1997]). However, the idea behind edge detection is to have the sum for a pixel be 0 where the pixel values are the same and be a nonzero value in areas where pixels are different. For example:

Output

$$\begin{bmatrix} -1 & -1 & -1 \\ -1 & 8 & -1 \\ -1 & -1 & -1 \end{bmatrix}$$

When pixels are all the same, the combination of neighboring pixels will result in a zero value because the sum of the weights is 0 (-8 for the neighboring pixels, +8 for the pixels being processed, which sums to 0). In areas where pixels are not the same (around edges), the sum will be nonzero, and the pixels will not be black as illustrated by the figure.

Sharpening

Sharpening an image consists of enhancing its edges so that the image appears crisper. To achieve this, we can simply add a pixel's value to the value computed by edge detection:

Output

$$\begin{bmatrix} -1 & -1 & -1 \\ -1 & 8 & -1 \\ -1 & -1 & -1 \end{bmatrix} + \begin{bmatrix} 0 & 0 & 0 \\ 0 & 1 & 0 \\ 0 & 0 & 0 \end{bmatrix} = \begin{bmatrix} -1 & -1 & -1 \\ -1 & 9 & -1 \\ -1 & -1 & -1 \end{bmatrix}$$

Where there are no edges, the edge detection part of the matrix returns 0 and the output pixel has the same value as the original. Where an edge is detected, the pixel value is modified, enhancing the difference with neighboring pixels: this makes the image look crisper.

Table 4.13 ■ Common convolution matrices (Continued)

CONVOLUTION MATRIX

Embossing

Embossing produces an effect similar to that of etched metal. This effect is achieved by use of a matrix where opposite coefficients have a combined weight of zero:

$$\begin{bmatrix} -2 & 0 & 0 \\ 0 & 1 & 0 \\ 0 & 0 & 2 \end{bmatrix}$$

Output

▼ **RescaleOp**   `RescaleOp` enables us to stretch or squeeze pixel components and alpha values. This manipulation can be used, for example, to adjust the color or brightness of an image, as illustrated by the example in Table 4.14.

Table 4.14 ■ RescaleOp used for adjusting brightness in an RGB image

```
// image is an RGB image: red, green and blue
// components will be increased by 50%. Because they
// are all equally increased, the image will be
// brighter, as this amounts to adding white to the
// image.
RescaleOp brighten = new RescaleOp(1.5f, 0, null);
brighten.filter(image, null);
```

Output

Red   □ x 1.5
Green □ x 1.5
Blue   □ x 1.5

Note that the semantics of a `RescaleOp` depend on the `ColorModel` of the filtered `BufferedImage`. For example, increasing all the color components in a CMYK model (which is a subtractive model) would not increase the image brightness, but would decrease it.

▼ **LookupOp**   This last `BufferedImageOp` (because the following `BandCombineOp` is not a `BufferedImageOp`, as we will discuss), provides a way to map pixel color components and alpha values to other values through a `LookupTable`. This can be used, for example, to invert an image, as in our example (see Table 4.15). It can also be used for thresholding (that is, to enhance color variations), as illustrated in our gallery (see Chapter 17, page 491).

Table 4.15 ■ LookupOp used for inverting an image

```
// Create lookup array
byte lookup[] = new byte[256];
for(int i=0; i<256; i++)
  lookup[i] = (byte)(255 - i);

// Create LookupTable for array
LookupTable table = new ByteLookupTable(0, lookup);

// Create LookupOp from lookup table
LookupOp inverter = new LookupOp(table, null);

// Filter source image
BufferedImage dst = inverter.filter(source, null);
```

Output

The process for computing the output pixel is illustrated in Figure 4.9, which shows how the output value for the red component is processed. The value of the input red component is used as an index into the `LookupTable`'s array: the value at that index is the value for the output pixel's red component. The `LookupTable` class enables us either to use one separate array for each color component in the filtered image or to use a single array, in which case it will be used for all components.

▼ **BandCombineOp**   `BandCombineOp` provides a way to combine the different bands of an image. This filter is not a `BufferedImageOp` implementation; it is a `RasterOp` implementation, which is the interface defined for `Raster` filters. To understand the difference between `RasterOp` and `BufferedImageOp`, we need to remember the difference between `Raster` and `BufferedImage`: `Raster` objects hold pixel data, but they have no semantics: there is no way to interpret the color semantics of the data. As we discussed, this color interpretation of pixel values is provided by the `ColorModel` class and its implementations. A `BufferedImage` is essentially a `Raster` coupled with a `ColorModel` for color semantics.

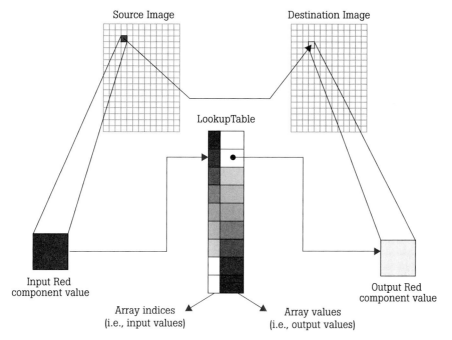

Figure 4.9 ■
The LookupOp process

`RasterOp` and `BufferedImageOp` both perform calculations on pixel values. However, the `BufferedImageOp` implementations typically interpret the color semantics, or at least have an option to do so. One common thing they do is to treat the alpha component differently than color components. `RasterOp` is a purely mathematical operation that is not related to the semantics of pixel samples.

All the filters we have presented so far are both `BufferedImageOp` and `RasterOp` implementations. This mean that they can be "color blind" (when operating as `RasterOp`) or they can treat pixels differently depending on the component semantics (for example, alpha or color component). There are no color semantics that can easily be attached to `BandCombineOp`, which is why `BandCombineOp` only implements the `RasterOp` interface.

Using a `RasterOp` is only slightly different from using a `BufferedImageOp`. The process is:

- Create a filter.
- Get the source and destination `Raster`.
- Invoke the `RasterOp`'s `filter` method.

Table 4.16 illustrates this process, which, as you can see, is simple.

Table 4.16 ■ BandCombineOp used to swap Raster bands of pixel samples

CODE

```
//
// Create a RasterOp, here a BandCombineOp
//
float matrix[][]
  = { { 0f, 0f, 1f},    // Red takes blue value
      { 0f, 1f, 0f},    // Green unchanged
      { 1f, 0f, 0f} };  // Blue takes red value

BandCombineOp combine
  = new BandCombineOp(matrix, null);

// Get source Raster.
// source contains the original image
Raster imageRaster = source.getRaster();

// Get destination Raster
WritableRaster dstRaster = imageRaster.createCompatibleWritableRaster();

// Invoke filtering process
combine.filter(imageRaster, dstRaster);
```

Output

There are a number of interesting points about this code segment.

1. BandCombineOp provides a way to do linear combinations of bands through a matrix definition.[17] It is possible to build Raster objects with an arbitrary number of bands (for example, 7 or 8) and use a BandCombineOp to mix them.

   In our example, the resulting red, green and blue values after the filtering are:

$$\begin{bmatrix} r' \\ g' \\ b' \end{bmatrix} = \begin{bmatrix} b \\ g \\ r \end{bmatrix} = \begin{bmatrix} 0 & 0 & 1 \\ 0 & 1 & 0 \\ 1 & 0 & 0 \end{bmatrix} \times \begin{bmatrix} r \\ g \\ b \end{bmatrix}$$

17. It is interesting to note that some color spaces are not linear: doing a linear combination of color components is not always accurate.

$$\begin{bmatrix} s'_1 \\ s'_2 \\ s'_3 \end{bmatrix} = \begin{bmatrix} c_{00} & c_{01} & c_{02} & c_{03} \\ c_{10} & c_{11} & c_{12} & c_{13} \\ c_{20} & c_{21} & c_{22} & c_{23} \end{bmatrix} \times \begin{bmatrix} s_1 \\ s_2 \\ s_3 \\ 1 \end{bmatrix}$$

Figure 4.10 ■
Combining Raster samples

2. `WritableRaster` is a subclass of `Raster` that provides write access to its `DataBuffer`. Because a `RasterOp` needs to write its data to the output, it requires a `WritableRaster` as a destination.
3. Filtering a `BufferedImage` with a `BandCombineOp` is possible. Just add the following lines of code after our code segment:

```
BufferedImage filteredImage
  = new BufferedImage(source.getColorModel(),
                      dstRaster, true, null);
```

The source `Raster` was already created from a `BufferedImage` (by the `source.getRaster` method invocation).

Again, `BandCombineOp` is a purely mathematical processing of the pixel samples. The width of the combination matrix must match the number of bands in the input `Raster`. If there is an extra column in the matrix, then an implicit 1 is appended at the end of the combined band samples, as illustrated in Figure 4.10. The height of the matrix must match the number of bands in the output `Raster`.

Summary

As we have seen, `BufferedImage` has a flexible design because the various concerns are well separated and can vary independently: pixel storage (`DataBuffer`), pixel organization (`SampleModel`), and color interpretation (`ColorModel` and `ColorSpace`). This design allows the Java 2D API to support a wide variety of color representations and storage strategies.

Filtering `BufferedImage` in itself could be the topic of a whole book, even though the process of filtering is quite simple. The filter implementations provided by default offer powerful capabilities, from spatial transformations (`AffineTransformOp`) to blurring or edge detection (`ConvolveOp`), to color adjustment (`LookupOp`, `RescaleOp`). Filters can be applied to `BufferedImage` or to `Raster` objects (as `BufferedImageOp` and `RasterOp` implementations), and `BandCombineOp` is the only filter that applies to `Raster` objects only. All other filters can work both with `BufferedImage` or `Raster`.

Note that both `RasterOp` and `BufferedImageOp` define single-source/single-destination filter interfaces. Some filter operations, such as add or multiply, actually use multiple sources. The Java Advanced Imaging API provides a framework for multiple source filters.

As with many other aspects of the API, the filtering model is extensible because it is built around interfaces (`BufferedImageOp` and `RasterOp`). As we illustrate in Chapter 9, we can create new types of filters and use them in the API just as easily as we use the default ones.

Table 4.17 summarizes the classes we discussed in this section.

Table 4.17 ■ Key BufferedImage related classes

CLASS OR INTERFACE	PURPOSE
`BufferedImage`	This is the highest-level construct. It encapsulates a `Raster`, which stores and organizes pixels, and a `ColorModel` for pixel color interpretation.
`Raster`	Contains and organizes pixels. It encapsulates a `DataBuffer`, which provides storage of pixels in arrays called banks, and a `SampleModel`, which contains the logic to organize pixel samples that make up a pixel.
`DataBuffer`	Provides raw data storage in one or several arrays of a given type. For example, the `DataBufferByte` class stores pixel values in byte arrays. Note that one data element in a `DataBuffer` (e.g., a byte) may contain several pixels (e.g., 8 in a binary image), exactly one pixel (e.g., the gray value in an 8-bit gray scale image), or a single pixel sample (e.g., the red component of an RGB pixel).
`SampleModel`	Controls the way pixels are organized in a `DataBuffer`. For example, different pixel samples (e.g., the Red, Green, and Blue values) may be packed in a single integer, as in the `SinglePixelPackedSampleModel` implementation, or spread across different data elements, as in the `ComponentSampleModel`.
`ColorModel`	Encapsulates the logic required to turn pixel samples into color components. The color components are relative to the associated `ColorSpace`.

Table 4.17 ■ Key BufferedImage related classes (Continued)

CLASS OR INTERFACE	PURPOSE
ColorSpace	Defines a specific system to measure color. For example, the sRGB ColorSpace refers to the standard RGB space, as defined by http://www.w3.org/pub/WWW/Graphics/Color/sRGB.html. The ICC_ColorSpace provides a way to create a ColorSpace from a standard ICC_Profile. For more details on the International Color Consortium, see http://www.color.org.
BufferedImageOp	Defines the interface for a BufferedImage filter. For example, the ConvolveOp filter implements the BufferedImageOp interface.
RasterOp	Defines the interface for a Raster filter. All the predefined image filters implement at least the RasterOp interface, and most implement the BufferedImageOp as well (see our discussion on "BandCombineOp" on page 104).

Text Manipulation

As we discussed in our overview on the Java 2D API, there are multiple ways to render text and several levels of text support. Drawing text can be as simple as using Graphics2D's drawString methods and as complex as adjusting individual glyph positions through a GlyphVector (glyphs are the visual representations of characters. See "Font" on page 156).

In our overview of text support, we categorized the features as follows:

1. Simple text rendering. Drawing a simple string of text follows the traditional rendering model of setting the relevant graphic context attributes (Font and Paint), selecting the object to render (a String or an AttributedString), and invoking the Graphics2D's drawString method.
2. Advanced text manipulation. The TextLayout and LineBreak-Measurer classes offer a very sophisticated way to manipulate text. For example, TextLayout handles bidirectional text display (text that runs from left to right or right to left) but also provides features relevant to user interfaces, such as caret management

and hit testing. `LineBreakMeasurer` provides a way to arrange text blocks.

3. Custom glyph layout. The API provides access to the individual glyphs that represent characters. This access allows us to manipulate individual glyph positions to implement custom layout algorithms.

Our overview in Chapter 2 explained simple text rendering (see "Simple text rendering" on page 19), and we also used simple text rendering to illustrate the Java 2D rendering model in Chapter 1 (see "The Java 2D API Rendering Model" on page 2). Please refer to these pages for details on this topic.

Here, we look in greater detail at the advanced text rendering capabilities that the API offers. First, we describe the `AttributedString` class, the various `TextAttribute` values that define style attributes, and the rendering of styled text. Then, we present `TextLayout` and `LineBreakMeasurer` which, combined with `AttributedString`, make sophisticated text layout and rendering possible. Finally, we show how to create a custom glyph layout algorithm.

AttributedString

Defining styled text consists of mapping style attributes to a range of characters in a string of text. Consider the following string of text: "Attributed Strings are fun!" We are going to manipulate it with the API so that it is rendered as shown in Table 4.18.

Table 4.18 ■ Styled text rendering

STYLEDTEXTRENDERING.JAVA

Attributed Strings are fun !

```
String text  = "Attributed Strings are fun !";
AttributedString styledText  = new AttributedString(text);

// Set font attributes for the whole string
styledText.addAttribute(TextAttribute.FAMILY, "serif");
styledText.addAttribute(TextAttribute.SIZE, new Float(40));
styledText.addAttribute(TextAttribute.FOREGROUND, Color.black);
```

Table 4.18 ■ Styled text rendering (Continued)

STYLEDTEXTRENDERING.JAVA

```
// Set font style attributes for different parts of the string.

// "Attributed" is in Bold
styledText.addAttribute(TextAttribute.WEIGHT,
                        TextAttribute.WEIGHT_BOLD, 0, 10);

// "fun" is underlined
styledText.addAttribute(TextAttribute.UNDERLINE,
                        TextAttribute.UNDERLINE_ON, 23, 28);

Color redColor = new Color(128, 0, 0);
Color blueColor = new Color(70, 107, 132);
Color yellowColor = new Color(236, 214, 70);

// Set text color
// "Attributed" is in dark red
styledText.addAttribute(TextAttribute.FOREGROUND, redColor, 0, 10);

// "String" is blue
styledText.addAttribute(TextAttribute.FOREGROUND, blueColor, 11, 18);

// "fun" is yellow on blue background
styledText.addAttribute(TextAttribute.FOREGROUND, yellowColor, 23, 28);
styledText.addAttribute(TextAttribute.BACKGROUND, blueColor, 23, 28);

// Paint background with white
g.setPaint(Color.white);
g.fillRect(0, 0, getSize().width, getSize().height);

AttributedCharacterIterator iter      // This is the iterator
   = styledText.getIterator();        // Graphics2D renders

LineMetrics metrics
   = font.getLineMetrics(iter, 0, iter.getEndIndex(),
                                g.getFontRenderContext());

g.drawString(iter, 20, 20 + metrics.getAscent());
```

The first step is to create an `AttributedString` object for the text we want to render:

```
String text = "Attributed Strings are fun !";
AttributedString styledText = new AttributedString(text);
```

This code builds an `AttributedString` with no defined attributes. We then set attributes relevant for the whole text:

```
styledText.addAttribute(TextAttribute.FAMILY, "serif");
styledText.addAttribute(TextAttribute.SIZE, new Float(40));
styledText.addAttribute(TextAttribute.FOREGROUND, Color.black);
```

This code sets the default font family (see Table 5.9 on page 165 for exact meaning of the font family name), size, and foreground `Paint`. Note that this is different from setting the default `TextAttribute.FONT` attribute—

```
Font font = new Font("serif", Font.PLAIN, 40);
styledText.addAttribute(TextAttribute.FONT, font);
```

—because the `FONT` attribute overrides all other font-related attributes. In other words, if the `FONT` attribute is set for the whole string, then setting the `Font` `SIZE` or `POSTURE`[18] attributes, for example, has no effect because they are over-ridden by the `FONT` attribute size and posture.

Also note that these attribute settings apply to the whole text. This first version of `addAttribute` takes no information about the range of characters to which the attribute applies, which means that it applies to the whole string. This explains why the attributes become the default setting.

The following attribute settings apply to subparts of the text. For example,

```
// "Attributed" is in Bold
styledText.addAttribute(TextAttribute.WEIGHT,
                        TextAttribute.WEIGHT_BOLD, 0, 10);
```

makes the "`Attributed`" substring bold, and

```
// "String" is blue
styledText.addAttribute(TextAttribute.FOREGROUND,
                        new Color(70, 107, 132), 11, 18);
```

makes "`String`" blue. Figure 4.11 shows how the different attribute settings in the code relate to the string and its visual aspect. Note that the character indices are those of the first character whose style is modified and the one *following* the last character whose style is modified. In other terms, this means that the first index is included and the last index is excluded from the set of characters to which the style applies.

There are more attributes than the ones we have used in this short example, and we discuss them in the next section. However, setting them is always done the same way, by invoking the `AttributedString.addAttribute` method. As we mentioned in our overview, `Graphics2D` does not render `Attributed-String` directly. Rather, it uses an `AttributedCharacterIterator` to walk through the styled text content and style attributes. In our example in

---

18. This attribute defines the slant of the italicized text.

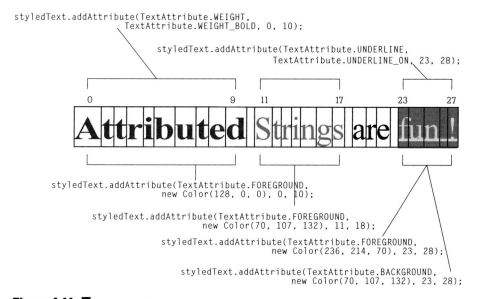

Figure 4.11 ■
Applying TextAttributes to ranges of characters

Table 4.18 on page 110, we get the iterator from the styled text in preparation of the rendering call:

```
AttributedCharacterIterator iter = styledText.getIterator();
```

The remainder of the code uses a `LineMetrics` object[19] to get the styled text height in order to place it properly:

```
LineMetrics metrics = font.getLineMetrics(iter, 0, iter.getEndIndex(),
                                          g.getFontRenderContext());
```

Finally, `Graphics2D` renders the styled text:

```
g.drawString(iter, 20, 20 + metrics.getAscent());
```

As for simple text, the coordinates (`20, 20 + metrics.getAscent()`) represent the leftmost point on the baseline about which the text is drawn. It is similar to the initial pen position before a line of text is written.

Our example used only a few of the `TextAttribute` style attributes. This class defines more attributes, and they sometimes have different purposes.

---

19. See "Accessing font metrics" on page 167 in Chapter 5 for more details.

A closer look at TextAttribute

The predefined `TextAttribute` values can be classified in the following categories:

- Font definition attributes
- Text layout control (not the class, the process)
- Rendering control

▼ **Font definition attributes**   Six attributes are relevant to `Font` creation: `FONT`, which completely defines a `Font` object, `FAMILY`, `SIZE`, `POSTURE`, `WEIGHT`, and `TRANSFORM` which define the font family, its size, how oblique and bold it is, and how glyphs should be transformed. These attributes are detailed in Chapter 5 (see "Font constructors" on page 164).

▼ **Text layout control**   Again, this is not a typo but a reference to the process of laying out lines of text, as opposed to the `TextLayout` class. Two attributes influence the layout process: `RUN_DIRECTION` and `JUSTIFICATION`. The first attribute specifies whether text dominantly runs from left to right or right to left. The second one defines how text can be justified (this is actually a ratio of the extra space to use when justifying text). Text run direction and justification are discussed in greater detail later in this section.

▼ **Rendering control**   As we have seen in our example, some attributes control the rendering process: for example, `FOREGROUND` and `BACKGROUND` specify the `Paint` object used to fill a glyph and its background, respectively. The `UNDERLINE` attributes that our example used also controlled drawing of a line under the glyphs. Note that this is not a `Font` attribute, but really a control of the rendering process, even though it is tied to a set of characters and is a text characteristic.

Additional attributes control the rendering process: `STRIKETHROUGH`, `SWAP_COLORS`, and `CHAR_REPLACEMENT`. The first attribute is similar to `UNDERLINE`, except that the strikethrough line appears at a different elevation relative to the baseline. Note that `LineMetrics` (built from a `Font` object) can return both the underline and the strikethrough elevations. In our code, if we substitute the line

```
styledText.addAttribute(TextAttribute.UNDERLINE,
                        TextAttribute.UNDERLINE_ON, 23, 28);
```

with

```
styledText.addAttribute(TextAttribute.STRIKETHROUGH,
                        TextAttribute.STRIKETHROUGH_ON, 23, 28);
```

the output becomes:

Similarly, if we add

```
styledText.addAttribute(TextAttribute.SWAP_COLORS,
                        TextAttribute.SWAP_COLORS_ON, 23, 28);
```
the output becomes:

The foreground and background colors have been swapped.

The `CHAR_REPLACEMENT` attribute allows substitution of glyphs by an arbitrary `GraphicAttribute` object. The idea is to render characters with an entity able to draw itself and provide metrics similar to the ones given by a glyph: baseline, ascent, descent, etc. There are two default implementations of the `Graphic-Attribute` abstract class: `ImageGraphicAttribute` and `ShapeGraphic-Attribute`, all in the `java.awt.font` package. The following addition to our example replaces the "A" glyph with its outline:

```
TextLayout aLayout = new TextLayout("A", font, frc);
Shape aShape = aLayout.getOutline(null);

ShapeGraphicAttribute aReplacement
    = new ShapeGraphicAttribute(aShape,
                                GraphicAttribute.ROMAN_BASELINE,
                                true);
styledText.addAttribute(TextAttribute.CHAR_REPLACEMENT, aReplacement, 0,
1);
```

We already introduced the `TextLayout` class in our overview of the API (see "Advanced text manipulation" on page 21). It provides many features, and later we describe it further. Here, we use its ability to return the shape of the glyphs it represents to build a `ShapeGraphicAttribute`. The `ShapeGraphic-Attribute` object we build aligns the shape about the baseline (because this is

English text, we use the roman baseline, which is how the baseline we are accustomed to is qualified) and strokes it rather than filling it. The output is:

Attributed Strings are fun!

You can use the ShapeGraphicAttribute to insert simple shapes into a text, to replace characters with a more sophisticated shape, or to use an alternate rendering method (as in our example, where we stroked the "A" glyph instead of filling it).

You can use ImageGraphicAttribute to insert Images within a text block. You can use it to provide a sophisticated rendering of a specific glyph. In the following code snippet, we use the base glyph "A" to create an image representing its cut-out shadow.

```
TextLayout aLayout = new TextLayout("A", font, frc);
Shape aShape = aLayout.getOutline(null);
Rectangle bounds = aShape.getBounds();

// Use the Shape size to build a BufferedImage
int blurWidth = 6;
BufferedImage image = new BufferedImage(bounds.width + blurWidth*4,
                  bounds.height + blurWidth*4,
                  BufferedImage.TYPE_INT_ARGB);
// Create a Graphics2D to paint into the BufferedImage
Graphics2D g2 = image.createGraphics();
int w = image.getWidth(), h = image.getHeight();

// Set the shadow color
g2.setPaint(Color.black);

// Translate to the glyph's origin before filling it
g2.translate(-bounds.x + (w - bounds.width)/2,
          -bounds.y + (h - bounds.height)/2);
g2.fill(aShape);

// Now, use a ConvolveOp to blur the shape
float k[] = new float[blurWidth*blurWidth];
for(int i=0; i<k.length; i++) k[i] = 1/(float)k.length;
Kernel kernel = new Kernel(blurWidth, blurWidth, k);
ConvolveOp blur = new ConvolveOp(kernel);
image = blur.filter(image, null);

// Clear the shape area to create the 'cut-out' effect
g2 = image.createGraphics();
g2.translate(-bounds.x + (w - bounds.width)/2,
```

```
                             -bounds.y + (h - bounds.height)/2);
      g2.setComposite(AlphaComposite.Clear);
      g2.fill(aShape);

      image = image.getSubimage(blurWidth, blurWidth,
                                 image.getWidth() - 2*blurWidth,
                                 image.getHeight() - 2*blurWidth);

      // Finally, build an ImageGraphicAttribute. Because we have added a
      // shadow which is blurWidth wide, we specify the exact origin
      // within the image. This corresponds to the lower left point
      // of the 'A' glyph.
      ImageGraphicAttribute aImageReplacement
          = new ImageGraphicAttribute(image, GraphicAttribute.ROMAN_BASELINE,
                                       blurWidth, blurWidth + bounds.height);

      // Set the replacement attribute to the image we just created
      styledText.addAttribute(TextAttribute.CHAR_REPLACEMENT,
                              aImageReplacement, 0, 1);
```

This example uses several techniques we introduced earlier. First, it creates an offscreen buffer, as we presented in Chapter 3, "Rendering to an Output Device: Screen, Printer, and Images." Second, it uses a `ConvolveOp` as we discussed on page 94. Our example creates an offscreen image that is bigger than the shape we draw by 2*`blurWidth` margin. The reason for this is as follows. First, the blur creates a shadow that extends up to `blurWidth` outside of the `Shape`, because the `ConvolveOp` kernel is `blurWidth` wide. Second, the `ConvolveOp` leaves out a margin the size of its convolution kernel. This explains the two additional `blurWidth` margins.

Once the image is created, an `ImageGraphicAttribute` can also be created. Its constructor lets us specify not only the baseline for aligning the `Image`, as did the `ShapeGraphicAttribute` constructor, but also the origin of the image. This is what `TextLayout` uses as an equivalent to the glyph origin. Here, because we do use a glyph, we simply set the actual origin of the "A" shape.

This completes our tour of `TextAttribute` values that control the rendering process. `TextAttribute` values are used to annotate `AttributedString` with style information, and we have seen that this information is used to control the layout process, the rendering process, and the definition of fonts.

We have seen how `AttributedSting` objects are rendered by a `Graphics2D` object, but styled text can also be rendered through a `TextLayout` object. `TextLayout`, with `LineBreakMeasurer`, provides extensive support for text rendering and also for text editing.

Advanced text rendering with TextLayout and LineBreakMeasurer

`TextLayout` provides an impressive set of features. Here is the list, from the API documentation.

- Implicit bidirectional analysis and reordering
- Cursor positioning and movement, including split cursors for mixed directional text
- Highlighting, including both logical and visual highlighting for mixed directional text
- Multiple baselines (roman, hanging, and centered),
- Hit testing
- Justification
- Default font substitution
- Metric information such as ascent, descent, advance, width, and leading
- Rendering

These features can be divided into three categories:

1. International text complexities—Bidirectional text support, multiple baselines[20]
2. Text editing support—Cursor positioning, highlighting, hit testing
3. Text rendering support—Justification, text drawing, text metrics, default font substitution

This book is about rendering techniques, so we are more interested in the last feature category, which is the one we will describe in the most detail. However, let's look at each group in turn, as they are all important.

▼ **International text complexities**   Supporting international text involves more than using Unicode to define any character in any language. Displaying international characters is a challenge of its own. The two biggest challenges are the way text flows and the way glyphs are arranged.

---

20. Note that even though we list international text support as a separate category here, all the features work correctly for international text.

Occidentals are accustomed to text that reads from left to right. However, the whole world does not use that model for text, and some scripts read from right to left. The direction in which text reads is called the run direction. `TextAttribute.RUN_DIRECTION` defines the way paragraphs of text should dominantly run and can be set to either `TextAttribute.RUN_DIRECTION_LTR` (left to right) or `TextAttribute.RUN_DIRECTION_RTL` (right to left). Different runs in an `AttributedString` could have different run directions. `TextLayout` handles those different situations and processes the text string so that the visual ordering or the different text runs fits the direction attributes. Refer to the Java 2D documentation and the Unicode standard [Unicode97] for further information on the topic.

We may also think that the way glyphs are laid out to form lines of text around a horizontal baseline is universal. It is not; there are other ways to organize glyphs. The API supports two others: one is the center baseline, used in scripts such as Chinese and Japanese, and the other is the hanging baseline, used in Devangiri and similar scripts. `TextLayout` handles those scripts properly, just as it does English.

▼ **Text editing features**　Text display is often coupled with text editing capabilities, for example, in word processor applications. In addition to displaying text, such applications must display carets (the caret marks the current text insertion point in a typical text editing application) and allow selection. `TextLayout` supports these features.

Again, these features go beyond our scope. However, they are key to any application providing custom text editing support, and it is important to remember that they are provided through the `TextLayout` class.

▼ **Text rendering support**　The feature-rich `TextLayout` class also provides text rendering support. It can render text, as we have seen in Chapter 2 (see "Advanced text manipulation" on page 21). It can also render more sophisticated text.

For one thing, `TextLayout` can render styled text, just as `Graphics2D` does. Second, it provides text metrics. Those two features make `TextLayout` easy to use because it gives a single interface to all the features needed to render text: styled text to define the text visual aspect and metrics to be able to place that text properly.

But there is more. Another feature `TextLayout` provides is text justification. In typical word processors, you can align text in several ways: left-aligned, right-aligned, centered, and justified. While aligning to the left, right, or center only requires that the text lines be translated, justifying text implies modification of character spacing, which is a complex process.

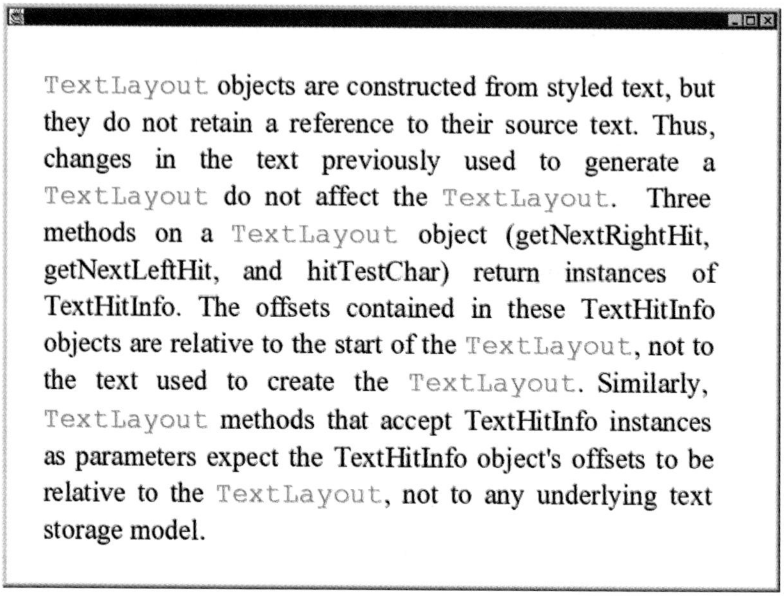

> `TextLayout` objects are constructed from styled text, but they do not retain a reference to their source text. Thus, changes in the text previously used to generate a `TextLayout` do not affect the `TextLayout`. Three methods on a `TextLayout` object (getNextRightHit, getNextLeftHit, and hitTestChar) return instances of TextHitInfo. The offsets contained in these TextHitInfo objects are relative to the start of the `TextLayout`, not to the text used to create the `TextLayout`. Similarly, `TextLayout` methods that accept TextHitInfo instances as parameters expect the TextHitInfo object's offsets to be relative to the `TextLayout`, not to any underlying text storage model.

Figure 4.12 ■
TextLayout rendering capabilities at work

Finally, used in conjunction with `LineBreakMeasurer`, `TextLayout` supports layout of paragraphs. Figure 4.12 shows a screen shot of a program (**Justified-TextBlock.java** on the CD–ROM) that draws a paragraph of text, using all of these features. It loads a text file and creates a styled text from it. Then, it breaks the text into individual lines that fit into a given width and justifies each line. Let us use this example to illustrate each of the `TextLayout` rendering features.

▼ **Creating and using an AttributedString**   To create text with style attributes for rendering, we again use the `AttributedString` class and set the default attributes for the whole string.

```
Font font = new Font(fontName, Font.PLAIN, fontSize);
AttributedString str = new AttributedString(text);
str.addAttribute(TextAttribute.FONT, font);
str.addAttribute(TextAttribute.FOREGROUND, Color.black);
```

Note that the `text` `String` object contains the whole paragraph of text. To change the color and font for all instances of "TextLayout," we parse the string, find each position where it appears, and set the `AttributedString` FONT and FOREGROUND attributes accordingly.

```
// tlFont and tlColor are the values used for the
// FONT and FOREGROUND attributes for all instances of
// "TextAttribute" inside text.
Font tlFont = new Font("monospaced", Font.PLAIN, fontSize);
Color tlColor = new Color(0, 128, 0);
int tlLength = "TextLayout".length();
int i = text.indexOf("TextLayout");
while(i != -1){
   str.addAttribute(TextAttribute.FONT, tlFont, i, i+tlLength);
   str.addAttribute(TextAttribute.FOREGROUND, tlColor,
                    i, i+tlLength);
   i = text.indexOf("TextLayout", i+1);
}
```

The `TextLayout` class provides an important feature to make sure that the text it renders is represented by proper glyphs: *font substitution*. If the `FONT` attribute is defined, as in our example, the `TextLayout` uses that `Font` object, and font substitution does not happen. However, we have seen earlier in this chapter that the font can also be specified through attributes (see "Font defini-tion attributes" on page 114). If attributes are used, the font might be only partly defined (that is, only its `SIZE` is specified, or its `FAMILY`) or not at all (that is, none of the font-related `TextAttributes` is set). In that case, `TextLayout` creates a `Font` that is the best match for the available attributes. But it also checks that all characters can be rendered by glyphs in that `Font` object. If not (that is, "missing character box" shows), `TextLayout` substitutes the `Font` instance with one that can render the character, if one is available. This ensures that text is displayed properly, with attributes that match the require-ments as closely as possible.

▼ **Creating a text paragraph**   The next step consists in breaking down the `AttributedString` content into lines of text that fit into a wrapping width. This capability is provided by the `LineBreakMeasurer` class. Just like the `Graphics2D` and `TextLayout` classes, it does not use an `AttributedString` directly but rather uses an `AttributedCharacterIterator` to walk through the styled text content and attributes.

```
AttributedCharacterIterator iter = str.getIterator();
FontRenderContext frc
   = new FontRenderContext(null,
                        true,    // Use antialiasing
                        true);   // Use fractional metrics
LineBreakMeasurer measurer = new LineBreakMeasurer(iter, frc);
```

`FontRenderContext` objects describe the text rendering environment, for example, whether or not antialiasing is used. Those settings influence the text spatial characteristics and are needed by `LineBreakMeasurer` to accurately determine the wrapping points.

The following lines prepare the main line-breaking loop.

```
float wrappingWidth = w - 2*MARGIN; // Leave some margin on each side
float curY = MARGIN;                // Controls the current line's
                                    // vertical position
Vector vLayouts = new Vector();     // Stores 1 TextLayout for each line
Vector vPenPositions = new Vector();// Stores the baseline origin for
                                    // each line
TextLayout layout = null;           // Variable used in following loop
Point2D.Float penPosition = null;   // Idem
```

The main loop can be summarized as:

```
while (measurer.getPosition() < iter.getEndIndex()) {
  // Get next line
  layout = measurer.nextLayout(wrappingWidth);

  // Process vertical position for the line
  ....

  // Store line layout and position
  ...
}
```

So, the loop is controlled by the current position (`measurer.getPosition`), that is, how many characters have already been placed into lines. The current position will not exceed the end of the text, defined by `iter.getEndIndex()`. Until the end of the text is reached, the measurer provides lines of text that fit in the requested wrapping width in the form of a new `TextLayout`:

```
layout = measurer.nextLayout(wrappingWidth);
```

The remainder of the loop consists in computing the vertical position where the layout should be drawn and justifying each line to the wrapping width.

```
while (measurer.getPosition() < iter.getEndIndex()) {
  layout = measurer.nextLayout(wrappingWidth);

  // Adjust current elevation
  curY += (layout.getAscent());

  // Justify previous layout if any: this way, all lines will
  // be justified, but the last one.
  if(vLayouts.size()>0){
      TextLayout previousLine
        = (TextLayout)vLayouts.elementAt(vLayouts.size()-1);
      previousLine = previousLine.getJustifiedLayout(wrappingWidth*2);
      vLayouts.setElementAt(previousLine, vLayouts.size()-1);
  }

  // Store layout position so that text block appears centered
  penPosition = new Point2D.Float(MARGIN, curY);
  vPenPositions.addElement(penPosition);
```

```
// Store layout
vLayouts.addElement(layout);

// Move to next line.
curY += layout.getDescent() + layout.getLeading();
}
```

The vertical position is based on the metrics returned by `TextLayout`'s `get-Ascent`, `getDescent`, and `getLeading` methods. All `TextLayout` instances have their origin on their baseline and on their left hand side. The layouts will be drawn at the computed pen positions, as illustrated in Figure 4.13.

Justifying each line is straightforward: simply invoke `TextLayout.getJusti-fiedLayout` with the justification width as an input parameter.

Once text positions have been computed and lines justified, all that is left is to render the individual lines at the proper location. Before this is done, the pen positions and layouts are copied into an array, for readability. Drawing the text is straightforward and relies on `TextLayout`'s rendering capability. Here, we draw into an offscreen buffer.

```
Point2D.Float lastPosition = penPositions[penPositions.length-1];
TextLayout lastLayout = layouts[layouts.length-1];
int bw = w;
int bh = (int)(lastPosition.y + lastLayout.getDescent() + MARGIN);
buf = new BufferedImage(bw, bh, BufferedImage.TYPE_INT_ARGB);
Graphics2D g = buf.createGraphics();

for(i=0; i<layouts.length; i++)
  layouts[i].draw(g, penPositions[i].x, penPositions[i].y);
```

As we will see in The Graphic Layers Framework, we can build on the `Text-Layout` and `LineBreakMeasurer` to format text paragraphs in various creative ways (for example, fit text into a disc; see Chapter 14).

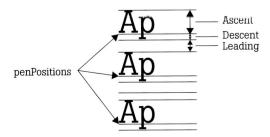

Figure 4.13 ■
Pen positions for the TextLayout lines

Custom glyph layouts

We just saw how `TextLayout` and `LineBreakMeasurer` provide both glyph layout (`TextLayout` positions and draws individual glyphs) and text paragraph layout (`LineBreakMeasurer` breaks down text into lines to form blocks of text). The API actually exposes some of the underlying features that `TextLayout` uses, in the form of the `java.awt.font.GlyphVector` class. `TextLayout` uses `GlyphVector` objects to create the glyph for each font used by the text it represents. `GlyphVector` instances are created by the `Font.createGlyphVector` method.

Besides supporting the `TextLayout` implementation, `GlyphVectors` can support the implementation of a customized glyph layout. Before we look more closely into an example of this, it is important to realize that glyph layout, which amounts to spacing characters properly, is a complex topic. Most fonts do not have fixed-size characters, so spacing characters depends on the type of character. For example, an "l" takes much less space than an "A," and even the spacing to the left and the right of glyphs depends on a number of factors. Sometimes, the spacing depends on the type of neighboring glyphs. Figure 4.14 illustrates a process, known as kerning, which maps a pair of glyphs (here "T" and "o") into a positioning offset. That technique produces a much more sophisticated layout, more pleasing to the eye. This section illustrates that there is a lot more to glyph layout than mere spacing: contextual and style information influence glyph layout.

So, it is usually best to rely on what the platform offers for glyph layout rather than to try to implement an alternate solution. However, there are situations where modifying the glyph layout logic might be useful, for example, to produce a specific visual effect. In our example in Table 4.19, we space glyphs evenly so that they can be drawn into fixed-size boxes. This might be useful, for example, to display text in a crossword.

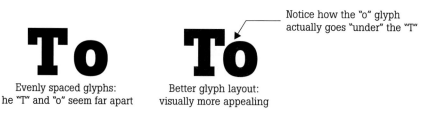

Notice how the "o" glyph actually goes "under" the "T"

Evenly spaced glyphs: he "T" and "o" seem far apart

Better glyph layout: visually more appealing

Figure 4.14 ■

Kerning: an illustration of glyph layout complexity

Table 4.19 ■ Custom glyph layout example

```
// First, create a GlyphVector from a Font object
Font font = new Font(fontName, Font.PLAIN, 90);

String text = "CrossWords"
FontRenderContext frc = new FontRenderContext(null, true, true);
LineMetrics metrics = font.getLineMetrics(text, frc);

GlyphVector glyphVector = font.createGlyphVector(frc);

// Modify the glyph positions: find the largest glyph width and space all
// glyphs so that they all appear inside a same size rectangle
int n = glyphVector.getNumGlyphs();

// First, find the largest glyph
for(int i=0; i<n; i++){
  Shape gBounds = glyphVector.getGlyphLogicalBounds(i);
  Rectangle2D bounds = gBounds.getBounds2D();
  maxWidth = Math.max(maxWidth,bounds.getWidth());
}


// Add some margin so that the largest glyphs do not appear squeezed
// in its box
maxWidth += 10;

// Now, center each glyph in its allocated maxWidth space
for(int i=0; i<n; i++){
  Shape gBounds = glyphVector.getGlyphOutline(i);
  Rectangle2D bounds = gBounds.getBounds2D();
  Point2D pos = glyphVector.getGlyphPosition(i);

  // Adjust x position to align in the maxWidth wide rectangle
  double xPos = i*maxWidth + (maxWidth - bounds.getWidth())/2;
  pos.setLocation(xPos, pos.getY());

  // Update glyph position
  glyphVector.setGlyphPosition(i, pos);
}

...

Graphics2D g = ...;
```

Table 4.19 ■ Custom glyph layout example (Continued)

CUSTOMGLYPHLAYOUT.JAVA

```
// Painting GlyphVector
Color grayishBlue = new Color(120, 120, 140);
g.setPaint(grayishBlue);
g.drawGlyphVector(glyphVector, 20, 20 + metrics.getAscent());

// Paint glyph boxes as a set of lines
int n = glyphVector.getNumGlyphs();
double boxHeight = metrics.getAscent() + metrics.getDescent();
double xPos=0; yPos=20;
for(int i=0; i<=n; i++){                    // Draw vertical edges
  xPos = 20 + i*maxWidth;
  g.draw(new Line2D.Double(xPos, yPos xPos,
                    yPos + boxHeight));
}

xPos = 20; yPos = 20;                       // Draw top edge
g.draw(new Line2D.Double(xPos, yPos,
                    xPos +n*maxWidth,
                    yPos));
yPos = 20 + boxHeight;
g.draw(new Line2D.Double(xPos, yPos,        // Draw bottom edge
                    xPos +n*maxWidth,
                    yPos));
```

▼ **Creating a GlyphVector**   In our example, we start by creating a Glyph-Vector, from a Font object.

```
Font font = new Font(fontName, Font.PLAIN, 90);
String text = "CrossWords";

FontRenderContext frc
   = new FontRenderContext(null,  // No optional AffineTransform
                    true,  // Use antialiasing
                    true); // Use fractional metrics

LineMetrics metrics = font.getLineMetrics(text, frc);
GlyphVector glyphVector = font.createGlyphVector(frc);
```

Note how both the LineMetrics (used later to get the height of the text line) and the GlyphVector creation require a FontRenderContext object. Remember that a FontRenderContext describes how text is intended to be rendered, that is, whether antialiasing is used,[21] whether fractional metrics are used, and whether a specific AffineTransform should be applied to the glyphs before

---

21. See "Antialiasing" on page 188 in Chapter 5 for a definition of antialiasing.

rendering. All these attributes influence both the spatial characteristics of the rendered text (which explains why Font used a FontRenderContext to create appropriate LineMetrics) and the glyph layout (which explains why Font uses a FontRenderContext also to create a GlyphVector).

▼ **Processing the largest glyph width**   The next operation consists in computing the width of the largest glyph.

```
int n = glyphVector.getNumGlyphs();

for(int i=0; i<n; i++){
  Shape gBounds = glyphVector.getGlyphVisualBounds(i);
  Rectangle2D bounds = gBounds.getBounds2D();
  maxWidth = Math.max(maxWidth, bounds.getWidth());
}
```

The getGlyphVisualBounds method returns a four-sided polygon with two edges parallel to the baseline. The returned shape is the smallest such polygon that includes all of the glyph at the given index. Note that this polygon is not necessarily a Rectangle (for example, if the glyph is oblique), which is why we use the getBounds2D method to convert to a rectangular area: it represents the smallest "box" into which the glyph would fit. The above loop simply keeps track of the largest of such smallest boxes for all the glyphs in our GlyphVector.

▼ **Custom glyph layout**   The following code performs the actual glyph layout.

```
for(int i=0; i<n; i++){
  Shape gBounds = glyphVector.getGlyphOutline(i);
  Rectangle2D bounds = gBounds.getBounds2D();
  Point2D pos = glyphVector.getGlyphPosition(i);

  // Adjust x position to align in the maxWidth wide rectangle
  double xPos = i*maxWidth  + (maxWidth - bounds.getWidth())/2;
  pos.setLocation(xPos, pos.getY());

  // Update glyph position
  glyphVector.setGlyphPosition(i, pos);
}
```

Here, we modify the x-axis position for each glyph so that it appears centered in a maxWidth-wide rectangle. The two key methods used in that process are getGlyphPosition and setGlyphPosition. Even though not used in our example, two additional classes in the java.awt.font package are important for glyph layout: GlyphMetrics and GlyphJustificationInfo. GlyphMetrics specifies the glyph type (such as white space character, ligature or normal) and its spatial attributes (such as its advance). GlyphJustificationInfo specifies how a given glyph should be used in a justification process (we illustrated such a process in Figure 4.12 on page 120). For example, white spaces typically absorb most of the extra space, but other glyphs can be given more space as well. Not all glyphs play the same role, and GlyphJustificationInfo defines the role of any given glyph. Both GlyphMetrics and GlyphJustification- Info can be retrieved from a GlyphVector (through the getGlyphMetrics and getGlyphJustificationInfo methods, respectively).

▼ **Rendering a GlyphVector**   Laying out glyphs is the hard part of the process, and drawing the result is as simple as drawing a plain text string.

```
g.setPaint(new Color(120, 120, 140));
g.drawGlyphVector(glyphVector, 20, 20 + metrics.getAscent());
```

This method is similar to the drawString method that Graphics2D provides for simple text and AttributedString. The remainder of the code simply draws lines around each glyph-enclosing box to create a crossword-like decoration.

Again, laying out glyphs is a sophisticated process, and it should only be tinkered with for very specific reasons. For example, our example would fail to support international text properly if the text required ordering (as in Hebrew or Arabic) or shaping (as in Arabic). However, this ability to customize glyph layouts is one more example of the API's extensible architecture, and it allows specific needs to be fulfilled, as our crosswords example illustrated.

Table 4.20 summarizes the key classes used for text rendering.

Table 4.20 ■ Key text rendering classes

CLASS	PURPOSE
Graphics2D	Its drawString methods render simple text (defined by a simple String object) or stylized text (text defined by an AttributedCharacterIterator object). Graphics2D can also render pre-processed text in the form of GlyphVector objects.
String	Simple way to define text for rendering by a Graphics2D object.
Font	One of the Graphics2D context attributes (see Chapter 5). The context Font defines the default style characteristics of text, such as its family (Helvetica, Times, etc.), its weight (e.g., bold) or its posture (e.g., italic). Note that this default attribute may be overridden by different settings in AttributedCharacterIterators. However, all the font characteristics apply for simple text string rendering.

Table 4.20 ■ Key text rendering classes (Continued)

CLASS	PURPOSE
AttributedString	Supports the definition of styled text strings, that is, text strings with variable style attributes. For example, parts of the string can have a different font, color, or size. An AttributedString is not rendered directly. Rather, an AttributedCharacterIterator is passed to a Graphics2D for rendering. The AttributedString.getIterator methods return an AttributedCharacterIterator that can be rendered.
TextAttribute	Contains a set of predefined text characteristic attributes that Graphics2D and TextLayout recognize. For example, TextAttribute defines attributes for the font, the foreground, the background, the weight. TextAttribute values are set in an AttributedString by the addAttribute method.
AttributedCharacter-Iterator	Used by Graphics2D to render a string of text with variable style attributes. Typically, an AttributedCharacterIterator is created from an AttributedString.
TextLayout	Provides extended support for international text layout (e.g., bidirectional text support), text editing capabilities (e.g., cursor management, text highlighting) and text metrics. This feature-rich class can also be used for both complex and simple text rendering.
GlyphVector	Contains a set of Shape instances corresponding to the visual representation of a character string. Note that glyphs are different from string characters: there is not necessarily a one-to-one correspondence. Use GlyphVector to create custom glyph layout algorithms and also to speed up the rendering process.
LineBreakMeasurer	Allows paragraph layout. Use this class to display a paragraph of text within a maximum width.

Table 4.20 ■ Key text rendering classes (Continued)

CLASS	PURPOSE
`FontMetrics,` `LineMetrics`	They provide text metrics information, that is, different spatial characteristics about the visual representation of text using a specific font. Such characteristics include, among others, the height, the advance (i.e., the horizontal space taken by the text). See "Font" on page 156. Note that `TextLayout` provides a convenient way to also retrieve metrics information.
`FontRenderContext`	Objects of this class are obtained through the `Graphics2D.getFontRenderContext` method. It describes the context in which text rendering happens. For example, it describes whether antialiasing is used or not. `FontRenderContext` influences the way text rendering is performed.

Conclusion

The Java 2D API covers a large part of the computer graphics field. There are many books that help you to better understand several aspects of the API, and Table 4.21 provides a list of references that provide insights on the different areas we have discussed.

Even though shapes, text, and images cover whole areas of computer graphics, they are surprisingly easy to manipulate in the API and all fit in the common rendering model we discussed in our introduction. The way they are rendered, however, is controlled by the attributes that make the graphic context, and those attributes are discussed in our next chapter.

Table 4.21 ■ Computer Graphics references

AREA	BOOK REFERENCE[*]	COMMENT
General	[Foley 1997] and [Hearn 1997]	These two famous books provide extensive coverage of the field of computer graphics. They are handy references.
Image processing	[Crane 1997]	This book contains a wealth of information about raster graphics and image filtering.
Vector graphics	[Adobe98]	The PostScript reference manual contains a lot of information about vector graphics. Even though PostScript is not directly related to the Java 2D API, there are many common concepts.
Text Management	[Unicode97]	This standard is a little intimidating. However, it contains explanations for many concepts behind the text classes in the API.
Color theory	[Cirogianni 1998]	This book explains the underlying concepts and difficulties related to color in general. Note that the two books listed as "General" in this table also contain information about color theory, but they are not as detailed.

*See bibliography for title and publisher.

chapter **5**

GRAPHIC CONTEXT ATTRIBUTES

In this chapter, we describe the different attributes that make the graphic context. We already presented and used them on several occasions, especially in Chapter 4. However, there is more to each of these attributes, and the following paragraphs detail the operation and interface of each of them. There are a total of seven attributes in the context, as shown in Figure 5.1.

Remember that the graphic context is attached to a specific Graphics2D instance. Therefore, it is possible to have several instances of Graphics2D with different rendering contexts. This might be useful for multithreaded programs where different threads might need to concurrently render on the same output device, but for different purposes.

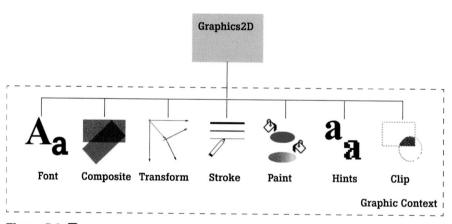

Figure 5.1 ■
Graphic context attributes

AffineTransform

Even though we have not formally defined `AffineTransform` yet, we have already encountered it several times and defined it in Chapter 4 (see "Affine-Transform definition" on page 64). First, we discussed its use to transform coordinates between the user space and the device space in the overview. Second, we saw how it is used to create transformed shapes in Chapter 4 (see "Shapes" on page 58), and also as a `TextAttribute` to modify font glyphs. Third, we discussed how it is used in the `AffineTransformOp` for spatial transformation of images. We will see, when we discuss the `Font` rendering context attribute, that `AffineTransform` is also used to derive `Font` objects.

In this chapter, we are going to look at `AffineTransform` from a more formal point of view and explain how different transforms can be composed and what the implications of composition are.

A formal definition of AffineTransform

Here is how the `AffineTransform` class is described in the Java 2 platform SDK software documentation:

This class represents a 2D affine transform which performs a linear mapping from 2D coordinates to other 2D coordinates in a manner which preserves the "straightness" and "parallelness" of lines. Affine transforms can be constructed using sequences of translations, scales, flips, rotations, and shears.

Such a coordinate transform can be represented by a 3 row by 3 column matrix with an implied last row of [0 0 1] which transforms source coordinates (x, y) into destination coordinates (x', y') by considering them to be a column vector and multiplying the coordinate vector by the matrix, according to the following formula:

$$\begin{bmatrix} x' \\ y' \\ 1 \end{bmatrix} = \begin{bmatrix} m_{00} & m_{01} & m_{02} \\ m_{10} & m_{11} & m_{12} \\ 0 & 0 & 1 \end{bmatrix} \begin{bmatrix} x \\ y \\ 1 \end{bmatrix} = \begin{bmatrix} m_{00} \cdot x + m_{01} \cdot y + m_{02} \\ m_{10} \cdot x + m_{11} \cdot y + m_{12} \\ 1 \end{bmatrix}$$

A straightforward example is translation. As we will see in the following section, a translation's matrix can be expressed as:

$$\begin{bmatrix} 1 & 0 & t_x \\ 0 & 1 & t_y \\ 0 & 0 & 1 \end{bmatrix}$$

So, if we apply the definition, the destination coordinates (x', y') after translation are:

```
x' = x + tx;
y' = y + ty;
```

AffineTransform gives us a generic way to compute the new coordinates of a point after it has been transformed. If we look back at the different uses of the class we discussed, we can understand that this is how things work. The transform object is the tool used to calculate the actual pixel location on an output device (that is, points in the device space), given a set of coordinates in the user space. Points that make up a transformed Shape object are computed the same way.

Types of elementary transforms

The AffineTransform class definition states that a transform can always be expressed as a combination of five elementary transforms. The following example illustrates each of them (Figure 5.2 and **AffineTransformTypes.java** on the CD-ROM).

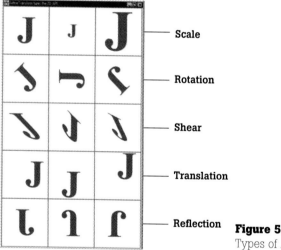

— Scale

— Rotation

— Shear

— Translation

— Reflection

Figure 5.2 ■
Types of AffineTransforms

▼ **Scale** A scale transform has the following mathematical form:

$$M = \begin{bmatrix} s_x & 0 & 0 \\ 0 & s_y & 0 \\ 0 & 0 & 1 \end{bmatrix}$$

A scale transform lets us do things like shrinking and enlarging.

A scale can be created with the `createScaleInstance` method. An `Affine-Transform` is set to be a scale with the `setToScale` method, and a scale is concatenated to an `AffineTransform` with the `scale` method, as in our example. The `setToScale` method resets an `AffineTransform` to a scale only, that is, it gets rid of what it was previously and only sets the scale factors, s_x and s_y.

▼ **Rotation** A rotation centered about the origin of angle α has the following mathematical form:

$$M = \begin{bmatrix} \cos(\alpha) & -\sin(\alpha) & 0 \\ \sin(\alpha) & \cos(\alpha) & 0 \\ 0 & 0 & 1 \end{bmatrix}$$

A rotation is created with the `createRotateInstance` methods. An `Affine-Transform` is set to be a rotation with the `setToRotation` methods, and a rotation is concatenated to an `AffineTransform` with the `rotate` method. All these methods have two versions: one for rotations about the origin, which only takes the rotation angle as a parameter, and one that takes the rotation center coordinates as additional parameters.

▼ **Shear** A shear transform has the following mathematical form:

$$M = \begin{bmatrix} 1 & sh_x & 0 \\ sh_y & 1 & 0 \\ 0 & 0 & 1 \end{bmatrix}$$

A shear transform can be used to skew shapes, images, and fonts. A shear is created with the createShearInstance method. An AffineTransform is set to a shear with the setToShear method, and a shear is concatenated to an AffineTransform with the shear method.

▼ **Translation**   A translation has the following mathematical form:

$$M = \begin{bmatrix} 1 & 0 & t_x \\ 0 & 1 & t_y \\ 0 & 0 & 1 \end{bmatrix}$$

A translation is created with the createTranslateInstance method. An AffineTransform is set to a translation with the setToTranslation method, and a translation is concatenated to an AffineTransform with the translate method.

▼ **Reflection**   A reflection has the following mathematical form:

$$M = \begin{bmatrix} +/\text{-}\ 1 & 0 & 0 \\ 0 & +/\text{-}\ 1 & 0 \\ 0 & 0 & 1 \end{bmatrix}$$

A reflection lets us flip shapes, images, and fonts either vertically or horizontally. There are no separate methods for reflections as they can be specified through the scale method by setting the s_x and s_y matrix elements to ±1.

Composing AffineTransforms

We now know all the elementary types of transforms. Let us see how they can be composed.

▼ **Transform composition defined: Transform stack**   Composing transforms means that we stack transforms that should be applied. For example, when we compose a translation with a rotation it means that we stack a rotation on top of a translation. When we apply the transform stack to a point, we pop one transform from the top of the stack after another and apply it. For example, we first pop the rotation that is at the top of the stack, and apply it. Then, we pop the translation and apply it. As we are using a stack, the last transform that has been piled up is the first one to apply, as illustrated by Figure 5.3.

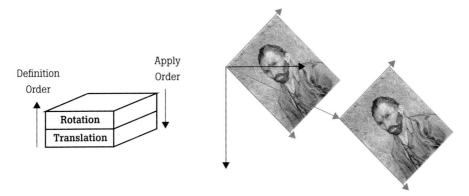

Figure 5.3 ◼
Transformation stack

In mathematical terms, composing two transforms t_1 and t_2 described by the matrices M_1 and M_2 means making their product $M_1 \cdot M_2$. This is also called concatenating transforms. Now, if we use the resulting matrix to transform a point (x, y):

```
P" = M·P = M₁·M₂·P = M₁·P' where P' = M2·P
```

Using our stack analogy again, what we are doing here is piling up M_2 on top of M_1, and we get the $M_1 \cdot M_2$ transform stack. Then, when we apply the transform stack to a point, the top of the stack applies first (that is, M_2). Simply put, it means that applying the composition of t_1 and t_2 is the same as first applying t_2 (which would result in P') and then applying t_1. In our code, we could write:

```
t1·concatenate(t2);
```

and t_1's matrix would become $M_1 \cdot M_2$. If we wanted M_1 to apply first, we would write:

```
t1·preConcatenate(t2);
```

and the matrix would become $M_2 \cdot M_1$. Preconcatenating amounts to inserting t_2 at the bottom of the transform stack.

The API actually contains several methods that make concatenations easy. The `rotate`, `scale`, `shear`, and `translate` methods in `AffineTransform` concatenate the transform object with, respectively, a rotation, a scale, a shear, and a translation. In the same way, the `rotate`, `scale`, `shear`, and `translate` methods in the `Graphics2D` class concatenate the current transform with a rotation, a scale, a shear, and a translation. Furthermore, the `Graphics2D.transform` method concatenates the input transform with the current one.

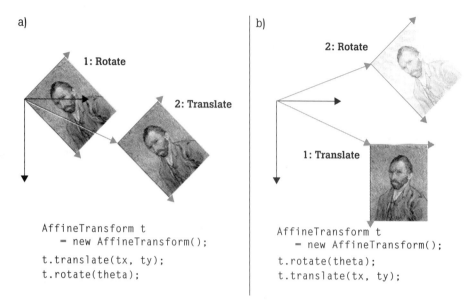

a)

1: Rotate

2: Translate

```
AffineTransform t
  = new AffineTransform();
t.translate(tx, ty);
t.rotate(theta);
```

b)

2: Rotate

1: Translate

```
AffineTransform t
  = new AffineTransform();
t.rotate(theta);
t.translate(tx, ty);
```

Figure 5.4 ■
Importance of transformation order

▼ **Composition order**   Because it is key to understand this well, let us stress the importance of the composition order: usually, the effect of applying transform t_1 and then transform t_2 is not the same as applying t_2 first and then t_1. This is illustrated in Figure 5.4 a) and b).

It may seem surprising that the transform that is specified last is the one that applies first, but we are building a stack of transforms: the one we specify last ends up at the stack top and, as we explained earlier, applies first.

▼ **Composing for more intuitive effects**   Sometimes, composition of transforms may be a little hard to grasp, and the result we get is "what we said" and not "what we meant." For example, we may want to scale an image and use the following transform:

```
AffineTransform t = AffineTransform.getScaleInstance(.5f, .5f);
```

We get the result shown in Figure 5.5: the image appears to be scaled and translated. This is what we asked for, but what we meant was: "scale at current position," that is, scale about the image center. In other words, leave the object where it is and apply the transform we want. To achieve this, we need to center the transform about the object's center, then apply the transform, and finally move the object back to its initial position:

```
AffineTransform t = new AffineTransform();
// Step 3: Move image back to its position
t.translate(image.getWidth(this)/2, image.getHeight(this)/2);
// Step 2 : Scale, while image is centered
t.scale(.5f, .5f);
// Step 1 : Center image about the origin
t.translate(-image.getWidth(this)/2, image.getHeight(this)/2);
```

Figure 5.5 illustrates that effect: the first row shows the results of applying a scale only, and the second one shows that combining the scale with translations results in the original image being scaled about its center. Note that scaling about the center may not be quite what you want, and sometimes, we may want the baseline to be preserved. We only used the center as an example to show that we often need to combine not only scales, but also shears, with translations to get the desired transformation effect (this depends on the context).

Note that the `Position` class, in the Graphic Layers Framework that we introduce in Part 2, contains convenience methods to place `Shapes` relative to a bounding `Rectangle` with notions that are more intuitive, such as Top, Top-Right, or Center. The underlying implementation uses the principles we just discussed to position `Shape` objects as requested.

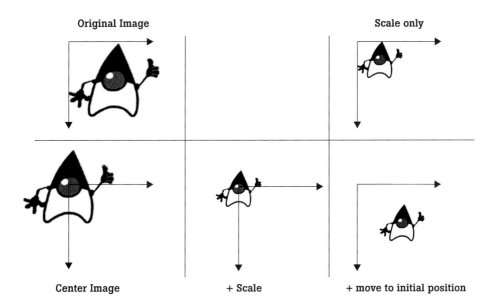

Figure 5.5 ■
Intuitive effects with transformations

Summary

`AffineTransform` is central to the Java 2D API and it is important to understand it well to enjoy the other features. It is essential to get a good mental representation of coordinate system transformations and of composition order.

One thing to remember about setting the `Graphics2D`'s `AffineTransform` attribute is that it may have a fairly high processing cost, especially when images are drawn (remember that there are different algorithms to perform pixel interpolation, as we explain in "RenderingHints" on page 182). Consequently, depending on the type of processing, it may be interesting to use other alternatives. For example, if an image needs to be rendered several times at double its size, it is better to first use an `AffineTransformOp` to enlarge it and then render the bigger image than to set the `Graphics2D`'s `AffineTransform` to a scale of factor two and render the image several times. In the first case, pixel interpolation is performed once, whereas it is done each time the image is drawn in the second one.

There are usually several ways to achieve any given rendering, and it is important to consider the different alternatives, especially if you encounter performance problems.

Strokes

The Stroke interface

The `java.awt.Stroke` interface is fairly short. Let us have a look at its definition.

```
public interface Stroke {
    /**
     * Returns an outline Shape which encloses the area that
     * should be painted when the Shape is stroked according
     * to the rules defined by the
     * object implementing the Stroke interface.
     * @param p a Shape to be stroked
     * @return the stroked outline Shape.
     */
    Shape createStrokedShape (Shape p);
}
```

What this definition tells us is that a `Stroke` implementation should define the outline of a `Shape` to be stroked, again, as a `Shape`. A `Stroke` implementation defines the geometrical form that a pen would make when used to draw along the path of a `Shape`. The exact nature of that form depends on the pen characteristics, for example, how wide the pen is or whether it produces a dashed pattern. This may seem surprising, but it makes a lot of sense when you think of what is involved in rendering the outline of a `Shape`. We need to know *what*

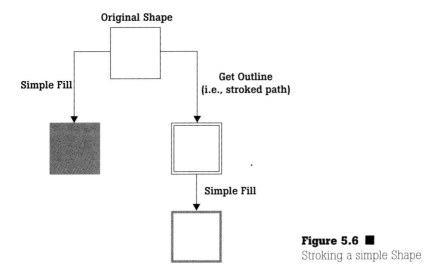

Figure 5.6 ■
Stroking a simple Shape

pixels should end up on the screen, and the `Paint` implementations define the "value" of the pixels. For example, if we are drawing a rectangle and use an orange `Color` for the `Paint` attribute, the `Color` defines that orange pixels should be used to paint the outline. But where should the pixels be drawn? This is what `Stroke` does: it defines the form whose inside represents the outline of the `Shape` being stroked.

The process for stroking a `Shape` can be described as:

■ Request the `Stroke` implementation to create the outline `Shape`.
■ Fill the outline with the current `Paint`.

So, stroking a `Shape` is almost similar to filling a `Shape`: in the end, the same process is used, and a `Shape` is filled in both cases. The difference is that when a `Shape` is stroked, the `Shape` that is filled is the stylized or decorated outline of the original `Shape` object (that is, the form of the mark created by a pen), as illustrated in Figure 5.6.

The following code produces two orange rectangles similar to the ones in Figure 5.6.

```
public void paint(Graphics _g){
  Graphics2D g = (Graphics2D)_g;
  Rectangle rect
    = new Rectangle(10, 0, 10, 100); // 100x100 rectangle, with
                                     // upper left corner in (10, 10)
  g.setPaint(Color.orange);
  g.fill(rect);                      // Simple fill of the
                                     // rectangular Shape
```

```
Stroke thickStroke = new BasicStroke(4.f);
g.setStroke(thickStroke);
g.translate(120, 0);              // Shift by 120 pixels to the right
g.draw(rect);                     // Actually calls getStrokedPath on
                                  // thickStroke and fills returned
                                  // shape.
}
```

The pseudocode for the `Graphics2D.draw` method can be written as:

```
void draw(Shape shape){
   Shape outline = currentStroke.createStrokedShape(shape);
   fill(outline);
}
```

The important things to remember are that `Stroke` is one of the rendering attributes used by the `Graphics2D` class, that it can be set through the `Graphics2D.setStroke` method, and that there is a default implementation, the `BasicStroke` class, which provides support for the common needs.

What happens if we do not set the `Stroke` attribute before we use `draw`? In that case, the default `Stroke` attribute, which is a solid stroke of width 1 (in user space), is used. This default attribute is important because it provides backward compatibility with previous versions of the JDK software, where drawing of geometrical forms was always done with a solid stroke of width 1 (there were no other options). Therefore, programs written for, let us say, JDK 1.1.x, will have the same behavior when running on the Java 2 platform.

The BasicStroke implementation

The `BasicStroke` implementation can create outlines of varying width and also supports dashes. That is, we can create thin or thick outlines with `BasicStroke` as well as dashed outlines. Table 5.1 details the parameters that control the outline created by a `BasicStroke`, and Table 5.2 illustrates the related visual aspect. The CD-ROM contains a program, **BasicStrokeControls.java**, that illustrates each of the `BasicStroke` settings.

Table 5.1 ■ Parameters that control outlines created by BasicStroke

	PURPOSE	POSSIBLE VALUES	DEFAULT VALUE
Width			
	Thickness of the outline, in user space.	Floating-point value	1

Table 5.1 ■ Parameters that control outlines created by BasicStroke (Continued)

PURPOSE	POSSIBLE VALUES	DEFAULT VALUE
End caps		
Style used for the end of path segments along the outline. This applies to unclosed parts of the outline and to dash segments, when a dash pattern is used.	`CAP_BUTT`, `CAP_SQUARE`, `CAP_ROUND`	`CAP_SQUARE`
Line joins		
Style used for line segment junctions.	`JOIN_MITER`, `JOIN_BEVEL`, `JOIN_ROUND`	`JOIN_MITER`
Miter limit		
When a `JOIN_MITER` line join is used, spikes can appear when segments connect at a sharp angle. The miter limit provides a way to cut off such spikes. Its value represents the ratio of the miter length (distance between the inner and outer elbows of a line connection) to the stroke width. The segment connection angle is related to the miter limit: `angle = 2.asin(1/miterlimit)` For example: a miter limit of 10 cuts off angles less than 11 degrees, and a miter limit of 3 cuts off angles less than 39 degrees. See Figure 5.10 on page 147 for more details on the miter limit.	Floating-point value	10
Dashing pattern		
Defines the succession of dashes and gaps.	Array of floating-point values, interpreted as successive length of dashes and gaps in the dash pattern.	null, i.e., solid line

Table 5.1 ■ Parameters that control outlines created by BasicStroke (Continued)

PURPOSE	POSSIBLE VALUES	DEFAULT VALUE
Dash phase		
Represents the distance from the start of the dashing pattern, in user space, to the beginning of the stroke. The dashing pattern represents a recursive pattern that is repeated along the stroked path, and the dash phase defines where to start in that pattern.	floating-point value	0

Table 5.2 ■ BasicStroke variations

Related code   Visual result

WIDTH

```
new BasicStroke(2.f),
new BasicStroke(4.f),
new BasicStroke(8.f),
new BasicStroke(16.f)
```

END CAPS

```
// No decoration
new BasicStroke(15.f, BasicStroke.CAP_BUTT,
          BasicStroke.JOIN_BEVEL),

// Square end
new BasicStroke(15.f, BasicStroke.CAP_SQUARE,
          BasicStroke.JOIN_BEVEL),

// Rounded end
new BasicStroke(15.f, BasicStroke.CAP_ROUND,
          BasicStroke.JOIN_BEVEL) };
```

Table 5.2 ■ BasicStroke variations (Continued)

LINE JOINS

```
// Connected with a straight segment
new BasicStroke(10.f, BasicStroke.CAP_SQUARE,
                BasicStroke.JOIN_BEVEL),

// Extend outlines until they meet
new BasicStroke(10.f, BasicStroke.CAP_SQUARE,
                BasicStroke.JOIN_MITER),

// Round of corner.
new BasicStroke(10.f, BasicStroke.CAP_SQUARE,
                BasicStroke.JOIN_ROUND)};
```

DASHING PATTERN

```
BasicStroke(8.f, BasicStroke.CAP_BUTT,
            BasicStroke.JOIN_BEVEL, 8.f,
            new float[]{ 6.f, 6.f }, 0.f);

BasicStroke(8.f, BasicStroke.CAP_BUTT,
            BasicStroke.JOIN_BEVEL, 8.f,
            new float[]{ 10.f, 4.f }, 0.f);

BasicStroke(8.f, BasicStroke.CAP_BUTT,
            BasicStroke.JOIN_BEVEL, 8.f,
            new float[]{ 4.f, 4.f, 10.f, 4.f }, 0f);

BasicStroke(8.f, BasicStroke.CAP_BUTT,
            BasicStroke.JOIN_BEVEL, 8.f,
            new float[]{ 4.f, 4.f, 10.f, 4.f }, 4f);
```

MITER LIMIT

```
// Actually cuts off all angles
BasicStroke(10.f, BasicStroke.CAP_SQUARE,
            BasicStroke.JOIN_MITER, 1f),

// Cuts off angles less than 60degrees
BasicStroke(10.f, BasicStroke.CAP_SQUARE,
            BasicStroke.JOIN_MITER, 2f),

// Cuts off angles less than 11 degrees
BasicStroke(10.f, BasicStroke.CAP_SQUARE,
            BasicStroke.JOIN_MITER, 10f)};
```

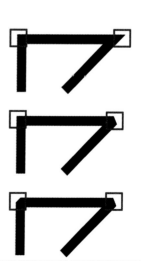

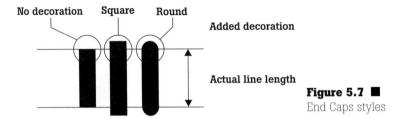

Figure 5.7 ■
End Caps styles

▼ **Stroke size**   This is the simplest style attribute and can be passed to the `BasicStroke` one-argument constructor. If the `Stroke` attribute is not set before we use `draw`, the default value, which is a solid stroke of size 1, is used. The `BasicStroke` constructor that takes no arguments creates the default `Stroke` attribute value.

▼ **End caps**   This decoration style applies to the terminations of unclosed path segments. Figure 5.7 illustrates the different styles in greater detail. Note how the decoration actually extends the segments beyond their length. In the figure, the double arrow on the right shows the length of the line that was drawn with different strokes. Except for the `CAP_BUTT` style (leftmost), where no decoration is added, the other two styles extend the line beyond its limits with the decorative element.

▼ **Line joins**   The line join parameter controls the style of connecting line segment joins. The bold lines in Figure 5.8 show how the different settings connect the outer line segment corners.

▼ **Dashing patterns**   The dashing pattern defines the sequences of dashes and gaps along the path. In Figure 5.9, we show a close-up of the dashing pattern defined by our rightmost stroke in Table 5.2 on page 144. Note that the

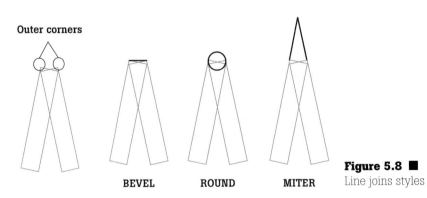

Figure 5.8 ■
Line joins styles

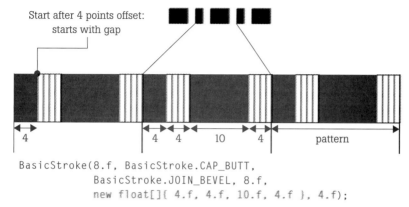

Start after 4 points offset:
starts with gap

4   4   4   10   4   pattern

```
BasicStroke(8.f, BasicStroke.CAP_BUTT,
            BasicStroke.JOIN_BEVEL, 8.f,
            new float[]{ 4.f, 4.f, 10.f, 4.f }, 4.f);
```

Figure 5.9 ■
Dashing pattern close-up

dash phase is the distance from the dash pattern start and not an offset in the array defining the pattern.

Note that the end caps style applies to the dashes. Therefore, if we select a decoration such as CAP_ROUND that extends beyond the segment limits, we need to account for that in the gaps that separate segments. Otherwise, the dashes may overlap.

▼ **Miter limit**   As we explained in Table 5.1, the miter limit defines the ratio between the distance between the inner and outer elbows to the stroke width. Figure 5.10 shows how the miter limit is related to the connection angle. The

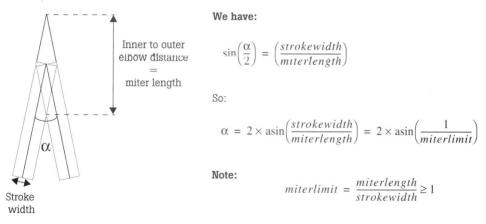

Inner to outer
elbow distance
=
miter length

Stroke
width

We have:

$$\sin\left(\frac{\alpha}{2}\right) = \left(\frac{strokewidth}{miterlength}\right)$$

So:

$$\alpha = 2 \times \operatorname{asin}\left(\frac{strokewidth}{miterlength}\right) = 2 \times \operatorname{asin}\left(\frac{1}{miterlimit}\right)$$

Note:

$$miterlimit = \frac{miterlength}{strokewidth} \geq 1$$

Figure 5.10 ■
Miter limit

formula relating the angle to the miter length and stroke width can be used to find the cutoff angle value: all angles smaller than α will be cut off. In other words, when the MITER join style is specified, all angles larger than α will indeed join, and angles smaller than α will have the BEVEL style, as we illustrated in Table 5.2 on page 144.

Summary

We have just seen how the Stroke interface provides a flexible and extensible way to define the kind of pen used to draw the outline of any shape. Because both Stroke and Shape are interfaces, the API can actually draw any kind of shape with any kind of pen or marker, as long as the desired implementations are provided. The BasicStroke class provides a sophisticated implementation of the Stroke interface and supports various outline widths, line termination decorations, connection policies (line joins), dashing patterns, and a way to eliminate spikes on connecting segments.

We will see in the Graphic Layers Framework presentation in Part II that writing a custom implementation of the Stroke interface can provide visually interesting results. For example, we will create an implementation, ShapeStroke, that repeats a set of Shape objects along the path of the shapes it strokes. For example, ShapeStroke can draw the outline of a Shape with a set of triangles and squares. Another implementation uses a text string that it repeats along a Shape's outline.

We discussed how the createStrokedShape method returns a Shape defining the form of the outline. We also mentioned that, when a Shape is drawn, that Shape is then filled with the current graphic context Paint attribute. The next paragraph looks into the Paint interface in further detail and explains how the API uses the Paint to fill shapes.

Paints

Before version 2 of the Java platform, all rendering was done by means of the Graphics object's Color attribute set by the setColor method. Subsequent rendering calls (like drawLine or fillRect) used this Color.

The same principle has been extended in 1.2: instead of a Color, a java.awt.Paint object is associated with the Graphics2D object through the setPaint(Paint paint) method. By Paint object, we mean an object that implements the new Paint interface.

But, what about backward compatibility and the setColor method? The Color class now implements the Paint interface. So, a call to setColor is strictly equivalent to a call to setPaint: the new API is backward compatible. We will describe the `Paint` interface later. For now, just remember that it provides the capability to create much more sophisticated filling patterns than just solid color, as we have seen in our example in Table 4.1 on page 59.

In this first part, we have seen on several occasions how `Paint` is used to fill and draw shapes and to render text (for example, the `TextAttribute.FORE-GROUND` and `TextAttribute.BACKGROUND` styled text attributes have values of type `Paint`). In this section, we introduce the different `Paint` implementations that the API provides, as well as the mechanics of the `Paint` interface.

What kinds of Paints are there?

Figure 5.11 shows a screen shot of a program that illustrates the different `Paints` provided in the API. We use this program (see **PaintTypes.java** on the CD-ROM) as a reference throughout this section. Each row shows a different type of `Paint` implementation: `Color` on the first row, `GradientPaint` on the second row, and `TexturePaint` on the last one. Each column illustrates a different usage of `Paint`: rectangle filling in the first column, `Shape` stroking in the second one, and filling in the last one.

▼ **Color**   We have mentioned that the `java.awt.Color` class now implements the `Paint` interface. It can be used as in previous versions of the JDK. In our example, we use blue, white, and red `Color Paints`:

```
Color redColor = new Color(160, 0, 0);
Color whiteColor = Color.white;
Color blueColor = new Color(0, 0, 128);
```

This is the same as what we had in previous JDK versions. The `Color` class contains a set of predefined `Color` instances as a convenience (we use the `white` predefined `Color` in our example).

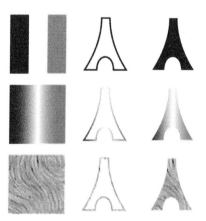

Figure 5.11 ■
Paints in the Java 2D API

Two classes derive from `Color`: `java.awt.SystemColor` and `javax.swing.plaf.ColorUIResource`.

`SystemColor` defines the color settings for GUI objects such as buttons, windows, text, etc. It is useful when it is important for the application to use the user's color settings (windowing environments such as Solaris™ and Windows let users define their favorite GUI objects' colors).

`ColorUIResource` is used in Swing with a similar, but more sophisticated intent: Swing supports the notion of look and feel, and the `javax.swing.UIManager` class (it has a `put` method) allows color settings for a look and feel.

By default, a `Color` object is defined in sRGB (Red Green Blue) and has an alpha value. The alpha value controls the color opacity: a value of 1 means that the `Color` is fully opaque, and a value of 0 means the color is fully transparent. When a `Color` is fully opaque, none of the background on which it is used will show through. When a `Color` is fully transparent, the background completely shows and the `Color` not at all. In other words, the value (`1.f - alpha`) represents the amount of background that shows through the `Color`. Figure 5.12 shows different alpha settings for the following code (**ColorTransparency.java** on the CD-ROM):

```
Color white = new Color(1f, 1f, 1f, alpha);
g.setColor(white);
g.fillRect(x, y, w, h);
```

Note that the above code is equivalent to using an `AlphaComposite` with the `AlphaComposite.SRC_OVER` rule and same alpha value, with a fully opaque white:

```
Color white = new Color(1f, 1f, 1f, 1f);
g.setColor(white);
g.setComposite(AlphaComposite.getInstance(AlphaComposite.SRC_OVER,
                                          alpha));
g.fillRect(x, y, w, h);
```

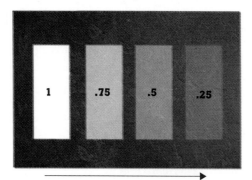

Background increasingly
dominates as alpha decreases

Figure 5.12 ■
Color transparency

Refer to "AlphaComposite rules" on page 172 for details on `AlphaComposite`.

A final word about `Color`: it is possible to define a `Color` in a different system than sRGB by using a specific `ColorSpace`. For example, a `Color` can be defined by its CMYK (Cyan-Magenta-Yellow-Black) components if the proper `ColorSpace` is used. Because `ColorSpaces` are able to convert `Color` components from their own space to and from the sRGB space, a `Color` created with components in the CMYK color space (that is, with values for Cyan, Magenta, Yellow, and Black) will simply convert those values to sRGB, using the `ColorSpace`'s conversion method `toRGB()`. For more details about `ColorSpaces`, refer to Chapter 4 (see "Rendering Images: BufferedImages" on page 77).

▼ **GradientPaint**   The second row in our example (see Figure 5.11) shows `GradientPaint` at work:

```
Color redColor = new Color(160, 0, 0);
Color whiteColor = Color.white;
Color blueColor = new Color(0, 0, 128);
Color transparentColor = new Color(0, 0, 0, 0); // Fourth value is alpha

Paint redGradient = new GradientPaint(0, 0, redColor,
                          CELL_WIDTH/2, 0, whiteColor);
Paint blueGradient = new GradientPaint(CELL_WIDTH/2, 0,
                          transparentColor,
                          CELL_WIDTH, 0, blueColor);
...

// g is a Graphics2D object
...
g.setPaint(redGradient);
g.fillRect(0, 0, CELL_WIDTH/2, CELL_WIDTH);
...
g.setPaint(blueGradient);
g.fillRect(CELL_WIDTH/2, 0, CELL_WIDTH/2, CELL_WIDTH);
```

A `GradientPaint` is defined by five parameters: two end points (A and B), two colors, (colorA and colorB), and a cycling strategy (this is an optional construction argument not used in our example). The color of a pixel depends on its position relative to the end points. As illustrated in Figure 5.13, the color progressively changes from colorA to colorB between A and B. For points outside the line (A, B), the color is the same as that of their projection on (A, B). If the gradient's cycling strategy is cyclic, then the color varies repeatedly between colorA and colorB (see Figure 5.14). Otherwise, all points "behind" A have the colorA value, and all points behind B have the colorB value.

▼ **TexturePaint**   This is the last of the three `Paint` implementations provided in the API. The last row in our example (see Figure 5.11) shows several shapes rendered with `TexturePaint`. Here is how the `texturePaint` object is created:

Behind A,
color is colorA

Between A and B,
same color as projection on the
(A, B) line

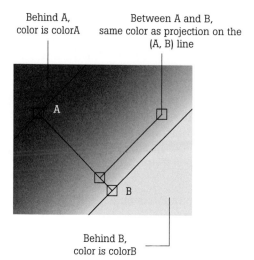

Behind B,
color is colorB

Figure 5.13 ■
GradientPaint controls

```
BufferedImage textureImage = ...;  // Create textureImage from existing
                                   // image or create one.

// Use the full image as the texture base.
texturePaint = new TexturePaint(textureImage,
                                new Rectangle(0, 0,
textureImage.getWidth(), textureImage.getHeight()));
```

There are two construction input parameters: a `BufferedImage` and an anchor.
The `BufferedImage` parameter defines the texture. The anchor parameter is a

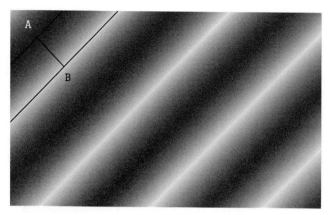

Figure 5.14 ■
Cyclic GradientPaint

`java.awt.Rectangle`, which defines where the texture "starts" in the user space. The texture image is resized to fit the anchor `Rectangle`. Then, the rectangle is repeated in all directions. In our example (Figure 5.11), the texture is anchored about the origin and is set to its "natural" size, that is, no resizing will happen before the texture is repeated.

Table 5.3 illustrates the impact of modifying the anchor parameter in the following code (see **TexturePaintControls.java** on the CD-ROM):

```
paint = new TexturePaint(texture, anchor);
...
public void paint(Graphics _g){
    Dimension dim = getSize();

    Graphics2D g = (Graphics2D)_g;
    g.setPaint(paint);
    g.fillRect(0, 0, dim.width, dim.height);
}
```

Table 5.3 ■ TexturePaint anchor

Texture

```
int iw = texture.getWidth();
int ih = texture.getHeight();
```

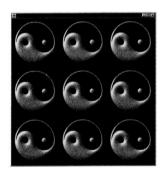 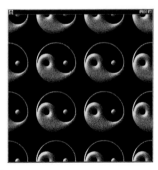 

Anchor about the origin, using the texture size. `anchor = new Rectangle(0, 0, iw, ih);`	Modified anchor origin (now about the image center): `anchor = new Rectangle(iw/2, ih/2, iw, ih)`	Modified anchor size: half the size of the texture. `anchor = new Rectangle(0, 0, iw/2, ih/2)`

Advantage of the Paint interface

We have seen how the Shape interface allows the definition of any type of geometrical form. Combined with the Paint interface, it becomes possible to fill or stroke any type of geometrical form with any kind of Paint. In our example in Figure 5.11, the second and third columns show how the same Shape object (an Eiffel tower) is rendered with very different Paint objects by the same two API calls, fill and draw.

```
// Eiffel Tower Shape
shape = new GeneralPath();
shape.moveTo(43.f, 5.f);
shape.lineTo(58.f, 5.f);
shape.quadTo(58.f, 50.f, 88.f, 95.f);
shape.lineTo(65.f, 95.f);
shape.curveTo(65.f, 65.f, 35.f, 65.f, 35.f, 95.f);
shape.lineTo(13.f, 95.f);
shape.quadTo(43.f, 50.f, 43.f, 5.f);
...
g.setPaint(redColor); // Fill with solid red
g.fill(shape);
...
g.setPaint(redGradient);// Fill shape with GradientPaint
g.fill(shape);
g.setPaint(blueGradient);
g.fill(shape);
...
g.setPaint(texturePaint); // Stroke Shape with TexturePaint
g.draw(shape);

g.setPaint(redColor);       // Stroke with solid red
g.draw(shape);
...
g.setPaint(redGradient);   // Stroke shape with GradientPaint
g.draw(shape);
g.setPaint(blueGradient);
g.draw(shape);
...
g.setPaint(texturePaint); // Stroke Shape with TexturePaint
g.draw(shape);
```

The code is similar to fill a Rectangle and to fill an Eiffel tower (g.fill in each case), and setting the Paint attribute is also identical (g.setPaint in each case).

There is an interesting twist in the above code: why is the redGradient fill not masked by the blueGradient fill? There are two successive calls to fill on the same Shape object, so why isn't the Eiffel Tower only blue and white? The answer is that the blueGradient Paint was defined (see Page 151) as a gradient between a blue Color and a fully transparent color. Therefore, the redGradient shows through the blue gradient where the gradient color is transparent (in our example, the left side of the Eiffel Tower).

Features of the Paint interface

We now know which `Paint` implementations are provided by default and when they are used. But we have not looked at the `Paint` interface very closely yet. It turns out that it has a single method:

```
public PaintContext createContext(ColorModel cm,
                        Rectangle deviceBounds,
                        Rectangle2D userBounds,
                        AffineTransform xform,
                        RenderingHints hints)
```

In other words, a `Paint` is requested to provide a `PaintContext`, which is the object actually responsible for delivering pixel values for a `Paint`. The `cm` parameter specifies the `ColorModel` that receives the `Paint` data. This is a hint for the `Paint` implementation, and it can be used to optimize `PaintContext` implementations. This attribute will make more sense when we have a look at the `PaintContext` interface.

The `deviceBounds` and `userBounds` parameters let the `PaintContext` developer know the extent of the area to be painted. Pixels lying outside the bounds typically won't need to be processed. Again, this can be used to improve performance.

The `hints` should be given to the `PaintContext` to choose between rendering alternatives. For example, a `PaintContext` developer could choose different processing strategies depending on whether `RenderingHints.KEY_RENDERING` is set to `RenderingHints.VALUE_RENDER_QUALITY` or to `Rendering-Hints.VALUE_RENDER_SPEED`.

Finally, the `transform` parameter defines the affine transform between the user space and the device space. A `PaintContext` operates in the device space (that is, with coordinates that match the device), and this parameter can be used to prepare a `PaintContext` with the proper attributes.

▼ **The PaintContext interface** The `PaintContext` interface itself contains three methods: `getColorModel`, `getRaster`, and `dispose`.

`getColorModel` defines the `ColorModel` instance to be used for the pixels that are generated by the `PaintContext`. This explains why a `ColorModel` was passed as an argument to the `createContext` method: ideally, a `PaintContext` will return pixel values in the same format as the destination uses. However, this behavior is not required.

`getRaster` is the heart of the `Paint` architecture. It is the method that is called to get the pixel values for a rectangle in the device space. The getRaster method is where pixel computing happens and, if you plan on implementing your own Paint, it is where the hard work goes: PaintContext is the place where the actual color pattern shown on the screen or printer is processed.

Summary

Like Composite and Stroke, Paint is a graphic context attribute defined by an interface. This makes it extensible, and we will see in the Graphic Layers Framework goodies package how this extensibility allows us to create new kinds of Paint implementations. We will present three Paint implementations that we will use like any other Paint in the API (several variations of gradient Paint, radial, multiple colors, etc.).

Paints render shapes and also text. The graphic context attribute that defines the text style is the Font attribute, which we discuss next.

Font

The Font attribute is used for text rendering: it defines the set of shapes, called *glyphs*, that are used to represent text information. Creating good-looking fonts is an art to which some designers have dedicated their life.[1] The choice of a font that matches an application's requirements in terms of style, size, and legibility is essential.

What are fonts?

As we just said, fonts represent a concatenation of all the shapes, called glyphs, that are used to represent text information. Even though we are accustomed to a one-to-one mapping between glyphs and characters, there are many instances where glyphs and characters do not correspond. For example, *ligature* is the generic name given to a glyph that represents two or more consecutive characters (Figure 5.15).

So, for ligatures, a single glyph represents several characters ("f" and "i" in our example).

---

1. For a fascinating history of font design, you may refer to Fred Smeijers's book "Counter Punch" [Smeijers 1996].

No ligature:
one glyph per character

Ligature:
one glyph for two
characters

Figure 5.15 ■
Glyph representing a ligature

There are different styles of fonts; the major categories are:

■ Serif. These fonts have decorative elements resembling the ones on roman
columns. The most famous one is the Times font.

Times is a Serif Font

Fonts of this type have a classic feel to them and are often used in traditional book publishing.

■ Sans Serif. These fonts do not have the decorative elements of the Serif
Fonts (which explains the name), and they have a more modern look. Helvetica is an example of a Sans Serif font.

Helvetica is a Sans Serif Font

■ Monospace. These fonts provide glyphs of equal width. Monospace fonts
have long been used in computers, especially in older command-line or
text-based applications that used a fixed-size rectangle to display characters. Courier is a popular example of such a font.

Courier is a Monospace Font

This book uses a monospace font for all the code segments because it provides a better alignment of code elements. Most programmers are familiar
with monospaced fonts because they use them to edit and display code.

- Display. These fonts are typically very heavy, very bold, and are visible from far away. They are used in advertising (for example, on billboards), but also as titles in magazines or software applications. The following font from Monotype, called Impact, is a display font.

Impact is a Display Font

- Script. These fonts mimic human script. They have a more natural look than other font types. An example is the Monotype French Script font.

French Script MT is a Script Font

- Decorative. These fonts cannot be classified in any of the other categories and are used to decorate graphical composition. An example is the Southwest Ornaments MT font, from Monotype.

Different font styles serve different purposes. For example, a Script font may be appropriate to announce a wedding or advertise a classy product, but it does not fit for code display, which usually requires monospace, legible fonts. Different fonts evoke different moods, and it is important to select the one that resonates with the message the application is trying to get across.

One important characteristic of newer fonts is that they support Unicode. Instead of mapping 8-bit characters to glyphs, they map Unicode characters (16 bits) to glyphs. Unicode fonts are much better because they fit well into the Java internationalization scheme based on Unicode. However, the Java platform also supports legacy fonts that are not Unicode based.

Available fonts

Fonts are defined in font files. The two most popular formats are *Type 1* fonts (also called PostScript™ fonts) and *TrueType* fonts. Installing a font on a computer so that it becomes available to applications is operating system dependent, and a different method is used on a Macintosh than on a Solaris workstation or a Windows personal computer.

The Java platform is responsible for interacting with the operating system to give the programmer access to the set of fonts installed on the system. That list can be obtained through the `java.awt.GraphicsEnvironment.getAllFonts` method. The following short program lists all the `Fonts` available to an application on a particular computer (see **FontLister.java** on the CD-ROM).

```
public class FontLister {
  public static void main(String args[]){
    GraphicsEnvironment env =
      GraphicsEnvironment.getLocalGraphicsEnvironment();
    Font fonts[] = env.getAllFonts();
    for(int i=0; i<fonts.length; i++){
      Font f = fonts[i];
      System.out.println(f.getName());
    }
  }
}
```

What happens if no font has been installed on the system where the Java platform runs? There are a number of fonts that are *guaranteed* to be available to the programmer; they are listed in Table 5.4. So, no matter what the platform supports, those default fonts are always available. They are typically provided in four styles: Regular, Bold, Italic, and Bold-Italic.

Table 5.4 ■ Default Fonts on the Java platform

FONT NAME BY EXAMPLE
serif
sans serif
monospace
dialog
dialog input
Lucida Bright
Lucida Sans
Lucida Sans Typewriter

Furthermore, the platform provides a way to make extra fonts loadable in an operating-system-independent way. The `java.awt.fonts` command-line option of the `java` application can be used to point to a directory where extra fonts, which are not necessarily loaded in the operating-system-dependent way, will be loaded from and made available to the Java application. Here is what the command line looks like:

```
java -Djava.awt.fonts=<extraFontsDirectory> MyApplication
```

For example:

```
java -Djava.awt.fonts=/local/FontTest/res/fonts FontTest
```

will make all the fonts from font files in the /local/FontTest/res/fonts directory available to the FontTest application, in addition to the default Java fonts and the platform-specific fonts.

Using fonts

One of the graphic context attributes is a Font. Therefore, the method to use a specific Font instance for rendering is:

1. Set the Font in the graphic context. Graphics.setFont does this.
2. Select the graphic object that uses Font and is to be rendered, for example, a String object.
3. Invoke a rendering method that uses Font, for example, Graphics.drawString.

The program listed (and illustrated) in Table 5.5 draws a simple string of text.

Table 5.5 ■ Setting the Graphics2D Font attribute

Output

Hello Curlz MT Font

```
Graphics2D g = ...;

// Create Font attribute
Font font
  = new Font("Curlz MT", Font.PLAIN, 40);

// Set Font attribute in graphics context
g.setFont(font);

// Select graphics object
String text = "Hello Curlz MT Font";

// Invoke rendering method that uses the Font attribute
g.drawString(text, 40, 50);
```

The first thing this code does is to build a Font object:

```
Font font = new Font("Curlz MT", Font.PLAIN, 40);
```

This is one of the methods for creating a Font. It uses the font name "Curlz MT," the font style Font.PLAIN, and the font size 40. The meaning of those parameters is detailed later in our paragraph on creating Fonts.

As we discussed in Chapter 4 (see "Text Manipulation" on page 109), there are several ways to render text:

1. Simple text rendering (`Graphics.drawString(String)`). There, the `Font` attribute translates the `String` characters into glyphs, which are then drawn to the output, using the current `Paint`.

2. `AttributedCharacterIterator` (`Graphics2d.drawString (AttributedCharacterIterator, int, int)`). This is, in a way, text with style information. Among the style attributes (defined in the `java.awt.font.TextAttribute` class), is the FONT attribute.

3. `TextLayout`. As we discussed, the `java.awt.font.TextLayout` can also render text (`TextLayout.draw(Graphics2D, float, float)`. `TextLayout` offers another way to render `Attributed-CharacterIterators`.

Our example in Table 5.5 used the first method to render text. The code example shown in Table 5.6 illustrates the other two and the use of `TextAttribute.FONT`.

Table 5.6 ■ Rendering AttributedCharacterIterator with Graphics2D or TextLayout

CODE

Both methods of rendering produce the same output

One Font-Another Font

```
// The example uses the following two Fonts
Font curlzFont = new Font("Curlz MT", Font.PLAIN, 40);
Font serifFont = new Font("serif", Font.PLAIN, 40);

// AttributedString rendering
AttributedString string
    = new AttributedString("One Font-Another Font");
string.addAttribute(TextAttribute.FONT, serifFont, 0, 8);
string.addAttribute(TextAttribute.FONT, curlzFont, 8, 21);
g.drawString(string.getIterator(), 0, 40);

=============================

// Alternate method: rendering through a TextLayout
TextLayout layout
    = new TextLayout(string.getIterator(), g.getFontRenderContext());
layout.draw(g, 0, 40);
```

Creating fonts

There are several ways of creating Font objects. One way is through the Font constructor and another way is through derivation. No matter what method is used to create, five attributes control what the font actually looks like: name, size, weight, posture, and transform. We next look at each of these attributes in turn.

▼ **Font name**   Several names define fonts.

First, there is the *logical name*. It refers to one of the six default fonts the Java platform guaranteed (there are now more, see later): Dialog, DialogInput, Monospaced, Serif, SansSerif, or Symbol. Such names are called logical because they do not directly represent font face names. Rather, the mapping between those logical names and the platform fonts are defined in the font.proper-ties file (in the <jdkDirectory>/jre/lib directory, where <jdkDirectory> is the directory in which the Java platform is installed). This property file is platform specific and comes with the Java platform distribution.

Second, there is the *font face name*, also called *font name*. It describes the host system font name, for example, *Times Roman Bold* or *French Script MT*. Those do not map to a specific style, as guaranteed with the logical Fonts.

Third, there is the *font family name*. The family describes a type of font, that is, a set of fonts that share a common design. For example, *Times Roman Bold*, *Times Roman Italic*, and *Times Roman Regular* all belong to the *Times Roman* family.

▼ **Font size**   This attribute describes how big the font is. The size unit is the point. On the Java platform, a point is 1/72 of an inch high, which is the size of a pixel on a typical monitor. Figure 5.16 illustrates three different font sizes: 14, 24, and 36 points. The drawing has been blown up so that pixels are visible, and the pixel grid is shown. As you can see, the font size matches the number of pixels (assuming the default transform between the user space and the device space).

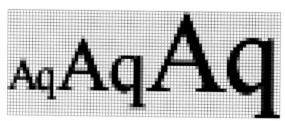

One point is equivalent to one screen pixel. A point has a size of 1/72 inch.

Figure 5.16 ■

Font size and the notion of point

▼ **Font weight**   This attribute describes how bold the font is. Currently, the weight attribute can be set to regular or bold. Note that the font face name may already imply some weight characteristics for the font. For example, *Helvetica Bold* is, as one would expect, a bold font. However, this is separate from the weight attribute that the Java platform uses to set any font as bold. So, if a font is already bold and you specify that its weight is bold, then it will appear even bolder.

▼ **Font posture**   This attribute describes the inclination of the font glyphs. Currently, the posture attribute can be set to regular or italic. The same remark as for the weight attribute applies for the posture. Some font faces, such as *Times Roman Oblique*, indicate the default posture of the font. However, this is separate from the posture attribute. So, if a font is already oblique by default, then it will be even more so if the posture attribute is set to italic.

▼ **FontTransform**   This attribute can be an arbitrary `AffineTransform` that is applied to the font glyphs before they are used. The program listed in Table 5.7 shows a `Font` object with its `AffineTransform` attribute set to a horizontal flip.

Table 5.7 ■ Creating a flipped Font

FONTFLIP.JAVA

Output

```java
// Rendering context parameters
Font font = new Font("serif", Font.BOLD | Font.ITALIC, 120);

// The following transform performs a flip
// about the x axis
AffineTransform flip = AffineTransform.getScaleInstance(1, -1);

Font flippedFont = font.deriveFont(flip);

// Text we render
String text = "The quick fox";
```

Table 5.7 ■ Creating a flipped Font (Continued)

```
// Use each font in turn
g.setFont(font);
g.setPaint(Color.black);
g.drawString(text, 20, 120);

g.setFont(flippedFont);
g.setPaint(new Color(0, 0, 0, 128)); // 50% transparent black
g.drawString(text, 20, 120);
```

Note that the transform is applied to the space whose coordinate system is shown in red. That coordinate has the default orientation we have seen for user and device spaces (that is, x axis to the right and y axis downwards). Its origin is on the string leading edge (here, the leftmost position in the text) and on the baseline (as we explain later, the baseline is the line on which most glyphs' bases align). So, if we had used a different transform, we would have had a different result. For example, had we used:

```
AffineTransform rotate = AffineTransform.getRotateInstance(Math.PI/8);
```

we would have seen the following result (the transformed space coordinate system is shown in green):

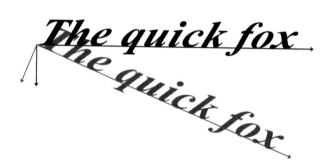

▼ **Font constructors**   The Font class has two constructors. The first one takes three parameters: the font name, its style, and its size.

```
Font(String name, int style, int size)
```

The name can be either the logical name (for example, serif) or the face name (for example, Helvetica Bold), as we explained earlier.

The style should be set to one of the following (or a combination of them): Font.PLAIN, Font.BOLD, or Font.ITALIC. Table 5.8 shows different settings

Table 5.8 ■ Font style settings

STYLE PARAMETER VALUE	STYLE
Font.PLAIN	Plain
Font.BOLD	**Bold**
Font.ITALIC	*Italic*
Font.BOLD | Font.ITALIC	***Bold and Italic***

for the different styles. In other words, the style parameter is a shortcut to specify both the font weight (Font.BOLD) and the font posture (Font.ITALIC). The default for each of those is regular, that is, a regular weight and a regular (non-italic) posture. Note that there is no way to specify the AffineTransform attribute through this constructor. However, it is possible with the second one:

```
Font(Map attributes);
```

A Map is an interface for objects able to store attribute key/value pairs, and the java.util.Hashtable is one implementation. The relevant attributes that the Font class understands are listed in Table 5.9.

Table 5.9 ■ TextAttributes relevant for the Font class

TEXTATTRIBUTE	VALUE TYPE	DESCRIPTION
FONT	java.awt.Font	Describes a complete Font.
FAMILY	java.lang.String	Describes the font family name. This is different from the font face name. For example, the family name should not hold style information as in *Helvetica Bold*. Rather, it should be limited to the type of font, as in *Helvetica*.
SIZE	java.lang.Float	Font size, in points.
WEIGHT	java.lang.Float. There are predefined values, such as TextAttribute.WEIGHT_REGULAR and TextAttribute.WEIGHT_BOLD.	Defines how bold the font is. At the time of this writing, "regular" and "bold" were supported in the reference implementations of the Java platform.

Table 5.9 ■ TextAttributes relevant for the Font class (Continued)

TEXTATTRIBUTE	VALUE TYPE	DESCRIPTION
POSTURE	`java.lang.Float`. There are predefined values, such as `TextAttribute.POSTURE_REGULAR` and `TextAttribute.POSTURE_OBLIQUE.`	Defines how "italic" the font is, i.e., its angle with the baseline. At the time of this writing, only the values defined by "regular" and "oblique" were supported in the reference implementation of the JDK.
TRANSFORM	`java.awt.geom.AffineTransform`	Defines how glyphs produced by the underlying Font objects are transformed before being used (see previous discussion on the transform attribute).

The code sample below illustrates the setting of the five Font attributes (we left out `TextAttribute.FONT`) using the Map-based Font constructor. The process is simple: build a map, put the relevant attributes into the map, create the Font with the map-based constructor:

```
AffineTransform flip = AffineTransform.getScaleInstance(1, -1);
Hashtable map = new Hashtable();
map.put(TextAttribute.FAMILY, "Times");
map.put(TextAttribute.SIZE, new Float(120));
map.put(TextAttribute.POSTURE, TextAttribute.POSTURE_OBLIQUE);
map.put(TextAttribute.WEIGHT, TextAttribute.WEIGHT_BOLD);
map.put(TextAttribute.TRANSFORM, flip);
Font font = new Font(map);
```

This code creates a Font similar to the one we used for our example in Table 5.7 on page 163.

▼ **Deriving fonts**   There is an additional way to create Font instances: derivation. Deriving a Font consists of using a base Font object and deriving another Font object with different attributes from it (we actually used that technique in the examples in Table 5.7 on page 163). Several deriveFont methods in the Font class do just that.

```
// Derives a Font with a different style
deriveFont(int style);

// Derives a Font with a different size
deriveFont(float size);
```

```
// Derives a Font with a different transform
deriveFont(AffineTransform);

// Derives a Font with a different size and style
deriveFont(int style, float size);

// Derives a Font with a different style and transform
deriveFont(int style, AffineTransform transform);

// Derives a Font with an arbitrary list of attributes
deriveFont(Map attributes);
```

Font derivation amounts to using a base Font as a set of default attributes. For example, the lines—

```
Font flippedFont = font.deriveFont(flip);
Font rotatedFont = font.deriveFont(rotate);
```

—where flip and rotate are AffineTransform instances, create Font objects that have all the attributes of the base font object, except for a different AffineTransform attribute. Other deriveFont methods are just variations on that same principle.

Font metrics

Anybody who tries for the first time to display text soon realizes that text placement is a challenge. How can we know how big a string of text is going to be when rendered to the screen or printer? Font metrics *preprocess* the spatial characteristics of text. They are then used to properly position the text in the output.

Rendered text has the spatial characteristics illustrated in Figure 5.17.

▼ **Vertical metrics**　The ascent represents the amount of space by which glyphs extend above the baseline. The descent represents the amount of space by which glyphs extend below the baseline. The leading (pronounced *ledding*) describes the amount of space between lines of text of the same font. The font height is the sum of the font leading, ascent, and descent.

▼ **Horizontal metrics**　The advance of characters describes the horizontal amount of space required to display text. The visible advance describes the amount of space needed to display the visible part of a text (that is, the text minus trailing white spaces).[2]

▼ **Accessing font metrics**　There are several ways to access font metrics. Before we look at the different ways to get that information, it is important to understand that accurate font metrics do not only depend on the font. They

2. Note that vertical direction text is not yet supported in Java 2D.

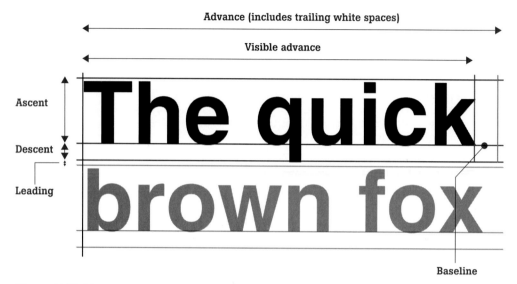

Figure 5.17 ■
Font metrics by example

also depend on the output device and how the rendering is done. For example, the font metrics might be different depending on whether antialiasing is done. Therefore, the FontRenderContext class, returned by the Graphics2D.get-FontRenderContext method or constructed directly, is always used to access accurate font metrics. It provides the link between the font, the output device rendering characteristics, and the font metrics.

There are two ways to access Font metrics.

1. The FontMetrics and LineMetrics classes.
   A Graphics object returns a FontMetrics object through its getFontMetrics method. The FontMetrics can provide all the vertical metrics for a text (getAscent(), getDescent(), getHeight()). It can also provide horizontal metrics for simple text (that is, text defined as a String, byte, or char arrays, through the bytesWidth, charsWidth, and stringWidth methods). Note that FontMetrics's way of processing metrics is based on what earlier Java platform versions were doing. Therefore, it is not as accurate as metrics the platform now supports. For more accurate metrics information, use the LineMetrics or Textlayout classes.

   LineMetrics can be obtained through a Font or FontMetrics object by calling one of their getLineMetrics methods. LineM-

`etrics` provides metrics for more sophisticated text (for example, defined as a `String` or `AttributedCharacterIterator`). `Line-Metrics`, like `FontMetrics`, provides the vertical metrics for text through its `getAscent`, `getDescent`, and `getLeading` methods. However, it does so more accurately than `FontMetrics`. `Line-Metrics`, though, does not provide horizontal metrics on text, and we need to turn to the `TextLayout` class to find that information.

2. The `TextLayout` class. This class provides a simple way to encapsulate both the text to be rendered and its metrics. As we explained in Chapter 2 (see "Advanced text manipulation" on page 21) and in Chapter 4 (see "Text rendering support" on page 119), a `TextLayout` can be built with either a `String` or an `AttributedCharacterIterator` (that class iterates through a text with style information). `TextLayout` contains methods to retrieve metrics information for the text it represents. Again, it provides vertical metrics through the `getAscent`, `getDescent`, and `getLeading` methods. It also provides horizontal metrics through its `getAdvance` and `getVisualAdvance` methods. `Text-Layout` also contains methods to get the bounding box of text, through its `getBounds` method.

These different ways of getting metrics information can be confusing. Remember that `FontMetrics` is mostly a legacy class, and unless you have a very specific reason to use it, don't. The `LineMetrics` class provides access to accurate vertical metrics information. Finally, `TextLayout` provides "one stop shopping" by both encapsulating styled character data and providing access to accurate font metrics.

Summary

Font design is a fascinating area of graphic design, and the Java 2D API now allows us to take advantage of the best Type 1 and TrueType fonts. We have shown that different types of fonts serve different purposes, and we can now use the ones that best serve our ends.

The API provides many ways to create `Font` objects, either through one of the class constructors or by derivation. It also provides many ways, through the `LineMetrics` and `TextLayout` classes, to access text metrics that can be used to properly position text on the output. It is important to understand the meaning of the different metrics to be able to manipulate text properly.[3]

As a graphic context attribute, `Font` influences only simple text string rendering. More elaborate types of text rendering that use `AttributedString` use the embedded style attribute in the styled text, not the graphic context attribute.

On the other hand, the `Composite` attribute, which we next present, influences all rendering operations on shapes, text, and images.

Composite

Compositing is the process of blending what is rendered with the background. If we use a traditional painting analogy, this blending is what happens with watercolors.

What is compositing?

If you use a heavily diluted blue to paint over, let us say, a red rectangle, then part of the underlying red square still shows through the blue paint (Figure 5.18).

This effect happens because the blue paint is actually partly transparent, so the red paint is partly visible. In the physical world, the phenomenon happens because the density of blue pigments is low enough: not all the red pigments are hidden by blue pigments. Visually, both the blue and red appear to blend. Using the Java 2D lingo, we would say that the blue paint has been composited with the red background.

Where is compositing used?

This painting analogy is very close to what compositing is about: blending a source (similar to our diluted blue paint) with a destination (similar to our red rectangle). Figure 5.19 shows how the `Composite` rendering context attribute is

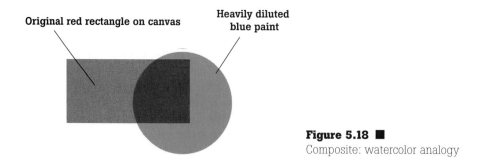

Original red rectangle on canvas

Heavily diluted blue paint

Figure 5.18 ■
Composite: watercolor analogy

3. The `GlyphMetrics` class also provides metrics, but on individual font glyphs. `GlyphMetrics` can be retrieved from a `GlyphVector`. See "Custom glyph layouts" on page 124 for an example of using `GlyphVector`.

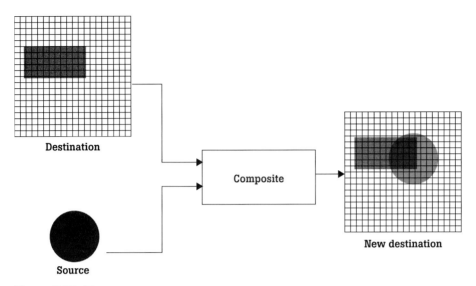

Figure 5.19 ■
Role of the Composite attribute in the rendering process

involved in the rendering process: it is responsible for blending the source and the destination according to its own rules. For example, the AlphaComposite implementation of the Composite interface supports different modes. One of them, SRC_OVER, enables us to get the exact result shown in Figure 5.18.

The process shown in Figure 5.19 is achieved by the following code.

```
// Acquire Graphics2D object
Graphics2D g = ...;

// Set context attributes: Paint
g.setPaint(red);

// Select graphic object to render: a rectangle
Shape redRect = new Rectangle(3, 3, 50, 25);

// Invoke rendering method: Graphics2D.fill
g.fill(redRect);

// Set context attributes: Paint and Composite
g.setPaint(blue);
g.setComposite(AlphaComposite.getInstance(AlphaComposite.SRC_OVER, .5f);

// Select graphic object to render: a circle.
Shape blueDisc = new Ellipse2D.Float(30, 0, 40, 40);

// Invoke rendering method: Graphics2D.fill
```

```
// This uses the blue Paint and the SRC_OVER Composite.
g.fill(blueDisc);
```

As for all the other rendering context attributes, the process is:

1. Set the rendering context attribute. In our example, we set the blue `Color Paint` attribute and the `AlphaComposite Composite` attribute in preparation for painting `blueDisc`.

   ```
   g.setPaint(blue);
   g.setComposite(AlphaComposite.getInstance(
                          AlphaComposite.SRC_OVER, 0.5f));
   ```

2. Select the graphic object to render. In our example, we prepare an `Ellipse2D` object to render the blue disc.

   ```
   Shape blueDisc = new Ellipse2D.Float(30, 0, 40, 40);
   ```

3. Invoke the rendering operation. We invoke the `fill` method on `Graphics2D`. The `fill` process uses the `Paint` and `Composite` we have set.

   ```
   g.fill(blueDisc);
   ```

The `AlphaComposite` instance used in the example has a "Source Over" rule (`AlphaComposite.SRC_OVER`) which means that the source (`blueDisc`) should be painted over the destination (the `redRect`). One thing we can do with a computer that we cannot do in the real world is to paint under the existing destination (for example, we could create an `AlphaComposite` with a `DST_OVER` rule, which means that the source should be painted under the destination).

In the example, our `AlphaComposite` instance also uses a transparency setting, the second parameter in the `getInstance` call. This parameter defines how opaque the source is. Here, we used a `0.5` floating-point value, which means that the source is 50% opaque. In other words, it only lets 50% of the underlying surface show through.[4]

`AlphaComposite` is the single implementation of the `Composite` interface that comes with the API. It offers a large number of rules (such as `SRC_OVER` and `DST_OVER` we just mentioned) that control how it blends a source and a destination. The following section describes the meaning of those various settings.

AlphaComposite rules

The class contains eight different composition rules that are defined after the work of Thomas Porter and Tom Duff (see [Porter 84, 253-259], or [Foley 1997, Chapter 17]). Each composition rule defines a different way to combine the

---

4. Note that if the source is already partly transparent (remember that colors can have an alpha component defining how opaque they are), then the `AlphaComposite.SRC_OVER` defines an extra alpha for the source. In our example, the source will be only 50% as opaque as it actually is.

source and the destination in a rendering operation. Before we look at the different rules, let's see how `AlphaComposite` instances are created (see **Alpha-CompositeRules.java** on the CD-ROM).

▼ **Creating an AlphaComposite**   The `AlphaComposite` class has no constructor. Instead, it has two factory methods that enable us to get instances: `getInstance(int rule)` and `getInstance(int rule, float alpha)`. The reason for having two factory methods instead of public constructors is that the `AlphaComposite` class is immutable (that is, it is final and has no methods to change its attributes). Therefore, it makes sense to make sure that `AlphaComposite` instances are shared whenever possible, and using a factory method is a good way to ensure this. For example, the `AlphaComposite` contains a number of predefined `AlphaComposite` instances, such as `AlphaComposite.SrcOver`. If the rule and alpha passed in any of the two factory methods match one of the predefined instances, then that instance is returned. Otherwise, a new `AlphaComposite` is created.

▼ **Visual representation of AlphaComposite rules**   To illustrate the eight composition rules that `AlphaComposite` provides, we created a simple program that performs the same rendering, but with varying composition rules. Each rule is used twice, once at full opacity (with an alpha of 1) and once at half opacity (with an alpha of 0.5, which is half transparent). Figure 5.20 shows the output produced by the program listed in Table 5.10.

As the figure shows, results are widely different. However, they all operate on the color and alpha components of the source and destination. Let's call a_s the transparency value of the source and c_s the value of one of the source color components. As all color components are treated the same way by an `AlphaComposite`, we will only use this generic representation of a color component. For example, in RGB, c_s might represent either red, green, or blue because the processing is the same for each. Let's call a_d the alpha component of the destination prior to composition and c_d the value of a color component prior to composition.

For all rules, the value of the destination alpha and color components is a fraction of the source alpha and color components (a_s and c_s) added to a fraction of the destination alpha and color components prior to composition (a_d and c_d). If we call f_s and f_d the fraction that the source and destination, respectively, contribute to the final destination, we have:[5]

$$a_d = a_d.f_d + a_s.f_s$$
$$c_d = c_d.f_d + c_s.f_s$$

---

5. These equations assume that the source and destination components have premultiplied alpha values.

Fully opaque   **Half opaque**

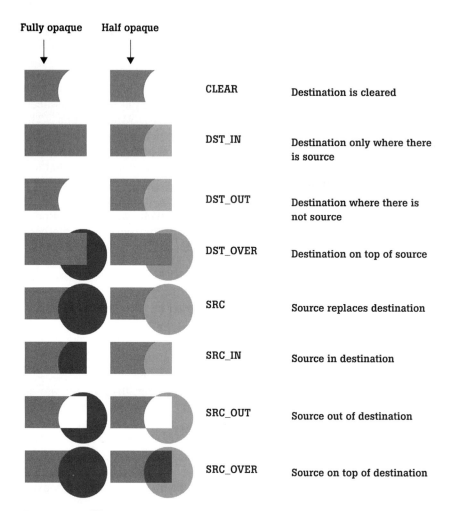

CLEAR — Destination is cleared

DST_IN — Destination only where there is source

DST_OUT — Destination where there is not source

DST_OVER — Destination on top of source

SRC — Source replaces destination

SRC_IN — Source in destination

SRC_OUT — Source out of destination

SRC_OVER — Source on top of destination

Figure 5.20 ■
AlphaComposite rules

The fraction values of f_s and f_d are what differentiate the different rules, listed in Table 5.10, as we next explain.

Table 5.10 ■ Illustration of the AlphaComposite rules

ALPHACOMPOSITERULES.JAVA

```
AlphaComposite alphaComposites[] = {
AlphaComposite.Clear,
AlphaComposite.getInstance(AlphaComposite.CLEAR, .5f),

AlphaComposite.DstIn,
AlphaComposite.getInstance(AlphaComposite.DST_IN, .5f),

AlphaComposite.DstOut,
AlphaComposite.getInstance(AlphaComposite.DST_OUT, .5f),

AlphaComposite.DstOver,
AlphaComposite.getInstance(AlphaComposite.DST_OVER, .5f),

AlphaComposite.Src,
AlphaComposite.getInstance(AlphaComposite.SRC, .5f),

AlphaComposite.SrcIn,
AlphaComposite.getInstance(AlphaComposite.SRC_IN, .5f),

AlphaComposite.SrcOut,
AlphaComposite.getInstance(AlphaComposite.SRC_OUT, .5f),

AlphaComposite.SrcOver,
AlphaComposite.getInstance(AlphaComposite.SRC_OVER, .5f),
};

...

Shape redRect = new Rectangle(3, 3, 50, 25);
Shape blueDisc = new Ellipse2D.Float(30, 0, 40, 40);
Rectangle bounds = redRect.getBounds();
bounds.add(blueDisc.getBounds());

//
// Iterate through the list of alphaComposites
//
Color red = new Color(200, 50, 50);
Color blue = new Color(50, 50, 120);
```

Table 5.10 ■ Illustration of the AlphaComposite rules (Continued)

ALPHACOMPOSITERULES.JAVA

```
int nComposites = alphaComposites.length;
for(int i=0; i<nComposites; i++){
// Set default composite and paint a red square
g.setPaint(red);
g.setComposite(AlphaComposite.SrcOver);
g.fill(redRect);

// Set current composite and blue paint
g.setPaint(blue);
g.setComposite(alphaComposites[i]);
g.fill(blueDisc);

if((i%2)==0)
  g.translate(bounds.width + 10, 0);
else
  g.translate(-bounds.width - 10, bounds.height + 10);
```

The CLEAR rule

Here f_s and f_d are equal to zero, which implies that:

$a_d = 0$
$c_d = 0$

As a result, the pixels in the destination are cleared, that is, set to all zeros. It is interesting to realize that this may produce different visual results in different contexts. For example, when you draw to a BufferedImage that has an alpha channel, all the pixels affected by the clear (pixels in the blueDisc Shape, in our example) become fully transparent. If there is no alpha channel, then the pixels become fully black. In our program, the rendering was done in a BufferedImage with an alpha channel:

```
BufferedImage buf = new BufferedImage(w, h,
BufferedImage.TYPE_INT_ARGB_PRE);
Graphics2D g = buf.createGraphics();
```

Then, the buf BufferedImage was painted onto a JComponent with a white background:

```
public void paint(Graphics g){
    g.drawImage(buf, 0, 0, null);
}
```

This explains why, in our example, clearing pixels resulted in the redRect Shape appearing to be clipped, and not in a black disc. If we had rendered to the screen directly, we would have had the output—

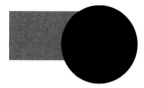

—because there is no alpha channel in the destination when rendering to the screen. We would have obtained a similar result if we had rendered to a BufferedImage with no alpha channel.

Finally, note how the CLEAR rule does not use the alpha setting. It is not used to compute the output; a_s is ignored. Therefore, it is pointless to use getInstance to build a CLEAR AlphaComposite. Instead, use the predefined AlphaComposite.Clear instance.

The DST_IN rule

Here, the fractions for the source and destination are $f_s = 0$ and $f_d = a_s$. Consequently:

$$a_d = a_s \cdot a_d$$
$$c_d = a_s \cdot c_d$$

When the source alpha is 1 (AlphaComposite.DstIn has an alpha of 1), the alpha and color of the destination are unchanged (here, the red rectangle remains unmodified). For an alpha of 50%, the destination, previously fully red, becomes half transparent, which is why some of the white background now becomes visible.

Note that composition only happens on the pixels affected by a rendering operation. In our example, only the pixels inside the blueDisc Shape are composited with the destination. So, we would get different results if we were rendering a similar content in a different way. For example, if we first create a BufferedImage with an alpha channel by drawing the blueDisc in that image and then drawing the BufferedImage in lieu of the blueDisc, we might expect the same result.

```
BufferedImage blueDiscBuf = new BufferedImage(bounds.x + bounds.width,
                                              bounds.y + bounds.height,

BufferedImage.TYPE_INT_ARGB);
Graphics2D g2 = blueDiscBuf.createGraphics();
```

```
g2.setPaint(blue);
g2.fill(blueDisc);
g2.dispose();

// Now, use the same Composition rule, but draw blueDiscBuf
// instead of filling blueDisc
for(int i...){
    g.setComposite(alphaComposites[i])
    g.drawImage(blueDiscBuf, 0, 0, null);
}
```

The following figure shows that the output is actually quite different:

Now, all the pixels that are covered by the `blueDiscBuf` are processed, not only those in the `blueDisc` Shape. Because pixels in the source `blueDiscBuf` outside the `blueDisc` Shape have an alpha value of 0 (this is the initial value, and nothing has been drawn in those pixels), the destination, in those pixels, also has a 0 alpha after composition. In other words, all pixels in the destination that are not in the source, that is, not in pixels where the source is not transparent, are cleared. This explains the name of the rule: Destination in Source, `DST_IN`.

The DST_OUT rule

For this rule, the fractions for the source and destination are $f_s = 0$ and $f_d = 1\text{-}a_s$. This results in:

```
a_d = (1-a_s).a_d
c_d = (1-a_s).c_d
```

All pixels in the destination that are on top of pixels in the source and that are transparent (that is, a_s=0), will keep the same value. On the other end, pixels in the destination on top of fully opaque source pixels (that is, $a_s = 1$) will be cleared because both a_d and c_d will become zero. Simply put, only pixels that are out of the source (not on top of the source's opaque pixels) are kept in the final destination. This explains the name of the rule: Destination Out of Source, `DST_OUT`.

The DST_OVER rule

For this rule, the fractions of the source and destination are $f_s = (1-a_d)$ and $f_d = 1$. This results in:

$$a_d = a_d + (1-a_d).a_s$$
$$c_d = c_d + (1-a_d).c_s$$

In places where the destination is fully opaque (for example, the `redRect` pixels), the source is completely hidden by the destination. In places where the destination is fully transparent, the source shows with its color and alpha value.

The SRC rule

For this rule, the fractions for the source and destination are $f_s = 1$ and $f_d = 0$. This results in:

$$a_d = a_s$$
$$c_d = c_s$$

The source completely replaces the destination. This is equivalent to replacing destination pixels with that of the source, which explains the rule's name: Source. If we had used the same alternate rendering solution as described in the `DST_IN` rule (that is, first render to a `BufferedImage`, then to the output, using the same composition rule), we would obtain:

Again, because compositing is performed for all pixels that are rendered, the result is different. When using an intermediate `BufferedImage`, we also have the `Composite` instance process more pixels. Therefore, all the pixels now replace the destination, not only those in the `blueDisc` Shape, and we end up with the `blueDisc` only.

The SRC_IN rule

For this rule, the fractions for the source and destination are $f_s = a_d$ and $f_d = 0$. This results in:

$$a_d = a_d \cdot a_s$$
$$c_d = a_d \cdot c_s$$

So, only pixels from the source that are on top of opaque pixels in the destination (that is, pixels in the redRect) replace the destination. This explains the rule's name: Source in Destination. Again, note that a different result would be obtained if we used an intermediate BufferedImage.

All the pixels outside the blueDisc in the intermediate BufferedImage that overlap the redRect replace the destination. Because they are transparent, they erase the redRect.

The SRC_OUT rule

For this rule, the fractions for the source and destination are $f_s = (1-a_d)$ and $f_d = 0$. This results in:

$$a_d = (1-a_d) \cdot a_s$$
$$c_d = (1-a_d) \cdot c_s$$

Only pixels from the source that overlap transparent pixels in the destination (that is, pixels out of the redRect) replace the destination. This explains the rule's name: Source out of Destination. Pixels inside the destination are cleared, and pixels outside reproduce the source. Again, note that using an intermediate BufferedImage would yield a different result.

Because all the pixels are now composited, all the `redRect` pixels are cleared, which explains why only `blueDisc` pixels remain.

The SRC_OVER rule

For this rule, the fractions for the source and destination are $f_s = 1$ and $f_d = (1-a_s)$. This results in:

$$a_d = (1-a_s)a_d + a_s$$
$$c_d = (1-a_s)c_d + c_s$$

If the source is fully opaque, then none of the destination shows. If the source is completely or partly transparent (a_s is less than 1), then some of the destination contributes to the final output, giving the illusion that the destination shows through the source. The `SRC_OVER` rule, with no extra alpha transparency, is the default `Graphics2D` setting.

Composite internals

Now that we have looked at the various rules for the `AlphaComposite` implementation, let us have a look at how `Composite` actually works: how does it blend pixels?

▼ **The Composite interface**   `Composite` is a short interface defined in the `java.awt` package.

```
public interface Composite {
    public CompositeContext createContext(ColorModel srcColorModel,
                                          ColorModel dstColorModel,
                                          RenderingHints hints);
}
```

This approach is similar to that taken by the `Paint`/`PaintContext` pair we discussed earlier. A `Composite` only holds the information necessary to create the object, a `CompositeContext` that will do the compositing in a given context. Again, there are several reasons for compositing in that way, among them:

1. Lightweight model. Until the compositing operation is actually needed, only a lightweight object (such as `AlphaComposite`, which holds only two variables, its rule and an alpha value) needs to be stored.
2. Flexibility. Depending on the context defined by the `createContext` parameters, a `Composite` implementation could decide to use different strategies for compositing. Those strategies might be implemented by different `CompositeContext` implementations. At least, it is a possibility.

So, for a given context, defined by the `ColorModel` of the source, the `Color-Model` of the destination, and hints on how the user wants the operation to be handled, the `Composite` instance is responsible for creating an appropriate `CompositeContext`. But why are `ColorModel` objects defining the context?

▼ **The CompositeContext interface** `CompositeContext` is also an interface in the `java.awt` package. Like `Composite`, it is very short.

```
public interface CompositeContext{
    public void dispose();

    public void compose(Raster src,
                        Raster dstIn,
                        WritableRaster dstOut);
}
```

The platform calls `dispose` when it no longer needs a `CompositeContext`, at least temporarily. This gives the `CompositeContext` an opportunity to do any cleanup or release resources if needed.

The `compose` method is called to actually combine the source and destination. The source pixels are contained in the `src` input `Raster`. The destination pixels are stored in the `dstIn Raster`, and the `CompositeContext` implementation is requested to store the results of the composition into the `dstOut Raster`. It is important to remember that `dstIn` and `dstOut` might be the same object. The `srcModel` and `dstModel`, which were part of the context used to create the `CompositeContext` from the `createContext` method in `Composite`, define the semantics of pixels in the source and destination `Raster`s. This is needed, for example, so that the `CompositeContext` implementation is able to distinguish between alpha and color components. See Chapter 4 ("ColorModels" on page 86) for more details on `ColorModel`s.

Summary

The `CompositeContext` interface has taken us deep into the internals of the Java 2D API. It is interesting to note how even this advanced feature can be easily extended and gives us an opportunity to add more features to the API. An example of a custom `Composite` and `CompositeContext` implementation is included in the Graphic Layers Framework goodies, and its operation is explained in Chapter 9 (see "Custom Composite" on page 328).

RenderingHints

`RenderingHints`, as we briefly mentioned, give the API programmer a chance to influence the various quality and speed trade-offs that Java 2D implementations may make. For example, the antialiasing strategy is one of the `RenderingHints` (`RenderingHints.KEY_ANTIALIASING`), and there are different values for this hint, depending on whether antialiasing should be used (`RenderingHints.VALUE_ANTIALIAS_ON`) or not used (`Rendering-Hints.VALUE_ANTIALIAS_OFF`). Antialiasing is one of the eight hints available in the current version of the API. Before we look at each of those hints, let us have a closer look at what it means to set a hint and how it is used by the platform.

Why RenderingHints?

`RenderingHints` reconciles the platform rendering capabilities and the programmer's rendering requests.

▼ **Platform rendering capabilities** Java 2D is part of the core Java platform. Therefore, it is available in many different environments: different operating systems, but also different graphic hardware support (for example, low color resolution, monochromatic displays). In these different environments, the rendering capabilities vary. If we take the antialiasing example again, there will be platforms where antialiasing will be supported and some where it will not.

▼ **Programmer's rendering ideal** By this we mean the ideal rendering options desired by the programmer. These will vary depending on the type of applications the programmer works on. Some applications will favor speed (for example, animations), and some applications will favor quality (for example, creation of rendering effects, such as those presented in this book). In our antialiasing example, some programmers will prefer to have antialiasing turned off, no matter what, because this will give them the best performance. Some will prefer to have it turned on if possible.

▼ **Reconciling capabilities and options** Because of the cross-platform nature of Java, it is not possible to guarantee that all rendering options will be available on all platforms, simply because on some platforms the options would not make sense, depending on the environment (for example, antialiasing does not make sense on a two-color display). On the other hand, programmers need a way to specify what they want. This is where `RenderingHints` fits in. The approach is that programmers provide hints as to what they would like to use when there is a potential rendering option. Then, the hints are used by the rendering engine to control the rendering process.

Be sure to keep this important distinction in mind: *hints are not options*. There is no guarantee that they will actually be used, especially if the underlying platform implementation cannot fulfill the requested option.

Where and how are RenderingHints used?

The most important class using hints is `Graphics2D`, but `RenderingHints` is also used in the internal operation of `Paint`, `Composite`, and `Buffered-ImageOp`.

▼ **Graphics2D** Three methods set or modify the `RenderingHints` in the graphics context.

1. `setRenderingHint(RenderingHint.Key key, Object hint-Value)`. This method sets one of the hints, defined by a `RenderingHints.Key` object (for example, `RenderingHints.KEY_ANTIALIASING`), to `hintValue` (for example, `Rendering-Hints.VALUE_ANTIALIAS_ON`).
2. `addRenderingHints(Map hintMap)`. This method is a convenience for adding the set of key/value pairs contained in the `hintMap` to the set of hints already set in `Graphics2D`.
3. `setRenderingHints(Map hintMap)`. This method removes any hints already defined in `Graphics2D` and replaces them with the set of key/value pairs in `hintMap`.

Hints are part of the rendering context, so they are used in the same way as the other context attributes:

1. Set the desired `RenderingHints`.
2. Select the graphic object to render.
3. Invoke the rendering method.

Table 5.11 illustrates two consecutive invocations of the same rendering method, but with different settings for the antialiasing hint.

▼ **Paint and Composite** We have seen that one of the parameters in the `Paint.createContext` and `Composite.createContext` methods is a `RenderingHints`. This is the value in the graphic context of the `Graphics2D` object for which the `PaintContext` or `CompositeContext` should perform rendering (remember that `PaintContext` and `CompositeContext` are the ones that actually paint the correct pixel pattern and blend source and destination pixels, respectively).

Table 5.11 ■ Setting RenderingHints in Graphics2D

CODE

```
Graphics2D g = (Graphics2D)_g;

// Set rendering context: Antialias ON
g.setFont(new Font("serif", Font.PLAIN, 30));
g.setRenderingHint(RenderingHints.KEY_ANTIALIASING,
                   RenderingHints.VALUE_ANTIALIAS_ON);

// Select object to render
String text = "a";

// Invoke rendering method
g.drawString(text, 20, 30);

// Modify rendering context: Antialias OFF
g.setRenderingHint(RenderingHints.KEY_ANTIALIASING,
            RenderingHints.VALUE_ANTIALIAS_OFF);
g.translate(0, 40);

// Render text again
g.drawString(text, 20, 30);
```

The same rendering call, drawString, produced different output qualities with different values set for the antialiasing strategy.

To better understand what happens, let's look at the following code segment:

```
// Set graphic context attributes
g.setRenderingHint(RenderingHints.KEY_XXX, hintValue);
g.setPaint(Color.blue);
g.setComposite(AlphaComposite.SrcIn);

// Select object to render: a rectangle
Rectangle rect = new Rectangle(30, 30, 50, 50);
g.fill(rect);
```

The Graphics2D object g processes the fill call as follows:

1. Creates a PaintContext from Color.blue, the Paint in the graphic context. It passes the hints as one of the parameters so that the Color object can decide which PaintContext implementation is best suited for the given hints.

2. Invokes the PaintContext's getRaster method (it may be called several times to cover the whole area to be filled) to get the pixel pattern that should be painted on the output. For the Color.blue, the pixels all have the blue value.

3. Creates a `CompositeContext` from `AlphaComposite.SrcIn`. Again, it passes the hints as one of the parameters so that the `AlphaComposite.SrcIn` object can decide which `Composite-Context` is best suited for the given hints.

4. Invokes the `CompositeContext.compose` method to combine the destination `Raster` with the `Raster` returned by the `PaintContext`'s `getRaster` method.

In `Paint` and `Composite`, `RenderingHints` gives those objects a chance to create the best `PaintContext` and `CompositeContext` to match the programmer's requirements. Note that those hints may not be of any use, depending on the `Paint` or `Composite` implementation: it actually depends on the kind of processing they do. However, it is key to have hints as a parameter so that their usefulness is a possibility.

▼ **BufferedImageOp**   The `BufferedImageOp` interface uses no `Rendering-Hints`. However, each of its implementations uses a `RenderingHints` in a constructor. For example, the `AffineTransformOp` documentation specifies that it accepts a hint about the algorithm for interpolating pixels (see "BufferedImageOp" on page 94). Other implementations use hints about the preferred dithering trade-offs and color conversion trade-offs (more on this later).

Available RenderingHints

Now that we have seen how and where `RenderingHints` is used, let us look at the hints that are actually available. Eight `RenderingHints` keys are defined in `RenderingHints`; this section explains each one.

▼ **Pixel interpolation**   When an image is transformed spatially and drawn into a destination, there might not be a one-to-one mapping between the pixel locations in the destination and the pixel location in the source. For example, if an image is scaled up (say, by a factor of two), one pixel out of two in the destination will not have an exact correspondence with a pixel in the source. The value for such pixels needs to be interpolated, and the `Rendering-Hints.KEY_INTERPOLATION` hint provides several options to control the preferred method.

The simplest method consists of using the value closest to the interpolated pixel location in the source. This is a fast method, but it produces poor results if many pixels need to be interpolated. For example, if an image is scaled up by a large factor, blocks of pixels (that is, all the interpolated pixels closest to the same pixels in the source) start to be very visible (see the left image in Figure 5.21).

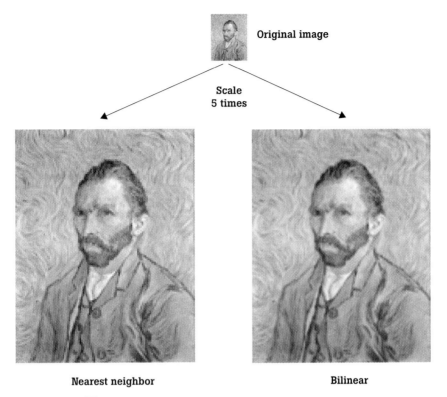

Original image

Scale
5 times

Nearest neighbor   Bilinear

Figure 5.21 ▪
Different interpolation algorithms

Two other methods, called bilinear and bicubic, produce increasingly better results, but are also more computation intensive. The image on the right in Figure 5.21 shows that the bilinear interpolation produces a better quality result than nearest neighbor.

The "right" setting really depends on the application. In an animation where an image rolls across the screen, it may be wiser to use the nearest neighbor interpolation because it is faster. For the examples in Part 3 of this book, we usually choose bilinear interpolation to get the best possible output quality.

▼ **Alpha interpolation** This hint is defined by the Rendering-
Hint.KEY_ALPHA_INTERPOLATION key and can be set to the platform default or to speed or quality (RenderingHints.VALUE_ALPHA_INTERPOLATION_XXX, where XXX can be DEFAULT, SPEED, or QUALITY). This hint controls the blending method in case different algorithms are available.

▼ **Antialiasing**   We have used antialiasing as our example for `Rendering-Hints` all throughout this first part. Antialiasing is the process of smoothing the staircase effect that happens as a side effect of drawing `Shapes` on a raster device, that is, a device made of a discrete set of controllable elements, usually square, that are filled with a color value. Setting `Rendering-Hints.KEY_ANTIALIASING` to `RenderingHints.VALUE_ANTIALIAS_ON` turns on the antialiasing process if it is supported by the platform. Figure 5.11 on page 149 illustrated the different outputs obtained with antialiasing turned on or off.

The `RenderingHints.KEY_ANTIALIASING` hint controls antialiasing for all rendering. The `RenderingHints.KEY_TEXT_ANTIALIASING` hint controls text antialiasing only. Therefore, it is possible to turn on antialiasing for text, but not for shapes.

▼ **Color rendering**   In our discussion on `BufferedImages` in Chapter 4, we explained how the Java 2D API allows conversion between different color spaces (see "ColorSpace" on page 88). There are actually several degrees of accuracy in color conversion. One is to consider that if a source is defined in sRGB, for example, and the destination is also defined in sRGB, then there is no need to convert when reproducing colors from the source to the destination. While this model works for some applications, it does not take device differences into account. In a more sophisticated model, to provide what is referred to as color matching, the API could actually convert color by using the ICC profiles for the source and destination to ensure highly accurate color matching (again, see Chapter 4 for more details on ICC profiles).

One thing `RenderingHints.KEY_COLOR_RENDERING` could control is how accurate color matching should be. The various `RenderingHints.VALUE_COLOR_XXX` values offer a choice between the platform default (`XXX = DEFAULT`), speed (`XXX = SPEED`), and quality (`XXX = QUALITY`). The default value will use whatever default setting the platform uses, the speed value will skip color matching when converting between color spaces of the same type (for example, source and destination are both sRGB), and quality will do all the necessary processing to ensure accurate color matching. Again, it is important to realize that not all platforms may implement all the options; for example, accurate color matching was not implemented in the first release of the Java 2 platform on either Windows or Solaris.

▼ **Dithering**   Dithering is a common technique to reduce the contouring effect that appears when colors are reproduced on an output with fewer levels of colors. The API allows us to decide which method we want to use through the `Ren-`

deringHints.KEY_DITHERING hint. We can either use the platform default or turn dithering on or off (VALUE_DITHER_ENABLED or VALUE_DITHER_DISABLED). The default setting might be a good option by which to take advantage of the underlying platform capabilities.

▼ **Fractional metrics** This hint (RenderingHints.KEY_FRACTIONAL-METRICS) can be either on or off (RenderingHints.VALUE_FRACTIONAL-METRICS_ON/OFF). When on, the rendering engine might use a floating-point calculation which, in effect, produces a more accurate placement for shapes and character glyphs. When turned off, metrics might be rounded off and the resulting error (due to the round-off approximation) might become visible.

▼ **Rendering** The general hint (RenderingHints.KEY_RENDERING) can take one of three settings: RenderingHints.VALUE_RENDER_DEFAULT, Rendering-Hints.VALUE_RENDER_SPEED, and RenderingHints.VALUE_RENDER_QUALITY. When set to default, the platform will likely use whatever it considers its default implementation for any given algorithm. A typical use for the implementation of, say, an interpolation algorithm, would be to first check the KEY_INTERPOLATION hint. If none is set, the implementation might check the value of the KEY_RENDERING hint and decide to use its default algorithm if the value is DEFAULT. Some platforms might choose to make the default the algorithm corresponding to the SPEED setting; some, the QUALITY setting or even some other alternative. The SPEED and QUALITY settings can be used by extensions of the API (for example, a custom implementation of the Composite interface) to discriminate between possible options.

Summary

Remember the following key things about RenderingHints. First, the hints allow us to define our preferences when there might be alternate algorithm choices. The hints constituting RenderingHints are not options: they are just indications of our preferences. Then, if the platform does support the option, the preference might be taken into account. Second, there are no correct settings for RenderingHints. The right setting depends on the type of application, and generally, it depends on whether speed or quality is more important.

Table 5.12 suggests settings for the different hints, depending on whether speed or quality is more important.

Table 5.12 ■ Suggestion for RenderingHints settings

HINT	CODE NAME	QUALITY SETTING	SPEED SETTING
Alpha interpolation	ALPHA_INTERPOLATION	Quality	Speed
Interpolation	INTERPOLATION	Bicubic or Bilinear	Nearest neighbor
Rendering	RENDERING	Quality	Speed
Antialiasing	ANTIALIASING	On	Off
Text antialiasing	TEXT_ANTIALIASING	On	Off
Dithering	DITHERING	Enabled	Disabled
Color matching	COLOR_RENDERING	Quality	Speed
Fractional Metrics	FRACTIONALMETRICS	On	Off

Clipping

The clip is the last of the attributes that, all together, make up the rendering context. It is a fairly simple attribute.

Clipping is the process of limiting the rendering to a specific area, known as the clipping area. Anything in the output device lying outside the clipping area is not affected by rendering operations.

Defining the clipping area

It used to be that the clipping region was limited to a rectangular area, set through the Graphics.setClip(x, y, w, h) method. This limitation has been removed, and it is now possible to set the clip to be any kind of Shape, thanks to the new setClip(Shape) and clip(Shape) methods. The former replaces the current clip attribute with a new Shape; the latter intersects the current clip with the Shape input parameter. The code example in Table 5.13 illustrates how the clip relates to the current AffineTransform attribute.

Table 5.13 ■ Setting the clipping area

CLIPPINGUSAGE.JAVA	CODE (CONT'D)

```java
Graphics2D g = ...

// Save original clip and transform
Shape clipShape = g.getClip();
AffineTransform transform
  = g.getTransform();

// Set simple clip : does not modify
// the output
g.clipRect(0, 0,
          size.width, size.height);
g.drawImage(image, 0, 0, null);

g.translate(w, 0);

// Intersect current clip with a
// smaller clip :
// show only the top right corner of
// the image
g.clipRect(w/2, 0, w/2, h/2);
g.drawImage(image, 0, 0, null);

// Restore default transform and clip
g.setTransform(transform);
g.setClip(clipShape);

// Move to next position
g.translate(2*w, 0);

// Scale before setting the same clip
g.scale(0.5, 0.5);
g.clipRect(w/2, 0, w/2, h/2);
g.drawImage(image, 0, 0, null);

// Restore transform and clip
g.setTransform(transform);
g.setClip(clipShape);

g.translate(3*w, 0);
```

```java
// Use a non-rectangle clipping
// area
Shape circle
  = new Ellipse2D.Float(0, 0,
                        w, h);
g.clip(circle);
g.drawImage(image, 0, 0, null);

// Restore transform and clip
g.setTransform(transform);
g.setClip(clipShape);

// Move to next position
g.translate(4*w, 0);

// Use a non-rectangle clipping
// area again,
// after setting a scale
// transform
g.scale(0.5, 0.5);
g.clip(circle);
g.drawImage(image, 0, 0, null);

// Restore transform and clip
g.setTransform(transform);
g.setClip(clipShape);

g.translate(5*w, 0);

// Use a non-rectangle clipping
// area again, before setting a
// scale transform
g.clip(circle);
g.scale(0.5, 0.5);
g.drawImage(image, 0, 0, null);
```

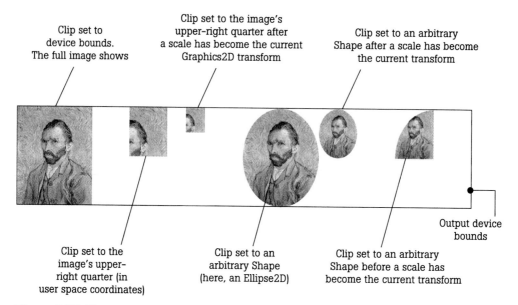

Clip set to device bounds. The full image shows

Clip set to the image's upper-right quarter after a scale has become the current Graphics2D transform

Clip set to an arbitrary Shape after a scale has become the current transform

Output device bounds

Clip set to the image's upper-right quarter (in user space coordinates)

Clip set to an arbitrary Shape (here, an Ellipse2D)

Clip set to an arbitrary Shape before a scale has become the current transform

Figure 5.22 ■
Different clip settings

Figure 5.22 illustrates the different clip settings.

It is important to understand that the clip is defined in user space when passed through one of the methods defining or modifying the clipping area. However, it is immediately transformed into device space and stored in device space. For example, when the clip is set by the setClip method, the input Shape is transformed, using the current AffineTransform to determine the clipping area in device space. Consequently, if the Graphics2D transform is modified later on, the clipping area is not affected.

In our example, the first image is drawn after the clip is set to the full size of the device: as expected, nothing is clipped, and the full image is drawn. The second image is drawn after intersecting the current clip (the device bounds) with a smaller clip corresponding to the upper-right quarter of the Image:

```
g.translate(w, 0);

// Intersect current clip with a smaller clip: show only
// the top right corner of the image
g.clipRect(w/2, 0, w/2, h/2);
g.drawImage(image, 0, 0, null);
```

Note that the clipRect method takes user space coordinates. Because the current transform is a translation to the right of image width (g.translate(w, 0)), the clip on the device is also shifted to the right.

The following image is painted after a different kind of transform—a 50%
scale—is set.

```
g.translate(2*w, 0);

// Scale before setting the same clip
g.scale(0.5, 0.5);
g.clipRect(w/2, 0, w/2, h/2);
g.drawImage(image, 0, 0, null);
```

Here again, the clip is set to the upper-right quarter of the image, in the user
space. Because the current `AffineTransform` at the time we set the clip is set to
a scale (composed with a translation), the clip is scaled and shifted to the right.

The remaining three images illustrate the use of an arbitrary `Shape` for the clip.
We used an `Ellipse2D`:

```
Shape circle = new Ellipse2D.Float(0, 0, w, h);
g.clip(circle);
```

Note the difference in the order used for setting up the context attributes for the
last two images. For the second-last one:

```
g.translate(4*w, 0);
g.scale(0.5, 0.5);
g.clip(circle);
```

For the last one:

```
g.translate(5*w, 0);
g.clip(circle);
g.scale(0.5, 0.5);
```

Because the transform is different at the time the clip is set, the clipping area is
different. Remember: the clipping area is transformed into device space, using
the current `AffineTransform`, at the time the clip is set or modified. So, for the
second-last image, the clip `Shape` is both scaled and translated. It is only translated for the last `Image`, not scaled.

Summary

The clipping area can be set to any kind of `Shape`,[6] and it is important to keep
in mind that the clip is converted to device space at the time it is set.

One limitation with the clipping mechanism is that it does not allow antialiasing along the boundaries of the clipping area, which may result in undesirable

---

6. Note, however, that there might be restrictions on some implementations. Please refer to the
javadoc documentation of the `java.awt.Graphics.setClip` method.

Figure 5.23 ■
Pixelation along the clipping path

pixelation along that path. Figure 5.23 shows a close-up on that effect along the Ellipse2D path in our previous example.

There are solutions to that problem, and the masking feature in the Graphic Layers Framework, described in Chapter 7, is an example (see "Layer masking" on page 233).

Parting thoughts

The graphic context and its related attributes are central to the Java 2D immediate rendering mode: rendering invocations produce different results depending on the state of the graphic context at the time the invocation happens. This mode provides the foundation for all kinds of rendering needs and fits the purpose of the Java 2 platform.

However, the resulting programming paradigm is sequential, meaning that programs using the API as it currently is must strictly follow the rendering model operation sequence: first, set the rendering context attributes; then, select the graphic object to render; and finally, invoke a rendering method on Graphics2D. When you chain several such sequences, you risk interference. For example, if you modify the Composite attribute to render an image and then render a Shape, the same Composite attribute will be reused for the Shape unless you modify the Composite attribute again for the second rendering operation. The rendering context attributes are persistent, and an individual rendering sequence is dependent on previous ones. It is often a good idea to restore default attributes when the state of the graphic context is uncertain or to implement some management of the graphic context attributes.

Table 5.14 shows the default values for a Graphics2D object.

An alternate approach is that of AttributedString rendering: the object to be rendered (a string of text) is associated with relevant rendering attributes (for

Table 5.14 ■ Graphic context attributes default values

ATTRIBUTE	VALUE
AffineTransform	Default transform as returned by the associated GraphicsConfiguration's getDefaultTransform method. This makes the user space's origin fit with the upper-left corner of the drawing area, with the positive side of the x-axis to the right and the positive side of the y-axis downwards.
Paint	Foreground Color for a Component or black (for printer or offscreen rendering).
Stroke	One point wide BasicStroke.
Clip	Rendering is limited to the drawing area.
Composite	AlphaComposite.SrcOver (no extra transparency).
Font	Font of the Component or Dialog 12 for printer and offscreen rendering.
RenderingHints	Depends on output device.

example, TextAttribute.FOREGROUND). When the object is rendered (through an intermediate AttributedCharacterIterator, for AttributedString), the rendered object actually encapsulates the relevant context attributes. There is a big difference between the two approaches: one provides the foundation for an efficient rendering engine, and the other (AttributedString) provides a more convenient programming model for a specific problem (styled text rendering). Note that the second rendering model relies on the default rendering model: rendering an AttributedString consists of using the style attributes to modify the context and render successive parts of the text. So, the two approaches are complementary: one provides the foundation, the other provides a higher-level and more convenient rendering model for a specific problem.

As we discuss in part 2, the same reasons that drove the styled text rendering to use a different rendering model explain the design of the Graphic Layers Framework, where the Java 2D rendering model is used as a foundation for a higher-level programming model for creating rendering effects.

End of Part I

In this first part, we have described in detail the foundation that the Java 2D API provides. This API can be used for many types of applications. In this book, we use it for creating visually appealing effects.

The next part explains how the Graphic Layers Framework takes advantage of Java 2D to build a framework to combine the different features of the API and also to take advantage of the API's extensible design: GLF includes many implementations of various interfaces, such as `Paint`, `Stroke`, and `Composite`.

THE GRAPHIC LAYERS FRAMEWORK

part **2**

6 THE GRAPHIC LAYERS FRAMEWORK FUNDAMENTALS

Purpose of the Graphic Layers Framework

The Graphic Layers Framework, GLF, provides a foundation for easy creation of rendering effects, such as *Recessed Shadow* or *Shape Texturizing* (see Chapter 17). The creation of such effects is characterized by:

- *Repetitive tasks*. Rendering operations (for example, filling Shapes) are repeated many times and are combined to obtain the desired results.
- *Large number of options*. The rendering options are numerous, from color settings, to transparency values, to transformation adjustments. Modifying and visualizing the result of various settings can be a daunting task.
- *Use of the API's extensible design*. The Java 2D API offers a lot of capabilities. Its open design allows it to be extended to achieve even richer rendering effects. For example, new types of fills can be added by creating new Paint implementations.

The Graphic Layers Framework addresses those three characteristics by providing the following:

1. *Layers as reusable rendering components.* (This is where the framework's name comes from.) The framework provides prepackaged rendering operations in the form of prepackaged `com.sun.glf.Layers`. For example, the `com.sun.glf.ShapeLayer` class supports automatic rendering of a `Shape`. Layers are natural building blocks for creating effects with 2D techniques, and this paradigm is used in many graphics tools.
2. *Configuration framework and utilities.* The framework provides utilities and tools to deal with the large number of configuration parameters and to enable experimentation with different settings.
3. *API extensions.* The framework provides several extensions to the Java 2D API: different `Paint` and `Stroke` implementations, but also `Buffered-Image` filters and `Composite` implementations.

When the framework is used, the visual output is described by stacking up `Layers`. The `Layers` stack can be configured by tools, saved, and loaded easily, and it can take advantage of the different API extensions. Figure 6.1 describes how to use the framework.

A given graphical composition is described in terms of `Layers`. Each `Layer` object has a number of options that control its rendering. For example, the bottom `Layer` in the figure can have the colors it uses configured. The configuration tools can modify these options to create a different configuration. Each configuration can be saved to a file and loaded later on. As we will see, the tools support different formats for different purposes. Finally, the tools and utilities can render a graphic composition defined by a stack of `Layers`.

In the following paragraphs, we look at the different packages that make up the Graphic Layers Framework and then show a first example of how they are used.

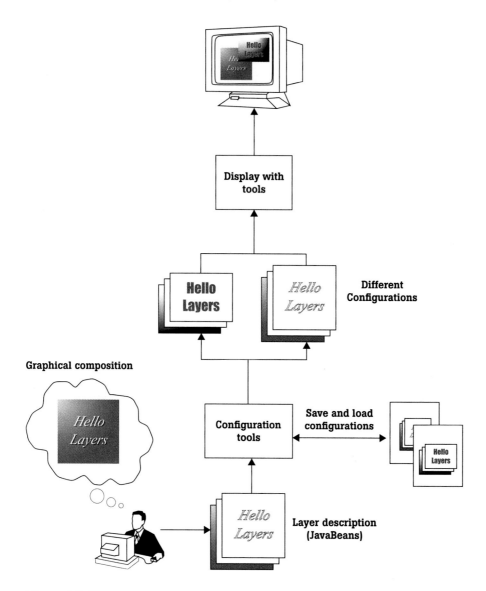

Figure 6.1 ■
Using the Graphic Layers Framework

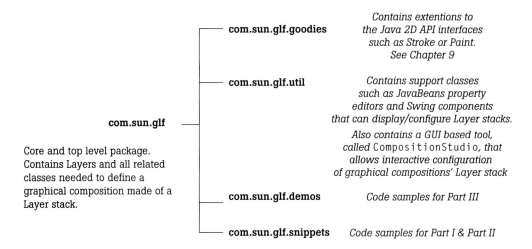

com.sun.glf.goodies — *Contains extentions to the Java 2D API interfaces such as Stroke or Paint. See Chapter 9*

com.sun.glf.util — *Contains support classes such as JavaBeans property editors and Swing components that can display/configure Layer stacks.*

Also contains a GUI based tool, called CompositionStudio, that allows interactive configuration of graphical compositions' Layer stack

com.sun.glf — *Core and top level package. Contains Layers and all related classes needed to define a graphical composition made of a Layer stack.*

com.sun.glf.demos — *Code samples for Part III*

com.sun.glf.snippets — *Code samples for Part I & Part II*

Figure 6.2 ■
The GLF packages

Overview of the GLF Packages

Figure 6.2 shows the different GLF packages and explains the main responsibility of each. Note that the snippets package is where all the code snippets for Part II can be found.

Our first example, "Hello Layers," illustrates the process of creating graphical compositions and experimenting with various options. In the process, it uses all of the GLF packages. This first example introduces the framework. The different packages are described in greater detail in the remaining chapters in Part II.

The "Hello Layers" Example

For the "Hello Layers" example, we want to display a text message centered in a rectangle. We want the background area to be filled with one of the GLF custom `Paint` implementations (`RadialGradientPaint`) and we want to create a shadow effect under the text. Figure 6.3 shows the desired output.

To achieve this result, we follow a three–step process:

1. Define the layer stack.
2. Create a *factory* that will generate the layer stack and define its set of options, such as colors and fonts.
3. Implement the factory.

Figure 6.3 ∎
"Hello Layers" Composition

Step 1. Defining the Layer stack

Our example can be described as a stack of three `Layer`s:

1. A background `Layer` consisting of a rectangle filled with a `RadialGradientPaint`
2. A text `Layer` displaying the text string
3. A shadow `Layer` displaying the text shadow

This stack[1] is depicted in Figure 6.4 in which we show the outline of the text so that the white text shows against the background.

Step 2. Creating a CompositionFactory and defining its option set

▼ **Creating a CompositionFactory**   In the Graphic Layers Framework, a `com.sun.glf.studio.CompositionFactory` creates a `com.sun.glf.Composition`. A `Composition` is an object able to perform arbitrary rendering on a `Graphics2D` object, just as the `SimplePainter` class we used in Chapter 3 (see "The SimplePainter class" on page 46):

```
public interface Composition{
  public Dimension getSize();
  // ...
  public void paint(Graphics2D g);
}
```

---

1. The order of layers in the stack is important. For example, if we rendered the background layer before the text layer (that is, the background layer *on top of* the text layer), then the text would be covered by the background and would no longer be visible.

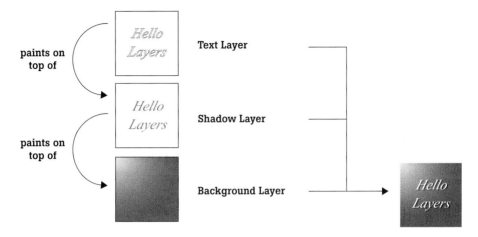

Figure 6.4 ■
"Hello Layers" layer decomposition

The CompositionFactory interface is further detailed in Chapter 7. It defines the size, in device space, of the area it renders through the getSize method and performs rendering through its paint method.

The LayerComposition class implements the Composition interface and performs rendering by drawing the different Layers in its stack.

Our HelloLayers class implements the CompositionFactory interface and creates a LayerComposition.

```
public class HelloLayers implements CompositionFactory{
  public Composition build(){
    // Create a layer composition where layers will be stacked.
    LayerComposition cmp = ...;

    // Return the LayerComposition we have created
    return cmp;
  }
}
```

Later in this chapter, we explain how the returned Composition is used by the different tools.

▼ **Defining the CompositionFactory option set**   There are a number of properties that describe the exact appearance of our "Hello Layers" example. So that they are modifiable through the GLF utilities, we make them attributes of the HelloLayers class and provide accessor methods to modify them:

```
public class HelloLayers implements CompositionFactory{
    //
    // Control parameters
    //
    String text = "Hello Layers";        // Displayed text
    Font textFont
        = new Font("serif",
                   Font.ITALIC, 90);      // Font used to display text

    Color textColor = Color.white;        // Color used to render text
    Color shadowColor
        = new Color(0, 0, 0, 128);         // Text shadow color

    Dimension size
        = new Dimension(400, 400);         // Overall composition size

    Color backgroundColorCenter
        = new Color(255, 234, 50);         // Yellow : radial gradient
                                           // center color
    Color backgroundColorOutside
        = new Color(153, 50, 0);           // Dark red : radial gradient
                                           // border color

    int shadowOffsetX = 7;
    int shadowOffsetY = 5;                 // Shadow offset, relative to
                                           // the text position

    //
    // Accessor methods for control parameters
    //
    public int getShadowOffsetX(){
      return shadowOffsetX;
    }

    public void setShadowOffsetX(int shadowOffsetX){
      this.shadowOffsetX = shadowOffsetX;
    }

    .... // Other accessors

    public Composition build(){
      ...
    }
}
```

The preceding code segment only shows accessor methods (that is, getProp-erty and setProperty methods) for the ShadowOffsetX attribute (getShad-owOffsetX, setShadowOffsetX). The actual code contains equivalent methods for all the other properties as well.

Note that we follow the JavaBeans™ naming pattern for the accessor methods: for a property called `propertyName` of type `propertyType`, the corresponding get and set methods have the following format:

```
public propertyType getPropertyName(){...}
public void setPropertyName(PropertyType newValue){...}
```

Chapter 8 explains how tools rely on this naming convention to automatically build a user interface for configuring a `CompositionFactory` object.

Step 3. Implementing the CompositionFactory: Creating and stacking Layers

Once we have decided on the set of control parameters, we can create `Layers` that make up our stack. This involves creating the individual `Layers` that we have identified and then stacking them up. Our example is made of three `Layers`: the background `Layer`, the text `Layer`, and the shadow `Layer`.

▼ **Creating a Layer stack**   Before creating any `Layer`, we create a `Layer-Composition` of a specific size (the canvas size), where the different `Layers` will be stacked.

```
LayerComposition cmp = new LayerComposition(size);
// size is one of the control properties
```

▼ **Background Layer**   We create a `ShapeLayer` to fill the background with a `RadialGradientPaint`. The `ShapeLayer` object can render any `Shape` with the help of a `Renderer`. A `Renderer` can, for example, fill or stroke a `Shape`. Here, we first create the `Shape` object that covers the background.

```
Rectangle rect = new Rectangle(0, 0, size.width, size.height);
```

Then, we create a `Paint` to fill that `Shape` object (remember that `Rectangle` is one of the `Shape` implementations. See Chapter 4, "Different types of shapes" on page 68).

```
Rectangle gradientRect
    = new Rectangle(-rect.width, -rect.height,
                2*rect.width, 2*rect.height);

RadialGradientPaint filling
    = new RadialGradientPaint(gradientRect,
                        backgroundColorCenter,
                        backgroundColorOutside);
```

We describe `RadialGradientPaint` in greater detail in Chapter 9 (see "Custom Paints" on page 304). The `gradientRect` parameter defines the bounds for the radial gradient. Here, the bounds are such that the gradient center matches the upper-left corner of the `Shape` object it fills, as illustrated in Figure 6.5.

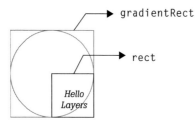

gradientRect

rect

Hello
Layers

Figure 6.5 ■
Creating a RadialGradientPaint

We then create a `Renderer` that will fill the `rect` `Shape`.

```
Renderer rectRenderer = new FillRenderer(filling);
// filling is the GradientPaint we just created
```

As we will see, `Renderer` defines the interface for objects able to perform atomic `Shape` rendering operations. Here, we use a `FillRenderer` that simply fills a `Shape` with a given `Paint` (the `filling` Paint), when requested.

The final step in creating the background `Layer` is the creation of a `ShapeLayer`.

```
ShapeLayer backgroundLayer = new ShapeLayer(cmp, rect, rectRenderer);
```

The `cmp` parameter specifies the `LayerComposition` instance this `Layer` is part of. The `rect` parameter specifies the `Shape` object this `ShapeLayer` object should render, and the `rectRenderer` specifies how the `Shape` object should be rendered (here, filled with a radial gradient).

▼ **Text Layer**   The second `Layer` that we create displays a string of text in the center of the composition.

```
TextLayer textLayer = new TextLayer(cmp,
                                    text,
                                    textFont,
                                    new FillRenderer(textColor));
```

As for `ShapeLayer`, the `cmp` parameter specifies the composition this `Layer` is part of. The `text` and `textFont` parameters describe the string to be displayed and the style of the character glyphs. Finally, as for `ShapeLayer`, we use a `FillRenderer` to fill the text block glyphs.

▼ **Shadow Layer**   To create the shadow effect, we reuse the `Shape` of the text block displayed by the `TextLayer` object:

```
Shape textBlock = textLayer.createTransformedShape();
```

The `createTransformedShape` method returns the text block as a `Shape` object, properly centered in the `LayerComposition` cmp. This object is used to create another `ShapeLayer`.

```
Renderer shadowRenderer = new FillRenderer(shadowColor);
ShapeLayer shadowLayer = new ShapeLayer(cmp, textBlock, shadowRenderer);

AffineTransform shadowTranslation
  = AffineTransform.getTranslateInstance(shadowOffsetX, shadowOffsetY);

shadowLayer.setTransform(shadowTranslation);
```

Note that this process is similar to the way in which the background Layer was created, except that a different Shape is used for the Layer and a different Paint is used for the FillRenderer. The textBlock Shape is defined in user space, and shadowTranslation is used to shift it.

▼ **Stacking Layers**   Once all the layers are created, the final step consists of stacking them in the desired order. Here, we put the background at the bottom, the shadow on top of it, and finally the text.

```
cmp.setLayers(new Layer[] {backgroundLayer, shadowLayer, textLayer});
```

Before returning the LayerComposition object we have created, we set the RenderingHints name/value pairs that should be used for rendering all the Layers in the Composition.

```
cmp.setRenderingHint(RenderingHints.KEY_ANTIALIASING,
                RenderingHints.VALUE_ANTIALIAS_ON);
```

Creating a Composition consists of the following actions:

1. Creating a LayerComposition of a given dimension
2. Creating the different Layers that, when drawn one on top of the other, produce the desired effect
3. Stacking layers in the order in which they should be drawn

Viewing the Hello Layers composition

We are at a point where we have code to build a LayerComposition. What do we do with it? The framework contains several classes that use Compositions for different purposes; these classes can naturally manipulate LayerCompositions as well because LayerComposition implements the Composition interface. For example, CompositionViewer displays in a JFrame Swing component the Composition built by a CompositionFactory. If we type the following at the command prompt[2]

```
java com.sun.glf.util.CompositionViewer com.sun.glf.snippets.HelloLayers
```

—we produce the frame shown in Figure 6.6.

2. The command assumes that glf.jar, included on the book CD-ROM, has been added to the CLASSPATH, as explained in the preface. Furthermore, the demorunner tool we describe in the book preface can run this code example.

Figure 6.6 ■
CompositionViewer

We did not use a Graphics2D object in this example. Why is that? The reason is that Layers allow us to describe *what* should be rendered and *how* it should be rendered. However, we are not doing any rendering. Rather, we are building a description. That description is used later by other components, such as CompositionViewer, to perform the corresponding rendering. We describe in detail how this works in Chapter 8 (see "The GLF Studio and Utilities: Experimenting with Layers" on page 278), but the core idea is simple.

CompositionViewer does the following:

1. Instantiates a HelloLayers CompositionFactory
2. Requests the HelloLayers instance to create a new Composition by invoking its build method (our implementation creates a LayerComposition)
3. Creates a Graphics2D object for the output (an offscreen buffer is used)
4. Requests the Composition object to render to the Graphics2D object

The LayerComposition object we return from the build method renders to the Graphics2D object by simply requesting each Layer to render itself to that Graphics2D object in turn. In our example, the background Layer fills a Rectangle, using a RadialGradientPaint, then the shadow Layer fills the text block using the shadow Paint, and finally, the TextLayer draws the text String using the text Paint.[3]

---

3. We will see later that LayerCompositions also have a backgroundPaint that can be used to fill the background. If you use the backgroundPaint, you need not create a ShapeLayer as we do in this example.

Modifying and experimenting with control properties

We use the CompositionStudio utility to tweak the composition control properties. To start it, we type the following at the command prompt.[4]

```
java com.sun.glf.studio.CompositionStudio com.sun.glf.demos.HelloLayers
```

This command summons the utility shown in Figure 6.7.

CompositionStudio allows easy modifications of a CompositionFactory properties (that is, properties of an object such as HelloLayers), previews the

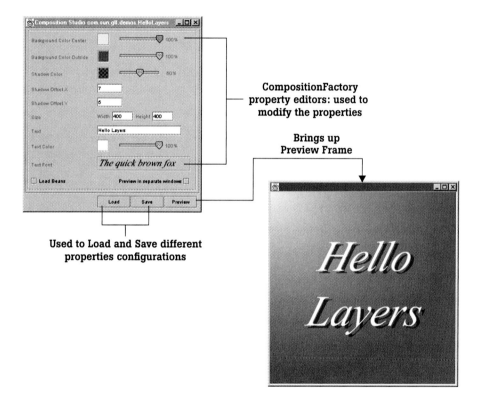

CompositionFactory property editors: used to modify the properties

Brings up Preview Frame

Used to Load and Save different properties configurations

Figure 6.7 ■
CompositionStudio

---

4. Again, this command assumes that you have the glf.jar file in the CLASSPATH.

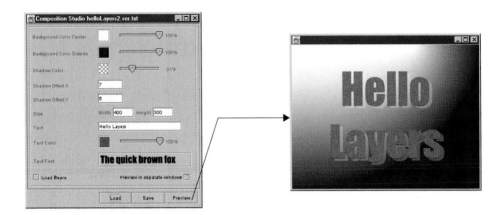

Figure 6.8 ■
Creating different configurations with CompositionStudio

effect of property changes, and loads or saves specific property settings. The different property editors are used to modify individual property values: Colors, text, Fonts, Strings, integers, etc.

For example, if we modify the attributes, as shown in Figure 6.8, and preview the corresponding output by selecting the Preview button, the output becomes quite different.

Conclusion

We have seen how the Graphic Layer Framework operates. It provides reusable rendering operations in the form of Layers: we used two types in our example: ShapeLayer and TextLayer. We have also seen how GLF provides supporting utilities, such as CompositionViewer, to render Layer stacks. Composition-Studio automatically scans a CompositionFactory object and creates a user interface that allows us to modify control parameters, preview the corresponding results, save and later load specific attribute configurations. Finally, we have used an extension of the Java 2D API, the com.sun.glf.goodies.RadialGradientPaint implementation of the Paint interface.

It is important to note the following key points about GLF:

1. *The core package is lightweight.* As we will see, there are only four types of `Layers`, and using them is straightforward.
2. *The utilities are helpers.* There is a lot more code in the `util` package than in the core `com.sun.glf` package. Those packages rely heavily on Swing and the JavaBeans specification. They are provided to ease the manipulation of the graphical compositions created in this book. However, we only discuss how to use them and not how they are designed, except when it is related to our main purpose of rendering effects.
3. *Extensions provided in GLF are not specific to GLF.* They can be used within GLF or directly with the Java 2D API.

The Graphic Layers Framework is simple, thin (core and goodies package), and easy to use (`util` package). The goal of GLF is to make it easy to combine the Java 2D features for specific rendering effects and also to be able to have fun modifying settings and visualizing results.

The "Hello Layers" example is typical of all the examples in the `com.sun.glf.demos` package: those examples are all `CompositionFactory` implementations, and we use `CompositionViewer` and `CompositionStudio` to display the `Compositions` they create. We describe how to use those tools in Chapter 8. Those tools rely on the design of the GLF core package that Chapter 7 describes. Our last chapter, Chapter 9, presents a number of extensions to the 2D API that our rendering effects in Part III use in combination with the standard API features, and also presents the `RadialGradientPaint` class.

While we are working to build a foundation for an easier programming model, appropriate for graphical compositions, we are going to address advanced Java 2D graphics issues. The most technically demanding sections in the following chapters are flagged with an "advanced" tag. Those sections typically detail how an internal feature of the Graphic Layers Framework is implemented and how it relies on the Java 2D features.

Understanding how the GLF is implemented is a good way to increase your command of Java 2D. However, you need not understand the GLF internal implementation to use GLF and have fun stacking up layers! Depending on your objectives, you can read or skip the advanced sections.

chapter 7

THE GLF CORE: WORKING WITH LAYERS

Introduction: Graphical Compositions

We said in the previous chapter that GLF addresses several needs. One is to simplify the creation of specific rendering effects, and another one is to simplify the management of configuration parameters. Those two needs are met by the `com.sun.glf.Composition` interface and its `com.sun.glf.LayerComposition` implementation shown in Figure 7.1. Utilities that manage properties rely on `Composition` and `LayerComposition`. As do all the classes we present in this chapter, `LayerComposition` and `Composition` belong to the GLF core package, the `com.sun.glf` package.

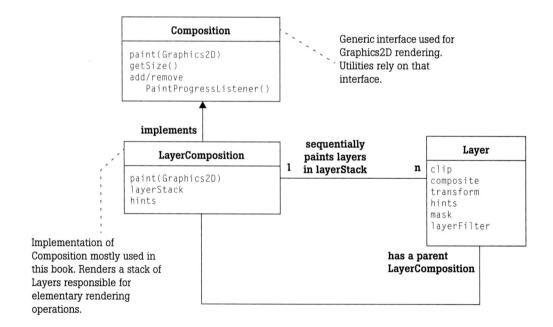

Figure 7.1 ■
Composition and LayerComposition

We saw with our "Hello Layers" example how the `CompositionStudio` utility relies on a `CompositionFactory` to build a `Composition`, which it displays and lets the user configure, and we discuss tools and utilities in Chapter 8.

In this chapter, we introduce the `Composition` interface and its responsibilities. Then, we introduce the `LayerComposition` implementation and discuss the `Layer` interface and its implementations. We will see that there are four extensions of the `Layer` class: `ShapeLayer`, `TextLayer`, `ImageLayer`, and `CompositionProxyLayer`. Each of these uses `Position` objects to ease placement of graphic objects (text, `Shapes`, or images) in a `Composition`, and we will explain how to use `Positions`.

The Composition interface

The following code describes the `Composition` interface.

```
public interface Composition{
  // Requests the composition to render into g
  // @param g the graphics into which drawing should happen.
  public void paint(Graphics2D g);

  // @return this composition's dimension, in device space
  public Dimension getSize();

  // @param listener object interested in paint progress updates
  public void addPaintProgressListener(PaintProgressListener l);

  // @param listener object no longer interested in paint
  //        progress updates
  public void removePaintProgressListener(PaintProgressListener l);
}
```

Translated into English, this code means that the responsibilities of a `Composition` are:

1. Be able to paint into a `Graphics2D` object. This is what the `paint` method is expected to do.
2. Define its size. The `getSize` method should return the size of the area drawn by the `Composition` object, in device space.
3. Allow interested parties to monitor progress of the painting operation. The `addPaintProgressListener` and `removePaintProgressListener` methods lets other objects (for example, tools using `Compositions`) to listen or stop listening to the paint progress of a `Composition`.[1]

---

1. This does not imply that painting is slow. However, some image manipulation techniques are time consuming and it is good to be able to monitor progress.

Most of the utilities we present in Chapter 8 ("The GLF Studio and Utilities: Experimenting with Layers") rely on the `Composition` interface. Because some rendering operations are time consuming, we felt that having a way for a tool to monitor the progress of a paint operation was important. This is what the `PaintProgressListener` interface allows:

```
public interface PaintProgressListener {
    public void paintStarted(Composition cmp, int paintSteps);
    public void paintStepStarted(Composition cmp, String stepDescription);
    public void paintFinished(Composition cmp);
}
```

A `Composition` implementation can decide to break down its `paint` operation into several steps and notify all its registered listeners when the `paint` operation starts, when it finishes, and every time an individual step is completed. This notification allows tools to give some feedback to the user.

It is important to note that the size of a `Composition` is defined in *device space* and starts at (0, 0) in that space (Figure 7.2).[2]

The `Composition` interface is at the center of the utilities that manipulate graphical compositions (such as `CompositionViewer` that we briefly introduced in Chapter 6 (see "Viewing the Hello Layers composition" on page 207). The Graphic Layers Framework comes with a single implementation of the `Composition` interface: the `LayerComposition` class.

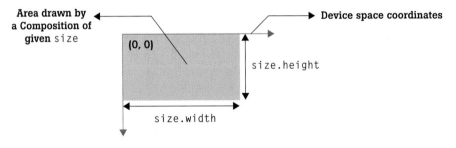

Figure 7.2 ■
Composition size and device space

---

2.   See "Coordinate spaces" on page 13 in Chapter 2 for a detailed discussion of user and device spaces.

Layers and LayerCompositions

We saw with the "Hello Layers" example that `LayerComposition` uses a stack of `Layers` such as `ShapeLayers` and `TextLayers` to describe what it renders. Figure 7.3 illustrates the relation between those classes and shows the four `Layer` implementations available in the framework: `ShapeLayer`, `TextLayer`, `ImageLayer`, and `CompositionProxyLayer`. Each of these implementations is described later in this chapter.

Using a layer paradigm is common in graphic tools and is a good mental representation of breaking down complex rendering effects.

In traditional drawing and painting, the layer paradigm takes the form of creating a complex drawing by stacking up transparencies, each one containing one simple element of the final artwork. This stacking approach provides flexibility to artists because they can change and replace some of the transparencies without redrawing the complete artwork.

Another advantage of transparencies is that they can be positioned relative to each other to create different results. For example, we can imagine having one transparency containing a background (for example, a beach), a character's outline (for example, your favorite cartoon mouse), and another with the color

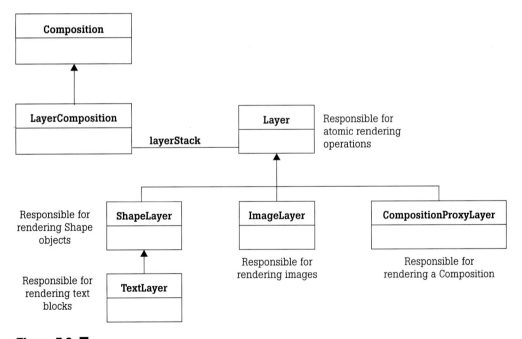

Figure 7.3 ■
LayerComposition and Layers

for the character's face and clothes. By modifying the content of the transparencies, we can change the color of the character's clothes, the background on which it appears (in a city), and the character itself (use your favorite duck now) and its position on the background. Layers provide a great deal of flexibility, even more so when translated to the computer environment.

In GLF, each Layer object (similar to a transparency) is responsible for an atomic rendering operation. The LayerComposition class is responsible for stacking and combining those operations.

The Layer abstract class

Layer is an abstract class that plays two roles:

1. *Defines the atomic rendering operation prototype.* The Layer class contains a paint method that is responsible for carrying out an arbitrary atomic rendering operation. For example, ImageLayer's paint method simply paints an image into a Graphics2D object.
2. *Holds a set of memento objects.* These memento objects (see next page) prepare the rendering context before a Layer's paint method is invoked (for example, clipping area, transform) and also define how a Layer combines with the underlying Layers (for example, filtered or masked).

The following pseudocode summarizes the Layer class.

```
public abstract class Layer {
  protected LayerComposition parent; // Parent composition

  //
  // Layer rendering context attributes
  //
  protected Composite composite;
  protected Shape clippingArea;
  protected RenderingHints hints;
  protected AffineTransform transform;


  //
  // If not null, the mask defines which parts of the Layer rendering
  // are actually painted to the output. Where the mask is transparent,
  // nothing is painted.
  //
  protected BufferedImage layerMask;

  //
  // The LayerFilter encapsulates either a BufferedImageOp
  // or a RasterOp that can be applied to a Layer
```

```
//
protected LayerFilter layerFilter;

//
// Accessor methods for memento attributes: get and set attributes
//
public Composite getComposite(){...}
public void setComposite(Composite composite){...}
public Shape getClippingArea(){...}
public void setClippingArea(Shape clippingArea){...}
public RenderingHints getRenderingHints(){...}
public void setRenderingHints(RenderingHints hints){...}
public void setRenderingHint(key, value){...}
public AffineTransform getTransform(){...}
public void setTransform(AffineTransform transform){...}

//
// Defining/Retrieving Layer mask
//
public BufferedImage getLayerMask(){...}
public void setLayerMask(BufferedImage mask, Rectangle maskRect){...}
public void setLayerMask(Shape shape, boolean invert){...}

// Performs the actual rendering
public abstract void paint(Graphics2D g);

// Returns the bounds of the area, in user space,
// that this Layer renders
public abstract Rectangle2D getBounds();

// @param parent the composition this layer belongs to. Should
// not be null.
protected Layer(LayerComposition parent){...}
}
```

We call the `Layer` attributes *mementos* because they are intended to be used by `LayerComposition`, not by the `Layer` extensions themselves. In other words, they are mementos for `LayerComposition` to remember how to set the context and combine the `Layers` in a `Composition`. The consequence for a `Layer` extension is that it need not bother setting up the graphic context in its `paint` implementation but just invoke rendering `methods`. The `Layer` abstract class implements all that is needed to support the attributes we just presented.

The `Layer` extensions, such as `ShapeLayer`, need only provide an implementation for the abstract `paint` and `getBounds` methods. The `paint` method should perform any rendering needed by the implementation. The `getBounds` method should return the area, in user space, that this `Layer` renders.

In the following section, we see how `LayerComposition` uses the different memento objects. Table 7.1 describes their meaning.

Table 7.1 ■ Description of Layer memento objects

MEMENTO	DESCRIPTION
composite	Composite attribute that should be set in the graphics context before painting this Layer on top of the other LayerComposition Layers.
clippingArea	Area, in *device* space,* outside which the Layer's rendering should have no effect.
hints	Hints that should be used for alternate rendering options this Layer might have.
transform	User space to device space transform for this Layer. This transform is set in the graphics context before this Layer is painted on top of the other LayerComposition Layers.
layerFilter	The LayerFilter class encapsulates either a BufferedImageOp or a RasterOp. If the layerFilter memento is set, then the output of the layer rendering is filtered before being combined with the underlying Layers in the layer stack.
layerMask	This image defines a mask. Only the part of the Layer rendering over opaque mask pixels (that is, white pixels for gray scale) are combined with the underlying Layers in the layer stack.

* Note that this is different from the clip in Graphics2D, which is defined in user space.

Using LayerCompositions

Building a LayerComposition is a four-step process:

1. Create a LayerComposition of a given size and set its back-groundPaint if needed.
2. Create various Layers that will be part of the stack.
3. Set the mementos for each Layer in the stack.
4. Set the LayerComposition RenderingHints if needed.

The resulting Composition can then be used for display. As in our "Hello Layers" example, the "Using Layers" example creates a LayerComposition in a CompositionFactory so that it can be used with the GLF utilities such as CompositionStudio.[3] This new example illustrates the different steps involved in using a LayerComposition. Here is its build method.[4]

```
public Composition build(){
  // Create a Composition of specific size. The size is based on
  // the mask Image size.
  BufferedImage mask
      = Toolbox.loadImage(maskImageFile, BufferedImage.TYPE_BYTE_GRAY);
  if(mask==null)
    throw new IllegalArgumentException("Cannot load : "
                                    + maskImageFile.getAbsolutePath());

  Dimension size = new Dimension(mask.getWidth(), mask.getHeight());
  LayerComposition cmp = new LayerComposition(size);
  cmp.setBackgroundPaint(Color.white);

  // Create an ImageLayer and set its mask memento
  BufferedImage image
      = Toolbox.loadImage(imageFile, BufferedImage.TYPE_INT_ARGB);
  if(image==null)
    throw new IllegalArgumentException("Cannot load : "
                                    + imageFile.getAbsolutePath());

  ImageLayer imageLayer = new ImageLayer(cmp, image);
  imageLayer.setLayerMask(mask);

  // Create a TextLayer and set its Composite memento
  Renderer textFill = new FillRenderer(textColor);
  Position textPosition
      = new Position(Anchor.BOTTOM, textMargins, textMargins);
  TextLayer textLayer
      = new TextLayer(cmp, text, textFont, textFill,
                      textPosition,
                      size.width,
                      TextAlignment.CENTER);

  textLayer.setComposite(ColorComposite.Hs);
                    // Hue and saturation of source.
                    // Brightness of destination

  // Create another layer for the textOutline
  Renderer textOutliner
      = new StrokeRenderer(textOutlineColor, textOutlineWidth);
  Shape textBlock = textLayer.createTransformedShape();
  ShapeLayer textOutlineLayer
      = new ShapeLayer(cmp, textBlock, textOutliner);

  // Stack up layers
  cmp.setLayers(new Layer[]{ imageLayer, textLayer, textOutlineLayer});
```

---

3. Refer to Chapter 8 for more details on these tools (see "Configuring a Composition" on page 297).
4. Variables such as `imageMaskFile`, `imageFile` or `textColor` are member variables in the `UsingLayers` class.

```
// Set LayerComposition RenderingHints. Consequently,
// antialiasing will be used on all layers.
cmp.setRenderingHint(RenderingHints.KEY_ANTIALIASING,
                     RenderingHints.VALUE_ANTIALIAS_ON);5
```

```
   return cmp;
}
```

The output of this LayerComposition is shown in Figure 7.4.

Note how the antialiasing setting applies to all the Layers in the stack: it is used both for textLayer and for textOutlineLayer. Also note that we are using some features that we have not yet seen in detail:

- ■ ImageLayer. This is one extension of the Layer class that renders an Image. We describe it further later in this chapter. We use this Layer type to render our Van Gogh painting.
- ■ ColorComposite. We use an instance of this Composite implementation in textLayer. This is one of the Java 2D extensions that comes with GLF. ColorComposite implements the Composite interface and composes a source and destination by mixing their Hue, Saturation, and Brightness components. Chapter 9 describes the operation of that Composite (see "Custom Composite" on page 328). The predefined Hs ColorComposite takes the hue and saturation of the source and the brightness of the desti-

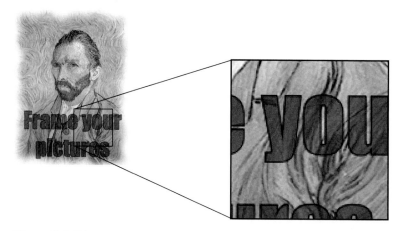

Figure 7.4 ■
UsingLayers output

5. Setting the RenderingHints in the LayerComposition object can be done at any time in the build method. RenderingHints settings are used when the LayerComposition object is rendered, not during the creation of the stack.

nation. Visually, it appears that the destination has the "edges" of the destination[6] and the "color" of the source. The `ColorComposite` class provides a kind of transparency effect that is different from the ones provided by the `AlphaComposite` class.

- `Toolbox`. We use this utility to load a `BufferedImage`. It is discussed on page 303.
- Masking. `ImageLayer` uses another image as a mask. To create the output shown in the figure, we used the following mask, which has the same size as the Van Gogh portrait. White pixels are interpreted as fully opaque and black pixels as fully transparent. Gray pixels are partly opaque: their opacity is proportional to their brightness. Only portions of the `Layer` on top of white of gray pixels show completely or partially through the mask.

gray scale
mask

The LayerComposition operation (Advanced topic)

Now that we have seen how to use `LayerComposition`, we turn to the way `LayerComposition` paints and we explain its operation.

`LayerComposition` has two attributes: a `backgroundPaint` attribute and `RenderingHints` attribute. Let us see how each is used in the `paint` process.

▼ **backgroundPaint**   The `backgroundPaint` fills the entire area rendered by `LayerComposition`, before any `Layer` is rendered.

```
public void paint(Graphics2D g){
    ...
    if(backgroundPaint != null){
        g.setPaint(backgroundPaint);
        g.fillRect(0, 0, dim.width, dim.height);
    }
    ...
}
```

6. Because the eye is more sensitive to brightness variations, our notion of edges tends to be associated with abrupt brightness changes more than with hue or saturation variations.

This method is really provided as a convenience because it is very common for the background of a Composition to be filled with a given Paint. Without this backgroundPaint, most LayerComposition would contain an equivalent background Layer. For example:

```
LayerComposition cmp = new LayerComposition(size);
Rectangle cmpRect = new Rectangle(0, 0, size.width, size.height);
ShapeLayer backgroundLayer = new ShapeLayer(cmp, cmpRect, new
FillRenderer(backgroundPaint);
....
cmp.setLayers(new Layer[] { backgroundLayer, ... });
```

Using the backgroundPaint attribute, we simply write:

```
LayerComposition cmp = new LayerComposition(size);
cmp.setBackgroundPaint(backgroundPaint);
```

The backgroundPaint attribute is provided for conciseness.[7]

▼ **RenderingHints** The LayerComposition hints are default rendering hints for all the Layers in the stack. However, if individual Layer Rendering-Hints are set, they take precedence. For example, in the execution of the following code segment—

```
LayerComposition cmp = new LayerComposition(size);
cmp.setRenderingHint(RenderingHints.KEY_ANTIALIASING,
                    RenderingHints.VALUE_ANTIALIAS_OFF);
Layer aliasedText = ...;
Layer antialiasedText = ...;
antialiasedText.setRenderingHint(RenderingHints.KEY_ANTIALIASING,
                                RenderingHints.VALUE_ANTIALIAS_ON);

cmp.setLayers(new Layer[] { .., aliasedText, .., antialiasedText, ..});
```

—the aliasedText will be rendered according to the default LayerComposition settings. Because the antialiasing is turned off by default in the Layer-Composition hints, the text will appear aliased. On the other hand, because the KEY_ANTIALIASING hint is set for the antialiasedText Layer, it takes precedence over the LayerComposition hint and the Layer will be rendered with antialiasing. We will see in the next section how this is managed inside LayerComposition's paint process.

▼ **The paint process** LayerComposition sequentially renders each Layer in its Layer stack. Even though each Layer has a paint method, that method will not be invoked on the same Graphics2D object as that of the LayerComposition if the layerMask or layerFilter is set. In that case, Layers are first rendered in an offscreen buffer.

---

7. As we noted earlier, the "Hello Layers" example could have used the backgroundPaint attribute.

Here is pseudocode describing the `LayerComposition` paint process.

```
public void paint(Graphics2D g){
  ...
  // Fill background with backgroundPaint
  // See earlier discussion

  // Create set of default rendering context attributes,
  // for the Composite, Clip, Transform, and RenderingHints

  // For example, for the Composite attribute
  Composite defaultComposite = g.getComposite();
  ...; // Get other default graphic context attributes

  // Default hints are handled differently: override
  // the Graphics2D default hints with this LayerComposition's
  // default hints.
  RenderingHints defaultHints = g.getRenderingHints();
  if(renderingHints != null) // renderingHints contains the
                              // LayerComposition hints
    defaultHints.putAll(renderingHints);

  // Now, render each Layer in turn
  for(int i=0; i<nLayers, i++){
    // layers contains the Layer stack. The bottom Layer is at index 0
    Layer layer = layers[i];

    // Set graphic context attribute, for example, the Composite
    Composite composite = layer.getComposite();
    if(composite != null) g.setComposite(composite);
    else g.setComposite(defaultComposite);

    ...; // Set other graphic context attributes

    //
    // Now, render layer
    //
    BufferedImage mask = layer.getLayerMask();
    LayerFilter filter = layer.getFilter();
    if(mask==null && filter==null)
      // No mask and no filter: render layer directly to Graphics2D
      layer.paint(g);
    else{
      // Create or reuse offscreen buffer
      BufferedImage offscreen = ...;

      // Render layer in offscreen buffer: offg is used to render
      // in offscreen
      Graphics2D offg = ...;
      ....
      layer.paint(offg);
```

Chapter 7 • The GLF Core: Working with Layers

```
        // If a filter is defined, filter now
        if(filterLayer != null)
            offscreen = filterLayer.filter(offscreen);

        // If a mask is defined, do masking now
        if(mask != null)
            doMasking(offscreen, mask);

        // Draw the offscreen buffer after filtering and masking
        g.drawImage(offscreen, ...);
    }
} // End of Layer painting loop
```

The graphic context is set up as follows before a `Layer` is rendered:

- Attributes (`Composite`, clip, transform, and hints) have their default values. For all those attributes, except `RenderingHints`, the default is the value of the input `Graphics2D` object at the time the `LayerComposition` paint method is invoked. For `RenderingHints`, the default input `Graphics2D` value can be overridden by the `LayerComposition`'s own default `RenderingHints`.
- If a `Layer` has a specific value for its attributes (that is, the mementos have been set), then that value is used. Otherwise, the default attribute is used.

This setup explains how the graphic context is prepared before `Layers` are requested to render into a `Graphics2D` object. Therefore, as we mentioned earlier, the `Layer` extensions need not bother with the graphic context, can assume the context is prepared properly, and should only invoke rendering methods.

The `Layer`'s paint method can be invoked with an offscreen buffer `Graphics2D` when filtering or masking is used. We first see how the smallest possible offscreen buffer is used. Then, we look at the filtering and masking processes.

▼ **Offscreen Layer rendering** Graphics rendering is expensive and some filtering operations are costly. It is important to limit rendering to just what is necessary, and this is what `LayerComposition` does for `Layer` offscreen rendering. Figure 7.5 illustrates the three rectangles `LayerComposition` uses to define the size of the offscreen buffer it needs: the `Composition`'s rectangle (`cmpRect`, in blue), the mask rectangle (`maskRect`, if a mask is defined, in green), and the `Layer`'s render rectangle (`renderRect`, in red), that is, the rectangle where the `Layer` performs rendering.

The following extract from the `LayerComposition` paint method shows how the appropriate offscreen buffer is calculated, as we illustrated.

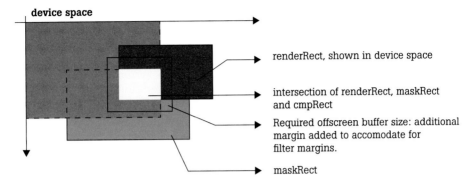

Figure 7.5 ■
Offscreen rendering

```
Rectangle cmpRect = getBounds();              // Device space
Rectangle maskRect = layer.getLayerMaskRect();  // Device space
Rectangle renderRect = layer.getBounds();     // User space

renderRect
  = transform.createTransformedShape(renderRect).getBounds();
                                              // Now in device space
                                              // Red rectangle in
                                              // figure.

renderRect = renderRect.intersection(cmpRect);  // Intersects red and
                                              // blue rectangles in
                                              // figure

if(maskRect!=null)                            // Intersect with green
   renderRect = renderRect.intersection(maskRect);// rectangle.

if(renderRect.width>0 && renderRect.height>0){  // If the renderRect is
                                              // empty, no need to
                                              // render anything.
   // Adjust size and position to accommodate for filter margin
   if(filter!=null){
      Dimension filterMargins
            = filter.getFilterMargins();       // Add filtering
                                              // margins if needed
                                              // and compute the size
      renderRect.x -= filterMargins.width;     // needed for the
      renderRect.y -= filterMargins.height;    // offscren buffer
      renderRect.width += filterMargins.width*2;
      renderRect.height += filterMargins.height*2;
   }

   ...
}
```

Next, we explain why it is useful to add margins around the area rendered by a Layer when a filter is defined.

At the end of the preceding code segment, renderRect defines the area, in device space, where rendering will actually happen with masking and filtering taken into account. This area is used to create, or reuse, an offscreen buffer.

```
// Create offscreen buffer
if(offScreen==null                              // No offScreen buffer
                                                // created yet
   ||
   offScreen.getWidth()<renderRect.width        // offScreen not wide enough
   ||
   offScreen.getHeight()<renderRect.height      // offScreen not high enough
   ||
   !isOffscreenCompatible(offScreen, layer      // offScreen not compatible
   )){                                          // with layer

     offScreen = createLayerCompatibleImage(layer, renderRect.width,
                                            renderRect.height);8
}

BufferedImage working
    = offScreen.getSubimage(0, 0, renderRect.width, renderRect.height);
offg = working.createGraphics();

// Clear working in case it has already been used
offg.setComposite(AlphaComposite.Clear);
offg.fillRect(0, 0, renderRect.width, renderRect.height);
offg.setComposite(AlphaComposite.SrcOver);
```

This code will create a new buffer only if one has not yet been created, if the existing one is not large enough or if the buffer type cannot be reused. If we are reusing a previously created offscreen buffer, chances are that it was of a larger but different size. The code uses getSubimage to retrieve a subpart of the offscreen buffer that has the appropriate size for the current Layer. The Alpha-Composite.Clear composition rule is used to reset all the pixels in the offscreen buffer to zero and start with a clean offscreen buffer.

At this, point, we can use working to render the current Layer object offscreen.

```
// Draw Layer offscreen
// Set offscreen transform to prepare offscreen rendering
offg.translate(-renderRect.x, -renderRect.y);
offg.transform(transform);

offg.setRenderingHints(hints);
layer.paint(offg);
```

8. createLayerCompatibleImage creates a BufferedImage.TYPE_INT_ARGB_PRE (i.e., alpha premultiplied standard RGB image) for all types of Layers, except for ImageLayers whose internal image is a BufferedImage. Then, the offscreen buffer is created with the same type as that image.

Figure 7.6 illustrates the purpose of the translation. The offscreen buffer has its own space that we refer to as the image space. The origin of the device space corresponds to the (–renderRect.x, –renderRect.y) point in image space. The layer transform is set after the translation, which means that it will apply first. The layer transform transforms coordinates from user space to device space, and the translation transforms coordinates from device space to image space where we are doing the rendering.

The offscreen buffer can now be used for filtering and masking.

▼ **Layer filtering**   One of the `Layer` mementos is a `LayerFilter` object. This class is a wrapper that accommodates either a `BufferedImageOp` or `RasterOp` and stores the filter margins.

```
static public class LayerFilter{
    private BufferedImageOp bFilter;
    private RasterOp rFilter;
    private Dimension filterMargins;

    public LayerFilter(BufferedImageOp filter){
      this.bFilter = filter;
      this.filterMargins = new Dimension(0, 0);
    }
```

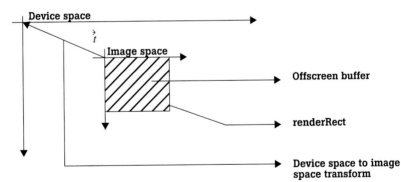

Device space to image space transform

$$T_{I \leftarrow D} = \vec{t}$$

User space to device space transform

$$T_{D \leftarrow U} = transform$$

User space to image space transform

$$T_{I \leftarrow U} = T_{I \leftarrow D} \otimes T_{D \leftarrow U}$$

Figure 7.6 ■
Defining the offscreen buffer size for a Layer

```java
    public LayerFilter(RasterOp filter){
      this.rFilter = filter;
      this.filterMargins = new Dimension(0, 0);
    }

    public LayerFilter(BufferedImageOp filter, Dimension filterMargins){
      this.bFilter = filter;
      this.filterMargins = (Dimension)filterMargins.clone();
    }

    public LayerFilter(RasterOp filter, Dimension filterMargins){
      this.rFilter = filter;
      this.filterMargins = (Dimension)filterMargins.clone();
    }

    boolean isRasterFilter(){
      return (rFilter != null);
    }

    public Dimension getFilterMargins(){
      return (Dimension)filterMargins.clone();
    }

    public BufferedImageOp getImageFilter(){
      return bFilter;
    }

    public RasterOp getRasterFilter(){
      return rFilter;
    }
}
```

BufferedImageOp vs. RasterOp

As we discussed in the first part of this book, there are two types of filters in Java 2D: `BufferedImageOp` and `RasterOp`. The first type operates on `BufferedImages` and the second one on `Rasters`. Because the `LayerComposition` uses an offscreen `BufferedImage` to render `Layers` for filtering, it can apply either a `BufferedImageOp` to the offscreen buffer or a `RasterOp` to the offscreen buffer's `Raster`. A `Layer` filter can be either of those, so we have two different methods to set the filter:

■ `setImageFilter` to set a `BufferedImageOp`
■ `setRasterFilter` to set a `RasterOp`

Here is how `LayerComposition` performs filtering of the offscreen buffer, using either a `RasterOp` or a `BufferedImageOp`.

```
LayerFilter filter = layer.getFilter();
if(filter!=null){
  if(filter.isRasterFilter()){
    //
    // RasterOp filter
    //
    RasterOp op = filter.getRasterFilter();
    WritableRaster workingRaster = working.getRaster();
    workingRaster
      = workingRaster.createWritableTranslatedChild(renderRect.x,
                                                    renderRect.y);

    WritableRaster filteredRaster
      = workingRaster.createCompatibleWritableRaster(working.getWidth(),
                                                     working.getHeight()
                                                     );

    op.filter(workingRaster, filteredRaster);

    working
      = new BufferedImage(working.getColorModel(),
                          filteredRaster,
                          working.isAlphaPremultiplied(),
                          null);
  }
  else{
    //
    // BufferedImageOp filter
    //
    BufferedImageOp op = filter.getImageFilter();
    working = op.filter(working, null);
  }

  offg = working.createGraphics();
}
```

Filtering as a `BufferedImageOp` (the `else` statement in the preceding code), is straightforward. The `filter.getImageFilter` method returns a `BufferedImageOp` object. Its `filter` method is invoked to carry out the filtering operation.

Filtering as a `RasterOp` is more sophisticated. The `filter.getRasterFilter` method returns the `RasterOp` object that should be used. Then, the `working Raster` is translated to the origin of the `renderRect` area.

```
WritableRaster workingRaster = working.getRaster();
workingRaster
  = workingRaster.createWritableTranslatedChild(renderRect.x,
                                                renderRect.y);
```

While all `BufferedImages` have their origin at (0, 0), this is not true for `Rasters`, which can have their origin anywhere. Some filters (for example, our `LightOp` filter, see "LightOp" on page 341) depend on the actual pixel locations. Creating a translated child with its origin at the "right" location in the device space ensures that such filters operate properly.

We mentioned that most of the filters provided in Java 2D are both `Buffered-ImageOp` and `RasterOp` implementations. When used with `Layer`s, should they be used as `BufferedImageOp` (that is, should the `setImageFilter` method be used) or should they be used as `RasterOp` (that is, should the `setRasterFil-ter` method be used)? When those filters have the same behavior in either form, it does not matter. However, most have different behaviors depending on whether they apply to `Raster`s or `BufferedImage`s. Consequently, we should set the filter through `setRasterFilter` when the `RasterOp` behavior is desired and use `setImageFilter` when the `BufferedImageOp` behavior is needed. You can refer to the filter documentation for details about differences in behavior for a specific filter. Furthermore, filters that have an operation related to the location of the pixels they process should be used as `RasterOp`s.

Most filters have a one-to-one mapping between pixels in the input image and pixels in the output image. However, some do not, and for those, the filter margins, which can be set together with a `Layer`'s filter, will prove useful.

▼ Filter margins What are filter margins? They are optional padding, defined in device space, that we add "around" the area rendered by a `Layer` offscreen before applying the filter.

Their purpose is to improve the results for filters such as `ConvolveOp` that process pixels areas. To get an accurate result, pixel processing should indeed extend beyond the limits of the image. For example, consider the following code example (**LayerMarginsUsage.java** on the CD-ROM).

```
Rectangle rect = new Rectangle(0, 0, rectWidth, rectHeight);
Renderer painter = new FillRenderer(color);

Dimension size
    = new Dimension(rectWidth + margins*2, rectWidth + margins*2);
LayerComposition cmp = new LayerComposition(size);
cmp.setBackgroundPaint(Color.white);

ShapeLayer blurredRect
    = new ShapeLayer(cmp, rect, painter, Position.CENTER);
ConvolveOp blur = new ConvolveOp(new GaussianKernel(blurRadius));
blurredRect.setImageFilter(blur, new Dimension(margins, margins));

cmp.setLayers(new Layer[]{blurredRect});
```

This code creates a `LayerComposition` with one `ShapeLayer` that contains a rectangle, centered in the composition. (The `Position.CENTER` parameter, in the `ShapeLayer` constructor, sets the `Layer` transform so that the input rectangle will be centered in the composition. Centering is described later in this chapter.) The area rendered by the `ShapeLayer` object will be filtered by a `ConvolveOp` object that uses a convolution kernel of specified radius.[9]

As we explained in Chapter 4 (see "ConvolveOp" on page 98), `ConvolveOp` does not convolve pixels at the image edges because the convolution kernel extends beyond the filtered image. It processes a subpart of the image, as illus-

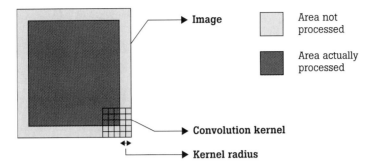

Figure 7.7 ■
ConvolveOp edge processing (A)

trated in Figure 7.7. The portion of the original image that is not processed can be set either to all zeros or to the values of the original image pixels.[10]

If we set filter margins, as in our example, we extend the area processed by the convolution (see Figure 7.8). If the margin is large enough, all the rendered area can be processed.

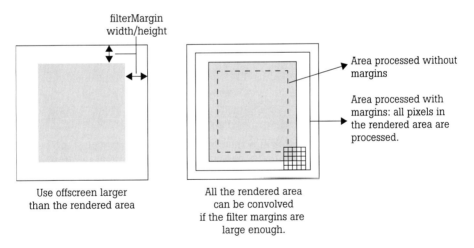

Figure 7.8 ■
ConvolveOp edge processing (B)

9. The GaussianKernel class is one of the com.sun.glf.goodies classes that extend the Java 2D API. It is a convenience class that builds a blurring convolution kernel of given radius. For a radius of blurRadius, the kernel matrix is (2*radius + 1) by (2*radius + 1) large.

10. This is a ConvolveOp option. See the API documentation for details.

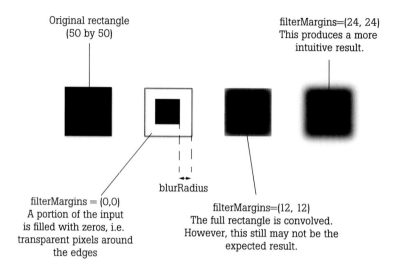

Original rectangle
(50 by 50)

filterMargins=(24, 24)
This produces a more
intuitive result.

blurRadius

filterMargins = (0,0)
A portion of the input
is filled with zeros, i.e.
transparent pixels around
the edges

filterMargins=(12, 12)
The full rectangle is convolved.
However, this still may not be the
expected result.

Figure 7.9 ■
Different values for the filter margins

Figure 7.9 shows the output of our code snippet with a kernel of radius 12 and various values for the filter margins.

The left rectangle shows the original rendering done by a Layer in the off-screen buffer. The second rectangle shows the result obtained with no margins. This result is equivalent to what ConvolveOp does by default: the edges are filled with zeros, and because we are using an alpha channel in the off-screen buffer, the edge pixels are transparent (alpha is zero). This explains why the input rectangle seems to have shrunk.

The third rectangle shows the result when the filter margins are set to (12, 12), that is, as wide as the blur radius. All the pixels in the original rectangle are convolved, but this still does not produce the expected result: the blurred edges seem to have been trimmed. Setting the margins to (24, 24), that is, twice as big as the blur radius, produces a more intuitive result—what we would call a blurred rectangle in the real world, which the other two rectangles are not.

The filter margins are useful for use in conjunction with convolutions. As a rule of thumb, the filter margins should be set to (0, 0) for most filters, except for convolutions where the best result is achieved with a margins twice as big as the convolution kernel radius, as we just showed.

We are now halfway through the LayerComposition paint process. We have seen how it can filter any of the Layers it paints. We are now going to see how it can mask Layers.

▼ **Layer masking**   A `Layer` mask is a gray scale `BufferedImage`. With the "Using Layers" example (see page 218) we saw that only the parts of the `Layer` object on top of white pixels in `layerMask` are rendered. In other words, `layerMask`'s black pixels mask the `Layer` object. Gray pixels partially mask the `Layer object`, in proportion to their brightness.

There are two situations where it is interesting to be able to mask out a `Layer`:

1. *Complex masks*. A good example of a complex mask is the one we used in the "Using Layer" program, where we created fuzzy edges around the masked image.

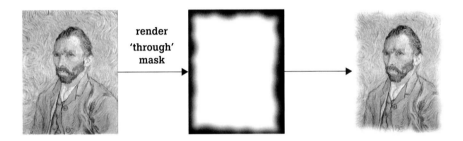

2. *Antialiased clipping*. As we mentioned in Chapter 5 (see "Clipping" on page 190), there are situations where clipping might not be satisfying because pixelation happens along the clipping path. Using a mask is a way to avoid this problem. For example, if we use the same `Shape` object as in Chapter 5, but use it to create a mask instead of setting the clip, we obtain the following result.[11]

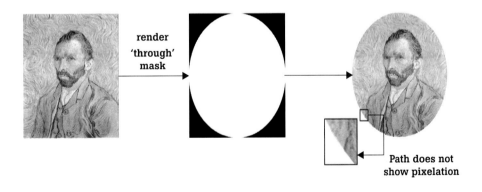

---

11. The ellipse is drawn in white, with antialiasing turned on. This is what creates an antialiased mask.

The mask is set in a `Layer` through one of its `setLayerMask` methods. There are four versions:

- `setLayerMask(BufferedImageOp mask)`. The `mask` parameter should be a gray scale image (or it will be converted to gray scale).
- `setLayerMask(BufferedImageOp mask, Rectangle layerMaskRect)`. The `layerMaskRect` parameter specifies where the mask should be anchored in device space.
- `setLayerMask(Shape shape)`. The input `shape` object is used to create a gray scale mask. Everything inside `shape` will be white (it will let the `Layer` show through), and everything outside the `shape` will be black (that is, it will mask out the `Layer`).
- `setLayerMask(Shape shape, boolean invert)`. The input `shape` is used to create a mask. If `invert` is false, the inside of the `Shape` object will be white (that is, it will not mask the `Layer` object). Otherwise, the inside of the `Shape` object will mask the `Layer` object. In both cases, a gray scale image is built.

All versions of `setLayerMask` call the second one in the preceding list. Here is its implementation.

```
public void setLayerMask(BufferedImage layerMask,
                         Rectangle layerMaskRect){
  .. // Check input arguments

  if(layerMask.getColorModel()!=maskColorModel){
    if(layerMask.getType()!=BufferedImage.TYPE_BYTE_GRAY){
      BufferedImage tmpMask
        = new BufferedImage(layerMask.getWidth(),
                            layerMask.getHeight(),
                            BufferedImage.TYPE_BYTE_GRAY);
      ColorConvertOp toGray = new ColorConvertOp(null);
      layerMask = toGray.filter(layerMask, tmpMask);
    }

    // At this point, we know that layerMask is TYPE_BYTE_GRAY.
    // Use the gray scale image to create a corresponding ARGB image,
    // with the alpha channel corresponding to the gray intensities.
    WritableRaster raster = layerMask.getRaster();
    layerMask = new BufferedImage(maskColorModel, raster, false, null);
  }

  this.layerMask = layerMask;
  this.layerMaskRect = layerMaskRect;
}
```

`maskColorModel` is a private `ColorModel` used by the `Layer` class to store mask data.

```
byte cmap[] = new byte[256];
for(int i=0; i<cmap.length; i++) cmap[i] = (byte)i;
maskColorModel = new IndexColorModel(8, 256, cmap, cmap, cmap, cmap);
```

The way in which `maskColorModel` is constructed will soon make sense. The `setLayerMask` implementation first checks whether the input mask already uses the internal mask model. If it does, it means that the input `BufferedImage` was created by a `Layer` object and need not be processed any further because it already has the right format. This behavior allows `Layers` to share the same mask object and not duplicate it.

If the input mask does not have the internal mask format, then it is processed. First, it is converted to a gray scale image if needed. This is what the `toGray` filtering does. Then, the gray scale raster is used to build a `BufferedImage` mask with `maskColorModel`. This is where the mapping between the gray scale pixel's brightness and an opacity happens. Using the gray scale `Raster` to build a `BufferedImage` that uses an `IndexColorModel` turns the gray scale values into indices in the color map. Black becomes index 0 and white becomes index 255. If you look at the color map, you can see that a pixel of intensity n becomes index n and maps to color (n, n, n, n) in the ARGB color space. This means that its opacity is proportional to its brightness. Black, at index 0, maps to (0, 0, 0, 0) and is fully transparent. White, at index 255, maps to (255, 255, 255, 255) and is fully opaque. At index 128, 50% gray maps to (128, 128, 128, 128) and is half transparent.

This transparency information in the mask that a `Layer` stores is used by `LayerComposition` to perform its masking operation. Here is how it happens in the `paint` method.

```
if(mask!=null){
    offg.setComposite(AlphaComposite.DstIn);
    offg.drawImage(mask, maskRect.x, maskRect.y,
                maskRect.width, maskRect.height, null);
    ...
}
```

The `DstIn` composition rule, which we discussed in Chapter 5 (see "Composite" on page 170), multiplies the destination pixels (here, our working offscreen buffer) by the source's alpha value (here, our mask). Because we have mapped our alpha values to the gray scale intensity of the mask, the result is that the offscreen buffer pixels become transparent when the mask is black and alpha is zero, and they will keep the same opacity when the mask is white and alpha is 255.

▼ **Finishing the paint process**   After masking the `Layer` object, we now have an offscreen `working` buffer that contains the `Layer`'s rendering as it should be combined with that of underlying `Layers` (or the `LayerComposition` background if processing the first `Layer` in the stack). Here is what the remainder of the paint process does.

```
g.clip(clip);
g.setComposite(composite);
g.drawImage(working, renderRect.x, renderRect.y, null);
```

The clip is applied at this time (remember that the `Layer` clip is defined in device space), as is the `Composite`. The offscreen buffer is drawn at the origin of the rendered area that `renderRect` describes.

We have gone into difficult issues of offscreen buffers and masking operations. Here, we have used those techniques in our `LayerComposition` implementations, but they can be reused in different contexts where the issues will be similar.

In the following sections, we present the different `Layer` implementations. They render the three elementary types of graphic objects: `Shapes`, text, images or `Compositions`. One of the objectives of GLF is to make programming easier, and one of the challenges of using Java 2D is to place graphics object properly. The `Position` class, in the core package (`com.sun.glf`), is used by the three `Layer` implementations to position objects properly inside a `Layer-Composition`. We explain how this class works before we introduce `ShapeLayer`, `TextLayer`, and `ImageLayer`.

Position

The `Shape` interface encapsulates the full geometrical description of an object, including the distinct aspects of form (for example, disc, square, Eiffel tower), size, and location.

Most people tend to mentally separate those notions, perhaps because in the real world, objects have a shape and can be moved around to be placed in different locations or in different positions. Moreover, we tend to think of location in relative terms: we put objects into others (for example, an envelope into a mailbox) or relative to each other (for example, a fork next to a plate). It is not very intuitive to think of object location relative to an absolute, fixed coordinate system.

The `Position` class offers a convenient way to reconcile the mathematical concepts of absolute coordinate systems and our mental process of relative placement. The idea is to easily determine `AffineTransforms` that will produce the desired result.

For example, imagine that we are using an arbitrary `Shape` object and that we want to draw it at the center of a given rectangle. Here is how you would code this positioning.

```
Graphics2D g = ...;              // Graphics2D where rendering
                                 // happens
Rectangle rect = ....;           // Rectangle where shape should
                                 // be centered
// First, draw rectangle
g.draw(rect);

//
// Process transform that will center shape in rect
//
Shape shape = ...;               // Arbitrary Shape object and bounding
                                 // rectangle
Rectangle shapeBounds = shape.getBounds();

AffineTransform t = new AffineTransform();
                                 // Center in rect
t.translate((rect.width-shapeBounds.width)/2,
          (rect.height-shapeBounds.height)/2);

t.translate(rect.x, rect.y);     // Move shape to rect's origin
t.translate(-shapeBounds.x,      // Move shape to origin[12]
          -shapeBounds.y);
g.transform(t);                  // Set centering transform
g.draw(shape);                   // Draws shape at the center of rect
```

This code is not overly complex, but centering is a simple case of positioning; even though centering is simple, it is easy to go wrong. Furthermore, it is common to position Shapes this way. The Position class contains a set of predefined values, and CENTER is one of them. By use of the predefined value for centering, the code becomes easier to write and read. The following code illustrates how Positions are used.

```
Graphics2D g = ...;              // Graphics2D where rendering happens
Rectangle rect = ....;           // Rectangle where shape should
                                 // be centered

// First, draw rectangle
g.draw(rect);

// Process transform that will center shape in rect
Shape shape = ...;               // Arbitrary Shape object
Rectangle shapeBounds
   = shape.getBounds()           // Shape's bounding rectangle

AffineTransform t
   = Position.CENTER.getTransform(shape, rect);
                                 // Returns the transform that will give
```

---

12. Remember that transform apply in the reverse order they are concatenated. Here, the move to the origin happens first. See "AffineTransform" on page 133 in Chapter 5 for details on AffineTransform.

```
                              // shape the desired position relative
                              // to rect.

g.transform(t);               // Set centering transform
g.draw(shape);                // Draws shape at the center of rect
```

This example illustrates the core idea of `Positions`: placement of `Shapes` relative to each other. A `Position` object can define the transform that will place a given `Shape` at a specified position within a rectangle.

The type of position is defined by an `Anchor` value, which defines an absolute relative placement definition, such as top, left, or bottom right. An object's position can be adjusted about its anchor with a vertical and horizontal adjustment. Finally, a `Position` can also apply a transform, *relative to the center of an object*, before or after positioning it. The following paragraphs explain each of these features in turn.

Anchoring objects

The `Anchor` class contains an enumeration of predefined absolute placement values. `Anchors` are used to build `Positions`. For example:

```
Position rightPosition = new Position(Anchor.RIGHT);
```

The following program places a `Shape`, our Eiffel tower, inside the rectangle defined by a background image. This program is reused several times in this section, as we vary the way the `Position` objects are created (see **Anchor-Placement.java** on the CD-ROM).

```
BufferedImage background
   = Toolbox.loadImage(backgroundImageFile, BufferedImage.TYPE_INT_RGB);
Graphics2D g = background.createGraphics();
AffineTransform defaultTransform = g.getTransform();

// Rectangle where shapes will be positioned
Rectangle rect
   = new Rectangle(0, 0, background.getWidth(), background.getHeight());

GeneralPath eiffel = new GeneralPath();
eiffel.moveTo(40.f, 20.f);
....; // Build Eiffel tower Shape.

// Create a GradientPaint to fill the Eiffel
// Tower. The top will be white and the bottom a pale orange.
Rectangle bounds = eiffel.getBounds();
GradientPaint gradient
   = new GradientPaint(0, bounds.y, Color.white,
                       0, bounds.y + bounds.height,
                       new Color(255, 185, 60));
```

```
Anchor anchors[] = { Anchor.TOP_LEFT,     Anchor.TOP,
                     Anchor.TOP_RIGHT,    Anchor.RIGHT,
                     Anchor.BOTTOM_RIGHT, Anchor.BOTTOM,
                     Anchor.BOTTOM_LEFT,  Anchor.LEFT,
                     Anchor.CENTER };

int n = anchors.length;
g.setPaint(gradient);

for(int i=0; i<n; i++){
   Position position = new Position(anchors[i]);
                   // Create new Position.

   g.transform(position.getTransform(eiffel, rect));
                   // Set Transform computed by Position
   g.fill(eiffel);     // Render Shape

   g.setTransform(defaultTransform);
                   // Restore default transform.
}
```

The output of this program is illustrated in Figure 7.10.

Note that the Position class also contains a set of predefined values, one for each of the Anchor values: Position.CENTER, Position.RIGHT, Position.LEFT, etc. Those values are for convenience, because classes that use relative positioning use Position objects and not Anchor objects. In other words, instead of creating this code—

```
Position rightPos = new Position(Anchor.RIGHT);
```

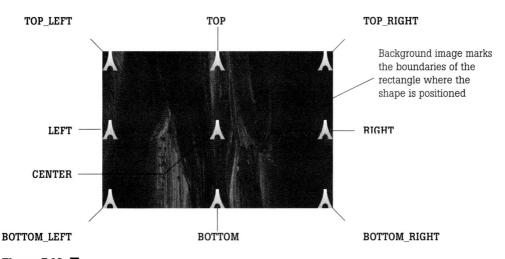

Figure 7.10 ■
The different Anchor values

—we can use the `Position.RIGHT` predefined `Position`. But why have both the notions of `Anchor` and `Position`? `Anchor` only captures an absolute placement. `Positions` can be adjusted about the anchor and, as we mentioned, can add an arbitrary transform relative to the center of the object to be placed.

Adjusting positions about the anchor

There are times when the `Anchor` placement needs to be adjusted to leave extra margins. `Position` allows this adjustment if the `hAdjust` (horizontal adjustment) and `vAdjust` (vertical adjustment) attributes are set. For example—

```
Position bottomRightPosition
    = new Position(Anchor.BOTTOM_RIGHT,
                    40,         // horizontal adjustment: right margin
                    60);        // vertical adjustment: bottom margin
```

—creates a `Position` that will place objects at the bottom right of the relative rectangle, adding a bottom margin (vertical adjustment) of 60 points and a right margin of 40 points (horizontal adjustment). The adjustment semantic is related to the `Anchor` value, as listed in Table 7.2. The values are best thought of as margins.

Table 7.2 ■ vAdjust and hAdjust Anchor adjustments

ANCHOR	HADJUST	VADJUST
Top Left	left margin	top margin
Top	NA	top margin
Top Right	right margin	top margin
Right	right margin	NA
Bottom Right	right margin	bottom margin
Bottom	NA	bottom margin
Bottom Left	left margin	bottom margin
Left	left margin	NA
Center	NA	NA

Figure 7.11 shows the result of positioning our Eiffel tower `Shape` relative to the background image's rectangle, using a vertical adjustment of 60 and a horizontal adjustment of 40 for the different `Anchor` values. The program that creates this output (**AdjustedAnchorPlacement.java** on the CD-ROM) is similar to our previous example, and only the `Position` creation differs.

```
for(int i=0; i<n; i++){
  Position position = new Position(anchors[i], 40, 60);
  ...
}
```

Applying transforms about an object's center

We mentioned in Chapter 5 (see "AffineTransform" on page 133) how some transforms are sometimes more intuitive when they apply about an object's center. For example, when we think of rotating an object, we usually think about rotating it about its center.

An object's placement can be further adjusted with a transform that applies about the object's center. For example:

```
AffineTransform shearNrotate =
AffineTransform.getRotateInstance(Math.PI/4);
shearNrotate.shear(-0.2f, -0.2f);
Position leftPosition = new Position(Anchor.LEFT, 40, 60, shearNrotate);
```

Figure 7.12 shows the output of our example program, now using an additional adjusting transform (see **AnchorPlacementTransform.java** on the CD-ROM).

```
Position position // Create new Position
  = new Position(anchors[i], 40, 60, shearNrotate);.
```

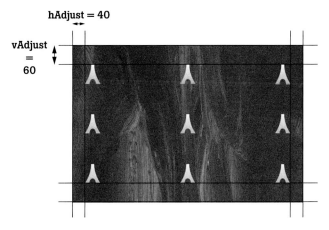

Figure 7.11 ▪
Adjusting positions about the anchor

Note how the `shearNrotate` transform applies about the Eiffel tower's center.

There is a final twist to the relative placement that `Positions` make: it is possible to control whether the adjusting, center-relative transform should apply to the `Shape` object before it is positioned or after. This distinction may be important, especially if the adjusting transform modifies the size of the object it transforms. When constructing a `Position` object, we can use a boolean parameter to define the desired behavior: place before transforming or transform before placing. For example—

```
AffineTransform scaleShearNrotate =
AffineTransform.getRotateInstance(Math.PI/4);
scaleShearNrotate.shear(-0.2f, -0.2f);
scaleShearNrotate.scale(5, 5);
boolean placeBeforeTxf = true;
Position leftPosition
    = new Position(Anchor.LEFT,   // Absolute anchoring position
              40,                 // Horizontal adjustment
              60,                 // Vertical adjustment
              scaleShearNrotate,  // Center-relative adjustment transform
              placeBeforeTxf);    // Transform before or after
                                  // positioning the Shape.
```

—creates a `Position` object that places the `Shape` object and then applies the transform about its center in that position. Figure 7.13 shows the influence of this setting. On the left, the transform is applied after the Eiffel tower has been placed at the desired position (that is, according to its `Anchor` and vertical and horizontal adjustments). On the right, the transform is applied before the `Shape` object is positioned relative to the rectangle.

`Positions` are very convenient for placing graphic object relative to one another. As we see in the next section, `ShapeLayer`, `TextLayer`, `ImageLayer`, and `CompositionProxyLayer` can all use `Positions`.

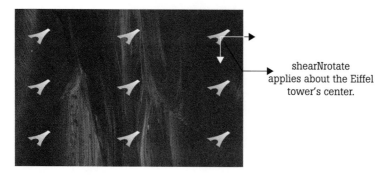

shearNrotate
applies about the Eiffel
tower's center.

Figure 7.12 ■
Adjusting positions with transform

Adjusting transform applies to the object's center after it has be positioned according to the Anchor, vertical and horizontal adjustments.

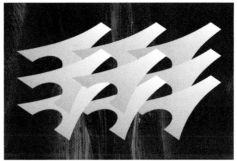

Adjusting transform is applied to the object. Then, the transformed object is positioned according to the Anchor, vertical and horizontal adjustments.

Figure 7.13 ■
Applying adjusting transform before or after positioning a Shape

ShapeLayer

Figure 7.3 on page 215 shows that the `ShapeLayer` class is responsible for rendering a `Shape` object. In the following paragraphs, we describe in detail how `ShapeLayer` operates and introduce the notion of `Renderer`. As we discuss how `ShapeLayer` operates, we will see how it uses `Positions` to easily place `Shape` objects inside a `LayerComposition`.

ShapeLayer operation: Placing Shapes and using Renderers

`ShapeLayer` provides two features to simplify `Shape` rendering: it places `Shapes` in the `LayerComposition` and it renders them. The automated `Shape` placement is optional and is provided by the constructor that uses a `Position` as an input parameter.

Rendering is delegated to `Renderers`: they are responsible for basic `Shape` rendering operations, such as: filling, stroking, etc. Figure 7.14 illustrates the three implementations of the `Renderer` interface that GLF provides:

■ `FillRenderer`
■ `StrokeRenderer`
■ `CompositeRenderer`

The `ShapeLayer` `paint` implementation is straightforward.

```
public void paint(Graphics2D g){
  renderer.render(g, shape);
}
```

ShapeLayer simply requests its associated Renderer to render its Shape. Note that the same Renderer instance can be used by different ShapeLayer objects: *Renderers provide reusable elementary rendering operations.* In our first examples, we have already used ShapeLayer. For example, the "Using Layers" example on page 218 used a ShapeLayer to outline the text block.

```
Renderer textOutliner
    = new StrokeRenderer(textOutlineColor, textOutlineWidth);
Shape textBlock = textLayer.createTransformedShape();
ShapeLayer textOutlineLayer
    = new ShapeLayer(cmp, textBlock, textOutliner);
```

A Shape and a Renderer are the only two required inputs to build a Shape-Layer. Another constructor takes an extra Position argument to place Shapes in the LayerComposition the Layer is part of, that is, to process the ShapeLayer's transform automatically. We now look at the different Renderer implementations and see how they can be used.

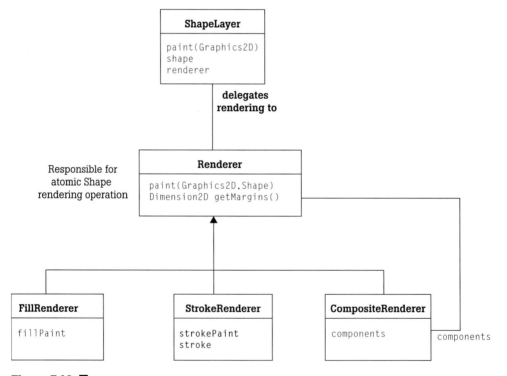

Figure 7.14 ■
ShapeLayer and Renderers

FillRenderer

FillRenderer fills a Shape with the Paint object it is given at construction time. Here is the code for FillRenderer's render method.

```
public void render(Graphics2D g, Shape shape){
    g.setPaint(filling);
    g.fill(shape);
}
```

Let us use a FillRenderer to render our Eiffel tower Shape as well as an Ellipse2D Shape. The program we describe next, **EiffelFill.java** on the CD-ROM, produces the output shown in Figure 7.15.

Creating the Shapes is straightforward.

```
GeneralPath eiffel = new GeneralPath();
eiffel.moveTo(40.f, 20.f);
...;

Rectangle bounds = eiffel.getBounds();

Ellipse2D ellipse = new Ellipse2D.Float(bounds.x, bounds.y,
                                        bounds.width, bounds.height);
```

Note how the ellipse Shape overlaps the eiffel Shape in the user space. Now, we use the two Shapes to compute the size of a LayerComposition. We want to position the two Shapes side by side, as illustrated in Figure 7.16, with some margins around the Shapes.

This positioning defines how the Shapes will appear in device space (that is, on the screen for screen rendering). The first step consists of computing the LayerComposition size—

```
int margins
    = (int)(0.10*bounds.height);            // Margins are 10% of the
                                            // Shape's height
Dimension size
    = new Dimension(2*bounds.width + 3*margins, // Margins to the left,
                                            // between the shapes and
                                            // to the right
            bounds.height + 2*margins);     // Top and bottom
                                            // margins.
```

Figure 7.15 ■
Using a FillRenderer

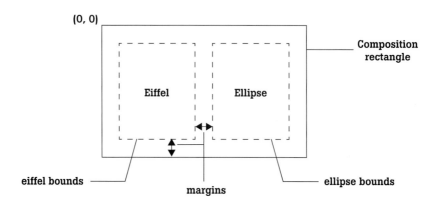

Figure 7.16 ■
Desired Shape positions

—which can be used to create the `LayerComposition`:

```
LayerComposition cmp = new LayerComposition(size);
cmp.setBackgroundPaint(Color.white);
```

Now, we can create a `FillRenderer` to fill our `Shapes`. The `FillRenderer` object is created with a `GradientPaint` from the top of the `Shape` to its bottom.

```
Color blue = new Color(100, 100, 200);
Color black = Color.black;
Paint gradientPaint
   = new GradientPaint(0, bounds.y, blue,
                       0, bounds.y + bounds.width, black);
FillRenderer filling = new FillRenderer(gradientPaint);
```

The `filling` object is used, as would be any other `Renderer`, to build `Shape-Layers` that are stacked in our `LayerComposition`.

```
Position eiffelPosition = new Position(Anchor.LEFT, margins, 0);
ShapeLayer eiffelLayer
   = new ShapeLayer(cmp,         // LayerComposition the layer belongs to
                    eiffel,      // Shape to be rendered
                    filling,     // Renderer to use to render the Shape
                    eiffelPosition);  // Shape position in cmp

Position ellipsePosition = new Position(Anchor.RIGHT, margins, 0);
ShapeLayer ellipseLayer
   = new ShapeLayer(cmp,
                    ellipse,
                    filling,
                    ellipsePosition);

cmp.setLayers(new Layer[]{ eiffelLayer, ellipseLayer }); // Stack up
                                                         // layers
```

```
cmp.setRenderingHint(RenderingHints.KEY_ANTIALIASING,
                     RenderingHints.VALUE_ANTIALIAS_ON);
// As we explained (see "Layers and LayerCompositions" on page 215),
// this will be used as the default aliasing hint for all layers
// in the stack.
```

The important things to note here are:

1. The Shape and Renderer parameters define what the layer renders (Shape) and how it renders it (Renderer).
2. The cmp parameter defines the LayerComposition instance of which the ShapeLayer object is a part.
3. The Position parameter is used by ShapeLayer to compute the appropriate Layer AffineTransform so that the input Shape objects appear at the desired relative position in the composition.

Position is an easy way to indirectly set the layer's AffineTransform memento. Internally, Position is used as we explained in the previous section.

```
public ShapeLayer(LayerComposition parent,
                  Shape shape, Renderer renderer, Position position){
  super(parent);

  if(shape==null||renderer==null)
    throw new IllegalArgumentException();

  this.renderer = renderer;
  this.shape = shape;
  if(position!=null)
    setTransform(position.getTransform(shape, parent.getBounds()));
}
```

Important Note

ShapeLayer does not require the use of Position, *and it has a constructor that takes no* Position *parameter. For example, we could have processed the appropriate placement transforms and written our example as follows.*

```
AffineTransform eiffelTransform
    = ...;           // Compute proper placement transform for Eiffel
AffineTransform ellipseTransform
    = ...;           // Compute proper placement transform for ellipse
ShapeLayer eiffelLayer = new ShapeLayer(cmp, eiffel, filling);
eiffelLayer.setTransform(eiffelTransform);
ShapeLayer ellipseLayer = new ShapeLayer(cmp, ellipse, filling);
ellipseLayer.setTransform(ellipseTransform);
```

The remainder of our example simply uses the LayerComposition object we have built for display in a frame. CompositionFrame is one of the utility classes we discuss in the following chapter.

```
CompositionFrame frame = new CompositionFrame("Filling Shapes with a
FillRenderer");
frame.setComposition(cmp);
frame.pack();

frame.addWindowListener(new WindowAdapter(){
  public void windowClosing(WindowEvent evt){
    System.exit(0);
  }
});
frame.setVisible(true);
```

We have seen several important points about ShapeLayer. First, it uses a Renderer to perform the appropriate Shape rendering, and our example showed how a GradientPaint is used (as could be any other Paint) by the FillRenderer implementation. Second, ShapeLayer can use Position objects to define the relative placement of the Shape it renders inside the LayerComposition it belongs to. This makes processing of AffineTransform transparent to the programmer since it automates computing of commonly needed transformations.

In the following sections, we present the other types of Renderer implementations, StrokeRenderer and CompositeRenderer. We also use each example as an opportunity to further illustrate the use of Position.

StrokeRenderer

This implementation of the Renderer interface renders a Shape by stroking its outline, using the Stroke and Paint objects it is given at construction time. The render method sets the Paint and Stroke context attribute and then invokes the Graphics2D draw method.

```
public void render(Graphics2D g, Shape shape){
  g.setStroke(stroke);
  g.setPaint(strokePaint);
  g.draw(shape);
}
```

The following example, **EiffelStroke.java** on the CD-ROM, is almost identical to the previous one, except in two regards:

■ It places the Eiffel tower and ellipse differently.
■ It uses StrokeRenderer instead of FillRenderer.

The output of the program is shown in Figure 7.17.

In this new example, the LayerComposition size is computed according to the desired layout—

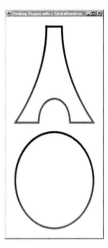

Figure 7.17 ■
Using a StrokeRenderer

```
Dimension size
   = new Dimension(bounds.width + 2*margins,    // Left & right margins
                   2*bounds.height + 3*margins);// Top, center & bottom
                                                // margins

LayerComposition cmp = new LayerComposition(size);
cmp.setBackgroundPaint(Color.white);
```

—and the Shape Positions are different:

```
Position eiffelPosition = new Position(Anchor.TOP, 0, margins);
Position ellipsePosition = new Position(Anchor.BOTTOM, 0, margins);
```

The following code creates the StrokeRenderers that are then used to build
the ShapeLayers.

```
Color blue = new Color(100, 100, 200);
Color black = Color.black;
Paint gradientPaint
   = new GradientPaint(0, bounds.y, black,
                       0, bounds.y + bounds.width, blue);
Stroke stroke = new BasicStroke(6);
StrokeRenderer outline
   = new StrokeRenderer(gradientPaint, // Paint used to fill the outline
                        stroke);       // Stroke used to generate the
                                       // outline Shape

ShapeLayer eiffelLayer
   = new ShapeLayer(cmp, eiffel, outline, eiffelPosition);

ShapeLayer ellipseLayer
   = new ShapeLayer(cmp, ellipse, outline, ellipsePosition);
```

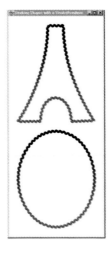

Figure 7.18 ■
StrokeRenderer can use any Stroke
implementation

Note that we use the `BasicStroke` implementation of the `Stroke` interface.
`FillRenderer` and `StrokeRenderer` can work with any implementation of
the `Stroke` and `Paint` interface just as `Graphics2D` can. For example, we could
have used our `WaveStroke`[13] implementation instead of `BasicStroke`—

```
Stroke stroke = new WaveStroke(6);
StrokeRenderer outline = new StrokeRenderer(gradientPaint, stroke);
```

—and obtained the result shown in Figure 7.18.

CompositeRenderer

This last implementation of the `Renderer` interface combines the rendering
operations of component `Renderer`s it is initialized with. Its `render` method is:

```
public void render(Graphics2D g, Shape shape){
  for(int i=0; i<components.length; i++){
    components[i].render(g, shape);
  }
}
```

where `components` is the array of `Renderer`s that `CompositeRenderer` combines.

Our new example, **EiffelComposite.java** on the CD-ROM, is another variation
on the same theme of Eiffel and ellipse rendering. The difference is again in
the way the `Shape`s are positioned and rendered. The output of the program is
shown in Figure 7.19.

---

13. See"WaveStroke" on page 325 in Chapter 9 for more details on `WaveStroke`.

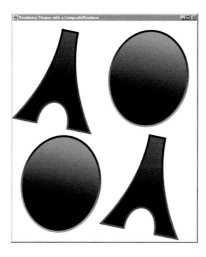

Figure 7.19 ■
Using a CompositeRenderer

Again, the `LayerComposition` size is based on the `Shape` size and the desired layout.

```
Dimension size
    = new Dimension(bounds.width*2 + margins*3,    // Left, center and
                                                   // right margins
                    bounds.height*2 + margins*3); // Top, center and
                                                   // bottom margins.
LayerComposition cmp = new LayerComposition(size);
cmp.setBackgroundPaint(Color.white);
```

Here, we need four different `Positions`, one for each of the rendered `Shapes`.

```
AffineTransform rotation
    = AffineTransform.getRotateInstance(Math.PI/16);

Position topEiffelPos
    = new Position(Anchor.TOP_LEFT, margins, margins, rotation);
Position bottomEiffelPos
    = new Position(Anchor.BOTTOM_RIGHT, margins, margins, rotation);
Position topEllipsePos
    = new Position(Anchor.TOP_RIGHT, margins, margins, rotation);
Position bottomEllipsePos
    = new Position(Anchor.BOTTOM_LEFT, margins, margins, rotation);
```

Note that we use a transform that does apply to the `Shape`'s center, when used. Creating `CompositeRenderers` implies that we first build simple `Renderers`. Here, we build four: two `FillRenderers` and two `StrokeRenderers`. The `StrokeRenderers` and `FillRenderers` use opposite `GradientPaints`, that is, `GradientPaints` with the same end points but opposite `Colors`.

```
Color blue = new Color(100, 100, 200);
Color green = new Color(100, 200, 100);
Color black = Color.black;

Paint blueStrokeGradientPaint
    = new GradientPaint(0, bounds.y, black,
                        0, bounds.y + bounds.width, blue);

Paint blueFillGradientPaint
    = new GradientPaint(0, bounds.y, blue,
                        0, bounds.y + bounds.width, black);

Paint greenStrokeGradientPaint
    = new GradientPaint(0, bounds.y, black,
                        0, bounds.y + bounds.width, green);


Paint greenFillGradientPaint
    = new GradientPaint(0, bounds.y, green,
                        0, bounds.y + bounds.width, black);

Stroke stroke = new BasicStroke(6);

// Build CompositeRenderer for 'blue' rendering
StrokeRenderer blueOutline
    = new StrokeRenderer(blueStrokeGradientPaint, stroke);
FillRenderer blueFilling
    = new FillRenderer(blueFillGradientPaint);
CompositeRenderer blueComposite
    = new CompositeRenderer(blueFilling, blueOutline);

// Build CompositeRenderer for 'green' rendering
StrokeRenderer greenOutline
    = new StrokeRenderer(greenStrokeGradientPaint, stroke);
FillRenderer greenFilling
    = new FillRenderer(greenFillGradientPaint);
CompositeRenderer greenComposite
    = new CompositeRenderer(greenFilling, greenOutline);
```

These Renderers are then used to build our ShapeLayers as we did before.

```
ShapeLayer topEiffelLayer
    = new ShapeLayer(cmp, eiffel, blueComposite, topEiffelPos);
ShapeLayer topEllipseLayer
    = new ShapeLayer(cmp, ellipse, greenComposite, topEllipsePos);
ShapeLayer bottomEiffelLayer
    = new ShapeLayer(cmp, eiffel, blueComposite, bottomEiffelPos);
ShapeLayer bottomEllipseLayer
    = new ShapeLayer(cmp, ellipse, greenComposite, bottomEllipsePos);

cmp.setLayers(new Layer[]{ topEiffelLayer,
                           topEllipseLayer,
                           bottomEiffelLayer,
                           bottomEllipseLayer });
```

Note that a `Renderer` instance can be used by multiple `ShapeLayers` (for example, `blueComposite` is used by two `ShapeLayers`) and also by multiple `CompositeRenderers`. Also, because it is common to combine exactly two `Renderers` for filling and stroking, as in our example, the `CompositeRenderer` class contains a convenience constructor that takes two `Renderers` instead of an array. However, if more `Renderers` should be combined, the array base constructor can be used.

```
CompositeRenderer composite
     = new CompositeRenderer(new Renderer[]{rendererA,
                                            rendererB,
                                            rendererC, ...});
```

Setting ShapeLayer mementos

The characteristics of `ShapeLayer` that we have just described are simple: `Renderers` encapsulate atomic rendering strategies that can be reused, and `Shape` objects can be positioned in a `LayerComposition` through the use of `Positions`. `ShapeLayer` also inherits the capabilities of the abstract `Layer` class it derives from; its mask, filter, `Composite`, clipping area, and hints attributes all influence rendering.

After a presentation of the `TextLayer`, `ImageLayer`, and `CompositionProxyLayer` classes, we next look at an example that shows how combining simple `Layers` and setting their mementos provides a powerful and concise description of complex rendering operations.

TextLayer

Figure 7.3 on page 215 shows that `TextLayer` extends `ShapeLayer`. In Chapter 4, we discussed how `Font` can turn characters into `Shapes` (see "Advanced text rendering with TextLayout and LineBreakMeasurer" on page 118). That technique is what `TextLayer` uses to provide convenience methods and constructors that make it easier to manipulate text: the actual rendering totally relies on the `ShapeLayer` implementation.

Operation

The `TextLayer` construction is similar to that of `ShapeLayer`, except that `Strings`, and `Fonts` or `AttributedStrings` are used as an input instead of `Shapes`. For example, the "Hello Layers" example used `TextLayer`.

```
Renderer filling = new FillRenderer(textColor);
TextLayer textLayer
    = new TextLayer(cmp,      // LayerComposition the textLayer is
                              // part of
                    text,     // Text drawn by this layer
                    textFont, // Font used to render text
                    filling); // Renderer responsible for
                              // rendering text.
```

The implementation of this constructor actually turns the input text into a `Shape` object, which we call a text block, and hands it to the `ShapeLayer` parent constructor.

```
public TextLayer(LayerComposition parent, String text, Font font,
Renderer renderer){
  super(parent,                       // Parent LayerComposition
        // makeTextBlock returns a Shape representing the text block.
        // By default, lines wrap at the LayerComposition's width and
        // are centered relative to each other.
        makeTextBlock(text, font,
                      parent.getSize().width,
                      TextAlignemtn.CENTER),
        renderer,                      // ShapeLayer Renderer parameter
        Position.CENTER);              // By default, text blocks
                                       // are centered.
}
```

Note that by default, a text block is centered in the `LayerComposition` it is part of.

The `makeTextBlock` method is the heart of the `TextLayer` implementation: it converts text into `Shape` objects, and it relies on the Java 2D features we introduced in the first part of this book. We describe its operation later. For now, let us see how to use `TextLayer`.

The `TextLayer` class contains three different constructors that provide control over different aspects of the text layout. These different aspects are detailed in Table 7.3.

The default values are used in constructors that do not give control over the parameter. For example, the constructor we used in our "Hello Layers" example does not use the text block position or text alignment parameters, and they default to `Position.CENTER` and `TextAlgnment.CENTER`, respectively.

The `TextLayerControls` example (**TextLayerControls.java** on the CD-ROM) is a `CompositionFactory` (as in "The "Hello Layers" Example" on page 201) that builds a single `Layer LayerComposition`. It displays the text loaded from a file

Table 7.3 ■ TextLayer controls

CONTROLLING CONSTRUCTION PARAMETER	DEFINITION	DEFAULT VALUE
Text content. e.g., "Hello" or "Hi there"	This parameter can be provided by a `String` or an array of `AttributedStrings`. `Strings` can contain line separators to separate different paragraphs.	NA
Font style e.g., Helvetica or Times	This parameter can be provided either by a `Font` object, when a `String` describes the text content, or by the input `AttributedStrings` `TextAttribute.FONT` settings. Note that `AttributedStrings` can have varying font styles along the text string.	None if text content is defined by a `String`: a `Font` object has to be provided. Default `FONT` `TextAttribute` value otherwise.
Wrapping width e.g., `LayerComposition`'s width	Maximum length, in user space, for a single line of text. The text block lines are wrapped so that they do not exceed that maximum width.	Parent `LayerComposition` width
Text block position e.g., Center, Right or Left	The text block is actually a `Shape`, and its position in the `LayerComposition` is controlled by the `Position` construction parameter. This parameter provides the same control on the text block `Shape` as we have seen on `Shapes` in `ShapeLayer`.	`Anchor.CENTER`
Text alignment. e.g., `TextAlignment.RIGHT`. All lines are aligned to the right.	Relative line alignments. The possible values are defined by the `TextAlignment` class: `LEFT`, `RIGHT`, `CENTER`, and `JUSTIFIED`.	`TextAlignment.CENTER`

in a `TextLayer` whose different control parameters can be adjusted with `CompositionStudio`. This example can be run as follows:[14]

```
java com.sun.glf.CompositionStudio com.sun.glf.snippets.TextLayerControls
```

Building the `LayerComposition` with the `TextLayer` is done as follows.

```
// Create LayerComposition with desired size
LayerComposition cmp = new LayerComposition(size);
cmp.setBackgroundPaint(backgroundColor);

String text = readFileAsString(textFile);
Renderer textPainter = new FillRenderer(textColor);

// Build text Position
AffineTransform transform =
AffineTransform.getRotateInstance(rotationAngle);
Position textPosition
    = new Position(textAnchor, hAdjust, vAdjust, transform);

// Build layer
TextLayer textLayer = new TextLayer(cmp,
                                    text,
                                    textFont,
                                    textPainter,
                                    textPosition,
                                    wrapWidth,
                                    textAlignment);

cmp.setLayers(new Layer[]{ textLayer });
textLayer.setRenderingHint(RenderingHints.KEY_ANTIALIASING,
                           RenderingHints.VALUE_ANTIALIAS_ON);

// Our LayerComposition only has one Layer in its stack
cmp.setLayers(new Layer[]{ textLayer });
```

Table 7.4 shows the output generated by this `LayerComposition` for different control parameter settings.

Our example describes the text style by using a `Font`. If we modify our example to use `AttributedString` instead, we get a text block with varying `Font` styles, as shown in Figure 7.20.

---

14. You can also use the tools we discussed in the Preface.

Table 7.4 ■ Visualizing the different TextLayer control parameters

PARAMETER SETTING & OUTPUT

Font

Curlz MT

> There are several parameters that control the behavior of the TextLayer. Of course, the text and its Font can be set, but you can also define the text alignment and the position of the text block in the Layer Composition it belongs to.

Serif

> There are several parameters that control the behavior of the TextLayer. Of course, the text and its Font can be set, but you can also define the text alignment and the position of the text block in the Layer Composition it belongs to.

Wrap width

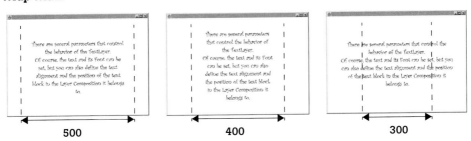

500   400   300

Positions, no adjustment

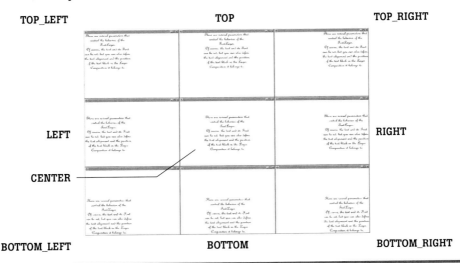

TOP_LEFT   TOP   TOP_RIGHT

LEFT   RIGHT

CENTER

BOTTOM_LEFT   BOTTOM   BOTTOM_RIGHT

Table 7.4 ■ Visualizing the different TextLayer control parameters (Continued)

PARAMETER SETTING & OUTPUT

Positions, vAdjust=10, hAdjust=20, transform set to rotation

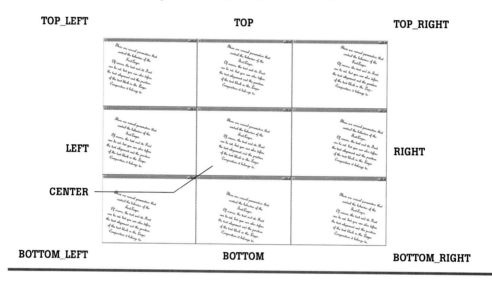

TOP_LEFT   TOP   TOP_RIGHT

LEFT   RIGHT

CENTER

BOTTOM_LEFT   BOTTOM   BOTTOM_RIGHT

```
protected AttributedString[] readFileAsAttributedString(File file){
  Font fonts[] = { font.deriveFont(Font.ITALIC),
                   font.deriveFont(Font.PLAIN) };
  int iCurFont = 0;
  Vector strings = new Vector();
  try{
    BufferedReader in = new BufferedReader(new FileReader(file));
    String line = "";
    while((line = in.readLine())!=null){
      AttributedString str = new AttributedString(line);
      str.addAttribute(TextAttribute.FONT, fonts[iCurFont]);
      iCurFont++;
      iCurFont %= 2;
      strings.addElement(str);
    }
    in.close();
  }catch(IOException e){
    String errorMessage = "Could not read : " + file + " : "
                          + e.getMessage();
    throw new IllegalArgumentException(errorMessage);
  }
```

Table 7.4 ■ Visualizing the different TextLayer control parameters (Continued)

PARAMETER SETTING & OUTPUT

TextAlignment

Right align **TextAlignment.RIGHT**	**Left align** **TextAlignment.LEFT**
There are several parameters that control the behavior of the TextLayer. Of course, the text and its Font can be set, but you can also define the text alignment and the position of the text block in the Layer Composition it belongs to.	There are several parameters that control the behavior of the TextLayer. Of course, the text and its Font can be set, but you can also define the text alignment and the position of the text block in the Layer Composition it belongs to.
There are several parameters that control the behavior of the TextLayer. Of course, the text and its Font can be set, but you can also define the text alignment and the position of the text block in the Layer Composition it belongs to.	There are several parameters that control the behavior of the TextLayer. Of course, the text and its Font can be set, but you can also define the text alignment and the position of the text block in the Layer Composition it belongs to.
Center align **TextAlignment.CENTER**	**Justified lines** **TextAlignment.JUSTIFY**

```
        AttributedString result[] = new AttributedString[strings.size()];
        strings.copyInto(result);
        return result;
    }

public Composition build(){
    ...; // As before

    AttributedString paragraphs[] = readFileAsAttributedString(textFile);
        TextLayer textLayer
            = new TextLayer(cmp, paragraphs, textPosition,
                        wrapWidth, justification,
                        new FillRenderer(textColor), transform);
```

As we mentioned, all the TextLayer constructors use one of the two make-
TextBlock methods of the TextLayer class, which we discuss next.

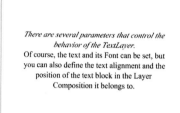

Figure 7.20 ■
Using AttributedStrings with TextLayer

makeTextBlock (Advanced topic)

▼ **Breaking lines into paragraphs**   The first version of `makeTextBlock` uses a `String` as an input and breaks it down into paragraphs along line breaks. Line breaks are defined by the "`line.separator`" `java.lang.System` property value.[15] Note that this definition is different on different platforms, and it is important to use the platform-specific value that the `line.separator` property gives. The other thing this first version does is to use the paragraph `Strings` and the input `Font` to build an array of "equivalent" `Attributed-Strings`. The code for this first version of `makeTextBlock` is:

```
public static Shape makeTextBlock(String text,
                                  Font font,
                                  float wrapWidth,
                                  TextAlignment alignment){

  // First, break input text into separate paragraphs. Paragraphs are
  // separated by line breaks.
  String lineSeparator = System.getProperty("line.separator", "\n");
  StringTokenizer st = new StringTokenizer(text, lineSeparator);
  int nParagraphs = st.countTokens();
  String paragraphs[] = new String[nParagraphs];
  for(int i=0; i<nParagraphs; i++)
    paragraphs[i] = (String)st.nextToken();

  // Now, create one AttributedString for each paragraph
  Hashtable stringAttrs = new Hashtable();
  stringAttrs.put(TextAttribute.FONT, font);
```

---

15. The `System` class contains a set of properties, from the operating system version to platform-specific variables, such as the line separator we use in `makeTextBlock` to detect paragraph boundaries.

```
AttributedString attributedStrings[]
   = new AttributedString[nParagraphs];
for(int i=0; i<nParagraphs; i++){
  attributedStrings[i]
     = new AttributedString(paragraphs[i], stringAttrs);
}

return makeTextBlock(attributedStrings, wrapWidth, alignment);
}
```

▼ **Turning text into a Shape**   The second version of makeTextBlock uses
the following process to turn an array of AttributedStrings into a Shape:

1. Wrap paragraph lines by using the wrapWidth and generate a
    Shape for each line.
2. Align lines according to the TextAlignment setting.
3. Concatenate line Shapes into a single text block.

Wrapping lines is done, as we explained in Chapter 4 (see "Advanced text rendering with TextLayout and LineBreakMeasurer" on page 118), by a
LineBreakMeasurer. The difference is that here we turn the TextLayouts into
Shapes. The following shows how a single paragraph (attributedString), is
processed.

First, we set the TextAttribute.JUSTIFICATION according to the TextAlignment parameter. Unless the text block should be justified (that is, TextAlignment is set to JUSTIFY), the TextLayout that we create later on should not be
justified.

```
// Force JUSTIFICATION attribute
if(alignment.equals(TextAlignment.JUSTIFY))
    attributedString.addAttribute(TextAttribute.JUSTIFICATION,
                                  TextAttribute.JUSTIFICATION_FULL);
else
    attributedString.addAttribute(TextAttribute.JUSTIFICATION,
                                  TextAttribute.JUSTIFICATION_NONE);
```

By default, the TextAttribute.JUSTIFICATION value is set to
JUSTIFICATION_FULL. Our code disables justification when it is not needed.

Second, we break the current paragraph into separate TextLayouts.

```
// iter is an AttributedStringCharacterIterator, frc a FontRenderContext
iter = attributedString.getIterator();
LineBreakMeasurer measurer = new LineBreakMeasurer(iter, frc);
int limit = iter.getEndIndex();
Vector vLayouts = new Vector();
while (measurer.getPosition() < limit) {
    vLayouts.addElement(measurer.nextLayout(wrapWidth));
}
```

Third, we justify the TextLayouts and get their outline, using the getOutline method.

```
int nLayouts = vLayouts.size();
for(int j=0; j<nLayouts-1; j++){
  layout = (TextLayout)vLayouts.elementAt(j);
  layout = layout.getJustifiedLayout(wrapWidth);
  t.translate(0, layout.getAscent());
  lineShape = layout.getOutline(t);
  vlines.addElement(lineShape);
  t.translate(0, layout.getDescent() + layout.getLeading());

  bounds = lineShape.getBounds();
  textBlockWidth = (int)Math.max(textBlockWidth, bounds.width);
  vlineBounds.addElement(bounds);
}
```

Note that getJustifiedLayout(wrapWidth) returns the layout unchanged when no line justification is allowed, that is, when TextAttribute.JUSTIFI-CATION is set to JUSTIFICATION_NONE. This is why the process started by setting this attribute to the appropriate value. The loop in the preceding code does not handle the last line because it is treated a little differently: no justification happens on the last line of the paragraph.

```
if(nLayouts>0){
  layout = (TextLayout)vLayouts.elementAt(nLayouts-1);
  t.translate(0, layout.getAscent());
  lineShape = layout.getOutline(t);
  vlines.addElement(lineShape);
  t.translate(0, layout.getDescent() + layout.getLeading());
  bounds = lineShape.getBounds();
  textBlockWidth = (int)Math.max(textBlockWidth, bounds.width);
  vlineBounds.addElement(bounds);
}
```

At this point in the makeTextBlock procedure, we have a Vector containing left-aligned Shapes representing each line in the text block. The remainder of the procedure aligns the lines according to their TextAlignment setting (t is an AffineTransform).

```
switch(alignment.toInt()){
  case TextAlignment.JUSTIFICATION_LEFT:
  case TextAlignment.JUSTIFICATION_JUSTIFY:
    break;
  case TextAlignment.JUSTIFICATION_CENTER:
    for(int i=0; i<nLines; i++){
      t.setToTranslation((textBlockWidth-lineBounds[i].width)/2, 0);
      lineShapes[i] = t.createTransformedShape(lineShapes[i]);
    }
    break;
  case TextAlignment.JUSTIFICATION_RIGHT:
    for(int i=0; i<nLines; i++){
      t.setToTranslation(textBlockWidth-lineBounds[i].width, 0);
```

```
      lineShapes[i] = t.createTransformedShape(lineShapes[i]);
    }
    break;
  default:
    throw new IllegalArgumentException("Illegal alignment: " +
                                        justification);
}
```

For left and justified alignment, there is no need to adjust line placement: lines are left-aligned by default and have already been justified, if required, by use of TextLayout.getJustifiedLayout. For center and right alignment, we use the width of the text block, which we computed when creating individual line Shapes to define how lines should be translated.

The remainder of the makeTextBlock method concatenates the individual line Shapes into a single text block Shape and returns that result.

```
GeneralPath textBlock = new GeneralPath();
for(int i=0; i<nLines; i++)
  textBlock.append(lineShapes[i], false);


return textBlock;
```

Note that the false value in the append calls means that the newly added line should not be connected to the current text block with a line.

Important Note

It is important to realize the implications of having our TextLayer *implementation rely on* ShapeLayer. *As we have seen, the* makeTextBlock *method uses* TextLayout *to generate* Shapes *for individual lines, which are later concatenated into a single text block* Shape.

The first consequence is that text metrics information is not available from a TextLayer. *Once it is built, a* TextLayer *is strictly equivalent to a* ShapeLayer, *and metrics information, for example, about individual lines, is not available. Second, the rendering process relies on* ShapeLayer, *which uses a* Renderer. *Therefore, the same* Renderer *is used for the full text block.*

If you compare this approach to rendering with TextLayout *(see "Text Manipulation" on page 109 in Chapter 4), you will discern a disadvantage and an advantage. The disadvantage is that text rendering attributes such as* TextAttribute.FOREGROUND *or* TextAttribute.BACKGROUND *are actually ignored: the text block is rendered by the* Renderer, *for example, a* FillRenderer. *Because the text block is seen as a single* Shape *object by the* Renderer, *the entire text block is rendered the same way. By contrast,* AttributedStrings *that are rendered by a* TextLayout *can have varying foreground* Paints, *as we saw in our example on page 110. The advantage of using a* Renderer *is that more sophisticated text rendering is possible. For example, if we use a* CompositeRenderer *that combines a* FillRenderer *and a* StrokeRenderer, *text is both outlined and filled, an effect that cannot be achieved with a* TextLayout.

Important Note (Continued)

Because our aim in this book is to show how to create appealing rendering effects, we designed TextLayer *to offer a simple and easy way to create text blocks with the desired alignment and position in the* LayerComposition *it is part of. So, although* TextLayer *is appropriate for our purpose, it may be inappropriate for other purposes, for example, for text editing features.*

ImageLayer

The ImageLayer class features are similar to those of ShapeLayer. The difference is that ImageLayer renders images instead of Shapes. It also provides a way to place images in the composition by means of Positions.

ImageLayer operation

ImageLayer is implemented as follows.:

```
public class ImageLayer extends Layer{
  // rendered image
  private Image image;

  // Requests the bounding box, in user space, of the area rendered
  public Rectangle getBounds(){
    return new Rectangle(0, 0,
                    image.getWidth(null), image.getHeight(null));
  }

  public void paint(Graphics2D g){
    g.drawImage(image, 0, 0, null);
  }

  //
  // @param parent the parent composition
  // @param image the image this layer should paint
  //
  // @exception IllegalArgumentException if image is null
  public ImageLayer(LayerComposition parent, Image image){
    this(parent, image, null);
  }

    // @param parent the parent composition
    // @param image the image this layer should paint.
    // @param position relative position this image should take in
    //        the composition.
    //
  public ImageLayer(LayerComposition parent, Image image,
                    Position position){
```

```
    super(parent);

    if(image==null)
      throw new IllegalArgumentException("Cannot paint null image");

    this.image = image;

    if(position!=null){
      Rectangle bounds = new Rectangle(image.getWidth(null),
                                       image.getHeight(null));
      setTransform(position.getTransform(bounds, parent.getBounds()));
    }
  }

  // @return image rendered by this layer
  public Image getImage(){
    return image;
  }
}
```

As for `ShapeLayer`, constructors that use a `Position` parameter use it to set the
Layer's transform. The rendering performed by `ImageLayer` only consists in
invoking the `Graphics2D drawImage` method.

Positioning images in a LayerComposition

`ImageLayer` provides an easy way to place images in a composition. The following example, **ImagePlacement.java** on the CD-ROM, places an image in all
the possible anchoring positions, using margins and a rotate transform.

```
// Load image
BufferedImage image = Toolbox.loadImage(imageFile,
BufferedImage.TYPE_INT_RGB);
if(image==null)
  throw new IllegalArgumentException("Could not load : " + imageFile);

// Create a LayerComposition
int w = image.getWidth();
int h = image.getHeight();
Dimension size = new Dimension(w*3 + 4*margins,
                               h*3 + 4*margins);
LayerComposition cmp = new LayerComposition(size);
cmp.setBackgroundPaint(backgroundColor);

// Create ImageLayers that render the same Image, but with
// different Positions.
int n = Anchor.enumValues.length;
Layer layers[] = new Layer[n];
AffineTransform rotator =
AffineTransform.getRotateInstance(rotateAngle);
```

```
for(int i=0; i<n; i++){
   Anchor imageAnchor = Anchor.enumValues[i];
   Position imagePosition
      = new Position(imageAnchor,
                     margins, margins,
                     rotator,
                     false);  // Rotate first, then place
   layers[i] = new ImageLayer(cmp, image, imagePosition);
}

cmp.setLayers(layers);
cmp.setRenderingHint(RenderingHints.KEY_INTERPOLATION,
                     RenderingHints.VALUE_INTERPOLATION_BILINEAR);
```

Note how we use the static `enumValues` array in the `Anchor` class to get the list of `Anchor` values. Otherwise, this is similar to the way we used `Position`s for `Shape`s or text. Figure 7.21 shows the output of the program with `rotateAngle` set to zero and Pi/4.

Note how the different images overlap. The `Anchor enumValues` are defined from the top left to the left, going clockwise around the rectangle.

No rotation

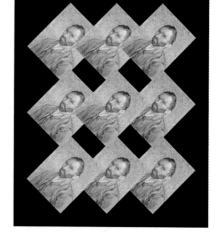

rotation = Pi/4

Figure 7.21 ■

Positioning images in LayerComposition with ImageLayer

```
public class Anchor {
    ...
    public static final Anchor enumValues[]{ TOP_LEFT,
                                             TOP,
                                             TOP_RIGHT,
                                             RIGHT,
                                             BOTTOM_RIGHT,
                                             BOTTOM,
                                             BOTTOM_LEFT,
                                             LEFT,
                                             CENTER };
    ...
}
```

The last `Anchor` value is `CENTER`, which is why this last `ImageLayer` is drawn
on top of the others.

CompositionProxyLayer

The `CompositionProxyLayer` class renders `Composition` objects. In particular, it can render a `LayerComposition`. As we discuss in this section, `Composi-
tionProxyLayer` makes it easy to reuse `LayerComposition` objects in other
`LayerCompositions` and to apply attributes to a set of `LayerCompositions`.

CompositionProxyLayer operation

The implementation of `CompositionProxyLayer` is straightforward.

```
public class CompositionProxyLayer extends Layer{
    // Area painted by this layer
    private Rectangle2D bounds;

    // Composition proxied by this Layer
    private Composition cmp;

    // Constructor
    // @param parent the parent composition
    // @param cmp the proxied composition
    // @param position relative position the proxied composition should
    //        have in the composition.
    public CompositionProxyLayer(LayerComposition parent,
                                 Composition cmp, Position position){
        super(parent);
        this.cmp = cmp;

        // Process bounds in user space
        Dimension size = cmp.getSize();
        bounds = new Rectangle(0, 0, size.width, size.height);
```

```
    if(position!=null)
      setTransform(position.getTransform(bounds, parent.getBounds()));
  }

  public Rectangle2D getBounds(){
    return bounds;
  }

  public void paint(Graphics2D g){
    cmp.paint(g);
  }
}
```

Again, as for `ImageLayer` and `ShapeLayer`, the constructor that takes a `Position` parameter uses it to set the `Layer`'s transform. The `CompositionProxy-Layer` class performs its rendering by simply requesting the proxied `Composition` to paint itself (see the `paint` method).

Reusing Compositions with CompositionProxyLayer

`CompositionLayerProxy` is deceptive in its simplicity: it is a very powerful class and we reuse it many times in Part III. The following example, **HelloLayerReuse.java** on the CD-ROM, illustrates how the same `Composition` (built by our `HelloLayer CompositionFactory` (see "The "Hello Layers" Example" on page 201), can be reused, positioned, and filtered easily because it is manipulated as a `Layer` object.

```
public Composition build(){
  //
  // Create a Composition object from HelloLayer
  //
  HelloLayers compositionFactory = new HelloLayers();
  Composition proxied = compositionFactory.build();

  //
  // Create a LayerComposition to display several layer compositions
  //
  Dimension proxiedSize = proxied.getSize();
  int w = proxiedSize.width;
  int h = proxiedSize.height;
  Dimension size = new Dimension(w*3, h*3);
  LayerComposition cmp = new LayerComposition(size);
  cmp.setBackgroundPaint(backgroundColor);
  Rectangle cmpRect = cmp.getBounds();
```

```
//
// Create CompositionProxyLayers that render the same composition,
// but with different Positions, filters, mask and attributes
//
Position positions[]
   = { Position.TOP_LEFT, Position.TOP, Position.TOP_RIGHT,
       Position.RIGHT, Position.BOTTOM_RIGHT, Position.BOTTOM,
       Position.BOTTOM_LEFT, Position.LEFT, Position.CENTER };

Shape mask = new Ellipse2D.Double(0, 0, w, h);

Shape masks[] = { positions[0].createTransformedShape(mask, cmpRect),
                  null,
                  positions[2].createTransformedShape(mask, cmpRect),
                  null,
                  positions[4].createTransformedShape(mask, cmpRect),
                  null,
                  positions[6].createTransformedShape(mask, cmpRect),
                  null,
                  positions[8].createTransformedShape(mask, cmpRect) };

AlphaComposite halfTransparent
 = AlphaComposite.getInstance(AlphaComposite.SRC_OVER, 0.5f);
Composite composites[] = { null, halfTransparent, null,
                           null, halfTransparent, null,
                           null, halfTransparent, null };

byte lookup[] = new byte[256];
for(int i=0; i<256; i++)
  lookup[i] = (byte)(255 - i);

LookupTable table = new ByteLookupTable(0, lookup);
LookupOp inverter = new LookupOp(table, null);

BufferedImageOp filters[] = { inverter, null, inverter,
null, inverter, null,
inverter, null, inverter };

int n = positions.length;
Layer layers[] = new Layer[n];

for(int i=0; i<n; i++){
  layers[i] = new CompositionProxyLayer(cmp, proxied, positions[i]);

  if(masks[i] != null)
    layers[i].setLayerMask(masks[i]);
```

```
   if(composites[i] != null)
      layers[i].setComposite(composites[i]);

   if(filters[i] != null)
      layers[i].setImageFilter(filters[i]);
}

cmp.setLayers(layers);
cmp.setRenderingHint(RenderingHints.KEY_ANTIALIASING,
                     RenderingHints.VALUE_ANTIALIAS_ON);

return cmp;
}
```

Note how the same `Composition` (proxied in the code) is reused nine times at different positions, and with different masks (every second `CompositionLay-erProxy` instance has its mask set to an ellipse), composites (some `Composi-`

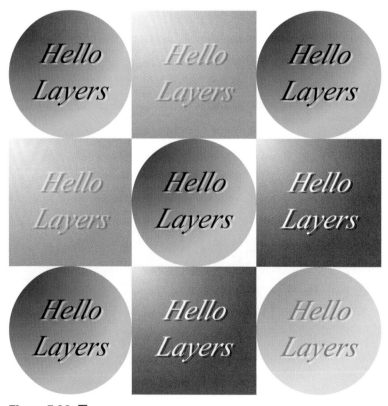

Figure 7.22 ∎

Reusing Compositions with CompositionProxyLayer

tionLayerProxy instances are rendered half-transparent), and filter attributes (some CompositionLayerProxy instances are inverted).

The important thing to remember about CompositionLayerProxy is that it provides a way to reuse Compositions *and* to apply generic Layer attributes to Compositions (such as mask, filter or Composite). Part III makes extensive use of these two features.

One Last Example

We worked to make GLF fun to program, and our final example shows how to create a sophisticated graphical composition with Layers. This example takes advantage of the different features we have presented in this chapter. We call this example the "Combining Layers" example (**CombiningLayers.java** on CD-ROM); its output is shown in Figure 7.23.

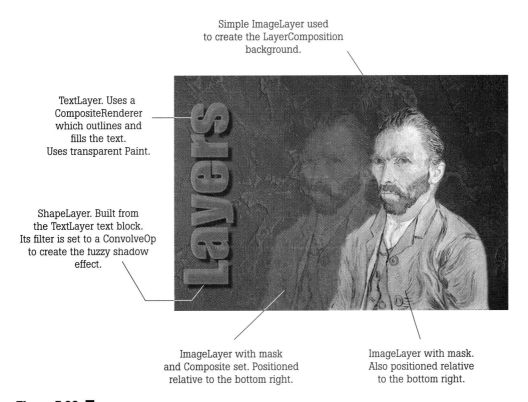

Simple ImageLayer used
to create the LayerComposition
background.

TextLayer. Uses a
CompositeRenderer
which outlines and
fills the text.
Uses transparent Paint.

ShapeLayer. Built from
the TextLayer text block.
Its filter is set to a ConvolveOp
to create the fuzzy shadow
effect.

ImageLayer with mask
and Composite set. Positioned
relative to the bottom right.

ImageLayer with mask.
Also positioned relative
to the bottom right.

Figure 7.23 ■
CombiningLayers output

As described in the figure, this LayerComposition is made of five Layers. Here is how they are created and stacked.

```
// First, load the images used in the Composition
BufferedImage background
    = Toolbox.loadImage(backgroundImageFile, BufferedImage.TYPE_INT_ARGB);
BufferedImage image
    = Toolbox.loadImage(imageFile, BufferedImage.TYPE_INT_ARGB);
BufferedImage imageMask
    = Toolbox.loadImage(imageMaskFile, BufferedImage.TYPE_INT_ARGB);

// If one the images could not be loaded, we cannot proceed
if(background==null ||
   image==null ||
   imageMask==null)
  throw new IllegalArgumentException("Could not load one of the images");

// Composition size is based on background image size
int width = background.getWidth();
int height = background.getHeight();
Dimension size = new Dimension(width, height);
LayerComposition cmp = new LayerComposition(size);

// Background layer
ImageLayer bkgLayer = new ImageLayer(cmp, background);

// Vertical TextLayer
AffineTransform textRotation = new AffineTransform();
textRotation.rotate(-Math.PI/2);

// Position to the left after applying transform
Position textPosition = new Position(Anchor.LEFT,
                                     textMargins, textMargins,
                                     textRotation,
                                     false);
Renderer textOutline = new StrokeRenderer(textOutlineColor, textOutlineWidth);
Renderer textFill = new FillRenderer(textFillColor);
Renderer textPainter = new CompositeRenderer(textOutline, textFill);
TextLayer textLayer
    = new TextLayer(cmp, text, textFont, textPainter, // Describes text's look
                    textPosition,                     // Text block's position
                    -1,                               // No line wrap
                    TextAlignment.CENTER);            // Does not matter for a
                                                      // single line.

// TextLayer shadow
Kernel gaussianKernel
    = new GaussianKernel(shadowRadius);               // GaussianKernel is a
                                                      // Kernel extension in GLF

ConvolveOp shadowBlur
    = new ConvolveOp(gaussianKernel);
```

```
Dimension shadowBlurMargins
    = new Dimension(shadowRadius*2, shadowRadius*2);  // Use filter margins
                                                      // (see page 227)
Shape textBlock = textLayer.createTransformedShape();
Renderer shadowFill = new FillRenderer(shadowColor);
AffineTransform shadowOffset
    = AffineTransform.getTranslateInstance(shadowOffsetX,
                                           shadowOffsetY);
ShapeLayer textShadow = new ShapeLayer(cmp, textBlock, shadowFill);
textShadow.setTransform(shadowOffset);
textShadow.setImageFilter(shadowBlur, shadowBlurMargins);


// Masked image
Position imagePosition = new Position(Anchor.BOTTOM_RIGHT, imageMargin, 0);
ImageLayer imageLayer = new ImageLayer(cmp, image, imagePosition);
Rectangle imageRect = new Rectangle(image.getWidth(), image.getHeight());
AffineTransform imageTransform = imageLayer.getTransform();
Rectangle maskRect
    = imageTransform.createTransformedShape(imageRect).getBounds();
imageLayer.setLayerMask(imageMask, maskRect);


// Image Shadow Reflection
Position imageShadowPosition
    = new Position(Anchor.BOTTOM_RIGHT, imageShadowMargin, 0);
ImageLayer imageLayerShadow = new ImageLayer(cmp, image, imageShadowPosition);
AffineTransform imageShadowTransform = imageLayerShadow.getTransform();
maskRect = imageShadowTransform.createTransformedShape(imageRect).getBounds();
imageLayerShadow.setLayerMask(imageMask, maskRect);
imageLayerShadow.setComposite(AlphaComposite.getInstance(
                                      AlphaComposite.SRC_OVER, .25f
                                      )
                             );


cmp.setLayers(new Layer[]{ bkgLayer,
                           imageLayerShadow,
                           textShadow,
                           textLayer,
                           imageLayer});
```

The bottom `Layer` is a simple `ImageLayer`.

```
ImageLayer bkgLayer = new ImageLayer(cmp, background);
```

Because the `LayerComposition` is given the background image's size, `bkgLayer` will fill the background entirely. The text on the left-hand side is both outlined and filled, and it also has a shadow. There are two `Layers`, one for the shadow and one for the text on top of it. The text is positioned to the left of the composition.

```
Position textPosition = new Position(Anchor.LEFT,
                                     textMargins, textMargins,
                                     textRotation,
                                     false);
```

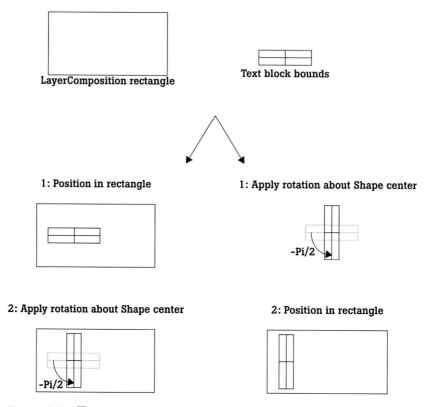

Figure 7.24 ■

Transforming text after or before positioning

The `false` parameter means that the text should be positioned to the left of the composition after the transform, `textRotation`, has been applied. Figure 7.24 illustrates what would have happened otherwise: the text would have shifted more to the right.

The text shadow uses the `filter` memento to create a realistic shadowing effect.

```
ConvolveOp shadowBlur            // GaussianKernel is a Kernel
    = new ConvolveOp(new GaussianKernel(shadowRadius));
Dimension shadowBlurMargins      // Use filter margins (see page 227)
    = new Dimension(shadowRadius*2, shadowRadius*2);
```

```
Shape textBlock = textLayer.createTransformedShape();
Renderer shadowFill = new FillRenderer(shadowColor);
AffineTransform shadowOffset
    = AffineTransform.getTranslateInstance(shadowOffsetX,
                                           shadowOffsetY);
ShapeLayer textShadow = new ShapeLayer(cmp, textBlock, shadowFill);
textShadow.setTransform(shadowOffset);
textShadow.setImageFilter(shadowBlur, shadowBlurMargins);
```

The `createTransformedShape` method (this is a `ShapeLayer` method—`Text-Layer` derives from `ShapeLayer`) returns the `Shape` object in device space. In other words, it returns the `Shape` object after transformation by the `Layer`'s transform. If the shadow `Layer` used the `textBlock` `Shape` as is, with no further transform, the shadow would appear exactly underneath the `textLayer`. However, a more realistic effect is obtained by shifting the shadow, and this is what the `shadowOffset` transform does. Note that the way the `textShadow` transform is set is an example of not using `Position`s for placing `Shape`s in a `LayerComposition` (or at least not directly—the original `textBlock` was indeed placed by means of a `Position`).

By default, the `textShadow` `Layer` would render sharp edges. To create fuzzy edges for the shadow, we set the `Layer`'s filter to a `ConvolveOp`. This is a concise way of requesting a fairly sophisticated operation: as we discussed in this chapter, it implies that `textBlock` will be rendered offscreen, filtered, and then combined with the underlying `Layer`s. We discussed the layer margins on page 227 ("Layer filtering"), and this is a example of how they can be useful.

The other two `Layer`s are `ImageLayer`s. They both use the masking memento in the `Layer` to limit the image rendering to the Van Gogh's outline. Note that the masking rectangle has to be processed to match the location where the images are rendered.

```
// Masked image
Position imagePosition
    = new Position(Anchor.BOTTOM_RIGHT, imageMargin, 0);
ImageLayer imageLayer = new ImageLayer(cmp, image, imagePosition);
Rectangle imageRect = new Rectangle(image.getWidth(),
                                    image.getHeight());
AffineTransform imageTransform = imageLayer.getTransform();
Rectangle maskRect =
    imageTransform.createTransformedShape(imageRect).getBounds();
imageLayer.setLayerMask(imageMask, maskRect);

// Image Shadow Reflection
Position imageShadowPosition
    = new Position(Anchor.BOTTOM_RIGHT, imageShadowMargin, 0);
ImageLayer imageLayerShadow
    = new ImageLayer(cmp, image, imageShadowPosition);
```

```
AffineTransform imageShadowTransform
    = imageLayerShadow.getTransform();
maskRect
    = imageShadowTransform.createTransformedShape(imageRect).getBounds();
imageLayerShadow.setLayerMask(imageMask, maskRect);
int srcOver = AlphaComposite.SRC_OVER;
imageLayerShadow.setComposite(AlphaComposite.getInstance(srcOver,
                                                .25f));
```

The last action consists in placing the layers we have created in a stack.

```
cmp.setLayers(new Layer[]{ bkgLayer, imageLayerShadow,
                    textShadow, textLayer, imageLayer});
```

The Layers are ordered as they will be rendered. Therefore, the textShadow Layer appears before the textLayer Layer in the stack, because it needs to be rendered "under" the text.

This last example demonstrates how a sophisticated output can be created in a very concise way. We hope this makes creating graphical compositions easier and fun.

Conclusion

We have now covered the heart of the Graphic Layers Framework design and key classes that provide a layering paradigm for creating graphical compositions. The Graphic Layers Framework can be used in different contexts, from generating postcards, to customizing calendars or generating advertisement banners.

The GLF layer-based programming model makes it easy and intuitive to build complex rendering effects by encapsulating many of the repetitive tasks into reusable objects such as Renderers and Layers. Those classes factor in the characteristics common to several types of rendering operations. For example, the Layer mementos define some of the graphic context attributes that should be used at rendering time.

It is important to keep in mind that the different programming model offered by GLF is tailored for our purpose: easy creation of rendering effects. Therefore, it should be easier to create graphical compositions with GLF than with the core Java 2D API. However, the GLF does not cover the broad range of other graphic rendering needs that the API addresses, such as medical imaging, geographical maps, or standard GUI development. The scope and strength of GLF and 2D are different, and GLF is a complement to the Java 2D API, not a replacement for it.

There is one aspect of creating graphical compositions that the core GLF classes do not address: the number of variables that are used to create any given output. Our last example uses fifteen different variables to create its output. Managing and experimenting with these variables is the primary need that the GLF utilities address. This is the subject of the next chapter.

8

THE GLF STUDIO AND UTILITIES: EXPERIMENTING WITH LAYERS

Introduction

The `com.sun.glf.util` package in the Graphic Layers Framework makes it easy to manipulate and configure rendering effects. As we have discussed, rendering effects are created by `com.sun.glf.Composition` implementations (such as `LayerComposition`), which have a `paint` method that performs rendering on the input `Graphics2D` object. The utilities in the `com.sun.glf.util` package help use `Compositions` and configure their output.

Three core features are provided in this package:

1. *Display* `Compositions`. The utilities can display `Compositions` in a graphical user interface environment.
2. *Save and restore* `Composition` *configurations*. The utilities provide support for saving and restoring `Composition` configurations in various formats and also saving and restoring the output created by a `Composition`.
3. *Configure* `Compositions`. The utilities help modify the properties that control the output created by a `Composition`.

Figure 8.1 shows the classes that deliver those three features. The classes shown in shades of blue are actual applications. The others are supporting classes.

Our goal is to explain how to use a set of classes that makes it easier to experiment and have fun with Java 2D and the Graphic Layers Framework. This chapter describes how those classes are used

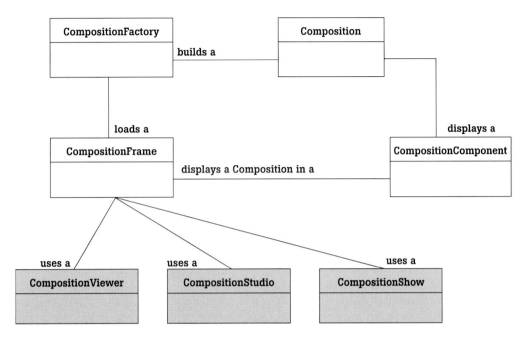

Figure 8.1 ■
Key utility classes and their relations

and how they are related. However, we do not detail how they are implemented because that subject is beyond the scope of this book. Their implementation makes extensive use of Swing, JavaBeans, and class reflection. Reflection allows tools to dynamically discover the attributes and methods of a class. Readers interested in learning more about the design and implementation of those utilities can refer to [Geary Swing1999] for Swing-related issues and to [Englander1997] for JavaBeans and class reflection issues.

Our next section explains how a `Composition` can be used in a typical graphical user interface (GUI) environment and introduces the `CompositionComponent` and `CompositionFrame` classes, which are used by utilities (`CompositionShow`, `CompositionViewer`, and `CompositionStudio`) to display the output of `Composition`s. After that, we describe how to save a `Composition`'s configuration as a serialized Java bean and how to save its output as an image. Finally, our last section details how to configure `Composition`s with `CompositionStudio`.

Viewing Compositions

Composition viewing is supported by the GLF utilities in two ways. First, there are supporting classes, CompositionComponent and CompositionFrame, that provide the display functionality. Those classes can be used in any program displaying Compositions. Second, there are several GLF utility applications that use the classes to show Compositions for different purposes. We first look at the supporting classes and then discuss the utilities that use them.

Supporting classes

▼ **CompositionComponent**   As illustrated in Figure 8.1, com.sun.glf. util.CompositionComponent can display a Composition. A Composition-Component can then be integrated in any graphical user interface application as would any other Swing component. CompositionComponent is an extension of the javax.swing.JComponent class that delegates its paint implementation to its associated Composition object. CompositionComponent has a preferred size equal to its Composition's size[1] (remember that a Composition has a size, see "Introduction: Graphical Compositions" on page 212).

The following code example reuses our "Hello Layers" example and displays it in two different CompositionComponents.

```
public class UsingCompositionComponent {
  public static void main(String args[]){
    // Reuse our HelloLayers example to build a Composition
    HelloLayers helloLayers = new HelloLayers();
    Composition composition = helloLayers.build();

    // Create a CompositionComponents
    CompositionComponent helloA
        = new CompositionComponent(composition);
                                  // Composition to display.
                                  // No rescaling

    Object interpolation
        = RenderingHints.VALUE_INTERPOLATION_BILINEAR;

    CompositionComponent helloB
```

---

1. In Java Graphics, user interface Components are displayed in Containers (e.g., a javax.swing.JFrame or a java.awt.Frame) which have a preferred size, i.e., a size that is optimal for their display. However, Containers can allocate more or less size to a Component. Therefore, a Component may have an actual size that is different from its preferred size. The actual size can be retrieved by the Component.getSize method.

```
                    = new CompositionComponent(composition,
                                          // Composition to display
                                     true,
                                          // Do rescaling to fit Component's
                                          // actual size
                                     interpolation);
                                          // Interpolation hint


        // Create a JFrame to display CompositionComponents
        JFrame frame = new JFrame();
        Container content = frame.getContentPane();
        content.setLayout(new GridLayout(1,2));
                                          // Use a 1 row by 2 column layout

        content.add(helloA);              // This Component does not rescale
        content.add(helloB);              // This Component rescales

        content.setBackground(Color.white);
                                          // Frame will have a white
                                          // background

        frame.pack();                     // Initial Frame size will
                                          // fit content.

        frame.setVisible(true);           // Show Frame
    }
}
```

Figure 8.2 shows the output of this program (see **UsingComponentComposition.java** on the CD-ROM). The first screenshot shows the initial screen output for the program. Both `CompositionComponents` have been allocated their preferred size because the `frame.pack` method sized the frame to give each `Component` its preferred size.

The second and third screenshots show the frame after it has been shrunk or blown up. The `CompositionComponent` that does not do rescaling simply displays the `Composition` object in its center. When the allocated size of the `CompositionComponent` is larger than the `Composition's` size, the `CompositionComponent` shows some extra margins. When its allocated size is smaller than the `Composition's` size, then only the center part of the `Composition` shows.

On the opposite (right-hand) side, the `CompositionComponent` was initialized with rescaling. When its allocated size is smaller than that of the `Composition`, the `Composition` is shrunk to fit the available size, keeping the aspect ratio of the `Composition`. Similarly, if the allocated size is larger than the `Composition's` size, then the output is blown up to fill the available size. Again, the original `Composition's` aspect ratio is kept constant (that is, the vertical and horizontal scale factors are the same).

Expand size: right composition is blown up.

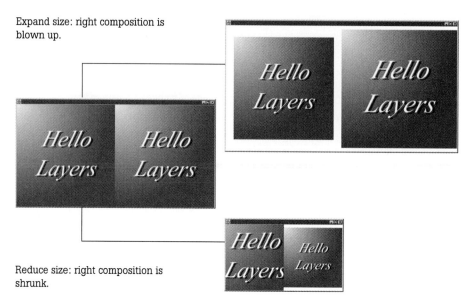

Reduce size: right composition is shrunk.

Figure 8.2 ■
Using ComponentComposition

CompositionComponent uses an offscreen buffer where it renders its associated Composition on the first paint method invocation (the paint method is invoked by the Swing framework the first time a JComponent needs to be rendered). Subsequent paint calls simply draw the offscreen buffer. This is why the third construction attribute used for constructing the right-hand CompositionComponent defines an interpolation hint: it is used for rescaling the offscreen buffer.[2]

▼ **CompositionFrame**   A CompositionComponent can be used in any GUI environment along with other Components: it can be used directly, as in our previous example. However, the CompositionFrame class might offer a better alternative. Many times, it is useful to display a Composition in a separate window; this is what CompositionFrame does. It displays a Composition in its center, using a CompositionComponent, as illustrated in Figure 8.1 on page 279.

---

2. See "RenderingHints" on page 182 in Chapter 5 for details on RenderingHints and their meaning.

CompositionFrame can either display a Composition directly (through its setComposition method) or it can load a Composition created by a CompositionFactory, as illustrated by the following code segment, again using our HelloLayers CompositionFactory.

```
HelloLayers helloLayers = new HelloLayers();
CompositionFrame cmpFrame = new CompositionFrame("Using
CompositionFrame");
cmpFrame.load(helloLayers);
cmpFrame.setVisible(true);
```

Under the hood, CompositionFrame does exactly what our previous example did: it uses the factory to build a Composition and a CompositionComponent to display it.

<hr>

Important Note

When CompositionFrame *loads a new* Composition, *it displays a progress bar that shows the percentage of* Layers *that have been drawn already. To do so, it takes advantage of the* PaintProgressListener *support we presented in the* Composition *class.*

<hr>

The other feature that CompositionFrame supports is to save the Composition it displays. As we describe later, two formats can be used to save a Composition: serialized CompositionFactory objects and images (for example, JPEG images). A right-click in a CompositionFrame will show a single item pop-up menu (see Figure 8.3). When the Save Image menu item is selected, a file chooser dialog opens; it lets the user select the file to use for saving and the desired format in which to save the file.

Figure 8.4 illustrates the CompositionFrame features. The offscreen buffer that the frame's CompositionComponent uses can be saved as an image. The CompositionFactory it loads can be serialized. We next explain why we serialize the CompositionFactory object and not the Composition itself.

Right clicking on CompositionFrame brings up a one item menu. Selecting 'Save Image' opens the 'File Save' dialog box.

Figure 8.3 ■
Saving Compositions from a CompositionFrame

Utilities that display Compositions

The `CompositionComponent` and `CompositionFrame` classes provide the instrumentation that let us display existing `Composition` configurations. However, they require us to write code to use them within our programs, as we have seen in our examples. This code is useful if you need to use `Compositions` from your application.

However, for running examples in this book or ones you create with GLF, you can use a number of utility applications that deal with `CompositionFactory` directly. The following utilities use those two classes and directly display the examples provided in this book or any other `Composition`.

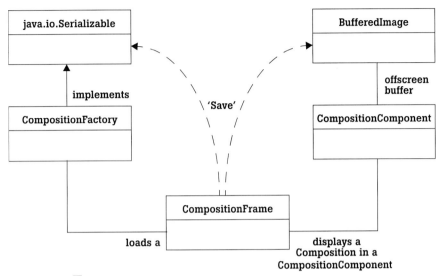

Figure 8.4 ■
CompositionFrame features

▼ **CompositionViewer** `CompositionViewer` is the simplest utility: it displays the `Composition` created by a `CompositionFactory` in a `CompositionFrame`. Here is how it is invoked.

```
java com.sun.glf.util.CompositionViewer <compositionFactoryBean>
```

For example:

```
java com.sun.glf.util.CompositionViewer com.sun.glf.snippets.HelloLayers
```

This command summons a window similar to the one in Figure 8.5. The `compositionFactoryBean` argument can be either a class name (as in the preceding example), a serialized bean name, or a text-based serialized bean.[3]

For example, all the demonstrations for the third part of this book are provided as serialized beans in text format. To view one of the examples (for example, the Image Drop Shadow example from Chapter 11), type the following at the command line.

```
cd <GLF Install Directory>
java com.sun.glf.util.CompositionViewer
res\com\sun\glf\beans\ch10\ImageDropShadowComposition.ser.txt
```

3. We explain this format in "Serializing Composition configurations" on page 288.

Figure 8.5 ■
Viewing an example with CompositionViewer

This command instantiates the serialized `CompositionFactory` from `Image-DropShadowComposition.ser.txt` and displays the `Composition` it creates, as shown in Figure 8.5.

▼ **CompositionShow**   The `CompositionShow` utility enables you to browse a set of `Compositions`. For example, to browse through all the examples provided in this book, type the following at the command-line prompt:

```
cd <GLF Install Directory>
cd code
java com.sun.glf.util.CompositionShow
```

This command displays a little frame (Figure 8.6).

If you select the Load button, a file chooser dialog appears so you can select either a file or a directory. If you select a directory, the utility searches for all serialized `CompositionFactories` in this directory and subdirectories. For example, if you select the `res\com\sun\glf\beans` subdirectory, all the examples from the third part of this book become available from the combo box. You can then use the left and right arrows to navigate between the different `Compositions`, or you can select the one you want directly from the combo box. As you select a new `CompositionFactory` bean, it is displayed in a `CompositionFrame` (see Figure 8.7).

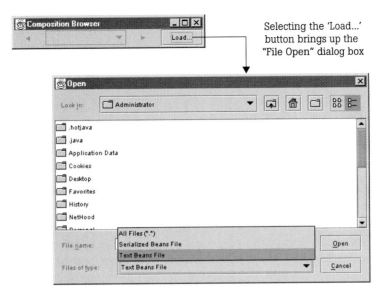

Selecting the 'Load...' button brings up the "File Open" dialog box

Figure 8.6 ■
CompositonShow's initial frame

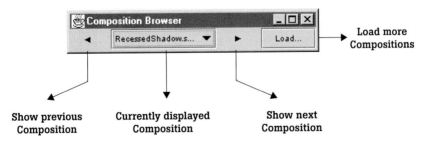

Load more Compositions

Show previous Composition

Currently displayed Composition

Show next Composition

Figure 8.7 ■
CompositionShow controls

▼ **CompositionStudio**   CompositionStudio is the other utility that displays Compositions using CompositionComponent and CompositionFrame. It also lets us configure CompositionFactory objects, as we discuss in detail on page 295.

Saving Compositions

On several occasions, we have said that a large number of properties control how any given Composition looks: size, colors, transparency values, text, etc. The framework provides support to help save and restore specific configurations through CompositionFactory objects. Our "Hello Layers" example (see Chapter 6) showed how different settings can result in dramatically different outputs.

As we explained, the framework can save CompositionFactory configurations as serialized JavaBeans objects. Composition output can be saved as well, in image format. The advantage of serialized objects is that they can later be restored by the framework for display or further configuration. The advantage of the image format is that the composition can be exported to other environments (for example, a graphic image tool, a Web page, or an email attachment). We introduce how to use each one of these formats, serialized and image, in turn.

Serializing Composition configurations

▼ **What is serialization?**   Serialization is a Java language feature that allows objects to be saved into binary storage (for example, a file) and later restored. All the processes of saving and restoring objects are taken care of by the Java virtual machine. The requirements for a class to be able to be serialized are:

1. Implement the java.io.Serializable interface
2. Only contain attributes that implement the java.io.Serializable interface or that are marked as transient (that is, should not be serialized)

▼ **Serializing CompositionFactories**   We mentioned earlier in this chapter that we are actually serializing CompositionFactory objects and not Compositions themselves. Why is this? There are three main reasons.

1. Composition instances contain a lot of object instances that are only used for rendering but that do not really describe the configuration. For example, a LayerComposition that contains an ImageLayer has a reference to a BufferedImage. The CompositionFactory object, used to generate that Composition, keeps a reference only to the name of the file from which the image should be loaded. It is lighter and less expensive to save a file name than a BufferedImage content.

2. Composition properties are interdependent. For instance, in our "Hello Layers" example we use a RadialGradientPaint to fill the background. The RadialGradientPaint's construction is bound to the size of the Composition. If we look back at the code that creates the Paint—

```
Rectangle rect = new Rectangle(0, 0,
                                   size.width, size.height);
Rectangle gradientRect
       = new Rectangle(-rect.width, -rect.height,
                           2*rect.width, 2*rect.height);
RadialGradientPaint filling
       = new RadialGradientPaint(gradientRect,
                                   backgroundColorCenter,
                                   backgroundColorOutside);
```

—we see that the filling attribute is dependent on the Composition's size.

3. Some of the Java 2D objects are not serializable. For example, the java.awt.GradientPaint class is not serializable.[4] Saving a CompositionFactory allows us to work around this issue: the factory has attributes that control the creation of a GradientPaint, for example, but does not contain a GradientPaint itself.

The process of serializing and restoring CompositionFactory objects is depicted in Figure 8.8.

---

4. This issue will likely be addressed in future revisions of the Java platform.

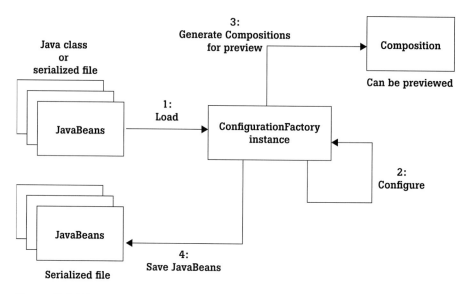

Figure 8.8 ■
Serializing CompositionFactories

Text-based serialization

Serialization is a powerful mechanism, but it has the following negative characteristics:

1.   Serialized files are not readable by a human because they are in binary format.
2.   Serialized files are version sensitive. When an object is serialized, it is tagged with the serial version unique identifier of the class it belongs to. By default, this identifier changes when incompatible changes are made to the class (such as deleting a field in the class), and a serialized object can only be restored if the serial version identifier in the saved object is the same as that in the class at the time the restoration happens. So, if an object is serialized, then when the class it belongs to is modified and recompiled, the serialized object can no longer be restored.

For graphical compositions, it is convenient to be able to read the configuration settings. Also, developing a CompositionFactory class usually takes many iterations to get right. At the same time, it is common to start creating and saving configurations that need to be loaded even when the class has had incompatible changes.

To address those issues, the framework comes with an alternate, text-based, and limited serialization scheme. In GLF, whenever a `CompositionFactory` is serialized, two files are saved: a .ser file and a .ser.txt file. The first file contains the regular, binary serialized version of the `CompositionFactory` object. The second contains the equivalent text-based version. For example, if we saved the configuration of `HelloLayers` that we will create on page 303 in a file called `helloLayers.ser`, a `helloLayers.ser.txt` file would be created in the same directory and would contain the following:

```
class=com.sun.glf.demos.HelloLayers
BackgroundColorCenter=ffffffff
BackgroundColorOutside=003333ff
ShadowColor=ffffff50
ShadowOffsetX=7
ShadowOffsetY=5
Size=400 300
Text=Hello Layers
TextColor=cc0033ff
TextFont=Impact/PLAIN/90
```

Our purpose is not to provide alternate serialization solutions, but to provide convenience. The scope of text-based serialization is limited to serve the purpose of persistent `CompositionFactory` objects and is not recommended for use outside that context.

Text-based serialization is implemented by a class called `TextBeans` in the `com.sun.glf.util` package. It can serialize properties of the classes and basic types described in Table 8.1. The right-hand column describes the text-based format and gives an example.

Table 8.1 ■ Text-based serialization formats

CLASS OR TYPE	FORMAT AND EXAMPLE
String	propertyName=<stringValue> e.g., Text=Hello Layer
Integer or int	propertyName=<intValue> e.g., Width=300
Double or double	propertyName=<doubleValue> e.g., Width=2.5

Table 8.1 ■ Text-based serialization formats (Continued)

CLASS OR TYPE	FORMAT AND EXAMPLE
Float or float	propertyName=\<floatValue\> e.g., Scale=2.3
Color	propertyName=\<aarrggbb\> e.g., for white background: BackgroundColor=ffffff
Font	propertyName=\<fontName\>/\<fontStyle\>/\<fontSize\> e.g., TextFont=serif/BOLD/90 fontStyle can be one of PLAIN, BOLD, ITALIC, or BOLDITALIC.
Dimension	propertyName=\<width\> \<height\> e.g., Size=300 200
File	propertyName=file:/\<fileName\> e.g., BackgroundImage=file:/C:/temp/myBackground.jpg
Enumerated type e.g., Anchor, TextAlignment	propertyName=\<toStringValue\> e.g., TextAnchor=TOP_RIGHT e.g., TextAlignment=RIGHT
Glyph	propertyName=\<unidoceValue\> \<fontValue\> e.g., Pictogram=34 serif/PLAIN/200

There are two important things to note about our text-based serialization scheme:

1. It is based on the JavaBeans naming patterns. That is, it saves only the properties that have accessor methods which follow the JavaBeans naming patterns. A class field x is saved if publicly accessible getX and setX methods exist and if x is one of the types or classes in the preceding table.

2. It supports simple properties. It does not support indexed properties or properties that are aggregates of the supported types.

Again, the text-based serialization scheme is not a generic solution, and it should not be used out of the context of this book. However, it is very handy in the process of developing `LayerCompositions`.

The last row in Table 8.1 shows the serialized text format of a `Glyph` object. `Glyph` is a utility class that can be used to extract individual character glyphs from a font. Here is the class definition.

```
public class Glyph implements Serializable{
  private static FontRenderContext frc
     = new FontRenderContext(null, true, true);
  private Font font;
  private char c;

  public Glyph(Font font, char c){
    if(font==null)
      throw new IllegalArgumentException();

    this.font = font;
    this.c = c;
  }

  public Shape getShape(){
    GlyphVector v = font.createGlyphVector(frc, new char[]{c});
    return v.getOutline();
  }

  public Font getFont(){ return font; }
  public char getChar(){ return c; }
}
```

Fonts contain a collection of glyphs that have decorative value, and some fonts are even specialized in that category (there is one category of font we described as decorative fonts, see page 156 in Chapter 5). A `Glyph` object provides a quick way to access a specific glyph's shape in a font, provided that its Unicode value is known. For example, to retrieve the glyph for "@", we can write:

```
Font glyphFont = new Font("serif", Font PLAIN, 50);
Glyph at = new Glyph(glyphFont, '@');
Shape atShape = at.getShape();
```

Saving Compositions as images

Our ultimate goal here is to create compelling graphical compositions that can then be shown to an end user. Although we can use tools such as `Composi-tionViewer` and `CompositionShow` to view our `Compositions`, it is also useful to be able to save our `Compositions` in popular image formats.

By default, `CompositionFrame` lets us save `Compositions` as JPEG images by means of the `com.sun.image.codec.jpeg` package.[5] You can add support for additional image formats to `CompositionFrame` by following these steps:

1. Create a class that implements the `com.sun.glf.util.ImageEncoder` interface.
2. Add the name of the encoder class to the encoder class in the `com\sun\glf\res\encoder.properties` file.

When the `CompositionFrame` class is first loaded by the Java virtual machine, it looks into the `encoder.properties` file and tries to load all the listed `ImageEncoder` implementations. Each implementation that is successfully loaded will be displayed as one optional format in the `CompositionFrame` File Save dialog that appears after you select the Save image pop-up menu on right click. This result is illustrated in Figure 8.9.[6]

In encoders.properties:
`list=com.sun.glf.util.JPEGEncoder com.sun.glf.priv.PNGImageEncoder`

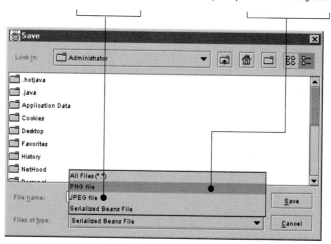

Figure 8.9 ■
Adding a custom ImageEncoder

---

5. See "Saving a JPEG file in CMYK" on page 92 in Chapter 4 for examples of how to use this package.
6. This architecture for adding different image format encoders is for this book only and is not meant as a generic solution to image encoding on the Java platform.

Configuring Compositions

To really have fun and understand the different parts of the Java 2D API, you'll want to exercise the many options various parameters can take: `AffineTransforms`, `Colors`, `Fonts`, etc. In the Graphic Layer Framework, the `CompositionStudio` utility provides a way to dynamically analyze the properties of a `CompositionFactory` Java beans and to build a user interface to modify, test, and save its configurations.

Figure 8.10 shows how `CompositionStudio` operates.

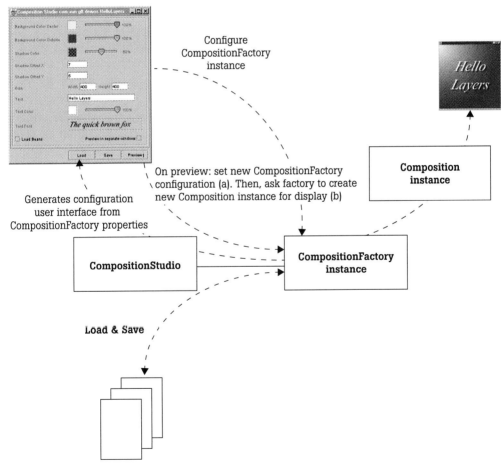

Figure 8.10 ■
Operation of the CompositionStudio utility

Loading a CompositionFactory

There are two ways to load a `CompositionFactory`: as a Java bean or as a file. Furthermore, `CompositionFactory` objects can be loaded either from the command-line argument or by clicking the Load button when the application has already started.

▼ **Loading a CompositionFactory as a Java bean** When the `CompositionFactory` utility starts, it can take the fully qualified name of a Java bean as an input and load the factory it contains. For example:

```
java com.sun.glf.util.CompositionStudio com.sun.glf.demos.HelloLayers
```

or

```
java com.sun.glf.util.CompositionStudio com.sun.glf.demos.helloLayers2
```

In the first case, the Java bean is the fully qualified name of the `Composition-Factory` class. In the second case, the Java bean is the fully qualified name of `helloLayers2`, that is, a serialized instance of the `HelloLayers` class. This means that the `com/sun/glf/demos/helloLayers2.ser` file can be found in the `CLASSPATH`.

To load a `CompositionFactory` Java bean when the application is already started, you need to first check the Load Beans check box and then click the Load button, as illustrated in Figure 8.11.

▼ **Loading a CompositionFactory as a file** Loading a serialized `CompositionFactory` as a JavaBeans requires that the serialized file be placed in the `CLASSPATH`. Sometimes, this is not convenient, so it is also possible to load a serialized file directly, without requiring that it be in the `CLASSPATH`. When you start the `CompositionFactory` utility, you can pass the file of the serialized file of the serialized `CompositionFactory` to load. For example:

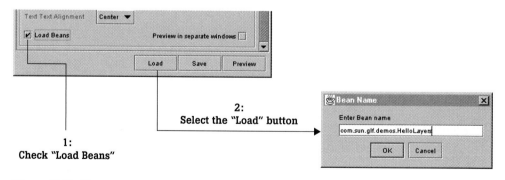

Figure 8.11 ■
Loading a CompositionFactory as a JavaBeans

```
java com.sun.glf.util.CompositionStudio helloLayers2.ser
```

or

```
java com.sun.glf.util.CompositionStudio helloLayers2.ser.txt
```

In the first case, we use the standard Java serialization format. In the second example, we use the text-based format we described earlier (see page 290). You can think of the text-based serialized format as a kind of recovery file that can be used to recover all or some of a `CompositionFactory`'s state if some incompatible changes have been made to the class after it has been serialized.

To load a `CompositionFactory` serialized file when the application has already started, you need to first check off the Load Beans check box and then click the Load button, as illustrated in Figure 8.12.

Configuring a Composition

No matter what the input format is for loading a `CompositionFactory` instance, `CompositionStudio` uses Java's reflection API to extract the properties it is able

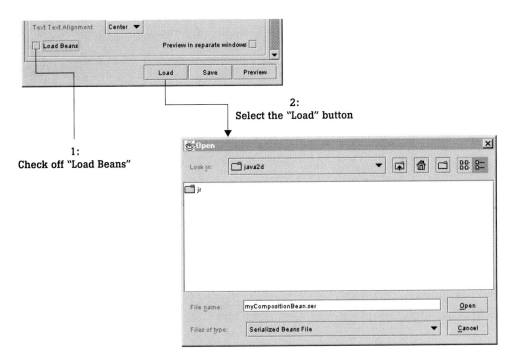

Figure 8.12 ■
Loading a CompositionFactory as a Java bean

to display (that is, of one of the supported types, listed later in this section) and that have accessor methods that follow the JavaBeans naming pattern from the CompositionFactory class. This use is similar to the TextBeans operation: CompositionStudio handles property x if x is one of the supported types and if there are publicly accessible getX and setX methods. For each such property, the utility adds a configuration control to the configuration window, as we saw for the "Hello Layers" example. Figure 8.13 shows how the Hello Layers properties are mapped to user interface controls. Those controls can be used, as we will see, to modify the CompositionFactory properties.

▼ **Mapping property names to UI label name**   A simple scheme is used to define the UI label name for a given property. The property name is defined in the CompositionFactory class. This name is parsed, and every time an uppercase letter is found, a white space is inserted before the letter. Finally, the first letter of the property is forced to be upper case.

A few examples: "size" maps to "Size"; "textAlignment" maps to "Text Alignment"; "whatDoYouWant" maps to "What Do You Want."

▼ **Supported property types and related user-interface controls**
Table 8.2 shows the different property types that are supported, the related user-interface controls, and a short explanation on how they operate. For the most sophisticated controls or those that need more explanation, a reference to the relevant paragraph replaces the explanation.

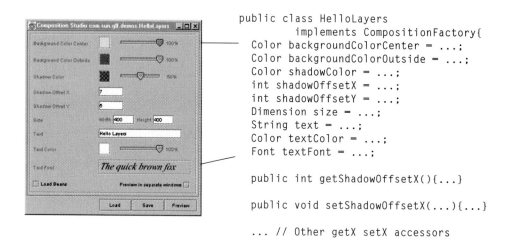

```
public class HelloLayers
            implements CompositionFactory{
    Color backgroundColorCenter = ...;
    Color backgroundColorOutside = ...;
    Color shadowColor = ...;
    int shadowOffsetX = ...;
    int shadowOffsetY = ...;
    Dimension size = ...;
    String text = ...;
    Color textColor = ...;
    Font textFont = ...;

    public int getShadowOffsetX(){...}

    public void setShadowOffsetX(...){...}

    ... // Other getX setX accessors
```

Figure 8.13 ■
CompositionStudio maps Java beans properties to UI controls

Table 8.2 ■ Property types and related user interface controls

Type	User interface control	Operation
String	String Property [Type your text here] [...]	Type the string value in text field. Select the button to pop up a dialog and enter strings that span multiple lines.
boolean or Boolean	Boolean Property ☑ On	
Integer or int	Int Property [1007]	Type the integer value into text field. Text field only accepts digit characters.
Double or double	Double Property [2.0]	Type in double value into text field. Text field only accepts valid double literals.
Float or float	Float Property [1.4]	Type in float value into text field. Text field only accepts valid float literals.
Color	Color Property ▨ ═══▽═ 75%	See page 300.
Font	Font Property **The quick brown fox**	See page 300.
Dimension	Dimension Property Width [400] Height [300]	Type the width in the left text field and the height in the right text field.
File	File Property [C:\work\Doc\java2d\book\priv\src\com\] [...]	See page 301.
Enumerated type e.g., Anchor, TextAlignment	Anchor Property [Top ▼]	Select the proper enumerated value from the combo box pull-down menu.
Glyph	Glyph Property @	See page 300.

▼ **Configuring a Font property**   The Font control displays the currently selected font in a preview rectangle. The size does not reflect the actual point size for the Font object but is fixed so that it is legible and the Font family can be recognized. If you move the cursor over the Font preview, a tooltip displays the actual Font details (see Figure 8.14). If you click on the Font preview, a Font selection dialog opens to enable you to select a different Font.

▼ **Configuring a Glyph property**   The Glyph control operates in a way very similar to the Font control. It displays a preview of the Glyph in a preview rectangle. Here also, the size does not reflect the actual Glyph size but is fixed so that it is legible in the preview dialog. If you move the cursor over the Glyph preview, a tooltip displays the Glyph details. If you click on the Glyph preview, a Glyph selection dialog opens. Its operation is illustrated in Figure 8.15.

▼ **Configuring a Color property**   As we have seen, a Color object can be defined by its red, green, blue, and alpha values. The Color control shows a preview of the Color and lets you modify its alpha value (see Figure 8.16).

Furthermore, if you click on the color preview rectangle, the Swing color chooser is displayed so you can modify the red, green, and blue components of the Color property (see Figure 8.17).

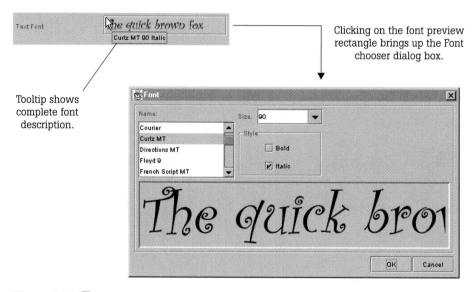

Figure 8.14 ■
Font selection dialog

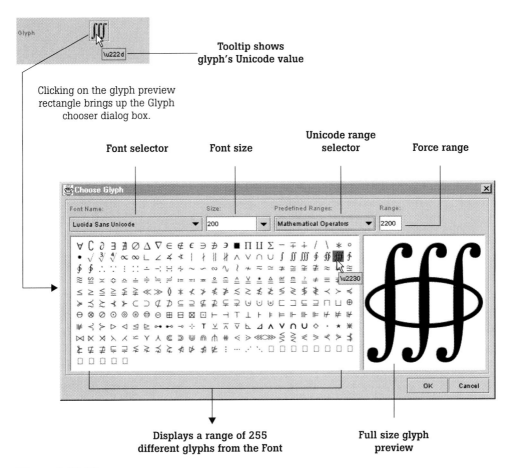

Tooltip shows
glyph's Unicode value

Clicking on the glyph preview
rectangle brings up the Glyph
chooser dialog box.

Font selector   Font size   Unicode range selector   Force range

Displays a range of 255
different glyphs from the Font

Full size glyph
preview

Figure 8.15 ■
Glyph selection dialog

▼ **Configuring a File**   The File user-interface control contains a text field and a button. The text field displays the current value for the File property. It can be edited directly to change which file the property represents. An alternate way to select the file is to select the ... button that opens a file dialog through which you can browse the file system. Note that the file name is entered in a platform-dependent format. For example:

■ on the Solaris platform: /home/myHomeDir/myFile.txt
■ on Microsoft Windows: c:\temp\myFile.jpg

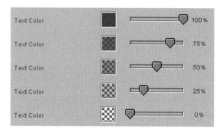

There is a tiled background under the color in the color preview to visualize the transparency setting: the more transparent the color is, the more visible the background is.

Figure 8.16 ■
Modifying the alpha value of a Color property

We have now seen all the different controls that can be used to modify a CompositionFactory's configuration. To visualize the effect of a configuration change, we use CompositionStudio's previewing feature.

Previewing a CompositionFactory configuration

The Preview button displays a CompositionFrame that shows the output created by the Composition object built by the CompositionFactory currently configured. The "Preview in separate windows" check box, at the bottom of the configuration window, defines whether successive previews should be displayed in

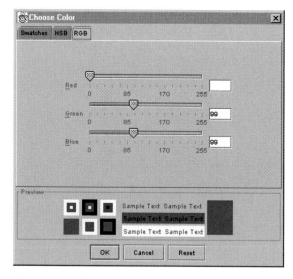

Figure 8.17 ■
Modifying the red, green, and blue components of a Color property

the same window (where they replace any previous preview) or in a separate window (which preserves the previous previews and enables comparisons).

Saving a CompositionFactory configuration

There are two ways to save a `CompositionFactory`'s configuration: by selecting the Save button in the `CompositionStudio` dialog or by clicking on a preview frame and selecting the "Save image..." menu item. In each case, a file dialog is displayed to enable you to select the file and the format in which the `Composition` object should be saved.

Conclusion

The utilities and tools we have presented will allow us to enjoy and experiment with the Java 2D features.

The core package we presented in Chapter 8 enables us to program graphical compositions by stacking layers. The utilities we described in this chapter let us manage the sometimes large number of configuration properties and enable us to save, restore, and share different configurations of our graphical compositions. In the next chapter, we take advantage of Java 2D's extensible design and create new `Paints`, `Strokes`, `Composites`, filters, and geometric transformations to enhance our graphical compositions.

Afterword about loading images

There is a class in the `com.sun.glf.util` package that we use repeatedly in this book to load images: the `Toolbox` class. This class can load an image from a `File` or a `URL` into a `BufferedImage` of any type. Its `loadImage` prototype is:

```
public BufferedImage loadImage(<File|URL> imageSource,
                               int imageFormat){...}
```

where `imageFormat` is one of the `BufferedImage` types, such as `TYPE_INT_ARGB` or `TYPE_BYTE_GRAY`. This class helps put images in the format that the application needs directly. For example, we typically work with images that are in the standard RGB format (that is, `TYPE_INT_ARGB`), but we also use gray scale images for masks. Therefore, we can load masks as follows:

```
BufferedImage mask
   = Toolbox.loadImage(maskFile, BufferedImage.TYPE_BYTE_GRAY);
```

Internally, `Toolbox` makes the `ColorConvertOp`[7] filtering needed to return the image in the requested format.

---

7. `ColorConvertOp` is described in Chapter 4 (see "ColorConvertOp" on page 98).

9

THE GLF GOODIES: TAKING ADVANTAGE OF JAVA 2D'S EXTENSIBLE DESIGN

Introduction

In this chapter, we are going to see Java 2D's extensible architecture at work. This is the third objective for the Graphic Layers Framework: to provide extensions to the Java 2D API.

The following sections show extensions for Paint, Stroke, Composite, and image filters. They also show how to add support for nonlinear geometrical transformations to the API. For each category of extension, a section explains what is involved in writing an extension: Which interfaces should be implemented? What are the important things to understand before starting to write anything? The section also explains how any given extension works. Readers interested more in using the extension can skip the first part of each section and jump to the description of the extension (for example, LightOp) to understand how to use it.

Custom Paints

Creating a custom Paint implementation (Advanced topic)

We saw in our Java 2D overview that two objects are involved in the painting process: a Paint object and a PaintContext object. The Paint object defines the characteristics of the style used to fill and draw Shape objects. A Paint object is defined in the user space and has no direct connection to the device space (that is, output device) where an actual pixel pattern needs to be generated. This pattern generation is the task of the `PaintContext` implementation, which works in the device space and generates pixel values in a specific context. Another way to look at the difference between `Paint` and `PaintContext` is that `Paint` is device independent and `PaintContext` is device dependent: a `PaintContext` object generates pixel values at a specific location on the output device, using a specific `ColorModel` for representing pixels.

Two steps are involved in creating a custom `Paint`:

1. Write an implementation of the `PaintContext` interface (or several).
2. Write an implementation of the `Paint` interface that uses the `PaintContext` implementation(s).

▼ **Writing an implementation of the PaintContext interface**　Here is the definition of the `PaintContext` interface.

```
public interface PaintContext{
    public void dispose();
    ColorModel getColorModel();
    Raster getRaster(int x, int y,
                     int w, int h);
}
```

It is important to understand the different methods well:

■ `getColorModel` defines the `ColorModel` for the `Raster` object returned by the `getRaster` method. For example, if the input `Raster` works in the default `ColorModel`, it could return `ColorModel.getRGBDefault()`. Note that this choice is left to the implementation to decide on and it might not be the same `ColorModel` as the one used by the destination. We will see later how the two are reconciled.

■ `getRaster` is the heart of the `Paint` design. This method returns a `Raster` containing the pixel values. For example, `java.awt.ColorPaintContext` returns a `Raster` where all pixels have the same value. `java.awt.GradientPaintContext`, for example, returns values that depend on the pixel location. Any custom `PaintContext` implementation will compute the pixel values in this method, based on some logic that it defines. The `getRaster` input arguments define the rectangle for which pixel values should be computed. Those arguments are in device space, which means that they refer to the physical location and size on the output device. For example, when rendering to the screen, a call to `getRaster(0, 0, 120, 40)` means that the `PaintContext` should provide the pixel values for a rectangle of 120 by 40 pixels at the top left of the screen. In raster output devices, a unit in device space corresponds to one pixel.

■ `dispose` is called by the platform when a `PaintContext` is no longer needed, or at least temporarily unneeded. This call allows the

PaintContext implementation to free up resources it may have allocated in the getRaster invocations. A typical example of a resource that can be freed is a working WritableRaster that PaintContext implementations use to store the pixel values and return from the getRaster method. This approach allows the implementations to avoid creating a new resource on each call.

As a result of this design, the higher the output device resolution, the bigger the number of pixels a PaintContext will have to process. Let us assume the following code:

```
Graphics2D g = ...;
g.setPaint(somePaint);
g.fillRect(0, 0, 4, 4);
```

If the output device attached to the Graphics2D object has a 72 dpi resolution, the PaintContext associated with somePaint will be invoked, one or more times, to fill a rectangle of (0, 0, 4, 4) in device space.[1] The reason is that one unit in user space has a size of 1/72nd inch. This is also the size of one pixel in a 72 dpi output device. Now, if the output device has a higher resolution, let us say 144 dpi, then a pixel has a size of 1/144th inch. Two pixels are used to cover one unit of user space. Therefore, the associated PaintContext will be invoked one or more times to fill in a rectangle of (0, 0, 8, 8) in device space. As the resolution increases, the size of the Raster object that needs to be filled also increases. Figure 9.1 illustrates these points.

When the resolution is doubled, the number of pixels the Paint needs to process is multiplied by four.

72 dpi: Raster will be
up to 4 by 4 pixels

144 dpi: Raster will be
up to 8 by 8 pixels

Figure 9.1 ■
Filling Shape at different resolutions

---

1. The rationale guiding invocations to the getRaster method is not part of the specification. Therefore, it is possible that to fill a given Shape with a Paint, the getRaster method is invoked several times.

Here are some important considerations to keep in mind when implementing a PaintContext:

■ A PaintContext operates in device space.
■ It implements the logic for processing pixel values: this is its added value.
■ It works in a specific ColorModel: the pixel values returned by the getRaster method must follow the SampleModel of the ColorModel returned by the PaintContext's getColorModel method.
■ It can use temporary resources, such as WritableRasters, to serve getRaster invocations. Those resources can be released on subsequent dispose invocations.

All the PaintContext implementations that come with the GLF work in the DirectColorModel, meaning that pixel values are packed in integers and the standard RGB color space is used. The following code snippet describes how a typical PaintContext implementation works.

```
public class MyPaintContext implements PaintContext{
  // Working Raster
  private WritableRaster working;

  // ColorModel this PaintContext uses. This is only an example
  private ColorModel myCM = ColorModel.getRGBDefault();

  public MyPaintContext(...){ // Implementation specific parameters
    ....
  }

  public void dispose(){
    // Set working to null so that it can be garbage collected
    working = null;
  }

  public Raster getRaster(int x, int y, int w, int h) {
    // Use working raster if it is big enough to accommodate
    // the requested area. Otherwise, create a new one.
    if (working == null
        || working.getWidth() < w
        || working.getHeight() < h)
      working = getColorModel().createCompatibleWritableRaster(w, h);

    //
    // Access raster internal int array. Because we use
    // DirectColorModel, we know the DataBuffer is of type
    // DataBufferInt and the SampleModel is
    // SinglePixelPackedSampleModel.
    // Adjust for initial offset in DataBuffer and also for the
    // scanline stride.
    //
```

```
DataBufferInt rasterDB = (DataBufferInt)working.getDataBuffer();
int pixels[] = rasterDB.getBankData()[0];
int off = rasterDB.getOffset();
SinglePixelPackedSampleModel sampleModel
   = ((SinglePixelPackedSampleModel)raster.getSampleModel());
int scanlineStride = sampleModel.getScanlineStride();
int adjust = scanlineStride - w;

// Now, process each pixel in turn
int pixel = 0;
for(int i=0; i<h; i++) {          // For each row
  for(int j=0; j<w; j++){         // For each column
    pixel = getPixelValue(j, i); // PaintContext specific: get pixel
                                 // value
    pixels[off + i*(w + adjust) + j] = pixel;
    }
  }

  return working;
}
```

There are a couple of interesting points to note about this code:

- The working Raster is reused if its size is big enough for the new request. It is released when dispose is invoked.
- PaintContext uses its knowledge of the ColorModel it uses to access its working Raster DataBuffer internal integer array. The working Raster might be bigger than the requested pixel area, that is, the number of data elements in the integer array between the start of two consecutive lines may be larger than w. The actual distance between two consecutive lines is defined by the scanline stride, as described in Figure 9.2.
- The initial offset in the array, retrieved from the DataBuffer's getOffset elements, defines the start of the Raster data. It is key to remember to always use this initial offset in the arrays, as it might not always be zero.

Requested Raster: w=2, h=2
Saved working Raster: w=5, h=2

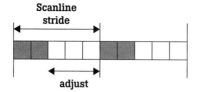

Figure 9.2 ■
Reusing a working Raster and scanline stride

▼ Writing an implementation of the Paint interface   As we described in Part I, the `Paint` interface has a single method:

```
public interface Paint extends Transparency {
    public PaintContext createContext(ColorModel cm,
                                      Rectangle deviceBounds,
                                      Rectangle2D userBounds,
                                      AffineTransform xform,
                                      RenderingHints hints);
}
```

and the `Transparency` interface it extends as well:

```
public interface Transparency {
    public final static int OPAQUE           = 1;
    public final static int BITMASK          = 2;
    public final static int TRANSLUCENT      = 3;
    public int getTransparency();
}
```

The requirement for `Transparency` is that a `Paint` implementation should declare which type of pixel opacity it supports. The type should be one of the following:

- `OPAQUE` – all the pixel values a `Paint` generates have an alpha component of 1.
- `BITMASK` — pixels are either fully opaque (alpha is 1) or fully transparent (alpha is O).
- `TRANSLUCENT` — pixels can have an arbitrary alpha value.

The right implementation for any `Paint` implementation depends on how it works. For example, all kinds of gradient `Paint`s make different kinds of linear color interpolation (that is, the pixel values they compute are some linear combination of configurable `Color`s). If the colors used for the interpolation are fully opaque, then the `Paint` can declare that it is only generating fully opaque pixel values. Otherwise, it will declare that it generates translucent pixel values.

The `createContext` method is invoked when the time comes to render a `Shape` with the `Paint`. The `Paint` is requested to create the appropriate `PaintContext` object that will do the job of generating pixel values. The parameters passed to `createContext` have the following purpose:

- The `ColorModel` parameter defines the `ColorModel` for which pixel values should be computed. Ideally, a `Paint` will create a `PaintContext` that is able to generate values for that `ColorModel`. However, this is not required, so we can think of the `ColorModel` as a hint.
- The `deviceBounds` argument defines the limits, in device space, of the area to be painted. This might help a `PaintContext` prepare the right resources to compute and store pixels in response to `getRaster` calls: the width and

height of the requested `Raster` should not exceed the `deviceBounds` width and `height` values.

■ The `userBounds` argument defines the limit, in user space, of the area to be painted. This limit might be used by a `Paint` implementation to choose between alternate `PaintContext` implementations. For example, the `GradientPaint` implementation could decide to return a `ColorPaintContext` if it found that the `userBounds` fell in a region of the gradient where all pixels have the same value.[2]

■ The `AffineTransform` argument defines the transform between the user space and the device space. This information is needed by `Paint`s that are tied to spatial coordinates. `Color` is not tied in that way because all pixels have the same value, no matter where they are located. Other `Paint`s are tied to spatial coordinates, such as `GradientPaint`, and all our custom implementations. For example, `RadialGradientPaint` uses a `Rectangle`, in user space, to define the bounds of the radial gradient. All points in the user space have a color interpolated, depending on their position relative to that bounding rectangle. Because colors are computed from the location of the pixel in user space, the `AffineTransform` argument is needed: The pixel's position in user space is computed, and then the user space position leads to the right interpolated color value.

■ The `RenderingHints` argument defines hints that the `Paint` or `PaintContext` implementation might use to choose between rendering alternatives. None of our custom `Paint` and `PaintContext` implementations use the incoming hints because there is a single algorithm used to implement them. However, other implementations might decide to use this information.

The following sections introduce the different `Paint` implementations provided in GLF and describe how they work.

GradientPaintExt

This first `Paint` implementation is in the same vein as the `GradientPaint` implementation that comes with the Java 2D API, except that it can use an arbitrary number of colors between the gradient control points. Its constructor parameters are explained in Table 9.1.

Figure 9.3 illustrates the `GradientPaintExt` constructor parameters.

---

2. Actually, `GradientPaintContext` does not return a `ColorPaintContext`, but it could.

Table 9.1 ■ GradientPaintExt construction parameters

PARAMETER	PURPOSE
Point2D origin	Coordinates for the gradient origin. Some constructors take the origin as two separate float values, x and y.
Point2D end	Coordinates for the gradient end. Some constructors take the end as two separate float values, dx and dy.
float I[]	Gradient intervals, along the gradient axis. These must be positive values. The sum of values is normalized to represent distance ratios between (x, y) and (dx, dy).
Color colors[]	Array of gradient colors. There is one for the gradient origin and one for the end of each gradient interval.
boolean cyclic (optional construction parameter)	If true, the colors cycle repeatedly between the colors defined in the colors array.

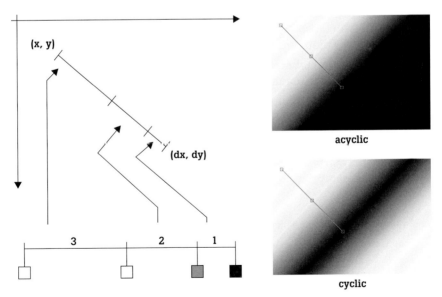

Figure 9.3 ■
GradientPaintExt constructor parameters

The following code snippet creates the `GradientPaintExt` instance illustrated in the figure (**GradientPaintExtUsage.java** on the CD-ROM).

```
Point start = new Point(40, 40);
Point end = new Point(300, 300);
float I[] = {3, 2, 1};
Color darkGreen = new Color(30, 120, 80);
Color darkBlue = new Color(10, 20, 40);
Color colors[] = {Color.white, Color.yellow, darkGreen, darkBlue};
GradientPaintExt paint
    = new GradientPaintExt(start, end, I, colors, cycleThrough);
```

That `paint` object can then be used as any other `Paint`. For example:

```
Rectangle rect = new Rectangle(0, 0, w, h);
g.setPaint(paint);
g.fill(rect);
```

Refer to Chapter 16 for examples of how `GradientPaintExt` is used to create texture effects such as copper. It is also used in Chapter 17 to create the sunset sky colors, in conjunction with the `RadialGradientPaintExt` `Paint` we describe later.

RadialGradientPaint

Our second `Paint` implementation provides a gradient between two `Colors`, as `GradientPaint` does. However, the color on any given point depends on a different rule. Here, it depends on the point's position relative to the ellipse bounding the gradient. The two focal points have the first gradient `Color`. Points on the ellipse boundary or outside the ellipse have the second gradient `Color` value. Points within the ellipse have a value proportional to their distance to the ellipse focal points.

Figure 9.4 contains a reminder of the mathematical concepts related to ellipses.

The following code snippet creates a `RadialGradientPaint` (**RadialGradient-PaintUsage.java** on the CD-ROM).

```
Rectangle gradientBounds
    = new Rectangle(margin, margin, w - 2*margin, h - 2*margin);
Color centerColor = Color.white;
Color boundsColor = new Color(20, 80, 60); // Dark green
RadialGradientPaint paint
    = new RadialGradientPaint(gradientBounds, centerColor, boundsColor);
```

`RadialGradientPaint` can be used as any other `Paint`.

```
Graphics2D g = ...;
g.setPaint(paint);
g.fillRect(0, 0, w, h);
```

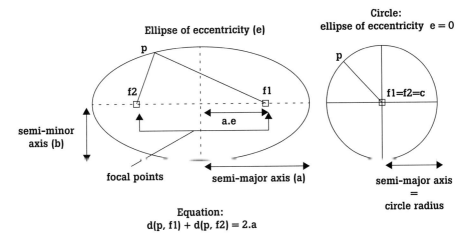

Ellipse of eccentricity (e)

Circle:
ellipse of eccentricity e = 0

p

p

f2

f1

f1=f2=c

a.e

semi-minor
axis (b)

focal points

semi-major axis (a)

semi-major axis
=
circle radius

Equation:
d(p, f1) + d(p, f2) = 2.a

Figure 9.4 ■
Ellipse mathematical concepts

Figure 9.5 shows the output of this snippet and illustrates how the color on a point is proportional to its distance to the ellipse focal points.

Note that one use of `RadialGradientPaint` is with square bounds, in which case the gradient is circular, as shown in Figure 9.6. The controlling ellipse being a circle, its eccentricity is zero, which means that the two focal points join in the circle's center.

Figure 9.5 ■
Using RadialGradientPaint

Figure 9.6 ■
Circular RadialGradientPaint

RadialGradientPaintExt

This last implementation of the Paint interface works in a way very similar to RadialGradientPaint except that it can use several Colors instead of just two. Its constructor parameters are explained in Table 9.2 and illustrated in Figure 9.7.

Table 9.2 ■ RadialGradientPaintExt control parameters

PARAMETER	PURPOSE
Rectangle2D bounds	Bounding rectangle for the ellipse defining the gradient bounds.
Color colors[]	Array of gradient colors. The first value defines the color of the focal points. The last value defines the color on the ellipse bounds. Other values define intermediate gradient interval colors.
float I[]	Gradient intervals, along the gradient axis. Those must be positive values. The sum of values is normalized to represent distance ratios between the focal points and the bounds, along the ellipse major axis.

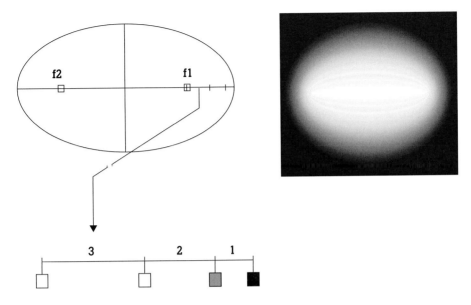

Figure 9.7 ■
RadialGradientPaintExt control parameters

The following code snippet creates the RadialGradientPaintExt illustrated in Figure 9.7 (**RadialGradientPaintExtUsage.java** on the CD-ROM).

```
Rectangle gradientBounds
    = new Rectangle(margin, margin, w - 2*margin, h - 2*margin);
double I[] = {3, 2, 1};
Color darkGreen = new Color(30, 120, 80);
Color darkBlue = new Color(10, 20, 40);
Color colors[] = {Color.white, Color.yellow, darkGreen, darkBlue};
Paint paint = new RadialGradientPaintExt(gradientBounds, colors, 1);
```

RadialGradientPaintExt can be used as any other Paint. For example:

```
g.setPaint(paint);
g.fillRect(0, 0, w, h);
```

Refer to Chapter 16 for an example of how RadialGradientPaintExt is used to create dramatic atmosphere and a sphere. It is also used in Chapter 17 to create the sunset sky colors, in conjunction with the GradientPaintExt Paint we describe earlier.

Custom Strokes

In Chapter 5 we saw what the `Stroke` interface is and how it is used in the `Shape` rendering process (see "Strokes" on page 140). A `Stroke` implementation creates the outline of the `Shape` it processes through its `createStrokedShape` method.

In this section, we see how to implement new types of `Strokes`. `CompositeStroke`, our first custom implementation, is simple yet handy, and we will see how it offers rendering options. `ControlStroke` is provided as an illustration of the typical process used by `Stroke` implementations. We detail how it is implemented.

The remaining custom `Strokes` available in the GLF, `ShapeStroke`, `WaveStroke`, and `TextStroke`, follow a process similar to that of `ControlStroke` to create a stroked `Shape`, even though they have more complex algorithms. We explain how those `Strokes` operate but we do not detail their implementation: doing so would take us deep into pure geometry and away from our focus on Java 2D and rendering effects. However, interested readers can refer to the source code accompanying this book to understand the details of those algorithms.

CompositeStroke

`CompositeStroke` combines two other `Strokes`:

```
public class CompositeStroke implements Stroke{
  private Stroke strokeA, strokeB;
  public CompositeStroke(Stroke strokeA, Stroke strokeB){
    if(strokeA==null || strokeB==null)
      throw new IllegalArgumentException();

    this.strokeA = strokeA;
    this.strokeB = strokeB;
  }

  public Shape createStrokedShape(Shape shape){
   return strokeB.createStrokedShape(strokeA.createStrokedShape(shape));
  }
}
```

In plain English, `CompositeStroke` means "outline the outline": it uses `strokeB` to create a stroked `Shape` from the stroked `Shape` created by `strokeA`. For example, consider the following `Stroke`, which we used in one of our first examples in Chapter 2 (see "Graphic Context Attributes" on page 34):

```
Stroke dashStroke
        = new BasicStroke(3f,
                          BasicStroke.CAP_ROUND,
                          BasicStroke.JOIN_ROUND,
                          0f, new float[]{0, 5}, 0);
```

If we use a CompositeStroke to combine it with another BasicStroke as follows (see **CompositeStrokeUsage.java** on the CD-ROM)—

```
BasicStroke simpleOutline
   = new BasicStroke();   // 1 point wide solid stroke
CompositeStroke compositeStroke
   = new CompositeStroke(dashStroke, simpleOutline);
```

—and modify our code sample to use that new Stroke instead of dashStroke,

```
Graphics2D g = ...;

GeneralPath eiffel = ...; // See page 62

// Draw the Shape with the default stroke
g.setPaint(new Color(60, 60, 80));
g.draw(eiffel);

// Create a border rectangle from the shape's bounds
Rectangle border = ...;

g.setStroke(compositeStroke);
g.draw(border);          // This actually draws the 'dots' outline
```

then we obtain the output shown in Figure 9.8: we have outlined the outline.

As for the custom Paint implementations, there is no difference between using
our custom Stroke implementation or the default BasicStroke included with
the 2D API: the Graphics2D.setStroke only depends on the Stroke interface.

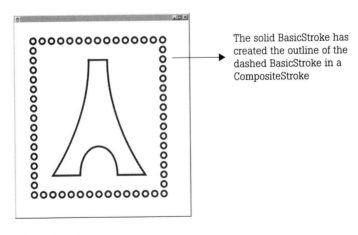

The solid BasicStroke has
created the outline of the
dashed BasicStroke in a
CompositeStroke

Figure 9.8 ■
Outline the outline with CompositeStroke

ControlStroke

The other implementation of the Stroke interface is more typical of how a custom Stroke implementation works. We saw in Chapter 4 (see "Shapes" on page 58) how Shapes provide a description of their form through a PathIterator that describes it in terms of path segments of different types. Each segment has different control points. For example, a line has two control points: the start and end points of the line segments. A quadratic Bezier curve segment has three control points. ControlStroke marks each of the control points with a control Shape, a small square by default.

ControlStroke creates a stroked Shape from a Shape by iterating along its path segments. Here is how it is implemented.

```
public class ControlStroke implements Stroke{
  // Default control Shape
  static Shape defaultControl = new Rectangle(0, 0, 3, 3);

  // Used to stroke the control points, see below
  BasicStroke basicStroke;

  // Control Shape
  Shape controlShape;

  // Control Shape bounds
  Rectangle2D controlBounds;

  // @param width stroke width
  public ControlStroke(float width){
    this(width, defaultControl);
  }

  // @param width stroke width
  // @param controlShape Shape that should be used to mark the control
  // points
  public ControlStroke(float width, Shape controlShape){
    basicStroke = new BasicStroke(width);
    this.controlShape
       = new GeneralPath(controlShape);  // Duplicate input controlShape
    this.controlBounds
       = this.controlShape.getBounds2D();// Used to center controlShape
                                         // about the control points
  }

  // Implementation of the Stroke interface.
  public Shape createStrokedShape(Shape shape){
    GeneralPath strokedShape
       = new GeneralPath();                 // Return value

    // Get path iterator to walk through the Shape path
    PathIterator pi = shape.getPathIterator(null);
```

```
  // Iterate through the path and process each
  // line segment.
  AffineTransform t = new AffineTransform();
  float seg[] = new float[6];
  int segType=0;
  while(!pi.isDone()){
    segType = pi.currentSegment(seg);
    switch(segType){
    case PathIterator.SEG_MOVETO:
      addControl(seg[0], seg[1], strokedShape, t);
      break;
    case PathIterator.SEG_LINETO:
      addControl(seg[0], seg[1], strokedShape, t);
      break;
    case PathIterator.SEG_CLOSE:
      break;
    case PathIterator.SEG_QUADTO:
      addControl(seg[0], seg[1], strokedShape, t);
      addControl(seg[2], seg[3], strokedShape, t);
      break;
    case PathIterator.SEG_CUBICTO:
      addControl(seg[0], seg[1], strokedShape, t);
      addControl(seg[2], seg[3], strokedShape, t);
      addControl(seg[4], seg[5], strokedShape, t);
      break;
    default:
      throw new Error("Illegal seg type : " + segType);
    }
    pi.next();
  }

  return basicStroke.createStrokedShape(strokedShape);
}

private void addControl(float x, float y,
                 GeneralPath path, AffineTransform t){
  t.setToTranslation((float)-controlBounds.getX() + x
                - (float)controlBounds.getWidth()/2,
                (float)-controlBounds.getY() + y
                - (float)controlBounds.getHeight()/2);

  path.append(t.createTransformedShape(controlShape), false);
}
}
```

Here is the common process followed by many `Stroke` implementations in their `createStrokedShape` method:

1. Create a `Shape` to hold the resulting stroked `Shape`.

   ```
   GeneralPath strokedShape
      = new GeneralPath(); // Return value
   ```

2. Then, use the `Shape`'s `PathIterator` to iterate along the `Shape`'s geometry and process each segment individually.

```
PathIterator pi = shape.getPathIterator(null);
float seg[] = new float[6];
int segType=0;
while(!pi.isDone()){
  segType = pi.currentSegment(seg);
  switch(segType){
  case PathIterator.SEG_MOVETO:
    // Process MoveTo
    break;
  case PathIterator.SEG_LINETO:
    // Process LineTo
    break;
  case PathIterator.SEG_CLOSE:
    // Process close
    break;
  case PathIterator.SEG_QUADTO:
    // Process QuadTo
    break;
  case PathIterator.SEG_CUBICTO:
    // Process CubicTo
    break;
  default:
    throw new Error("Illegal seg type : " + segType);
  }
  pi.next();
}
```

3. Process each segment. Each `Stroke` implementation has its own strategy. Here, we simply append a control `Shape` to our stroked `Shape`.

```
private void addControl(float x, float y, GeneralPath path,
                        AffineTransform t){
    t.setToTranslation((float)-controlBounds.getX() + x
                       -(float)controlBounds.getWidth()/2,
                       (float)-controlBounds.getY() + y
                       -(float)controlBounds.getHeight()/2);

    path.append(t.createTransformedShape(controlShape),
                false); // Do not connect
}
```

The input `AffineTransform` is a working object used to avoid the need to create a local `AffineTransform` for each invocation of the method. The input `path` is the stroked `Shape` that the `Stroke` is creating and the (x, y) point is the control point to mark. The preceding code centers `controlShape` about the control point (x, y) and appends it to `path`.

4. At the end, return the `Shape` object that was constructed by processing the successive segments. Here, we combine the `Shape` we created with a `BasicStroke` (to get the markers' outline):

```
return basicStroke.createStrokedShape(strokedShape);
```

In our example, processing a segment consists of adding a control `Shape`, centered about the control points, to the stroked `Shape`. For example, for a quadratic Bezier segment:

```
addControl(seg[0], seg[1], strokedShape, t);
addControl(seg[2], seg[3], strokedShape, t);
```

Remember that the `pi.currentSegment(seg)` call writes the control points coordinates into the `seg` array and that the number of relevant points depends on the returned segment type: none for a close, one for a move or a line, two for a quadratic curve, and three for a cubic curve (refer to the description of `QuadCurve2D` and `CubicCurve2D` on page 68 for an explanation of what the control points mean).

Remember also that the iteration starts implicitly at (0, 0) and that all the segments are in reference to the current position. This is why a line segment only returns one control point: the line start is the current position in the iteration. It is very common for `Stroke` implementations to keep track of the current position. Doing so is done as follows.

```
PathIterator pi = shape.getPathIterator(null);
float seg[] = new float[6];
int segType=0;
float curX=0, curY=0;
float lastMoveX=0, lastMoveY=0;
while(!pi.isDone()){
  segType = pi.currentSegment(seg);
  switch(segType){
  case PathIterator.SEG_MOVETO:
    curX = seg[0];
    curY = seg[1];
    lastMoveX = curX;
    lastMoveY = curY;
    ...
    break;
  case PathIterator.SEG_LINETO:
    curX = seg[0];
    curY = seg[1];
    ...
    break;
  case PathIterator.SEG_CLOSE:
    curX = lastMoveX;
    curY = lastMoveY;
    ...
    break;
  case PathIterator.SEG_QUADTO:
```

```
    curX = seg[2];
    curY = seg[3];
    ...
    break;
  case PathIterator.SEG_CUBICTO:
    curX = seg[4];
    curY = seg[5];
    ...
    break;
  default:
    throw new Error("Illegal seg type : " + segType);
  }
  pi.next();
}
```

The current position usually becomes the last control point on the current segment. The only special segment type is the close segment that moves the current position to the location of the last move, which explains why the code keeps track of the last move location with the `lastMoveX` and `lastMoveY` variables.

The following code snippet illustrates the use of `ControlStroke` on two different `Shapes`, a `Rectangle` and a `GeneralPath` (**ControlStrokeUsage.java** on the CD-ROM).

```
Graphics2D g = ...;

GeneralPath eiffel = ...; // See page 62

// Create a border rectangle from the shape's bounds
Rectangle border = ...;

// Draw the Shapes with the default stroke
g.setPaint(new Color(60, 60, 80));
g.draw(eiffel);
g.draw(border);

// Now draw shapes with ControlStrokes
g.setStroke(new ControlStroke(strokeWidth));
g.draw(eiffel);
g.draw(border);
```

We obtain the output shown in Figure 9.9.

All the other `Shape` implementations that we next discuss follow the same processing pattern. We discuss their specific features.

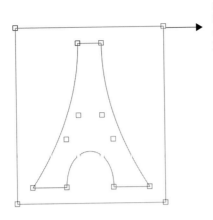

Control Shapes
have been placed
along the stroked
path by ControlStroke

Figure 9.9 ■
Using ControlStroke

ShapeStroke

The `ShapeStroke` implementation repeats a `Shape` pattern along the path of
the `Shapes` it strokes. It takes an array of `Shapes` as an input as well as the size
of the gap between the `Shapes`:

```
public ShapeStroke(Shape pattern[], float gap)
```

If we use the following `Shapes` to build a pattern—

```
Shape smallDot = new Ellipse2D.Float(0, 0, 12, 12);
Shape smallRect = new Rectangle(0, 0, 12, 12);
GeneralPath smallTriangle = new GeneralPath();

smallTriangle.moveTo(6, 0);
smallTriangle.lineTo(12, 12);
smallTriangle.lineTo(0, 12);
smallTriangle.closePath();

Shape pattern[] = { smallDot, smallRect, smallTriangle };
```

—then build a `ShapeStroke` with it—

```
ShapeStroke shapeStroke = new ShapeStroke(pattern, 20);
```

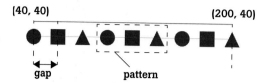

Figure 9.10 ■
Drawing a line with ShapeStroke

and use that stroke to draw a line—

```
Graphics2D g = ...;
g.setStroke(shapeStroke);
g.drawLine(40, 40, 200, 40);
```

—then we obtain the output shown in Figure 9.10.

With the following Shapes—

```
Rectangle rect = new Rectangle(40, 40, 200, 200);
g.draw(rect);

Ellipse2D disc = new Ellipse2D.Double(280, 40, 200, 200);
g.draw(disc);
```

—we obtain the result shown in Figure 9.11 (**ShapeStrokeUsage.java** on the CD-ROM).

The pattern Shapes are centered about the current segment and spaced at regular intervals defined by the gap construction attribute. ShapeStroke is useful in creating many kinds of borders and border effects.

Figure 9.11 ■
Drawing Shapes with a ShapeStroke

WaveStroke

The WaveStroke implementation is a different variation on the same idea. Here, a wave form is integrated into the path of the stroked Shape. Its constructor takes three parameters:

```
public WaveStroke(float waveLength, float waveAmplitude,
                  float waveThickness)
```

If we use a WaveStroke to render a simple line—

```
Stroke stroke
   = new WaveStroke(3, 10, 4), // 10 point length
                               // 4 in amplitude and 3 points thick.
Graphics2D g = ....;
g.setStroke(stroke);
g.drawLine(20, 20, 100, 20);
```

—we obtain the result shown in Figure 9.12, which also illustrates the meaning of the different construction parameters (**WaveStrokeUsage.java** on the CD-ROM).

WaveStroke is not limited to stroking lines, as we already illustrated in Chapter 7 (see "StrokeRenderer" on page 248) and as shown in Figure 9.13; it can be used with any Shape object. The figure actually shows the WaveStroke unit testing output that can be exercised by running the WaveStroke class:

```
java com.sun.glf.goodies.WaveStroke
```

WaveStroke, like ShapeStroke, is useful for creating borders and border effects.

TextStroke

This last implementation of the Stroke interface is the most complex, but it is as easy to use as the other ones. The idea of TextStroke is to repeat a text pattern along the path of a Shape. The TextStroke constructor takes the text it should repeat along the stroked Shape as an input.

```
public TextStroke(String text, Font font, boolean cycle, float cycleGap)
```

Figure 9.12 ■
Stroking a line with WaveStroke

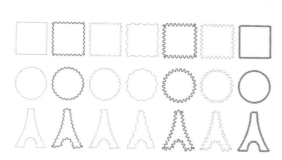

Each column in the figure shows different Shapes stroked with the same WaveStroke. Each column uses a WaveStroke with different settings for the width, waveLength, and waveHeight. The first column is displayed for reference and uses a BasicStroke.

Figure 9.13 ■
Different settings with WaveStroke

The `text` and `font` parameters define the text to draw along the stroked path. The `cycle` and `cycleGap` parameters control whether or not the text should be repeated after it has been "written" completely once and, if it should be, how much space should be inserted before the next text string starts.

The following code snippet (**TextStrokeUsage.java** on the CD-ROM) shows how to use a `TextStroke`.

```
// First, create the Shape object that will be stroked
Rectangle rect = new Rectangle(40, 40, 200, 200);
Ellipse2D disc = new Ellipse2D.Double(280, 40, 200, 200);
GeneralPath triangle = new GeneralPath();
triangle.moveTo(620, 40);
triangle.lineTo(720, 240);
triangle.lineTo(520, 240);
triangle.lineTo(620, 40);

// Build a first TextStroke that will repeat the text string
// along the Shape path, and use it to stroke the rectangle, disc and
triangle
Font font = new Font("dialog", Font.PLAIN, 20);
Stroke cycleTextStroke
   = new TextStroke("Text Strokes are fun", font, true, 10);
g.setStroke(cycleTextStroke);

g.draw(rect);
g.draw(disc);
g.draw(triangle);
```

```
// Stroke Shapes with BasicStroke for reference
g.setStroke(new BasicStroke());
g.translate(0, 240);

g.draw(rect);
g.draw(disc);
g.draw(triangle);

// Build a second TextStroke that will not repeat the text string along
// the Shape path.
// Use it to stroke the rectangle, disc and triangle
Stroke textStroke
  = new TextStroke("Text Strokes are fun", font, false, 0);
g.setStroke(textStroke);

g.translate(0, 240);
g.draw(rect);
g.draw(disc);
g.draw(triangle);
```

Figure 9.14 shows this example's output.

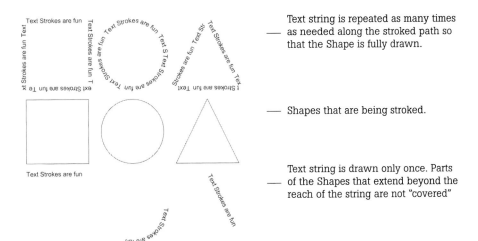

Text string is repeated as many times as needed along the stroked path so that the Shape is fully drawn.

Shapes that are being stroked.

Text string is drawn only once. Parts of the Shapes that extend beyond the reach of the string are not "covered"

Figure 9.14 ■
Using text to stroke Shapes with TextStroke

Custom Composite

We saw in Chapter 5 (see "Composite" on page 170) that Composites are responsible for "blending" the source of a rendering operation (that is, "what" we paint) with the destination of the rendering operation (that is, "where" we paint). Two classes are involved in this operation: Composite and Composite-Context. Both are interfaces, which makes it possible to create new kinds of blending rules for the Java 2D platform.

Typically, the Composite implementation encapsulates the rule of the blending operation. It is independent of the output device, and it must be able to create a CompositeContext for a given pair of ColorModels that describe how pixels are organized in the Rasters that the CompositeContext will later have to mix. The CompositeContext implementation is where the pixel blending happens.

Creating a custom Composite implementation (Advanced topic)

As with Paints, two steps are involved in creating a custom Composite:

1. Write one or several implementations of the CompositeContext interface that implements the desired blending rule.
2. Write an implementation of the Composite interface that defines the blending rule(s) and uses the CompositeContext implementation(s).

▼ **Writing an implementation of the CompositeContext interface**
Here is the definition of the CompositeContext interface.

```
public interface CompositeContext {
  public void dispose();          // Releases resources the context
                                  // might have allocated

  public void compose(Raster src, // 'what' is rendered. This is
                                  // the source.

             Raster dstIn,        // 'where' we are rendering.

             WritableRaster dstOut);
                                  // where to store the result
                                  // of the composite operation.
}
```

It is common for a CompositeContext implementation to define the Color-Model it operates in. For example, java.awt.AlphasCompositeContext operates in the DirectColorModel, as does our custom implementation, ColorCompositeContext. There are no constructors in interfaces, so there are no syntactical requirements for CompositeContexts to be constructed with the

`ColorModels` of the `src`, `dstIn`, and `dstOut` `Rasters` that will be passed to compose invocations. However, it is standard for `CompositeContext` implementations to take those `ColorModels` as construction parameters and determine whether they are compatible with its working `ColorModel`. That information can be used to define whether or not the input and output `Rasters` will need to be converted during the `compose` operation.

Converting `ColorModels` to the appropriate model that the implementation uses can be handled by `ColorConvertOp` filters. Here is a template for a `CompositeContext` implementation.

```
public class MyCompositeContext implements CompositeContext{
    ColorModel myCM;
    boolean srcNeedsConvert;
    boolean dstNeedsConvert;
    ColorConvertOp srcToMyCm, dstToMyCM, myCMToDst;

    public MyCompositeContext(ColorModel srcCM, ColorModel dstCM,
                              RenderingHints hints,
                              //Other implementation specific
                              // parameters
                              ){
        myCM = ...; // Depends on CompositeContext implementation
        if(!srcCM.equals(myCM)){
          srcNeedsConvert = true;
          srcToMyCM = new ColorConverOp(srcCM.getColorSpace(),
                                        myCM.getColorSpace(), hints);
        }
        if(!dstCM.equals(myCM)){
          dstNeedsConvert = true;
          dstToMyCM = new ColorConvertOp(dstCM.getColorSpace(),
                                         myCM.getColorSpace(), hints);
          myCMToDst = new ColorConvertOp(myCM.getColorSpace(),
                                         dstCM.getColorSpace(), hints);
        }

        ...; // Other implementation-dependent code
    }

    public void compose(Raster src, Raster dstIn, WritableRaster dstOut){
        int w = src.getWidth();
        int h = src.getHeight();
        int x = src.getMinX();
        int y = src.getMinY();

        // Convert src if needed
        if(srcNeedsConvert){
          WritableRaster newSrc
             = myCM.createCompatibleWritableRaster(w, h);
          newSrc = newSrc.createWritableTranslatedChild(x, y);
          src = srcToMyCM.filter(src, newSrc);
        }
```

```
        // Convert dst if needed
        WritableRaster dstOutOrig = dstOut;
        if(dstNeedsConvert){
          WritableRaster newDstIn
            = myCM.createCompatibleWritableRaster(w, h);
          newDstIn = newDst.createWritableTranslatedChild(x, y);
          dstIn = dstToMyCM.filter(dstIn, newDstIn);

          WritableRaster newDstOut
            = myCM.createCompatibleWritableRaster(w, h);
          newDstOut = newDstOut.createWritableTranslatedChild(x, y);
          dstOut = dstToMyCM.filter(dstOut, myDstOut);
        }

        // .... Implement mixing of src and dstIn. Write result in dstOut
        //      This is implementation dependent

        // Convert dstOut if needed
        if(dstNeedsConvert)
          dstOut = myCMToDst.filter(dstOut, dstOutOrig);
    }
}
```

Note how the conversion is made with a `ColorConvertOp`: the input and output `ColorSpaces` are used to build the `ColorConvertOp` object.

```
srcToMyCM = new ColorConvertOp(srcCM.getColorSpace(),
                        myCM.getColorSpace(), hints);
```

Furthermore, to ensure that the converted `Raster` has a `SampleModel` compatible with the working `ColorModel` (`myCM` in the example), the destination `ColorModel` creates the color conversion destination `Raster`.

```
WritableRaster newSrc = myCM.createCompatibleWritableRaster(w, h);
newSrc = newSrc.createWritableTranslatedChild(x, y);
```

There might be different `SampleModel`s that are compatible with a given `ColorSpace`. When the filter method of `ColorConvertOp` is invoked with a null argument for the destination, it creates a destination `Raster` that is compatible with the destination `ColorSpace`. However, there is no guarantee that it will be the one we want if there are several options, so we create the destination `Raster` from the `ColorModel` we use to ensure that the converted `Raster` has the format we expect.

`createWritableTranslatedChild` puts the `Raster` at the same (x, y) location as the filtered `Raster`. Remember that `Raster`s can be anywhere in the coordinate space and do not necessarily start at, nor include, the origin. `createWritableTranslatedChild` does not duplicate the `DataBuffer` used by the input `WritableRaster`. Instead, the `SampleModel`, `DataBuffer`, and size in the returned `WritableRaster` object are unchanged: only the `WritableRaster`'s origin has been modified.

Finally, once a compatible destination `WritableRaster` is ready, the conversion happens:

```
src = srcToMyCM.filter(src, newSrc);
```

Besides the color conversion needed to enable the `CompositeContext` implementation to work in the `ColorModel` it chooses, the actual "mixing" of the `src` and `dstIn Rasters` into new pixel values stored in `dstOut` depends on the `CompositeContext` implementation. Here is the pseudocode for composing the source and destination.

```
for(int i=0; i<h; i++){          // Iterate through each row
  for(int j=0; j<w; j++){        // Iterate through each
                                 // column in the row

    Object pixelSource
      = src.getPixel(j, i, ...);   // Get source pixel value,
                                   // column j, row i
    Object pixelDestination
      = dstIn.getPixel(j, i, ...); // Get destination pixel value
    Object pixelDestinationOut
      = compose(pixelSource,
              pixelDestination);  // Combine source and
                                  // destination pixels

    dstOut.setPixel(j, i,
          pixelDestinationOut);   // Write result in output Raster
  }
}
```

Implementations typically use a faster method than `getPixel` and `setPixel` to access or set pixel values, depending on the `ColorModel` they use. For example, an implementation that uses the default `ColorModel` (as returned by `ColorModel.getRGBDefault`) can rely on the fact that this model uses a `SinglePixelPackedSample` model and therefore a `DataBufferInt` to access the integers where pixels are stored directly.

Writing the `CompositeContext` implementation is the hard part of creating a custom composition rule for source and destination. Writing a `Composite` implementation is simpler.

▼ **Writing a Composite implementation**   As we mentioned earlier, the `Composite` implementation encapsulates the rule for a given type of compositing and creates a `CompositeContext` for a given pair of source and destination `ColorModels`.

For example, the `AlphaComposite` class defines a composition rule where the output is a linear combination of the source and destination `Rasters`.[3] The `ColorComposite` class, which we introduce later, defines a different type of

---

3.   See "AlphaComposite rules" on page 172 in Chapter 5.

linear combination of the source and destination that operates on the HSB components of the pixels it mixes. This definition is output device independent and is used by the `Composite` implementation, along with the source and destination `ColorModels`, to create the proper `CompositeContext` in its implementation of the `createContext` method.

```
public interface Composite {
    public CompositeContext createContext(ColorModel srcColorModel,
                                          ColorModel dstColorModel,
                                          RenderingHints hints);

}
```

For example, the `AlphaComposite` implementation is straightforward:

```
public CompositeContext createContext(ColorModel srcColorModel,
                                      ColorModel dstColorModel,
                                      RenderingHints hints) {
  return new AlphaCompositeContext(srcColorModel, dstColorModel,
                                   rule, extraAlpha);
}
```

where `rule` and `extraAlpha` describe the Porter and Duff rule (for example, Source Over or Destination In, see page 172) and the transparency setting (for example, 0.5 for half transparent). Our implementation, `ColorComposite`, does something very similar:

```
public CompositeContext createContext(ColorModel srcColorModel,
                                      ColorModel dstColorModel,
                                      RenderingHints hints){
  return new ColorCompositeContext(rule, alpha, srcColorModel,
                                   dstColorModel, hints);
}
```

where `rule` and `alpha` describe the type of compositing and transparency values, as we explain later. The created `CompositeContext` can then use the input `ColorModels` (and hints) to determine whether it should perform color conversions and use the input rule and alpha to perform the appropriate pixel compositing.

There are a number of important things to understand about the `Composite` design. Separating the `Composite` rule definition from the algorithm implementation allows the two to evolve separately:

- When used in a multithreaded environment, a `Composite` implementation can create a separate `CompositeContext` for each thread. The `Composite-Context` implementation can then assume it is used by a single thread.
- Even though `AlphaComposite` and `ColorComposite` do not use this technique, the `Composite` implementations have an opportunity to decide between alternate `CompositeContext` implementations depending on the context. For example, an implementation could use two different `CompositeContext` implementations: an accurate but slower one and a fast

but less accurate one. If the `RenderingHints.KEY_RENDERING` is set to `RenderingHints.VALUE_RENDER_SPEED`, it would use the fast implementations; if it is set to `RenderingHints.VALUE_RENDER_QUALITY`, it would use the highly accurate implementation. Another example would be a `Composite` implementation that uses different `CompositeContexts` for different `ColorModels`. One could operate in the default RGB `ColorModel` and the other one in a gray scale `ComponentColorModel`. Depending on the source and destination `ColorModel`, the `Composite` implementation could use one or the other.

Creating a custom compositing strategy requires a good command of the underlying concepts used in Java 2D: `DataBuffers`, `SampleModels`, `Rasters` and `WritableRasters`, and `ColorModels`. However, most programmers do not have to write a custom `Composite` implementation and can use existing ones without needing to understand, or even know about, the underlying implementations. For example, the `ColorComposite` implementation, which we introduce next, can be used just as easily as `AlphaComposite`.

ColorComposite: Combining HSB values

The idea of the `ColorComposite` class is to combine source and destination such that, for example, we could modify the color of the destination without modifying its brightness. We first look at the definition of `ColorComposite` and explain how it mixes source and destination. Then, we see how to use it from a program.

▼ **ColorComposite defined**   This implementation of the `Composite` interface combines the source and destination according to the following rules and works by reference to the Hue, Saturation, and Brightness components of the source and destination it combines:

1. *Hue Composite.* The destination takes the hue of the source and the brightness and saturation of the destination.
2. *Brightness Composite.* The destination takes the brightness of the source and the hue and saturation of the destination.
3. *Saturation Composite.* The destination takes the saturation of the source and the hue and brightness of the destination.
4. *Color Composite.* The destination takes the hue and saturation of the source and the brightness of the destination.

For each type, the rule is modulated by the alpha value. Assuming that we work in the HSB color space and that we call `sa, sh, ss, sb` the components of the source, `dia, dih, dis, dib` the components of the destination before composition, then the destination components are, after composition (destination out):

1. Hue Composite.
```
doh = sh
dos = dis
dob = dib
```
2. Brightness Composite.
```
doh = dih
dos = dis
dob = sb
```
3. Saturation Composite.
```
doh = dih
dos = ss
dob = dib
```
4. Color Composite.
```
doh = sh
dos = ss
dob = dib
```

Alpha composition is made in the standard RGB space (pseudocode).
```
dor = HSVtoRGB(doh, dos, dob).red;   // Destination out red
dog = HSVtoRGB(doh, dos, dob).green; // Destination out green
dob = HSVtoRGB(doh, dos, dob).blue;  // Destination out blue

a = sa*alpha;            // sa is the source pixel alpha value
                         // sa*alpha is the actual
                         // contribution of the source to the destination

ac = 1-a;                // Contribution of the destination to
                         // the final output

dor = a*dor + ac.dir     // dir = Destination in red
dog = a*dog + ac*dig     // dig = Destination in green
dob = a*dob + ac*dib     // dib = Destination in blue
doa = dia;
```

▼ Using ColorComposite   From this explanation, it may be hard to visualize what this implementation actually does. Let us see how to use the `Color-Composite` class.

`ColorComposite`, as `AlphaComposite`, contains a number of predefined, static `Composite` instances: `ColorComposite.Hue`, `ColorComposite.Saturation`, `ColorComposite.Brightness`, and `ColorComposite.Hs` (Hue and Saturation, that is, what we called color composite earlier). Those predefined values are fully opaque, that is, they use an alpha value of 1, and they can be used easily. For example:
```
Graphics2d g = ..;
g.setComposite(ColorComposite.Hue);
```

When transparency is needed, the ColorComposite.getInstance(rule, alpha) method can be used. The rule is defined by a ColorCompositeRule instance, and the alpha value is a floating-point numeric. To exercise the different values of ColorComposite and illustrate how it works, we created the following CompositionFactory that combines an image and draws a color rectangle on top of it, using a configurable ColorComposite (**ColorComposite-Usage.java** on the CD-ROM).

```
BufferedImage image
   = Toolbox.loadImage(destinationImageFile,
                       BufferedImage.TYPE_INT_RGB);
Dimension size = new Dimension(image.getWidth(), image.getHeight());
LayerComposition cmp = new LayerComposition(size);

ImageLayer destination = new ImageLayer(cmp, image);

ShapeLayer source = new ShapeLayer(cmp, cmp.getBounds(),
                                   new FillRenderer(sourceColor));
ColorComposite composite
   = ColorComposite.getInstance(compositeRule, compositeAlpha);
source.setComposite(composite);

cmp.setLayers(new Layer[]{destination, source});
```

Figure 9.15 shows the output obtained for different settings, using our Van Gogh portrait and painting a pure red rectangle on top of it.

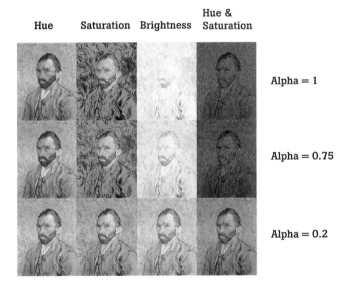

Hue	Saturation	Brightness	Hue & Saturation	
				Alpha = 1
				Alpha = 0.75
				Alpha = 0.2

Figure 9.15 ■
ColorComposite usage

▼ **About the ColorComposite implementation** The `ColorComposite` and `ColorCompositeContext` classes are implemented in line with the comments made at the beginning of this section. There is an interesting point to note about color composite—the way in which alpha composition is done. Alpha composition, at the end of the process, is done in the RGB color space and not using the HSV value. An alternate solution would have been to do the alpha compositing in HSV and then convert to RGB.

```
doh = a*doh + ac*dih;
dos = a*dos + ac*dis;
dob = a*.dob + ac*dib;

dor = HSVtoRGB(doh, dos, dob).red;     // Destination out red
dog = HSVtoRGB(doh, dos, dob).green;   // Destination out green
dob = HSVtoRGB(doh, dos, dob).blue;    // Destination out blue
```

While the saturation and brightness components would be the same, the hue would have been very different. The reason is that the hue represents the angle in the color palette. A linear combination of the hues produces an average of the angle value that is not our intuitive way of mixing colors, even though the result is mathematically accurate. For example, mixing the red and blue hue produces yellow. This issue is the problem of color interpolation: given two colors, what are the intermediate color values (interpolated colors)? As we just illustrated, this value depends on the color space, and the set of colors reached by linear combinations of the two colors will vary.

In the `ColorComposite` implementation, we chose to interpolate colors in the RGB space because interpolation produces a fairly good result; it is also the technique used for other algorithms in the Java 2D API that perform color interpolation (`GradientPaint`, and our custom `Paints`: `GradientPaintExt`, `RadialGradientPaint`, and `RadialGradientPaintExt`). The reader can refer to [Foley1997] for further reading on color interpolation.

The `ColorComposite` class shows that sophisticated techniques can be added seamlessly to Java 2D: we can use `ColorComposite` as easily and in the same way as we would `AlphaComposite` or any other `Composite` implementation. Next, we see how another type of Java 2D feature, image filtering, can be extended as well.

Custom BufferedImageOps and RasterOps

`BufferedImageOp` and `RasterOp` are filter interfaces; we introduced the implementations provided by the API in Chapter 4 (see "BufferedImageOp" on page 94). In this section, we look at what those interfaces define and explain their semantics. Then, we introduce an implementation: the sophisticated `LightOp` filter, which we will use to cast spotlights and to texturize the images we filter. Finally, we describe how other implementations included in GLF work: `ToneAdjustmentOp`, `CompositeOp`, and `CompositeRasterOp`.

The BufferedImageOp and RasterOp interfaces

These two interfaces are fairly similar. Here is the `RasterOp` definition.

```
public interface RasterOp {
    public Rectangle2D getBounds2D(Raster src);
    public Point2D getPoint2D(Point2D srcPt, Point2D dstPt);
    public RenderingHints getRenderingHints();

    public WritableRaster filter(Raster src, WritableRaster dest);
    public WritableRaster createCompatibleDestRaster(Raster src);
}
```

And here is the `BufferedImageOp` definition:

```
public interface BufferedImageOp {
    public Rectangle2D getBounds2D (BufferedImage src);
    public Point2D getPoint2D (Point2D srcPt, Point2D dstPt);
    public RenderingHints getRenderingHints();

    public BufferedImage filter(BufferedImage src, BufferedImage dest);
    public BufferedImage createCompatibleDestImage(BufferedImage src,
                                             ColorModel destCM);
}
```

▼ **Hints**   The first thing to note is that filters can have associated `Rendering-Hints`. Those are passed at construction time to the filter implementation and can be used by the filter to decide between alternate rendering algorithms.

▼ **Spatial information**   The `getBounds2D` method returns the bounding box of the output `BufferedImage` or `Raster`. The `getPoint2D` method returns the location of a destination point given a location in the input image. Note that `BufferedImage`s always have their origin at (0, 0). Therefore, a filtered image also has its origin at (0, 0). As a consequence, if the filter makes some kind of spatial transformation (as `AffineTransformOp` does), the output `BufferedImage` bounding box will start at (0, 0) and extend to encompass the spatially transformed image.

▼ **Creating a compatible destination**   Both `BufferedImageOp` and `RasterOp` offer a way to create a compatible destination to receive the result of a filtering operation through their `createCompatibleDestImage` and `createCompatibleDestRaster` methods. These methods are typically called internally by the implementation when their `filter` implementation is invoked with a null destination to create a destination `BufferedImage` or `Raster` that will hold the filtering result.

▼ **Filtering** Both types of filters have a `filter` method that takes a `BufferedImage` or `Raster` as input. In each case, the implementation is required to create an appropriate destination if one is not provided (that is, the destination argument is null). The `filter` method is the heart of a filter's implementation, and this is where pixel processing happens to create the filtered result. This is the method we used in our filtering examples in Chapter 4 (see these examples starting on page 94).

There are several requirements that a filter implementation must follow:

1. The documentation must specify whether or not the filter supports in-place filtering, that is, whether it is able to serve a filter invocation where the source and destination are the same image objects. Some filters, such as `RescaleOp`, can do this, and some, such as `ConvolveOp`, cannot. Typically, a filter can support in-place filtering when there is a one-to-one mapping between the source and destination and there is no spatial modification of pixels.

2. An implementation should throw an `IllegalArgumentException` if the input source or destination is not in a format it can work with. Note that implementations could also decide to perform appropriate conversions and serve the request. However, this is not always possible. For example, `BandCombineOp` needs to have a destination that has a specific number of bands. If not, there is no way a proper, temporary output could be converted to a different number of bands.

Implementing a custom filter (Advanced topic)

What is involved in implementing an image filter?

▼ **BufferedImageOp or RasterOp** The first thing is to decide whether you are implementing a `BufferedImageOp`, `RasterOp`, or both. As we have seen, most of the default implementations implement both (except `BandCombineOp`), and this is usually a good idea. Our `LightOp` implementation implements both interfaces.

▼ **Hints** The second thing is to implement `getHints`. If the filter uses hints to determine the filtering algorithms it uses, those will typically be passed as construction parameters. The `getHints` method should return this value.

▼ **Spatial characteristics** The third thing is to implement the `getBounds2D` and `getPoint2D` methods. Unless the filter is a spatial filter (that is, a filter that modifies pixel location, such as `AffineTransformOp`), those methods are straightforward, that is, they return the input points or the image/raster bounds unmodified.

▼ **Supported formats**   The fourth thing is to define the `ColorModel`(s) (and `SampleModels`, for `RasterOps`) on which the filter will work. As for `Paints` and `Composites`, it may be a good idea to operate in the default RGB `ColorModel` (and `DirectColorModel`) if possible, because this is the default `ColorModel` in Java 2D. However, using the default may not always make sense. Once the compatible `ColorModels` have been identified, you need to decide how to handle filter invocations that use input sources with unsupported models. For example, our `LightOp` implementation operates both on RGB and ARGB `DirectColorModel`s for `BufferedImages` and `SinglePixelPackedSample-Model` with three or four components with eight significant bits each for `Rasters`. When used as a `BufferedImageOp`, the source and destination are converted to the compatible standard RGB `ColorModel` if they are not compatible to begin with.

```
public BufferedImage filter(BufferedImage src, BufferedImage dest){
  if (src == null)
    throw new NullPointerException("src image is null");

  // First, convert src image if necessary
  SampleModel model = src.getSampleModel();
  if(!isCompatible(model)){
    BufferedImage tmp
      = new BufferedImage(src.getWidth(), src.getHeight(),
                          BufferedImage.TYPE_INT_ARGB);
    ColorConvertOp toRGB = new ColorConvertOp(null);
    toRGB.filter(src, tmp);
    src = tmp;
  }

  // Now, check destination. If compatible, it is used as is. Otherwise
  // a temporary image is used.
  BufferedImage finalDest = dest;
  if(dest==null){
    dest = createCompatibleDestImage(src, null);
    finalDest = dest;
  }
  else{
    // Check that the destination ColorModel is compatible
    SampleModel destModel = dest.getSampleModel();
    if(!isCompatible(destModel))
      dest = createCompatibleDestImage(src, null);
  }

  // We now have two compatible images. We can safely filter the source
  filter(src.getRaster(), dest.getRaster());

  // If we had to use a temporary destination, copy the result into the
  // real output image
  if(dest != finalDest){
    ColorConvertOp toDestCM = new ColorConvertOp(null);
```

```
    toDestCM.filter(dest, finalDest);
  }

  return dest;
}
```

When used as a `RasterOp`, `LightOp` throws an `IllegalArgumentException` if the input and destination `Raster`s do not have a supported `SampleModel`.

```
public WritableRaster filter(Raster src, WritableRaster dest){
  //
  // First, check input arguments
  //
  checkCompatible(src.getSampleModel());
  if(dest!=null) checkCompatible(dest.getSampleModel());
  else dest = createCompatibleDestRaster(src);
    ...
}
..

public void checkCompatible(SampleModel model){
  boolean compatible = false;

  .... // Set compatible to true if SampleModel can be used by filter

  if(!compatible)
    throw new IllegalArgumentException("Incompatible SampleModel");
}
```

▼ **Implementation**   Finally, the last thing involved in implementing a filter is the filtering algorithm itself. As in the preceding code, it is common for a filter that implements both the `BufferedImageOp` and the `RasterOp` interfaces to use a single processing method. The image filter uses the `Raster` filter.

```
public BufferedImage filter(BufferedImage src, BufferedImage dest){
  // Check source and destination. Color convert if necessary and
  // possible
  ....

  // We now have two compatible images. We can safely filter the source
  filter(src.getRaster(), dest.getRaster());

  // Color convert destination if necessary
  ...

  return dest;
}
```

The implementation of the filter varies, depending on the pixel format it works with and the type of filtering it implements. This is what makes each filter unique, as we now illustrate with the `LightOp` filter.

LightOp

LightOp provides a way to cast light on the filtered image and, optionally, add texture to it. It is similar to positioning lights on or around the filtered image to create a specific lighting condition. In addition, LightOp uses a notion of elevation map that gives a third dimension to filtered images. As a result, it can add texture to the images it filters. This section explains how each of those filtering effects can be obtained with the LightOp filter: casting light and texturizing. We first look at the different classes used by the filter to describe lighting conditions and texture information. Then, we present helper classes and methods that make using LightOp easy.

▼ **Operation/Design**   The LightOp class implements the Buffered-ImageOp and RasterOp interfaces as we described in the previous paragraphs. It works in the default RGB ColorModel and, when used as a BufferedImageOp, performs color conversion to the RGB ColorModel.

Figure 9.16 shows a class diagram containing all the classes related to LightOp.

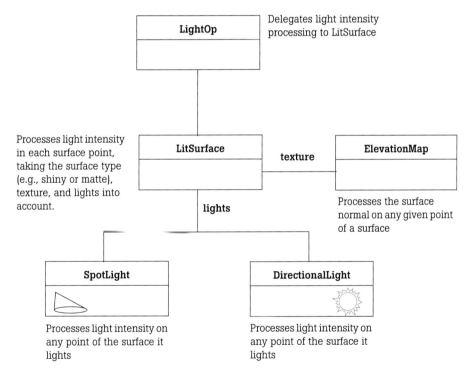

Figure 9.16 ■
LightOp classes

The `LitSurface` class that `LightOp` uses has three roles:

- First, it contains a description of the filtered image surface type: Is the surface reflective or matte? Is it shiny or not?
- Second, it contains a description of the surface geometry: Is it flat or does it have texture? If it has texture, that texture is described by an `ElevationMap` object.[4]
- Third, it defines the lighting conditions: What is the ambient light? Are there spotlights; if yes, what is their color, intensity, and location? Are there directional lights; if yes, what is their color, intensity, and direction?

In a nutshell, a `LitSurface` object describes an infinitely large virtual surface of a given type (for example, matte or metallic) that may have a texture and that has lights shining on it: this explains the name *Lit*Surface. The feature that `LightOp` uses is that a `LitSurface` can compute the red, green, and blue light intensity in any point. This light intensity is what its `getXXIntensity` method computes. For performance reasons, two methods compute light intensity: `getFlatIntensity` and `getTexturedIntensity`. The first one ignores the texture information, even if there is a texture, and the other one uses it (and fails if there is no `ElevationMap`).

The following pseudocode illustrates the heart of the `LightOp` filtering process.

```
minX = srcRaster.getMinX();  // x axis origin of the filtered Raster.
minY = srcRaster.getMinY();  // y axis origin of the filtered Raster.
double I[] = {0, 0, 0};      //  Will store red, green and blue
                             // light intensity
if(litSurface.isTextured()){
   for(int i=0; i<h; i++){     // For each row in the filtered Raster
      for(int j=0; j<w; j++){ // For each column in the row
         r = .., g = , b = ... // Get source red, green and blue components

         // Get light intensity at the current pixel location
         litSurface.getTexturedIntensity(j + minX, i + minY, I, Iwork);

         // Modify red, green, and blue value depending on intensity
         // and check for value overflow
         r = scale(r, I[0]);
         g = scale(g, I[1]);
         b = scale(b, I[2]);


         ...
      }// for each column
   }// for each row
```

---

4. In the context of `LightOp`, *texture* refers to a 3D lighting concept. When a surface has a texture, it means that it is not flat, and the texture defines the elevation in each point of the surface. Note that *texture* is sometimes used with a different meaning, for example in the `TexturePaint` class, where *texture* refers to an image whose pixel values are used to fill and draw `Shape` objects.

```
}// if(litSurface.isTextured())

else{                            // Surface has no texture, use
                                 // getFlatIntensity

   for(int i=0; i<h; i++){  // For each row in the filtered Raster
      for(int j=0; j<w; j++){// For each column in the row
         r = .., g = , b = ...// Get source red, green, and blue components

         // Get light intensity at the current pixel location
         litSurface.getFlatIntensity(j + minX, i + minY, I, Iwork);

         // Modify red, green, and blue value depending on intensity
         // and check for value overflow
         r = scale(r, I[0]);
         g = scale(g, I[1]);
         b = scale(b, I[2]);

         ...
      }// for each column
   }// for each row
}// if(litSurface.isTextured())
```

The reason for having two separate loops for textured and flat surfaces is that LightOp is an extremely computation intensive filter that uses 3D techniques, so it was important to be able to make the intensity calculation in a final method to avoid the additional cost of a virtual method. Furthermore, it was also important that LightOp need not check whether it has an associated texture on each request for intensity values. Having two separate methods, one for textured processing and one for untextured processing, allows each to be optimized and final, at the cost of having two separate loops.

The filtering done by LightOp relies on the ability of LitSurface to compute intensity on any given point of a surface. We said that there are three aspects to a LitSurface: the lights that illuminate the surface, the surface texture, and the surface type. Let us see how each influences the intensity values LitSurfaces compute.

▼ **Adding lights to a LitSurface**   Three types of lights can illuminate a LitSurface:

■ Ambient light — Has the same intensity in all viewing directions.
■ Directional light — Equivalent to the light produced by the sun if we assume all the rays are parallel, which is a fair approximation in most contexts. The incident light intensity is uniform across the surface and has a fixed direction.
■ Point light — Equivalent to the light project by a spotlight. The incident light intensity depends on the position of a point relative to the light source.

The incident light defines the lighting conditions. However, the light we perceive from an object is the reflected light. Objects reflect lights in different

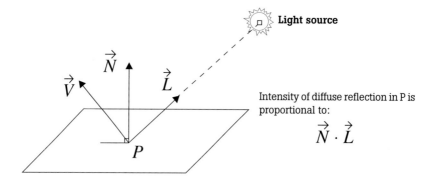

Figure 9.17 ■
Light vector, surface normal, and light intensity

ways, and there are several models for light reflection. In the diffuse reflection model, an object reflects light equally in all directions, and the intensity perceived by the viewer will be the same from all viewing angles. Figure 9.17 shows how in this model, the reflected light intensity on a given point is related to the product of the light vector (L, vector toward the light source) by the normal (N) to the surface at that point. The vector V points to the viewer.

Ambient light

For ambient light, the light intensity is the same in all directions. Therefore, no matter what the surface normal is, the product of the light vectors and the surface normal is constant. This explains why ambient light is always described by a constant.

In a `LitSurface`, the ambient light is one of the `LitSurface` attributes. For example, the following code snippet creates a `LitSurface` with a controllable ambient light (see **LightOpUsage1.java** on the CD-ROM).

```
LitSurface litSurface = new LitSurface(ambientLight);
LightOp lightOp = new LightOp(litSurface);
BufferedImage image = ...; // e.g. load Van Gogh image
BufferedImage filteredImage = lightOp.filter(image, null);
```

Because the intensity in each point is constant, this code only modifies the filtered image intensity, as shown in Figure 9.18.

This is an expensive way of adjusting the intensity; the ambient light is never used alone, but always in combination with other types of lights.[5]

---

5. In a 3D world, ambient light has an intensity I_a and 3D objects have an ambient reflection coefficient, k_a. The ambient light on an object is $k_a.I_a$. In our context, we only have a single object, the lit surface, and we have combined k_a and I_a in a single constant we call the ambient light.

0.25   0.5   0.75

1   1.5

Figure 9.18 ∎
Different settings for ambient light

Directional light

Light cast from directional lights has a constant direction in all points of the surface. Figure 9.19 illustrates how the reflected intensity depends on the illuminated surface type. On a flat surface, all points have the same normal, and the resulting intensity will be constant in all points. However, if the surface is not flat, the normal vector will vary, as will the resulting reflected light intensity.

The `DirectionalLight` class encapsulates all the information about a directional light. It is created with a light vector, a light intensity, and a light `Color`. The light vector has three dimensions. Figure 9.20 illustrates how the third-dimension axis is perpendicular to the image and pointing toward the viewer. This coordinate system is the one used internally by `LightOp` and related classes for all the 3D geometry calculations.

The following code snippet creates a `LightOp` object with one `Directional-Light` (**LightOpUsage2.java** on the CD-ROM).

```
double L[] = {-1, -1, 1};  // Light comes from the top-left corner
float I = ...;             // Intensity.
DirectionalLight eveningSun = new DirectionalLight(L, I, color);
LitSurface litSurface = new LitSurface();
litSurface.addLight(eveningSun);
LightOp lightOp = new LightOp(litSurface);
```

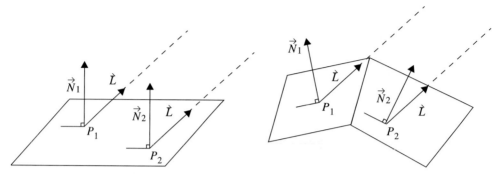

The light vector is constant over the surface (e.g., sunlight). When the surface is flat, the normal is constant over the surface, i.e., $N_1 = N_2$. Therefore, the reflected light intensity is the same on any point of the surface.

The light vector is constant over the surface (e.g., sunlight). Here, the surface is not flat: e.g., N_1 is not equal to N_2 in the figure. Therefore, the reflected light intensity is different in each point of the surface and depends on the normal on that point.

Figure 9.19 ■
Directional light on flat surface and on nonflat surface

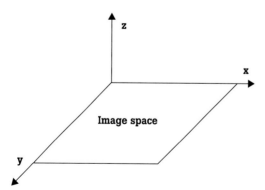

Figure 9.20 ■
3D Coordinate system used in LightOp

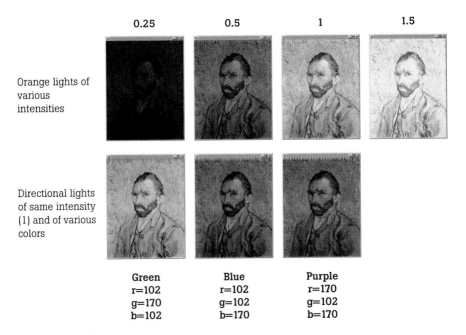

Figure 9.21 ■
Using DirectionalLights with different intensities and colors

Figure 9.21 shows the result produced when filtering with different settings for the light color and intensity.

By default, the surface is flat, so the directional light intensity is the same in all points. Therefore, our lighting operation is similar to a `RescaleOp`. Directional lights are typically used with textures in the surface, and the following example shows how much difference it makes on the output (**LightOpUsage3.java** on the CD-ROM).

```
BufferedImage image = Toolbox.loadImage(imageFile,
BufferedImage.TYPE_INT_RGB);
if(image==null)
  throw new IllegalArgumentException("Could not load imageFileName");
BufferedImage textureMap = Toolbox.loadImage(textureFile,
BufferedImage.TYPE_BYTE_GRAY);
if(textureMap==null)
  throw new IllegalArgumentException("Could not load textureMapFile");
```

```
double L[] = {-1, -1, 1};                    // Light comes from the
                                             // top-left corner

float I = lightIntensity;                    // Intensity.

DirectionalLight eveningSun = new DirectionalLight(L, I, lightColor);

LitSurface litSurface = new LitSurface(0); // No ambient light

litSurface.addLight(eveningSun);
LightOp lightOp = new LightOp(litSurface);
BufferedImage filteredImage = lightOp.filter(image, null);

// Create another image of the same size.
int w = image.getWidth();
int h = image.getHeight();
BufferedImage buf = new BufferedImage(w,h, BufferedImage.TYPE_INT_RGB);
Graphics2D g = buf.createGraphics();
g.setPaint(Color.gray);
g.fillRect(0, 0, w, h);

// Filter with no texture
BufferedImage noTexture = lightOp.filter(buf, null);

// Now, set a texture
ElevationMap texture
    = new ElevationMap(textureMap, true, 5);   // This is explained later

litSurface.setElevationMap(texture);

BufferedImage withTexture = lightOp.filter(buf, null);
BufferedImage withTexture2 = lightOp.filter(image, null);
```

Figure 9.22 shows the resulting images. We explain how `ElevationMap`s work later on.

Spotlights

`SpotLight` is the name we give to point light sources in the Graphic Layers Framework. A point light is the name used in computer graphics for describing a light that has an infinitely small source at a specific location. The point radiates light. Because it is not common for point lights to radiate light of equal intensity in all directions, models have been created to represent realistic point light sources such as spotlights. The most popular model was developed by Warn (see [Foley97], Chapter 16), and this is the model used by the `SpotLight` class for processing point light intensity.

LitSurface uses a green DirectionalLight but no ElevationMap texture (filteredImage).

LitSurface uses a green DirectionalLight but no ElevationMap texture to light a plain gray rectangle. Note the color shift because of the light color (noTexture).

LitSurface uses a green DirectionalLight with ElevationMap texture that creates the bumps (withTexture2).

LitSurface uses a green DirectionalLight with ElevationMap texture that creates the bumps. Note color shift as well (withTexture).

Figure 9.22 ■
Using DirectionalLight with or without texture

Figure 9.23 illustrates the important variables describing a point light source. The point light source in the Warn model is defined by a point (R) on a virtual reflecting surface. The vector L' is the normal to that surface. The intensity of the light in a point P is proportional to the cosines of the angle between L' and the (PR) vector, to the power of p. The higher the value of p is, the more focused the modeled light will appear (because the light intensity will drop more rapidly about the main light projection axis). We can therefore think of p as the light's focus factor.

The other important characteristic of a spotlight is the limiting cone: to create a more realistic effect, no light is projected outside the limiting cone starting at the light source and of angle delta. The light intensity reaches zero as the value of gamma reaches delta.

According to this light model, the intensity of the light reflected on any given point depends on:

■ The light's focus
■ The light's angle with the surface normal
■ The light's angle with the projector's surface normal

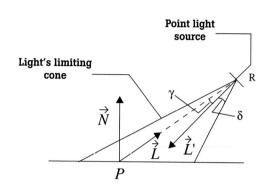

$\vec{N}$ Surface normal in P

$\vec{L'}$ Direction of the light's maximum intensity

δ Limiting cone: no light is projected outside the cone

$\vec{L}$ Light vector in P. The light intensity is proportional to:

$$(-\vec{L} \times \vec{L'})^{p} = \cos(\gamma)^{p}$$

p can be thought of as the light's focus

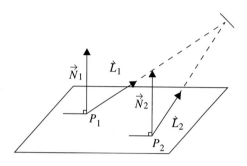

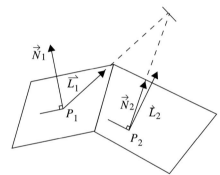

The light vector's intensity and direction is different in each point of the surface (e.g., L_1 and L_2 are different). When the surface is flat, the normal is constant over the surface, and the reflected intensity on any given point only depends on the position of the point relative to the light source.

When the surface is not flat, the normal is different in each point. Therefore, the reflected light intensity in a point of the surface depends both on the normal on that point and on the position of the point relative to the light source.

Figure 9.23 ■

Spotlight on a flat surface and on a nonflat surface

The `SpotLight` class encapsulates information about spotlights. It is defined by:

- Its intensity
- Its color
- The ellipse bounding the lit area
- The light's focus

The first two parameters are similar to those used by `DirectionalLight`. The bounding ellipse is the intersection of the light's limiting cone with the lit surface. In a two-dimensional world, it is easier to define the area that is lit than it is to determine where the spotlight should be positioned in a three-dimensional space. Internally, `SpotLight` uses the bounding ellipse to compute the light's location (R), but this is not of interest to the class user: we care about which part of the image is affected by the light, less about where that light exactly is.

The bounding ellipse is defined by a bounding rectangle and a rotation angle. Figure 9.24 illustrates how the bounding ellipse is defined. For a horizontal rectangle or a square, the rotation is about the center of the left side of the bounding rectangle. For a vertical rectangle, the rotation is about the center of the top side of the rectangle. Those parameters are passed to the `SpotLight` constructor.

```
public SpotLight(Rectangle2D boundingEllipse, Color color, double I,
                 double angle, int np)
```

The following code snippet illustrates the use of different `SpotLight` parameters (see **SpotLightUsage.java** on the CD-ROM); Figure 9.25 shows the result of the code.

```
Rectangle spotLightRect
    = new Rectangle(margin, margin, width, height);
LitSurface litSurface
    = new LitSurface(0, LitSurfaceType.NORMAL, null);
                        // Surface types are discussed later
SpotLight spot
    = new SpotLight(spotLightRect, spotColor, spotIntensity,
                    spotAngle, spotFocus);
litSurface.addLight(spot);
LightOp lighting = new LightOp(litSurface);
```

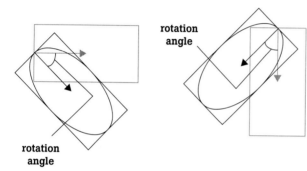

Light source R

The light vectors of constant intensity define a cone. The intersection of that cone with the lit surface is an ellipse. In GLF, the ellipse used to define a SpotLight is the ellipse where intensity reaches zero.

rotation angle

rotation angle

When the bounding ellipse's rectangle is horizontal, the light source is placed toward the left part of the ellipse and the rotation angle is about the center of the rectangle's left side.

When the bounding ellipse's rectangle is vertical, the light source is placed toward the top side of the ellipse, and the rotation angle is about the center of the rectangle's top side.

Figure 9.24 ■
Specifying the SpotLight lit area as an ellipse

The following example, **LightOpUsage4.java** on the CD-ROM, illustrates how a `LightOp` might use `SpotLights` to cast a specific light on an image. The example creates two different lighting conditions with `SpotLights`: first, a spot at the top of the filtered image; second, a set of two colored spots at the top of the image.

```
BufferedImage image = ...;  // e.g., Plain solid color image
                            // or Van Gogh portrait
Color spotColor = Color.white;
int w = image.getWidth();
int h = image.getHeight();
Rectangle topSpotArea
    = new Rectangle(0, 0, w, 2*h);
SpotLight topSpotLight
    = new SpotLight(topSpotArea,
                    spotColor,
                    spotIntensity, 0);  // no rotation
```

```
margin = 40
width=200, height=300
spotColor=orange
spotFocus=8
spotIntensity=10
spotAngle=0, +/- Pi/4
```

```
margin = 40
width=300, height=200
spotColor=orange
spotFocus=8
spotIntensity=10
spotAngle=0, +/-Pi/4
```

```
margin = 40
width=200, height=300
spotColor=orange
spotFocus=4, 16, 32
spotIntensity=10
spotAngle=0
```

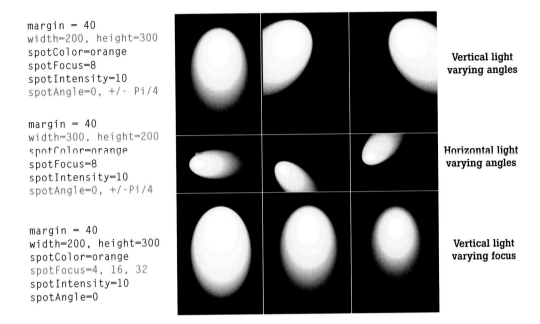

Vertical light varying angles

Horizontal light varying angles

Vertical light varying focus

Figure 9.25 ■
Different bounding rectangle, angle, and focus settings for SpotLight

```
LitSurface litSurface
    = new LitSurface(0.2);                // Some low intensity ambient
                                          // light
litSurface.addLight(topSpotLight);
LightOp lightOp = new LightOp(litSurface);
BufferedImage imageOneSpot = lightOp.filter(image, null);

// Now, modify LitSurface: remove all lights and add a SpotLight in
// the left and in the right angles
Color leftSpotColor = new Color(200, 200, 120);
Color rightSpotColor = new Color(150, 255, 150);
litSurface.removeAllLights();
Rectangle leftSpotArea = new Rectangle(-w/2, 0, w, 2*h);
SpotLight leftSpot
    = new SpotLight(leftSpotArea,
                    leftSpotColor,
                    spotIntensity,
                    -Math.PI/5);

Rectangle rightSpotArea = new Rectangle(w/2, 0, w, 2*h);
SpotLight rightSpot
    = new SpotLight(rightSpotArea,
```

```
                        rightSpotColor,
                        spotIntensity,
                        Math.PI/5);

litSurface.addLight(leftSpot);
litSurface.addLight(rightSpot);
BufferedImage imageTwoSpots = lightOp.filter(image, null);

this.imageOneSpot = imageOneSpot;
this.imageTwoSpots = imageTwoSpots;
```

The resulting `imageOneSpot` and `imageTwoSpots` are shown in Figure 9.26 for different settings of the variables.

The right column in the table shows the result when we use an `ElevationMap` texture in the `LitSurface`. We next describe how elevation maps work.

Elevation maps

In 3D graphics, volumes are described by polygons that have vertices used in the lighting computations. In our environment, there is no such thing as 3D models. We provide texture by using gray scale images as elevation maps. In

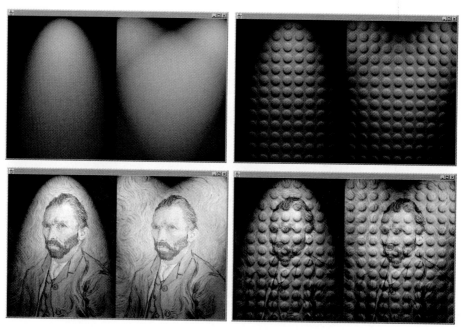

Figure 9.26 ■
Using SpotLights in different positions

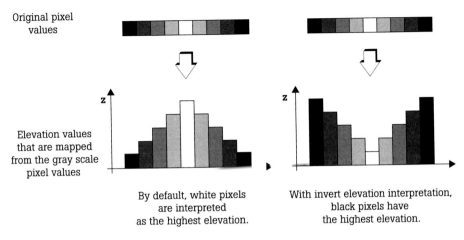

Original pixel
values

z

Elevation values
that are mapped
from the gray scale
pixel values

By default, white pixels
are interpreted
as the highest elevation.

With invert elevation interpretation,
black pixels have
the highest elevation.

Figure 9.27 ■
Mapping gray scale values to elevations

other words, we use a gray scale value as an indication of "how high" or "how low" a given point is. This definition is handled by the `ElevationMap` class. Let us see how it works.

An `ElevationMap` computes the surface normal at any given point. It uses a gray scale value to compute these normals. The pixel values are interpreted as elevations: by default, white is the highest and black is the lowest (left part of Figure 9.27). However, this can be changed to be the other way around (right part of Figure 9.27) where black pixels are mapped to the highest elevation.

By using the elevation on any point of the surface and then one of its neighbors, it is possible to compute the surface normal at any given point. These normal values are in turn used by `LitSurface` to compute the reflected light intensity on the surface. Note that we said a `LitSurface` was conceptually infinite. How does `ElevationMap` accommodate this concept?

The `ElevationMap` class has an anchor point that defines where the texture's origin is in the image space. Conceptually, the texture is then tiled on the surface, to the infinity. In practice, every time the normal in a point outside the texture area is requested, the value corresponding to its location in the corresponding tile is returned (Figure 9.28).

We already used a texture map in our previous examples (see page 349). Figure 9.29 illustrates the image that we used.

As you can see, the image starts black, that is, low on its outside, and becomes white, that is, high on the inside. This creates the little bump volume we saw in our previous examples. Here is how we created this `ElevationMap`.

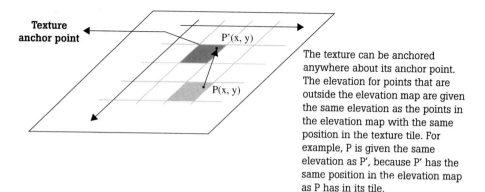

Texture anchor point

P'(x, y)

P(x, y)

The texture can be anchored anywhere about its anchor point. The elevation for points that are outside the elevation map are given the same elevation as the points in the elevation map with the same position in the texture tile. For example, P is given the same elevation as P', because P' has the same position in the elevation map as P has in its tile.

Figure 9.28 ■
Tiling texture maps

```
BufferedImage textureMap = Toolbox.loadImage(textureFile,
                                  BufferedImage.TYPE_BYTE_GRAY);
ElevationMap texture = new ElevationMap(textureMap, true, 5);
```

The first parameter contains the gray scale image, and each pixel value is interpreted as an elevation. The second parameter defines whether white pixels are the highest or the lowest, as we illustrated in Figure 9.27. Finally, the last parameter defines a height scale used to scale elevation differences between pixels. A value of 1 makes elevation differences subtle, and the surface appears

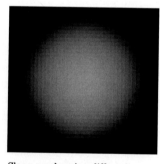

Actual gray scale image   Close-up showing different gray scale pixel values

Figure 9.29 ■
Texture image used for creating bump texture

heightScale

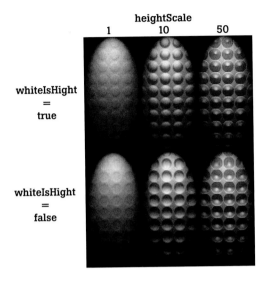

Figure 9.30 ■
Varying whiteIsHight and heightScale
parameters

flatter. A high value makes the elevation difference greater and makes the surface appear more mountainous. Variations of these two parameters for the same elevation map are illustrated in Figure 9.30, the output from the **ElevationMapUsage.java** snippet.

Figure 9.31 shows different examples of gray scale elevation maps.

Note that the map is not shown at the same scale as the output it was used for. On the left-hand side, the elevation maps have been blown up to distinguish the details of the gray scale variations. On the right-hand side, the maps have been shrunk.

We have now discussed two aspects of a `LitSurface`: the lighting conditions, described by the ambient light, spotlight, and directional lights, and the texture described by an `ElevationMap`. The last aspect of a `LitSurface` is the surface material description.

Describing the surface type

Surfaces do not all reflect light the same way—we have all experienced this. For example, a chunk of chalk does not reflect light with the same intensity as does a piece of polished metal. In computer graphics, several characteristics are attached to a material to describe how it reflects light. Those characteristics are then used to compute the light intensity reflected by a surface of that type. Three parameters control the type of material for a surface:

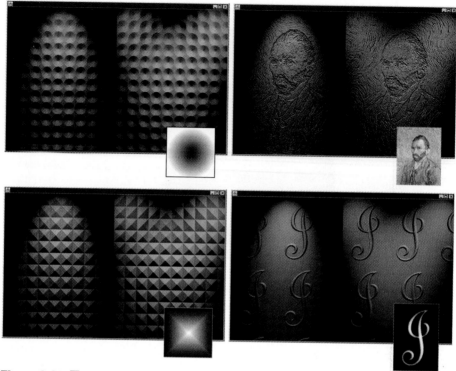

Figure 9.31 ■
Different types of elevation maps

- Diffusion coefficient
- Specular reflection coefficient
- Specular reflection exponent

In computer graphics there are two common types of reflection: diffuse reflection and specular reflection. We introduced diffuse reflection earlier to explain the relation between incident light and reflected light.

Diffuse reflection is the type of reflection that matte materials exhibit: the reflected intensity is equal in all directions and is completely unrelated to the viewing angle. The diffusion coefficient describes how much diffuse reflection a given material has.

Dull surfaces, such as chalk, reflect light in a way that diffuse reflection describes well and will have a high diffusion coefficient. However, this is not a proper model for metallic or shiny surfaces, which reflect light differently in different directions.

Light source

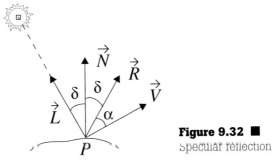

Figure 9.32 ■
Specular reflection

This type of reflection is called specular reflection and is the shiny spot we see on illuminated metallic or plastic objects.

As illustrated in Figure 9.32, the light is fully reflected along the direction of R. If the viewer is looking along that direction, then she sees the fully reflected light—the shiny spots on shiny surfaces. If the viewer looks from a different angle, then she sees a decrease in the reflected intensity as the angle alpha increases. It can be shown that the amount of light reflected in a given direction is proportional to:

$$(\vec{R} \times \vec{V})^{n_s}$$

where n_s is called the specular reflection exponent, one of the characteristics of a material. The higher the values of n_s, the smaller the range of alpha values for which the specular reflection will be significant and the shinier the material will look: the shiny spots will be smaller and contrast more with the neighboring areas. The specular reflection coefficient describes how much specular reflection a material has.

The LitSurface class has three separate properties for each of the above characteristics. They are:

- k_d: the diffusion coefficient
- k_s: the specular reflection coefficient
- n_s: the specular reflection exponent

While it is possible to set each of those parameters separately, it is difficult to find the right settings. The LitSurfaceType class encapsulates predefined settings for those properties that match four surface types: matte, normal, shiny, and metallic.

The following code sample illustrates how using each of those predefined values makes the textured surface appear different (**LightOpUsage5.java** on the CD-ROM); output is shown in Figure 9.33.

```
BufferedImage textureMap
   = Toolbox.loadImage(textureFile, BufferedImage.TYPE_BYTE_GRAY);
...
int w = size.width;
int h = size.height;
BufferedImage buf = new BufferedImage(w,h, BufferedImage.TYPE_INT_RGB);
Graphics2D g = buf.createGraphics();
g.setPaint(color);
g.fillRect(0, 0, w, h);
ElevationMap texture = new ElevationMap(textureMap, true, 10);

LitSurfaceType surfaceType
   = LitSurfaceType.NORMAL; // or MATTE, SHINY or METALLIC
LitSurface litSurface
   = new LitSurface(.2, surfaceType, texture);

double L[] = {-1, -1, 1};   // Light comes from the top left corner
DirectionalLight sunLight = new DirectionalLight(L, 1, Color.white);
litSurface.addLight(sunLight);
LightOp lightOp = new LightOp(litSurface);
BufferedImage withTexture = lightOp.filter(buf, null);
```

Note that the higher the diffusion factor is, the duller the matte surface looks. Also note that reflective and shiny surfaces have a comparatively higher specular reflection factor and coefficient.

There are a lot of concepts used in the `LightOp` filter. As we have seen, its operation fully rests on the construction of an appropriate `LitSurface` that describes the surface, texture, and lighting conditions. The following paragraphs present helper methods, constructors, and classes that make using `LightOp` easy.

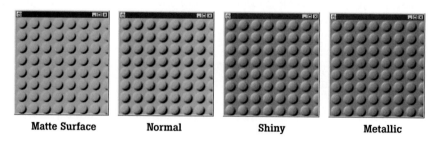

| Matte Surface | Normal | Shiny | Metallic |

Figure 9.33 ∎

Different LitSurfaceType values by example

Helper classes and methods

Manipulating `LightOp` requires several tasks that may be tricky, for example, positioning lights correctly and creating texture maps. The following classes make these tasks simpler.

LightStudio class

The `LightStudio` class, in the `com.sun.glf.util` package, provides a number of helper methods to create directional lights and spotlights.

Table 9.3 shows how each of these helper methods can be used to create `DirectionalLights` and `SpotLights`.

Table 9.3 ■ LightsStudio factory methods

METHOD & EXAMPLE USAGE   OUTPUT WHEN USED IN A LIGHTOP

getSunLight (see GetSunLightUsage.java on the CD-ROM)

```
DirectionalLight sunLight
    = LightsStudio.getSunLight(anchor, lightIntensity, lightColor);

texturedSurface.addLight(sunLight);
LightOp lighting = new LightOp(texturedSurface);
```

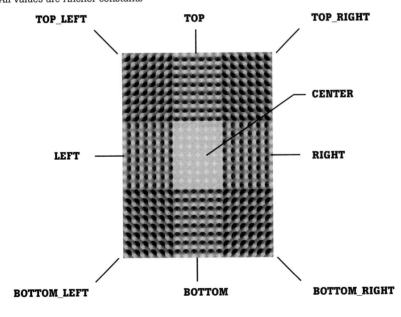

All values are Anchor constants

Table 9.3 ■ LightsStudio factory methods (Continued)

METHOD & EXAMPLE USAGE	OUTPUT WHEN USED IN A LIGHTOP

getSpotLight (see GetSpotLightUsage.java on the CD-ROM)

```
SpotLight light
    = LightsStudio.getSpotLight(litRect,   // Rectangle where the spot
                                           // light is placed
                               anchor,      // Placement within
                                           // litRect, e.g., TOP
                               spotSize,    // Size of the light's
                                           // ellipse on LitSurface
                               lightIntensity, // Spot's intensity
                               lightColor); // Spot light color
```

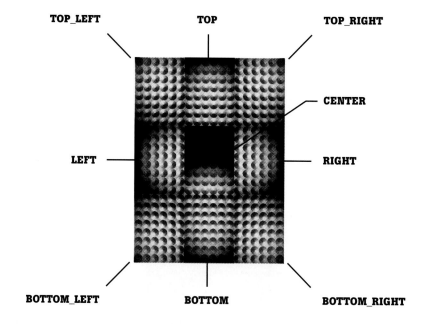

Table 9.3 ■ LightsStudio factory methods (Continued)

METHOD & EXAMPLE USAGE	OUTPUT WHEN USED IN A LIGHTOP

getLightRamp (see GetLightRampUsage.java on the CD-ROM)

```
SpotLight lights[]
  = LightsStudio.getLightRamp(litRect,      // Rectangle where the ramp
                                            // is placed
                             nLights,       // Number of lights in ramp
                             anchor,        // Ramp position in litRect
                             lightIntensity, // Spot intensity
                             lightColor,    // Spot color
                             0f);           // Overlap between spots
texturedSurface.addLights(lights);
```

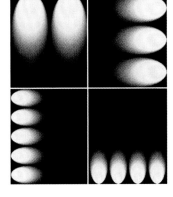

anchor = TOP
nLights = 2

anchor = RIGHT
nLights = 3

anchor = LEFT
nLights = 5

anchor = BOTTOM
nLights = 4

Table 9.3 ■ LightsStudio factory methods (Continued)

METHOD & EXAMPLE USAGE	OUTPUT WHEN USED IN A LIGHTOP

getHotSpotLightRamp

```
SpotLight lights[]
    = LightsStudio.getHotSpotLightRamp(litRect,    // Rectangle where
                                                   // the ramp is placed

                           nLights,                // Number of lights
                                                   // in ramp

                           anchor,                 // Ramp position
                                                   // in litRect

                           lightIntensity,         // Spot intensity

                           lightColor,             // Spotlight color

                           Of,                     // No overlap
                                                   // between spots

                           hotSpot);               // Spots are directed
                                                   // to hotSpot
```

In the figure, the hot spot is the center of each rectangle. For clarity, the hot spot to which lights point is represented by a black or white square.

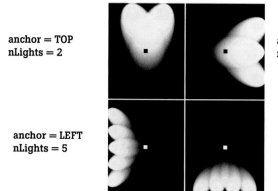

anchor = TOP
nLights = 2

anchor = RIGHT
nLights = 3

anchor = LEFT
nLights = 5

anchor = BOTTOM
nLights = 4

Figure 9.34 ■
Creating an elevation map from a Shape object

ElevationMaps: Shape-based constructors

There are at least two common uses for ElevationMaps in rendering effects. One is for texturizing, which is done with an arbitrary gray scale image. The other one is to extrude graphics, for example, text. This use being very common, the ElevationMap class provides a constructor that uses a Shape object to create a gray scale elevation map.

The process used to create the elevation map from a Shape is illustrated in Figure 9.34 and described below:

- Create a BufferedImage large enough to hold the Shape. The original Shape is shown on the left.
- Fill the Shape object with white and blur it with a ConvolveOp, using a Kernel of controllable dimension. This is the second, blurred shape in the figure.
- Trim the outside of the Shape so that it starts on sharp edges, as shown in the third shape in the figure.

This last gray scale image is then used as any other texture image, as we have discussed earlier. The last shape, the rightmost in the figure, shows the result of using an elevation map created from a Shape.

```
ElevationMap map
   = new ElevationMap(shape, shapeRect, Anchor.CENTER, 0, 0,
                      blurRadius, true, 10);

LitSurface litSurface
   = new LitSurface(ambientLight, LitSurfaceType.METALLIC, map);

litSurface.addLight(LightsStudio.getSunLight(Anchor.TOP_LEFT,
                                             lightIntensity,
Color.white));
LightOp lighting = new LightOp(litSurface);
// ... Use lighting
```

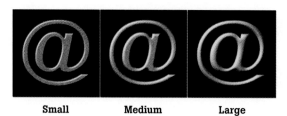

Small   **Medium**   **Large**

Figure 9.35 ■
Different settings for the blur radius

In the preceding `ElevationMap` construction, the last two parameters are `whiteIsHight` and `heightScale` we discussed earlier. The `shapeRect`, `anchor`, and adjustment values (both at zero in the example) place the `Shape` object in a bounding rectangle before building the gray scale image: the image will have the size of `shapeRect`, and the `Shape` object will be positioned according to its anchor and adjustment values. The blur radius can be used to control how round the texture should appear: the larger the blur radius, the rounder the resulting texture will appear. Figure 9.35 shows various settings for the blur radius.

The appropriate blur radius depends on the size of the shape that is used. The larger the shape, the larger the radius needs to be to create a rounder effect. For example, the shape used in Figure 9.35 is 250 points high (this is a 300 dpi image). The blur sizes used in the figure are 5 for small, 10 for medium, and 20 for large. The larger the blur radius, the longer the filtering takes because convolution time increases exponentially with the kernel size, which is equal to 2*blurRadius + 1. Note that `ElevationMap` uses `GaussianKernel`, which is separable; that use could allow the convolution to run more quickly (see [Crane97, Chapter 3] for more details on separable kernels. Also, see Chapter 15). At the time of this writing, the Java 2D platform did not take advantage of kernel separation, but it will in the future.

Further reading

There is no need to understand 3D graphics to use `LightOp` and its related classes. However, readers interested in learning more about the related concepts or about the way in which `LightOp` is implemented can refer to [Foley97] or [Hearn97] for further information.

The ToneAdjustmentOp filter

The `ToneAdjustmentOp` filter is used to tint an image. For example, it can be used to antique a photograph (see Chapter 15).

`ToneAdjustmentOp` operates as follows. It uses the brightness of the pixels it filters as an index in a color map that it builds from a set of color and interval values. The color map can be seen as a gradient of colors, as illustrated in Figure 9.36.

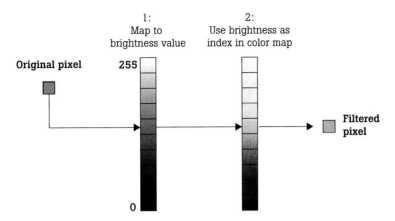

Figure 9.36 ■
ToneAdjustmentOp operation

The color map used by `ToneAdjustmentOp` is defined as a multicolor gradient paint: by a set of colors and intervals. For example, the color map used in Figure 9.36 is defined as described in Figure 9.37. Note that intervals a normalized to represent ratios of the color map entries. For example, the intervals in the figure sum to 11. The first interval will use 1/11th of the 256 entries. This means that the bottom of the map will have colors interpolated from black to dark red in 256.1/11 = 23 steps.

`ToneAdjustmentOp` has a constructor that takes the colors and intervals as input parameters.

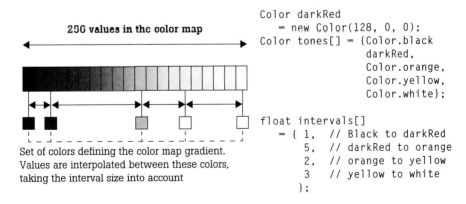

256 values in the color map

Set of colors defining the color map gradient.
Values are interpolated between these colors,
taking the interval size into account

```
Color darkRed
    = new Color(128, 0, 0);
Color tones[] = {Color.black
                 darkRed,
                 Color.orange,
                 Color.yellow,
                 Color.white};

float intervals[]
    = { 1,   // Black to darkRed
        5,   // darkRed to orange
        2,   // orange to yellow
        3    // yellow to white
      };
```

Figure 9.37 ■
Defining a color map for ToneAdjustmentOp

```
public ToneAdjustmentOp(Color tones[], float toneIntervals[],
                        boolean nullDestAsSource){ ... }
```

The `boolean` parameter indicates which behavior the filter should have when used with a null destination. If `nullDestAsSource` is `true`, then `ToneAdjustmentOp` will create a destination that has the same `ColorModel` as the source it filters. Otherwise, it will create a destination that uses an `IndexColorModel`, corresponding to the color map we just described. Using the `IndexColorModel` is faster but may not be the desired format. For example, it does not support transparency. The boolean parameter lets the user decide which behavior fits his or her needs.

It is very common to use `ToneAdjustmentOp` to simply tint an image. In such a case, black is mapped to black and white to white. Only the midtones, highlights, and shadows are adjusted and sometimes only the midtones are. As a convenience, `ToneAdjustmentOp` provides constructors that correspond to these common adjustments.

```
public ToneAdjustmentOp(Color midTone){
  this(new Color[]{Color.black, midTone, Color.white},
      new float[]{1, 1}, true);
}


public ToneAdjustmentOp(Color shadowTone, Color midTone,
                        Color highlightTone){
    this(new Color[]{Color.black, shadowTone,
                     midTone, highlightTone, Color.white},

                     new float[]{1, 1, 1, 1}, true);
   }
```

The **ToneAdjustmentUsage.java** example on the CD-ROM illustrates how to use `ToneAdjustment`. It creates a `LayerComposition` with a single `Image-Layer` object to which a `ToneAdjustmentOp` filter is attached. (See Figure 9.38 for examples of images created by this example.)

```
//
// First, load image to filter
//
BufferedImage image
  = Toolbox.loadImage(imageFile, BufferedImage.TYPE_INT_ARGB);
if(image == null)
  throw new Error("Could not load : " + imageFile);


//
// Now, build a ToneAdjustmentOp filter
//
Color tones[] = { tone1, tone2, tone3, tone4, tone5 };
float toneIntervals[] = {interval1,  // tone1 to tone2
                         interval2,  // tone2 to tone3
                         interval3,  // tone3 to tone4
                         interval4}; // tone4 to tone5
```

```
ToneAdjustmentOp toneAdjuster
   = new ToneAdjustmentOp(tones, toneIntervals);

//
// Build a composition the size of the filtered image
//
Dimension size = new Dimension(image.getWidth(), image.getHeight());
LayerComposition cmp = new LayerComposition(size);

ImageLayer imageLayer = new ImageLayer(cmp, image);
imageLayer.setImageFilter(toneAdjuster);

cmp.setLayers(new Layer[]{ imageLayer });
```

Two close but still different sets of colors and intervals. On the right hand side, light tones have more weight.

On those two images, bright tones are mapped to dark colors, and dark tones are mapped to light colors. This produces different kinds of negatives of the original picture.

Those two image use the same colors but different interval values. On the left hand side, dark tones have a large weight. On the right hand side, both the dark and light tones have been given a bigger weight than the midtone intervals. As a result, the image appears to have more contrast.

Figure 9.38 ■
ToneAdjustmentOp produces widely different results

The CompositeOp and CompositeRasterOp filters

`CompositeOp` and `CompositeRasterOp` let us compose a set of `Buffered-ImageOp` filters and `RasterOp` filters, respectively. In other words, they let us chain filters, as described in Figure 9.39. The filtered output is created by successively using each of the filters in the chain: the output of one filter is used as an input for the next one, until the end of the chain is reached.

Using `CompositeOp` and `CompositeRasterOp` is straightforward, as illustrated by the following code sample.

```
ConvolveOp blur = new ConvolveOp(...);
LookupOp invert = new LookupOp(...);
CompositeOp blurAndInvert = new CompositeOp(blur, invert);
// or:
// BufferedImageOp filters[] = { blur, invert };
// CompositeOp blurAndInvert = new CompositeOp(filters);
...
LightOp lightCast = new LightOp(...); // LightOp is a RasterOp
BandCombineOp combine = new BandCombineOp(...);
CompositeRasterOp lightAndCombine = new CompositeRasterOp(lightCast,
combine);

// or:
// RasterOp rasterFilters[] = { lightCast, combine };
// CompositeRasterOp lightAndCombine
//   = new CompositeRasterOp(rasterFilters);
```

Note that these two filter implementations can chain an arbitrary number of filters. However, they have convenience constructor to chain two filters, which is a common case.

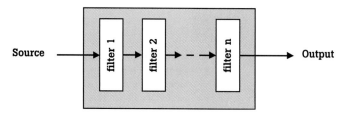

Figure 9.39 ■
Chaining filters with CompositeOp and CompositeRasterOp

Nonlinear Transformations

There are no nonlinear transforms in the Java 2D API. `Graphics2D` uses `AffineTransforms`, which support only linear coordinate transformations. However, it is possible to add support for nonlinear transformations, and the Graphics Layers Framework defines a `Transform` interface.

Transform and AbstractTransform

The `Transform` interface is simple.

```
public interface Transform {
  public Shape transform(Shape shape);
  public void concatenate(Transform t);
  public void preConcatenate(Transform t);
}
```

Translated to English, this code means that a `Transform` implementation should be able to do the following:

1. Transform a `Shape` according to its spatial transformation logic and return the transformed `Shape`.
2. Apply another transform object before or after itself. This task is similar to the `AffineTransform` concatenate and preConcatenate methods.

Here is an abstract implementation of the `Transform` interface.

```
public abstract class AbstractTransform implements Transform{
  Transform preTransform;
  Transform postTransform;

  final public void concatenate(Transform t){
    if(preTransform==null)
      preTransform = t;
    else
      preTransform.concatenate(t);
  }

  final public void preConcatenate(Transform t){
    if(postTransform==null)
      postTransform = t;
    else
      postTransform.preConcatenate(t);
  }
```

```
/**
 * transform implementation. Takes care of applying any pre or post
 * transform if needed.
 * @see #transformImpl
 */
final public Shape transform(Shape shape){
  if(preTransform!=null)
    shape = preTransform.transform(shape);

  shape = transformImpl(shape);

  if(postTransform!=null)
    shape = postTransform.transform(shape);

  return shape;
}

  public abstract Shape transformImpl(Shape shape);
}
```

As shown in the code, extensions of `AbstractTransform` only need to implement its abstract `transformImpl` method. This is what the `WaveTransform` and `BumpTransform` implementations do.

Using a `Transform` implementation with the Java 2D API or GLF is easy.

```
Transform transform = ...;        // e.g., new WaveTransform(...)
Shape shape = ...;                // get Shape that should be
                                  // transformed

shape = transform.transform(shape);// create a transformed version
                                   // of the original Shape.

// Use transformed Shape as any other Shape with GLF and/or Java 2D
```

WaveTransform

The `WaveTransform` implementation performs a sinusoidal transformation of the `Shape` coordinates. The transformation is controlled by the wave's height and length. There are two operation modes for `WaveTransform`: it can either use a fixed wave length or adapt its wave length to fit a specific number of waves in the width of the `Shape` object it transforms.

The following code snippet illustrates how a `WaveTransform` might be used to transform a text block (**WaveTransformUsage.java** on the CD-ROM).

```
Shape textBlock = TextLayer.makeTextBlock(text, textFont, textWrapWidth,
                                          TextAlignment.JUSTIFY);

// Use a WaveTransform to modify textBlock's shape
WaveTransform transform = null;
if(useWaveLength)
```

```
    transform = new WaveTransform(waveLength, waveHeight);
else
    transform = new WaveTransform(waveNumber, waveHeight);
```

```
textBlock = transform.transform(textBlock);
```

Figure 9.40 illustrates the different outputs obtained depending on whether the waves have a specified length or whether there should be a specific number of waves in the transformed Shape.

Note how the x-axis components are left unmodified by the transforms and how the y-axis coordinate transformation is dependent on the corresponding x-coordinate. Internally, the y-axis transformation is tied to the x-coordinate by a sinusoidal function.

BumpTransform

The BumpTransform implementation performs a more sophisticated geometrical transformation of the input Shape coordinates. It wraps the shape around an imaginary disc bump at the center of the shape base, so that when wrapped, the shape covers a specified angle on the bump (see Figure 9.41).

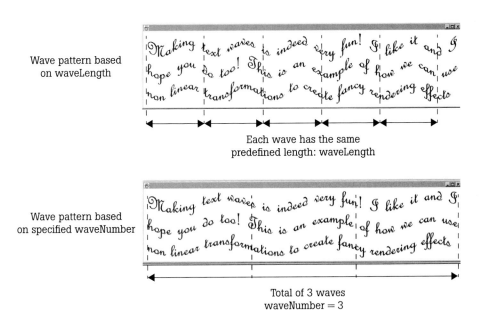

Figure 9.40 ■

Different operation modes for WaveTransform

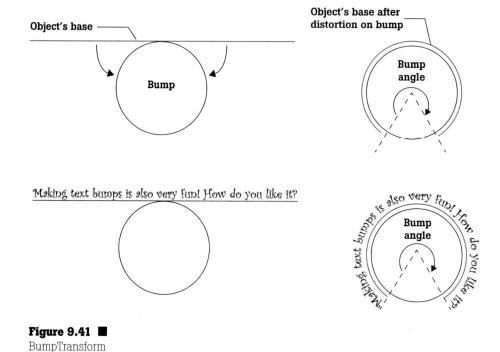

Figure 9.41 ■
BumpTransform

The following code snippet (**BumpTransform.java** on the CD-ROM) creates the output depicted in Figure 9.41.

```
Shape textBlock
  = TextLayer.makeTextBlock(text, textFont, -1, TextAlignment.CENTER);

// Use a BumpTransform to modify textBlock's shape
BumpTransform transform = new BumpTransform((float)bumpAngle);

textBlock = transform.transform(textBlock);
```

Nonlinear Transforms approximations

The two nonlinear transformations we defined create a transformed Shape by modifying the coordinates of the input Shapes. They do not modify the segment types. This approach does not produce an accurate result; the inaccuracy is not noticeable on some Shapes (as in our previous examples), but it can be very visible on other ones (for example, on rectangles). The reason for this visibility is that these Transforms are nonlinear and do not transform lines into lines, but, in those two examples, into curves. So, transforming coordinates of segment control points is not accurate.

The `MunchTransform` class, a `Transform` implementation, breaks down `Shapes` into linear segments that do not exceed a specified length. When used in conjunction with other `Transforms`, it attenuates the limitation we just described, as illustrated by the following example.

```
Rectangle rect = new Rectangle(0, 0, width, height);
BumpTransform bumpTransform = new BumpTransform(bumpAngle);

if(munchSize>0){
  MunchTransform munchTransform = new MunchTransform(munchSize);
  bumpTransform.concatenate(munchTransform);
}

Shape bentRect = bumpTransform.transform(rect);
```

The output is shown in Figure 9.42. Note that the approximations we use here are acceptable in our context of rendering effects and allow us to create pseudo-nonlinear transformations with minimum effort. However, they are not recommended for use in other contexts where a mathematically accurate transformation might be needed.

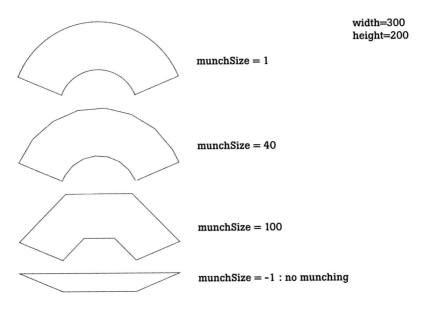

width=300
height=200

munchSize = 1

munchSize = 40

munchSize = 100

munchSize = -1 : no munching

Figure 9.42 ■
Using MunchTransform to approximate proper nonlinear transformations

End of Part II

This chapter completes the second part of this book, and we are now ready to enjoy the Java 2D features. We have built a framework to easily combine rendering operations (the GLF core package that we discussed in Chapter 8), we have tools that let us experiment with different configuration settings, and we have a set of custom Paint, Stroke, Composite, and image filters that we use to enhance the Java 2D platform capabilities.

All the things we covered in Part II are the foundation for Part III where all the examples compose Layers in LayerCompositions. We will refer to the viewer tools and configuration tools systematically as a way to run those examples and experiment with them. Finally, we will use extensions we have presented here to enhance the graphic compositions we will create.

part 3

RENDERING EFFECTS

chapter 10

INTRODUCTION

In the first two parts, we went through a lot of technical explanations on how the Java 2D API and GLF work and on how to use them. This may have been hard at times, but it was all in preparation for what we are going to present in this third part. This is the fun part: we have built a framework and we are now going to use it fully to create specific rendering effects! So, you can now sit back and enjoy!

In the following chapters, we explain how to create various rendering effects, such as shadows or photo tinting. Rendering effects combine multiple features and techniques, and this is what we concentrate on.

Note that this part does not pretend to give an exhaustive list of rendering effects. Rather, the effects that it describes are illustrations of the kind of appealing things that can be done. They provide hints and should be considered seeds for developing other rendering effects.

How to Read This Part

This part presents six sophisticated examples of the kind of graphical compositions we can create with Java 2D and GLF. Unlike the first two parts, there is no strong logical continuity between the chapters: this part is a sort of catalog of rendering effects. Browse through it and read the sections that describe the rendering effects in which you are interested. There is an exception to this advice: the last chapter is more complex than the others, and you may find easier to follow after you read one or two other chapters.

Chapter Format

Each chapter has a main theme. It presents a single example that illustrates this main theme and a number of additional techniques.

For instance, the first chapter discusses how to create compelling shadows. It presents several techniques for creating shadows which are directly related to the main theme. But it also presents other techniques (such as embossing or photograph tinting) that are not related to the main topic but are commonly used in many compositions.

Furthermore, each chapter presents a suggestion on how the composition might be used. For instance, the first example discusses how shadows might be used to enhance the different states of a user interface button. These suggestions are food for thought.

The first page of each chapter highlights key points: a bar on the left-hand side describes the main objective of the chapter (Objective), a suggestion on how the composition might be used (Purpose), and the list of techniques that are used and detailed (Techniques).

Technical Content

In Part II, we introduced the Graphic Layers Framework, its core components, extensions, and utilities. Part III relies heavily on GLF, and each code example it presents implements the `CompositionFactory` interface.

The different chapters discuss the content of the `build` method of such implementations. Please refer to Part II if you are not familiar with `CompositionFactory` implementations and how they can be configured with the GLF utilities (such as `CompositionStudio`) before reading this part: all chapters assume familiarity with GLF.

Chapters introduce one main example, which may, in turn, use simpler examples. Because we discuss the `build` method of those `CompositionFactory` implementations, the discussion revolves around techniques for creating the right set of `Layer` objects for a particular effect.

For instance, the first example explains how to use `ShapeLayer` to render shadows for `Shape` objects. It discusses how to initialize the class with the right `Shape`, `Renderer`, and filter.

The examples show the results created with a specific configuration of the `CompostionFactory` implementations. Remember that the GLF utilities allow you to create widely different results by using `CompositionStudio`[1] or other strategies to configure the parameters and obtain different results.

---

1. See Chapter 8, "The GLF Studio and Utilities: Experimenting with Layers," for a description of these tools.

Rendering Effects Index

Table 10.1 lists the various rendering effects introduced in Part III and briefly describes each effect and related techniques.

Table 10.1 ■ Catalogue of rendering effects

Chapter and effects	Description
Chapter 11: "Creating Realistic Shadows" on page 384	Create shadows of different kinds (drop shadow, cast shadow, etc.) and for different types of objects.
■ Image, text, and shape shadow	Create shadows for images, shapes, and text.
■ Drop shadow	Drop shadows show under objects lying flat above a surface.
■ Cast shadow	Cast shadows show behind objects positioned perpendicular to a surface.
■ Recessed shadow	Recessed shadows show within holes in a surface that has cut-outs.
■ Embossing with directional light	Use LightOp to emboss any shape or text, as a piece of metal.
■ Tinting an image	Use ToneAdjustmentOp to apply a given tint to an image.
■ Inexpensive border embossing	Combined with the recessed shadow effect, gives a sense of thickness to a cut-out surface by stroking the outline of the cut-out area.
Chapter 12: "Making Text Stand Out" on page 408	Make text more legible against different types of backgrounds.
■ Image, text, and shape glow effect	Create a glow behind images, text, and shapes, as if they were backlit by a neon light.
■ Adjusting brightness	Use RescaleOp to adjust the brightness of a line of text and increase the contrast with its background.

Table 10.1 ■ Catalogue of rendering effects (Continued)

CHAPTER AND EFFECTS	DESCRIPTION
■ Masking	Use a gray scale image to mask out part of a layer and hide parts of a background texture.
■ Texturizing with shapes	Using only text, transforms, and colors, build a background texture from scratch.
■ Using an image as a texture	One of the many ways to use an image as a background texture and fit it into the composition.
Chapter 13: "Sculpting with Light" on page 420	Create different realistic lighting conditions.
■ Carving	Use `LightOp` to carve a surface with a spotlight.
■ Embossing with a spotlight	Use `LightOp` to emboss an object with a spotlight.
■ Extruding	Use `LightOp` to extrude or punch a surface with a spotlight.
■ Adjusting colors	Use `RescaleOp` to increase the color contrast between text and its background.
Chapter 14: "Fancy Text Layouts" on page 430	Unusual text layouts.
■ Circular text layout	Lay out text in a circle.
■ Triangular text layout	Lay out text in a triangle.
■ Multiple stroking	Use strokes of various sizes and colors to make decoration elements stand out.
■ Combining `LayerCompositions`	Reuse `CompositionFactory` implementations in a single composition.
Chapter 15: "Tinting Photographs" on page 442	Use `ToneAdjustmentOp` to tint or antique a photograph.
■ Setting tones in a photograph	Use `ToneAdjustmentOp` to set the tones of an image and create different moods.

Table 10.1 ■ Catalogue of rendering effects (Continued)

CHAPTER AND EFFECTS	DESCRIPTION
■ Masking as a way to create a border	Build a mask with gradient paint to create a border effect.
■ Fast blur technique	Speed up large convolutions and obtain faster blurs for shadows or glows.
■ Using an extra layer to make text legible	Use an extra layer to increase contrast between text and its background.
Chapter 16: "Creating a Sense of Volume" on page 452	Use various gradient paints creatively to create realistic 3D effects and give a sense of volume and depth.
■ Creating 3D shapes	Use transforms, shapes, and gradient paints to build cylinders, spheres, and bars.
■ Using gradients to suggest volume and texture	Creative use of gradients give a sense of texture to objects.
■ Writing text along an arbitrary path	`TextStroke` at work to draw text along a curve.
■ More sophisticated combinations of compositions	Combine and group `LayerComposition` objects, using `CompositionProxyLayer` and `CompositionFactory` beans.

More Rendering Effects: The Gallery

The last example in Part III is followed by a gallery of compositions that illustrate more rendering effects (see Chapter 17). Each is briefly described to highlight the key techniques or tricks it uses.

The code for each of the gallery compositions is provided on the CD-ROM that comes with this book; you might want to refer to the source code for specific details.

Important Note on Performance

The examples shown in Part III are sophisticated and use techniques that are computation intensive. At the top of the list are convolutions and lighting effects that require many calculations per pixels and, as a consequence, slow down processing. Even though we discuss techniques to speed up these intense processing operations (for example, see the "fast blur" technique discussed in Chapter 15), our primary goal for this part is to create a sophisticated visual output, sometimes at the cost of speed. In the performance/quality trade-off, we favor the quality.

Depending on the type of application you are writing, you can limit the number of effects or use them appropriately to increase performance. For example, in an animation, it might be a good idea to use `LightOp` to create a texture. However it would not be a good idea to use this same filter on every frame of the animation because the filter is not fast enough to guarantee a satisfying frame rate.

In summary, you should understand the cost of a rendering operation or filter and decide whether it can be used in your context.

chapter 11

CREATING REALISTIC SHADOWS

■ OBJECTIVE
Create compelling shadows for all kinds of graphic objects: images, text, and shapes.

■ PURPOSE
Render the different states of user interface buttons.

■ TECHNIQUES
  ■ Image, shape, and text shadow
  ■ Drop shadow
  ■ Cast shadow
  ■ Recessed shadow
  ■ Embossing with directional light
  ■ Tinting an image
  ■ Inexpensive border embossing

Shadows are ever present in sophisticated graphics because they contribute to a sense of depth and add to the realistic look of a composition. For example, the different shadows you see in the above graphic create various impressions of depth (higher or lower) and dimension (the phones seem to be above a flat surface but the "email us" graphic seems to be orthogonal to the same surface).

Shadows can be used, for example, to create the various states of user interface buttons: the elements on the left row show potential buttons in their "up" state, elements in the middle represent the "hot" state (that is, when the mouse is over the button) and elements on the right represent the "down" state (that is, when the button is pressed).

The above composition shows three different types of shadows: a drop shadow, which is simply offset under the phone image, a cast shadow, which is offset and sheared under the embossed oval graphic, and a recessed shadow, which gives the feeling that the GO text is punched through the gray surface, letting the blue or yellow background show.

This chapter describes how to create each of these shadow types in turn. In the process, it explains how to create shadows for different graphic objects: images, text, and shapes.

Additional techniques are used in each of these different types of shadows. The phone image is tinted to different color shades, the graphic is embossed by LightUp, *and the rims of the recessed shadow text are embossed by a simple but effective technique. These techniques are discussed as well.*

Our first section describes the simplest shadow type, but it also covers the shadow basics, which are reused in subsequent sections.

Creating a Drop Shadow

The phone drop shadow example is used for the first row (the phone buttons) shown on page 384. This effect is created by the **ImageDropShadowComposition.java** example on the CD-ROM.

A drop shadow is one that is shifted under the supposedly lit object. The other types of shadows also imply an offset to create a sense of light direction and depth. Furthermore, a shadow effect is much more effective when edges are blurred, as we explain later.

Shadow basics

▼ **Creating a sense of light and depth**   Figure 11.1 illustrates how a shadow indirectly provides a sense of the light direction (top of the figure) and of the object elevation above the surface (bottom part of the figure). The figure shows the same object, a blue square, above a white surface, lit from different directions.

The direction in which the shadow is shifted implicitly tells the viewer that the light comes from the opposite direction. For example, if the shadow is offset down and to the right, the viewer will intuitively think the light comes from the upper-left direction. Similarly, the more offset the shadow is, the higher the object seems to be above the surface.

Different shadow offsets imply different light directions

Different shadow offsets also imply different elevations

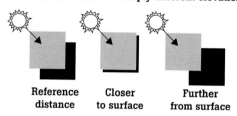

| Reference distance | Closer to surface | Further from surface |

Figure 11.1 ■

Creating a sense of light and depth with a drop shadow

▼ **Creating a realistic shadow**   Most of the shadows we encounter in the real world have fuzzy edges because of the effect of light diffraction on the edges of lit objects.

To create a realistic shadow, it is important to match this effect, and blurring a shadow provides a satisfying result.

Furthermore, shadows rarely block out light completely, but simply make the surface darker because they only block out part of the light.[1]

To create a more realistic shadow that matches this characteristic, we can paint the shadow partly transparent.

Figure 11.2 illustrates how an increasingly better result is achieved when a shadow is drawn on top of a background image.

Now that we know the basic visual tricks involved in creating an appealing shadow, let us start creating one type, a drop shadow, for images.

---

1. This is caused by the ambient light. Light would only be completely blocked out by a shadow if there was no ambient light.

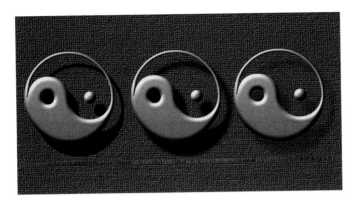

Figure 11.2 ■
Creating realistic shadows

The image shadow layer stack

Figure 11.3 shows the stack of layers involved in creating the image shadow and the most important parameters that control them.

Before starting creating `Layer` objects, we first get the raw material, images, and curved text, and then compute the composition size based on them.

Getting the raw material

By getting the raw material, we mean getting the basic graphic objects used in the composition.

▼ **Loading an image and its mask**   We start by loading a base image and its mask.

```
BufferedImage image
    = Toolbox.loadImage(imageFile, BufferedImage.TYPE_INT_ARGB_PRE);

BufferedImage imageMask
    = Toolbox.loadImage(imageMaskFile, BufferedImage.TYPE_BYTE_GRAY);
```

Note that we are loading `image` in premultiplied ARGB format because this is the format used by the GLF internally.[2]

---

2. This format is used by the `LayerComposition` class, see "The LayerComposition operation (Advanced topic)" on page 221 in Chapter 7.

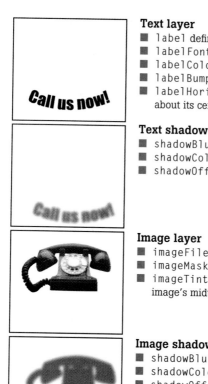

Text layer
- ■ label defines the displayed text.
- ■ labelFont defines the text font.
- ■ labelColor defines the text color.
- ■ labelBumpAngle controls how bent the label is.
- ■ labelHorizontalAdjust controls the label's adjustment about its centered bottom position.

Text shadow layer
- ■ shadowBlurRadius defines how large the shadow blur is.
- ■ shadowColor defines the color used to fill the shadow.
- ■ shadowOffset controls the shadow offset under the text.

Image layer
- ■ imageFile defines the image displayed.
- ■ imageMaskFile defines the image's transparency information.
- ■ imageTint defines the color to use as replacement for the image's midtone.

Image shadow layer
- ■ shadowBlurRadius defines how large the shadow blur is.
- ■ shadowColor defines the color used to fill the shadow.
- ■ shadowOffset controls the shadow offset under the image.
- ■ imageMaskFile is used to build shadow.

Figure 11.3 ■

ImageDropShadowComposition layer stack

▼ Creating and transforming the composition label To create the curved label, we first rely on TextLayer's makeTextBlock utility method to convert the text into a Shape object representing the text as one straight line.

```
Shape labelShape = TextLayer.makeTextBlock(label, labelFont);
```

Then, we use the nonlinear transformation, BumpTransform, to *bend* the label at a given angle.

```
BumpTransform labelBender = new BumpTransform(labelBumpAngle);
MunchTransform munchTransform = new MunchTransform(1);
labelBender.concatenate(munchTransform);
labelShape = labelBender.transform(labelShape);
```

Note how we use the `MunchTransform` class to increase the transformation quality: remember that the nonlinear transformation is only approximated.[3] Breaking down a `Shape` object into small segments before it is transformed improves the quality of the straight line segments transformation.

Computing the composition size

Now that we have the elements we are going to use in the composition, we can compute the `LayerComposition`'s size based on them,[4] as illustrated in Figure 11.4. In our example, we want to display the bent text label at the bottom of the image and add some margins around the composition.

```
Rectangle labelBounds = labelShape.getBounds();
int width = (int)(Math.max(image.getWidth(),
                          labelBounds.width) + 2*margin);

int height = image.getHeight() + labelImageGap
            + labelBounds.height + 2*margin;
Dimension size = new Dimension(width, height);
```

Once we know the size we want for the composition, we build a `LayerComposition` object.

Figure 11.4 ■
Computing ImageDropShadowComposition size

3. This is described in Chapter 9 (see "Nonlinear Transforms approximations" on page 374).
4. Note that this is one of many alternate solutions. It is also possible to chose an arbitrary size for the composition and not tie it to the elements it contains. However, it is often a good idea to fit the overall size to what is being drawn.

```
LayerComposition cmp = new LayerComposition(size);
```

At this point, we are ready to create the different Layer objects that we will stack into the composition.

Creating the composition layers

▼ **The label layer** For the label layer, we use labelShape and a FillRenderer to fill the label with a configurable color. The label is positioned at the bottom of the composition, leaving a margin so that it does not rest on the bottom edge.

```
Position labelPosition = new Position(Anchor.BOTTOM, 0, margin);
FillRenderer labelPainter = new FillRenderer(labelColor);
ShapeLayer labelLayer
    = new ShapeLayer(cmp, labelShape,
                     labelPainter,
                     labelPosition);
```

▼ **The label shadow layer** To build the shadow layer, we use labelShape again. We want to render it offset so as to provide a sense of light and depth. We also want to blur it to create a more realistic shadow effect.

The offset is provided by offsetting the shadow about its position. Here is how we create the shadow position: we first create a translation and then use it to build the label shadow Position.

```
AffineTransform shadowShiftTxf
    = AffineTransform.getTranslateInstance(shadowOffset.width,
                                           shadowOffset.height);
...
Position labelShadowPosition
    = new Position(Anchor.BOTTOM, 0, margin, shadowShiftTxf);
```

Note how we use the Position class to place the shadow at the same position as the label and then offset it about its position. For details on how the Position class works, refer to Chapter 7 (see "Position" on page 236).

Translated into English, the Position constructor means: "*Place the shadow at the bottom of the composition area, leaving a margin between the bottom of the label and the bottom edge of the composition. Then, apply the shadow-ShiftTxf transform, which shifts the shadow by applying a translation.*"

At this point, we can create a ShapeLayer object that will render the shadow.

```
ShapeLayer labelShadowLayer
    = new ShapeLayer(cmp, labelShape,
                     new FillRenderer(shadowColor),
                     labelShadowPosition);
```

If we were stopping there, the shadow would have sharp edges. To obtain fuzzy edges, we attach a blur filter to the layer. As we have discussed, blurring can be performed by the `ConvolveOp` filter, and we use our convenience `GaussianKernel` to quickly create a `Kernel` for that filter.

```
Kernel blurKernel = new GaussianKernel(shadowBlurRadius);
ConvolveOp blur = new ConvolveOp(blurKernel);
Dimension blurMargins
    = new Dimension(shadowBlurRadius*2, shadowBlurRadius*2);
labelShadowLayer.setImageFilter(blur, blurMargins);
```

▼ **The tinted image layer**   Creating the tinted image layer involves the following: create a base `ImageLayer` that renders the image (a phone, in our example), sets its mask so that we do not show the transparent parts of the image, and attaches a filter that will tint the image before it is drawn to the output.

```
// We draw the image at the top of the composition,
// leaving some margin.
Position imagePosition = new Position(Anchor.TOP, 0, margin);

// Create the Layer that will render the image at
// the right position.
ImageLayer tintedImageLayer = new ImageLayer(cmp, image, imagePosition);

// Set the Layer mask
Point imageLeftCorner = new Point(0, 0);
tintedImageLayer.getTransform().transform(imageLeftCorner,
                                          imageLeftCorner);
Rectangle imageRect
    = new Rectangle(imageLeftCorner.x, imageLeftCorner.y,
                    imageMask.getWidth(), imageMask.getHeight());
tintedImageLayer.setLayerMask(imageMask, imageRect);

// Create the tinting filter
ToneAdjustmentOp tinter = new ToneAdjustmentOp(imageTint);

// Set the Layer filter
tintedImageLayer.setImageFilter(tinter);
```

Note how the mask is positioned at the same position as the image. By default, the mask has its upper-left corner in (0, 0) in the device space. However, because we are drawing the image at the top of the composition and with some margin, the upper-left corner of the image will appear at a different position in the device space. To compute what that position is, we use `tinted-ImageLayer`'s transform to compute the device space coordinate of the image's upper-left corner.

```
Point imageLeftCorner = new Point(0, 0);
tintedImageLayer.getTransform().transform(imageLeftCorner,
                                          imageLeftCorner);
```

We then use that upper-left corner to build the device space rectangle where the mask is positioned.

```
Rectangle imageRect
    = new Rectangle(imageLeftCorner.x, imageLeftCorner.y,
                    imageMask.getWidth(), imageMask.getHeight());
```

Important Note

Here, the mask image defines the parts of the image that are opaque and those that are not. If the image format you are using contains transparency information (for example, PNG), then it is not necessary to use a separate mask image: all the transparency information is contained in the image. Note that masks are used for other things as we see in Chapter 15.

Setting the tone of the image so that the midtones have a configurable value is done by the `ToneAdjustmentOp` GLF filter. See Chapter 9 ("The ToneAdjustmentOp filter" on page 366) for details on that filter. To have the filter applied to the image before it is drawn to the output, we attach one instance to the `Layer` object.

```
// Create the tinting filter
ToneAdjustmentOp tinter = new ToneAdjustmentOp(imageTint);

// Set the Layer filter
tintedImageLayer.setImageFilter(tinter);
```

▼ **The image shadow layer**   The image shadow layer is the tricky one. We use the mask to create the blurry shadow. The first step is to create an image where we will draw the shadow.

```
BufferedImage imageShadow
    = new BufferedImage(imageMask.getWidth(), imageMask.getHeight(),
                        BufferedImage.TYPE_INT_ARGB_PRE);
```

Then, we paint the mask into the image.

```
Graphics2D g = imageShadow.createGraphics();
g.drawImage(tintedImageLayer.getLayerMask(), 0, 0, null);
```

Note how we draw the `tintedImageLayer`'s mask, not the mask we loaded as a gray scale image. We do this because the gray scale image is converted to an RGB image with alpha by the `Layer` class when the mask is set, as we explained in Chapter 7 (see "Layer masking" on page 233). Therefore, all the black pixels have been converted to transparent pixels, and all white pixels have been converted to opaque white pixels. Gray pixels have been converted to gray, partly transparent pixels. We are using that property and the `Alpha-Composite.SrcIn` compositing rule to replace the color components of all the pixels in the offscreen buffer.

```
g.setComposite(AlphaComposite.SrcIn);
g.setPaint(shadowColor);
g.fillRect(0, 0, imageMask.getWidth(), imageMask.getHeight());
g.dispose();
```

In effect, this code applies the alpha channel of the source (the mask image) to the destination (the rectangular area that has the `shadowColor`), as illustrated in Figure 11.5.

At this point, we have an offscreen buffer that contains the shadow of our image. However, its edges, if any, are as sharp as those of the original image. To obtain a more realistic look, we attach our `blur` filter to `imageShadowLayer`, as we did for `labelShadowLayer`.

```
imageShadowLayer.setImageFilter(blur, blurMargins);
```

As a result, `shadowImage` will be convolved before it is drawn to the final output when `imageShadowLayer` is painted.

▼ **Stacking up layers**   Now that we have created all the `Layer` objects we need for the composition, we stack them up in the composition.

```
cmp.setLayers(new Layer[]{ imageShadowLayer,      // First painted
                           tintedImageLayer,      // Second painted
                           labelShadowLayer,      // Third painted
                           labelLayer });         // Fourth painted
```

When `cmp` is rendered, the `Layer` objects in the stack will be painted in the order they appear in the array.

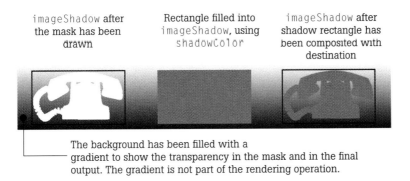

imageShadow after the mask has been drawn

Rectangle filled into imageShadow, using shadowColor

imageShadow after shadow rectangle has been composited with destination

The background has been filled with a gradient to show the transparency in the mask and in the final output. The gradient is not part of the rendering operation.

Figure 11.5 ■
Using the image transparency information to create the image shadow

Creating a Cast Shadow

Cast shadows are illustrated on the second line of the image at the top of page 384. The three examples are all created by `ShapeCastShadowComposi-tion`, the `CompositionFactory` implementation we describe in this paragraph.

Layer stack description

Figure 11.6 shows the different layers that make our composition and illustrates the most important parameters that control it.

Getting the raw material

The composition uses two shapes: the wavy text label and the cookie-cutter cut ellipse.

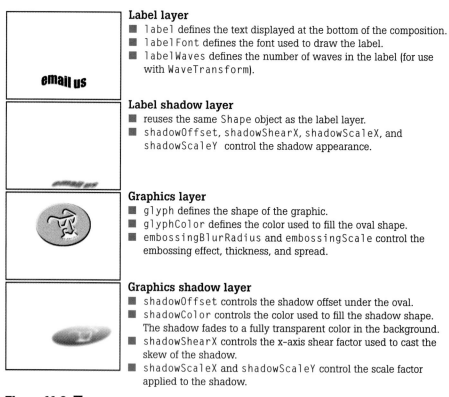

Label layer
- `label` defines the text displayed at the bottom of the composition.
- `labelFont` defines the font used to draw the label.
- `labelWaves` defines the number of waves in the label (for use with `WaveTransform`).

Label shadow layer
- reuses the same `Shape` object as the label layer.
- `shadowOffset`, `shadowShearX`, `shadowScaleX`, and `shadowScaleY` control the shadow appearance.

Graphics layer
- `glyph` defines the shape of the graphic.
- `glyphColor` defines the color used to fill the oval shape.
- `embossingBlurRadius` and `embossingScale` control the embossing effect, thickness, and spread.

Graphics shadow layer
- `shadowOffset` controls the shadow offset under the oval.
- `shadowColor` controls the color used to fill the shadow shape. The shadow fades to a fully transparent color in the background.
- `shadowShearX` controls the x-axis shear factor used to cast the skew of the shadow.
- `shadowScaleX` and `shadowScaleY` control the scale factor applied to the shadow.

Figure 11.6 ■
ShapeCastShadowComposition layer stack

▼ **Creating the wavy label**   This process is similar to what we did in our previous example: we first use `TextLayer` to convert the label text into a `Shape` object. Then, we use one of the `Transform` implementations to perform a non-linear transformation of that `Shape`.

```
Shape labelShape = TextLayer.makeTextBlock(label, labelFont);
WaveTransform labelWaver
   = new WaveTransform(labelWaves, labelWaveHeight);
MunchTransform munchTransform = new MunchTransform(1);
labelWaver.concatenate(munchTransform);
labelShape = labelWaver.transform(labelShape);
```

Note how, as in our previous example, we use the `MunchTransform` again to get a better nonlinear transformation of line segments.

▼ **Creating the cookie-cutter cut ellipse**   We use a `Shape` object as a cookie cutter to cut out a hole in an ellipse. First, we get the base `Shape` object from a `Glyph` object.

```
Shape symbol = glyph.getShape();
```

Then, we create an ellipse that encompasses this object and leaves some extra margin around it.

```
Rectangle symbolBounds = symbol.getBounds();
Shape ellipse
   = new Ellipse2D.Float(symbolBounds.x - ovalMargin*2,
                         symbolBounds.y - ovalMargin,
                         symbolBounds.width + ovalMargin*4,
                         symbolBounds.height + ovalMargin*2);
```

Finally, we use the `Area` class to subtract `symbol` from the ellipse, as illustrated in Figure 11.7.

```
Shape cutOutSymbolArea = new Area(ellipse);
cutOutSymbolArea.subtract(new Area(symbol));
```

Figure 11.7 ■
Using Area as a cookie cutter

Computing the composition size

We want to position the embossed graphic at the top of the composition and the wavy label underneath, leaving some gap in between, as illustrated in Figure 11.8.

This is similar to what we did in `ImageCastShadowComposition` example, except that we are using the `cutOutSymbolArea` bounds instead of an image size.

```
Rectangle labelBounds = labelShape.getBounds();
int width = (int)(Math.max(cutOutSymbolBounds.width,
                           labelBounds.width)
             + 2*margins.width);

int height = cutOutSymbolBounds.height + labelGap +
             labelBounds.height + 2*margins.height;

Dimension size = new Dimension(width, height);
LayerComposition cmp = new LayerComposition(size);
```

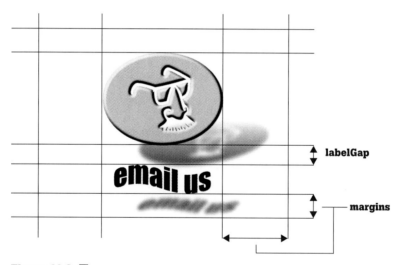

Figure 11.8 ■
Computing ShapeCastShadowComposition size

Creating the composition layers

▼ **Label layer**   We position the label at the bottom, leaving some margin.

```
Position labelPosition = new Position(Anchor.BOTTOM, 0, margins.height);
ShapeLayer labelLayer
   = new ShapeLayer(cmp, labelShape,
                       new FillRenderer(labelColor),
                       labelPosition);
```

▼ **Label shadow layer**   This is the first occasion where we create a cast shadow. We use the ability of the `Position` class to apply a transformation about an object's center *after* it is positioned in the composition. In our example, the transform is provided by the `getBottomLeftShearTransform` method.

```
Position labelShadowPosition
   = new Position(Anchor.BOTTOM, 0, margins.height,
                     getBottomLeftShearTransform(labelShape));

ShapeLayer labelShadowLayer
   = new ShapeLayer(cmp, labelShape,
                       new FillRenderer(shadowColor),
                       labelShadowPosition);

Kernel blurKernel = new GaussianKernel(shadowBlurRadius);
ConvolveOp blur = new ConvolveOp(blurKernel);
Dimension blurMargins
   = new Dimension(shadowBlurRadius*2, shadowBlurRadius*2);
....
labelShadowLayer.setImageFilter(blur, blurMargins);
```

As in our previous example, the `blur` filter will create a more realistic shadow with fuzzy edges.

Let us have a look at the `getBottomLeftShearTransform` method implementation.

```
private AffineTransform getBottomLeftShearTransform(Shape shape){
    AffineTransform shear = new AffineTransform();
    Rectangle bounds = shape.getBounds();

    // 5: Add offset
    shear.translate(shadowOffset.width, shadowOffset.height);
```

```
    // 4: Align bottom left point with original Shape
    shear.translate(-bounds.width/2f, bounds.height/2f);

    // 3: Shear
    shear.shear(shadowShearX, 0);

    // 2: Scale
    shear.scale(shadowScaleX, shadowScaleY);

    // 1: Move bottom left to origin
    shear.translate(bounds.width/2f, -bounds.height/2f);

    return shear;
}
```

Note how this code positions the sheared shape to the bottom left of the original shape, with some offset, as illustrated in Figure 11.9.

▼ **Symbol cast shadow**   The symbol shadow is built much like the label shadow is, except that a more sophisticated `Paint` is used so that the shadow fades into the background.

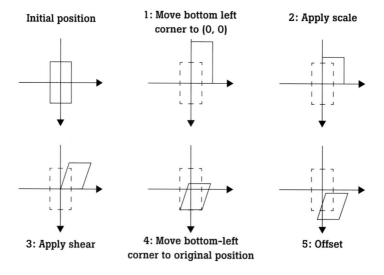

Figure 11.9 ■
Cast shadow: transform sequence

```
Shape symbolShadow = cutOutSymbolArea;

//
// Create a GradientPaint that fades into the background
//
Rectangle symbolShadowBounds = symbolShadow.getBounds();

// Build the transparent equivalent of shadowColor
Color transparentShadowColor
    = new Color(shadowColor.getRed(), shadowColor.getGreen(),
                shadowColor.getBlue(), 0);

GradientPaint symbolShadowPaint
    = new GradientPaint(0, symbolShadowBounds.y, transparentShadowColor,
                        0, symbolShadowBounds.y +
                        symbolShadowBounds.height, shadowColor);
```

We create a new `ShapeLayer` that will render the cast shadow with this `Paint`.

```
// Now, create a layer for the symbol shadow
Position symbolShadowPosition
    = new Position(Anchor.TOP, 0, margins.height,
                   getBottomLeftShearTransform(symbolShadow));

ShapeLayer symbolShadowLayer
    = new ShapeLayer(cmp, symbolShadow,
                     new FillRenderer(symbolShadowPaint),
                     symbolShadowPosition);

// Use blur to get fuzzy edges
symbolShadowLayer.setImageFilter(blur, blurMargins);
```

Note that the `GradientPaint` object is created relative to the `symbolShadow` bounds in user space and follows the shear transformation to device space. Remember to always define interdependent objects (such as `GradientPaint` and `Shape`) in the same space so that their dependency remains after transformation. We discuss this in greater detail in Chapter 16.

▼ **Embossed symbol layer**   The layer we are looking at now uses the `LightOp` filter. We use `LightOp` to emboss a `Shape` object, as we explained in Chapter 9 (see page 361).

First, we create an `ElevationMap` from the symbol.

```
Position symbolPosition = new Position(Anchor.TOP, 0, margins.height);
Shape cutOutSymbol
    = symbolPosition.createTransformedShape(cutOutSymbolArea,
                                            cmp.getBounds());
```

```
ElevationMap embossingMap
    = new ElevationMap(cutOutSymbol, embossingBlurRadius,
                       true, extrusionScale);
```

Because `LightOp` operates in device space, we position the symbol to its device space position, using `Position.createTransformedShape`. Then, we create a `LitSurface` with no ambient light and add a directional light to it, using one of the `LightsStudio` factory methods. We attach the `ElevationMap` object we just created to the `LitSurface` to get the texturizing we need.

```
// Now, create a LightOp to extrude our cutOutSymbol
LitSurface litSurface = new LitSurface(0);
DirectionalLight sunLight
    = LightsStudio.getSunLight(Anchor.TOP_LEFT, 1, Color.white);

litSurface.addLight(sunLight);
litSurface.setElevationMap(embossingMap);
LightOp embosser = new LightOp(litSurface);
```

We can now create a `ShapeLayer` and attach the `embosser` filter to it.

```
ShapeLayer extrudedSymbolLayer
        = new ShapeLayer(cmp, cutOutSymbol.getBounds(),
                         new FillRenderer(glyphColor));
extrudedSymbolLayer.setRasterFilter(embosser);
extrudedSymbolLayer.setLayerMask(cutOutSymbol);
```

There are two important things to notice here:

1. `ShapeLayer` renders the `cutOutSymbol` bounds, not `cutOutSymbol` itself. `LightOp` works better if it is applied to the bounds first and the result masked to hide the areas outside the desired `Shape`. An alternate way to obtain a similar result, but of lesser quality, would be to have `ShapeLayer` render `cutOutSymbol` and use no mask.

   ```
   ShapeLayer extrudedSymbolLayer
           = new ShapeLayer(cmp, cutOutSymbol,
                            new FillRenderer(glyphColor));
   extrudedSymbolLayer.setRasterFilter(extruder);
   ```

   The result is of lesser quality (see Figure 11.10) because antialiasing happens before filtering, and filtering the antialiased pixels produces a not-so-smooth result (right side of the figure). Using masking is a trick to get antialiasing on the filtered shape.

2. The filter is applied as a `RasterOp`, not a `BufferedImageOp`. In Chapter 7, we explained how filtering is applied to offscreen buffers. `LightOp` has a spatial meaning (that is, the location of pixels

Figure 11.10 ■
Filtering bounds and using a mask versus filtering shape directly

relative to light sources and elevation map is relevant) and should be used as a `RasterOp` when attached to `Layer` objects (see "LightOp" on page 341, in Chapter 9).

▼ **Stacking up layers**   At this point, we have created all the `Layers` we need for the composition. So, we stack them up in the order they should be rendered.

```
cmp.setLayers(new Layer[]{ symbolShadowLayer, extrudedSymbolLayer,
                           labelShadowLayer, labelLayer });
```

The cast shadow is sometimes called projected shadow. Usually, this qualifier is used for shadows that are cast in front of the lit object, instead of behind it. With our code, a negative value for the `shadowScaleX` parameter produces a projected shadow (see Figure 11.11) because it flips the shadow about the x-axis.

Figure 11.11 ■
Projected shadow

Creating a Recessed Shadow

The drop shadow and cast shadow are both used to draw shadows under an object. The recessed shadow is used to paint shadows in holes and gaps in a surface. It may seem complicated, but it is not: the `TextRecessedShadowComposition` example is the simplest of the three examples we cover in this chapter.

In this example, we explain not only how to create a recessed shadow but also how to create a slight embossing effect on the borders of the recessed area.

Layer stack description

The recessed shadow effect creates the impression that a surface has been "punched through," allowing us to see some of the other surface underneath. To differentiate the top surface and the one supposedly behind, we use two tricks. First, we use different colors for the top and background surfaces so that they can be easily distinguished. Second, we use a shadow effect to reinforce the separation between them and give a sense of the amount of space in between.

Figure 11.12 shows the different layers and illustrates the most important parameters that control them.

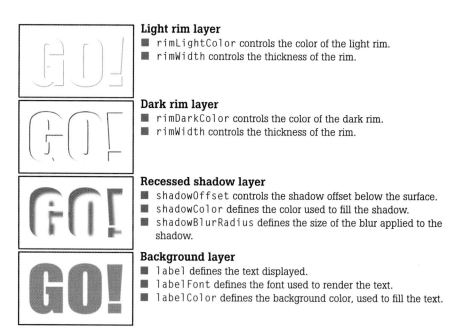

Light rim layer
- `rimLightColor` controls the color of the light rim.
- `rimWidth` controls the thickness of the rim.

Dark rim layer
- `rimDarkColor` controls the color of the dark rim.
- `rimWidth` controls the thickness of the rim.

Recessed shadow layer
- `shadowOffset` controls the shadow offset below the surface.
- `shadowColor` defines the color used to fill the shadow.
- `shadowBlurRadius` defines the size of the blur applied to the shadow.

Background layer
- `label` defines the text displayed.
- `labelFont` defines the font used to render the text.
- `labelColor` defines the background color, used to fill the text.

Figure 11.12 ■
TextRecessedShadowComposition layer stack

Getting the raw material

In this example, we use one string of text and manipulate it as a `Shape` object.

```
Shape labelShape = TextLayer.makeTextBlock(label, labelFont);
```

Computing the composition size

The size of the composition is computed from the `labelShape` bounds, leaving some extra margin around it (see Figure 11.13). That size is used to create a `LayerComposition` object.

```
Rectangle labelShapeBounds = labelShape.getBounds();
Dimension size
   = new Dimension(labelShapeBounds.width + 2*margin,
                   labelShapeBounds.height + 2*margin);
LayerComposition cmp = new LayerComposition(size);
```

Creating the layers

▼ **Label layer**　To create the label `Layer` object that will represent the underlying surface, we first center `layerShape` in the composition and then build a `ShapeLayer` with it.

```
labelShape
   = Position.CENTER.createTransformedShape(labelShape,
                                            cmp.getBounds());

ShapeLayer labelLayer
   = new ShapeLayer(cmp, labelShape, new FillRenderer(labelColor));
```

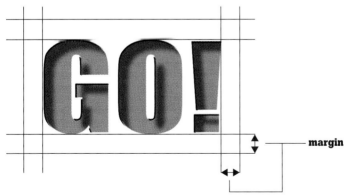

Figure 11.13 ■
Computing TextRecessedShadowComposition size

This code fills the centered `labelShape` object. Note that we could as well have done the following:

```
ShapeLayer labelLayer
    = new ShapeLayer(cmp, labelShape, new FillRenderer(labelColor),
                     Position.CENTER);
```

We would have obtained the exact same result. Neither of those two solutions is better than the other. However, we chose the first one here because we needed to center `labelShape` in the composition to create the following layer.

▼ **Label shadow layer**   The centered `labelShape` is subtracted from the composition rectangle to form the base of the shadow `Layer`.

```
Area cutOutLabelShape = new Area(cmp.getBounds());
cutOutLabelShape.subtract(new Area(labelShape));
FillRenderer shadowPainter = new FillRenderer(shadowColor);
ShapeLayer labelShadowLayer = new ShapeLayer(cmp, cutOutLabelShape,
                                             shadowPainter);
```

As we have seen in previous examples, we create fuzzy edges by attaching a convolution to the `Layer`.

```
Kernel blurKernel = new GaussianKernel(shadowBlurRadius);
ConvolveOp blur = new ConvolveOp(blurKernel);
Dimension blurMargins
    = new Dimension(shadowBlurRadius*2, shadowBlurRadius*2);
labelShadowLayer.setImageFilter(blur, blurMargins);
```

Only the part of the shadow that is inside `labelShape` should show, and we set the `Layer`'s mask to that end.

```
labelShadowLayer.setLayerMask(labelShape);
```

Finally, to create a sense of depth, we offset the shadow by setting the `Layer`'s `AffineTransform` attribute to a translation.

```
AffineTransform shadowShiftTxf
    = AffineTransform.getTranslateInstance(shadowOffset.width,
                                           shadowOffset.height);
labelShadowLayer.setTransform(shadowShiftTxf);
```

▼ **Dark rim and light rim**   To reinforce the sense of depth in the recessed effect, we are going to emboss the edges of the recessed area. The technique we are showing here provides an inexpensive embossing solution (from a computational perspective). It is fast because it only involves stroking. However, it does not provide the high-quality result we could get with `LightOp` at an extra computing cost.

The technique involves creating two `ShapeLayer` objects that stroke the outline of the recessed area with different colors.

Using mask   Using clip

Figure 11.14 ■
Pixelation when clipping

```
StrokeRenderer darkSideStroke
   = new StrokeRenderer(rimDarkColor, rimWidth);
StrokeRenderer lightSideStroke
   = new StrokeRenderer(rimLightColor, rimWidth);
Layer rimDarkSide = new ShapeLayer(cmp, labelShape, darkSideStroke);
Layer rimLightSide = new ShapeLayer(cmp, labelShape, lightSideStroke);

AffineTransform t
   = AffineTransform.getTranslateInstance(-rimWidth/2f, -rimWidth/2f);
rimDarkSide.setLayerMask(t.createTransformedShape(labelShape));

t.setToTranslation(rimWidth, rimWidth);
rimLightSide.setLayerMask(t.createTransformedShape(labelShape));
```

Note how we are setting the mask on each of the rim Layers to create a smooth clipping. Had we set the clip instead, we would have seen pixelation where the light and dark rim meet (see Figure 11.14).

▼ **Stacking up layers**   The final step consists in stacking up the layers in the order we want them painted.

```
cmp.setLayers(new Layer[]{ labelLayer, labelShadowLayer,
                           rimDarkSide, rimLightSide });
```

Putting It All Together

The composition we showed on page 384 is yet another LayerComposition that combines the three examples we have seen in this chapter. This is the ShadowsComposition example.

Combining LayerComposition objects involves the following steps.

1. Load a `CompositionFactory` bean.
2. Configure the `CompositionFactory` object.
3. Build a `Composition` from the configured `CompositionFactory` object.
4. Build a `CompositionProxyLayer` to render the `Composition` object in another `LayerComposition`.

Loading a CompositionFactory bean

Once a given `CompositionFactory` bean, such as a specific configuration of `ImageCastShadowComposition`, has been saved with the GLF utilities, that bean can be instantiated by the `CompositionFactoryLoader` utility class.

```
ImageDropShadowComposition dropShadowFactory =
(ImageDropShadowComposition)CompositionFactoryLoader.loadBeanFile(dropSh
adowBean);
```

This class takes care of loading the bean in the appropriate format, whether it was saved as a regular serialized object (`.ser` extension) or using our text format (`.ser.txt` extension), as we explained in Chapter 8.

Configuring and building a CompositionFactory object

Before using a `CompositionFactory` bean inside another composition, we might want to set some of its properties. For example, in `ShadowsComposition`, we set the color the `ImageDropShadowComposition` factory should use to tint the image.

```
dropShadowFactory.setImageTint(buttonUpColor);
Composition dropShadowHot = dropShadowFactory.build();
```

As a result, the `dropShadowHot` Composition will use the `Color` we desire for tinting the image (`buttonUpColor`).

Using CompositionProxyLayer

To get this `Composition` to display into a `LayerComposition`, we use the `CompositionProxyLayer` extension of the `Layer` class. `CompositionProxyLayer` delegates rendering to the `Composition` it proxies. However, because it has all the attributes of a `Layer`, we can set its various attributes, such as its `AffineTransform`. Therefore, the proxied `Composition` can be rendered at any location in the `LayerComposition` it is part of.

This is what we do in ShadowsComposition.

```
proxiedComposition
   = new CompositionProxyLayer(cmp,
                               dropShadowHot, // Proxied Composition
                               position);     // Position in
                                              // LayerComposition
```

ShadowsComposition uses this four-step process of reusing a Composition-Factory bean to render the nine elements it displays, as shown on page 384.

Conclusion

In this chapter, we have seen how to create different types of shadows for all kinds of graphic objects. Shadows are a powerful tool to create realistic effects, but some operations can be expensive: blurring shadow edges involves a computation-intensive convolution (especially when we use large convolution kernels), and transparent shadows involve alpha compositing, which is more computation intensive than opaque rendering.

If speed is the main objective of the rendering, it might be necessary to degrade the quality of the shadow to increase the rendering speed. If degrading quality is not an option, we can apply creative solutions to approximate large convolutions with a satisfying result, as we see in Chapter 15.

12

MAKING TEXT STAND OUT

■ OBJECTIVE

Make text stand out in a graphical composition so that it is legible.

■ PURPOSE

The same compositions can render the different states of a menu.

■ TECHNIQUES
- ■ Image glow
- ■ Text and shape glow
- ■ Brightness adjustment
- ■ Masking
- ■ Texturizing with shapes
- ■ Using an image as texture

Text is present in most of the compositions we create for either the Web or regular user interfaces. We put text in our compositions to convey a message to the reader, so it is important to make this message easily accessible and the text highly legible.

For example, the different menus at the top of this page could be used on a Web page, to help a user navigate a site. There are two different menus, each rendered twice with different settings: one to render the off state (no mouse on top of the menu item) and one to render the hot state (the mouse is on top of the menu item, which becomes hot, to notify the user it can be selected). Note how the text is easily readable, even though different colors and backgrounds are used.

Generally, text can be made legible by high contrast between the text and the background it is written on. For example, typical reading material, such as books and newspapers, uses a black ink for the text over white paper.

In the above composition, we see different types of glows used around text and images with very different visual impacts. Although this is a fancy effect, it is used functionally to increase contrast and improve text legibility.

In this chapter, we look at two different ways to create glowing edges around graphic objects. We also discuss additional techniques to further the goal of legibility.

Creating a Simple Glow

Layer stack

Figure 12.1 shows the stack of layers involved in creating a simple glow effect. It reflects the process of creating the leftmost menu on our composition on page 408 and the most important parameters that control the output.

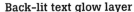

Text layer
- `menuLabels`, `menuLabels-Font`, and `menuLabels-Alignment` define how the text looks, filling it with the background texture.
- `menuLabelsScale` controls the text's brightness adjustment.

Back-lit text glow layer
- `menuLabels`, `menuLabels-Font`, and `backlitColor` paint the glow before it is blurred and rescaled.
- `backlitRadius` controls the glow spread, and `glowScale` controls the brighness adjustment.

Background paint
- `backgroundImageFile` defines the background's texture.

Image layer
- `imageFile` defines the image to be displayed at the bottom of the menu.
- `imageMaskFile` defines the outline of the object contained in `imageFile`.

Back-lit image glow layer
- `imageMaskFile` defines the image object's outline.
- `backlitRadius` controls the glow spread, and `glowScale` controls the brigntness adjustment.
- `backlitColor` defines the glow color.

Figure 12.1 ■
BacklitGlowMenuComposition layer stack and background fill

Getting the raw material

The raw material in this composition consists of:

- An image used for the background texture
- A second image and its mask for the object at the bottom of the menu
- A block of text whose alignment can be controlled

Here is how the images are loaded.

```
BufferedImage backgroundImage
    = Toolbox.loadImage(backgroundImageFile,
                        BufferedImage.TYPE_INT_ARGB_PRE);

BufferedImage image
    = Toolbox.loadImage(imageFile,
                        BufferedImage.TYPE_INT_ARGB_PRE);

BufferedImage imageMask
    = Toolbox.loadImage(imageMaskFile,
                        BufferedImage.TYPE_INT_ARGB_PRE);
```

Creating the text block relies on the `makeTextBlock` utility method in the `TextLayer` class.

```
int doNotWrap = -1;
Shape textBlock
  = TextLayer.makeTextBlock(menuLabels,    // List of labels that should
                                           // be displayed, defined as a
                                           // single string of text.
                            menuLabelsFont,// Used for the labels
                            doNotWrap,     // Each paragraph on a
                                           // single line: no line wrap
                            menuLabelsAlignment);
Position menuPosition
    = new Position(Anchor.TOP, 0, margins.height);
textBlock
    = menuPosition.createTransformedShape(textBlock, cmp.getBounds());
```

Note that `menuLabel` may contain several paragraphs of text, that is, several lines separated by line separators. In our example, each of the menu labels is a separate paragraph. Therefore, each label appears on a separate line because, `TextLayer` places different paragraphs on different lines.

Computing the layer size

The composition's size depends on the elements it contains, adding some margins around them, as illustrated in Figure 12.2.

menuImageGap

margins

Figure 12.2 ■
BacklitGlowMenuComposition size

```
Rectangle textBlockBounds = textBlock.getBounds();
Dimension size = new Dimension();
size.width = (int)Math.max(textBlockBounds.width,
                       image.getWidth()) + 2*margins.width;
size.height = textBlockBounds.height + menuImageGap
            + image.getHeight() + 2*margins.height;
LayerComposition cmp = new LayerComposition(size);
```

Before turning to creating `Layer` objects for the composition, we use the texture image to create a `TexturePaint` object and fill the composition's background.

```
// Fit background image to composition size
int iw = backgroundImage.getWidth();
int ih = backgroundImage.getHeight();

if(iw>size.width)
   backgroundImage = backgroundImage.getSubimage(0, 0, size.width, ih);

iw = backgroundImage.getWidth();

if(backgroundImage.getHeight()>size.height)
   backgroundImage = backgroundImage.getSubimage(0, 0, iw, size.height);
```

```
ih = backgroundImage.getHeight();

AffineTransform backgroundScale
    = AffineTransform.getScaleInstance(size.width/(float)iw,
                                    size.height/(float)ih);

AffineTransformOp backgroundScaler
    = new AffineTransformOp(backgroundScale,
                         AffineTransformOp.TYPE_BILINEAR);
backgroundImage = backgroundScaler.filter(backgroundImage, null);

// Create texture paint with background image
TexturePaint texturePaint = new TexturePaint(backgroundImage,
                                         cmp.getBounds());

cmp.setBackgroundPaint(texturePaint);
```

There are two things to note here: the strategy used to fit the texture image to the background area and the way this texture is used to fill the background.

In the code, the texture image is either sliced if it is bigger than the area it will cover or blown up if it is smaller. There are alternate solutions, such as shrinking the image if it is too big, instead of slicing it, or tiling the image instead of blowing it up if it is too small.

The other notable point is that we create a `TexturePaint` and set the background attribute of the composition. There are other ways to do the exact same thing. For example, we could have created an `ImageLayer` object and produced a similar result.

```
ImageLayer backgroundTextureLayer
    = new ImageLayer(cmp, backgroundImage, Position.CENTER);
```

Creating the composition layers

▼ **Text glow layer** Creating a glow is somewhat similar to creating a shadow: it involves blurring the graphic object for which we build the effect. However, for a glow, we apply a `RescaleOp` filter in addition to the blur filter.

In our example, we first create a `ShapeLayer` object.

```
FillRenderer glowRenderer = new FillRenderer(backlitColor);
ShapeLayer backlitTextLayer
    = new ShapeLayer(cmp, textBlock, glowRenderer);
```

Then we create the filter that will create the glow effect.

```
GaussianKernel blurKernel = new GaussianKernel(backlitRadius);
ConvolveOp blur = new ConvolveOp(blurKernel);
```

```
Dimension blurMargins = new Dimension(backlitRadius*2, backlitRadius*2);
RescaleOp alphaScale
= new RescaleOp(
      new float[]{glowScale, glowScale, glowScale, glowScale},
      new float[]{0, 0, 0, 0},
      null
      );

CompositeOp glowFilter = new CompositeOp(blur, alphaScale);
backlitTextLayer.setImageFilter(glowFilter, blurMargins);
```

Here, we do two important things. First, we use `CompositeOp` to combine two successive filters, the blur, and then the rescale operation. Second, we rescale the four bands of the image equally. That is, we apply the same scale factor for the red, green, blue, and alpha components of the image. The purpose of the rescale operation is the following: when we apply a blur, the resulting effect is rather subtle around the edges (see Figure 12.3) and is not satisfactory: it does not really qualify as a glow! To get a better effect, we need to spread the glow and its brightness. This is what `RescaleOp` does by increasing the alpha value of the pixels and their brightness, giving us a very effective glow effect.

Figure 12.3 ■
Glow with no rescaling

Note: Actually, the pixel's brightness is only adjusted on pixels where the alpha value is scaled enough to exceed 1. On other pixels, the brightness is not modified. The reason is that GLF operates in premultiplied ARGB format. Let us call "s" the scale factor, "a" the alpha value, and "c" one of the color component's values. Before scaling, the value stored for the alpha component is "a" and for the color component it is "a.c". The values stored after scaling are "s.a" for the alpha component and "s.a.c" for the color component. Where the scaled alpha value does not exceed 1, the new color component value simply reflects the new alpha value. Where it exceeds 1, the new color component's value is also increased.

▼ **Text layer**　The previous layer simply creates the glow around the edge of the text, and the following `Layer` renders the text itself, using the `TexturePaint` object we created for the background.

```
ShapeLayer menuLabelsLayer
   = new ShapeLayer(cmp, textBlock, new FillRenderer(texturePaint));
```

Figure 12.4 ■
Low contrast between
glow and text

This, however, is not enough to make the text legible with some glow colors because the contrast might not be sufficient between the texture and the glow (see Figure 12.4).

To increase the contrast, we use `RescaleOp` again, this time to brighten (or darken) the text we paint.

```
float menuScales[] = {menuLabelsScale,
                      menuLabelsScale,
                      menuLabelsScale,
                      1};
float scaleOffsets[] = {0, 0, 0, 0};
RescaleOp brightener
   = new RescaleOp(menuScales,
                   scaleOffsets, null);

menuLabelsLayer.setImageFilter(brightener);
```

▼ **Image glow** We create the image glow by reusing the composite filter we created for the text glow. However, we apply it to a different object. This time, we apply it to the image's mask.

```
// Create an image to paint the glow
BufferedImage imageGlow
   = new BufferedImage(imageMask.getWidth(), imageMask.getHeight(),
                       BufferedImage.TYPE_INT_ARGB_PRE);

// Paint the image's outline, using its mask
Graphics2D g = imageGlow.createGraphics();
g.drawImage(imageLayer.getLayerMask(), 0, 0, null);
g.setComposite(AlphaComposite.SrcIn);
g.setPaint(backlitColor);
g.fillRect(0, 0, imageMask.getWidth(), imageMask.getHeight());

Position imagePosition = new Position(Anchor.BOTTOM, 0, margins.height);

// Create an ImageLayer with the glow base and attach our glow filter
ImageLayer backlitImageLayer
   = new ImageLayer(cmp, imageGlow, imagePosition);
backlitImageLayer.setImageFilter(glowFilter, blurMargins);
```

As for shadows, we use the image's transparency information, provided by its mask image, to paint the glow. Then, that image is blurred and rescaled, as we have seen for the text.

▼ **Image layer**   The final layer in the composition is a simple `ImageLayer` object that we render on top of the image glow.

```
ImageLayer imageLayer = new ImageLayer(cmp, image, imagePosition);
```

▼ **Stacking up layers**   Now that we have created all the layers we need in the composition, we stack them up in the order they should be rendered.

```
cmp.setLayers(new Layer[]{ backlitTextLayer,
                           menuLabelsLayer,
                           backlitImageLayer,
                           imageLayer });
```

Creating a Sophisticated Glow

Our first example showed how to create a nice glow effect. However, we can make that effect more sophisticated by combining several, single-color glows. This is how the two menus on the right of page 408 were created.

The `NeonGlowMenuComposition` example created that output. Its layer stack is illustrated in Figure 12.5, where the layers are shown from left to right, the left-most layer being the first rendered.

The example is similar to the previous example except in two regards: the glow effect is more sophisticated (it resembles a real neon glow more closely), and the background texture is rendered by the program (and does not come from an

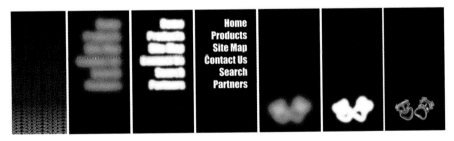

Figure 12.5 ■
NeonGlowMenuComposition layer stack

image file). This section explains how those two different aspects are implemented in turn.

Creating a more sophisticated glow

To render a more sophisticated glow, we use a trick and actually create two glows: one, the inner glow, with a smaller spread than the other one, the outer glow. The small glow is then rendered above the large one in the layer stack.

```
// Create inner blur
GaussianKernel innerBlurKernel = new GaussianKernel(neonRadius/2);
ConvolveOp innerBlur = new ConvolveOp(innerBlurKernel);
Dimension innerBlurMargins = new Dimension(neonRadius, neonRadius);
RescaleOp innerAlphaScale
    = new RescaleOp(
        new float[]{glowScale, glowScale, glowScale, glowScale},
        new float[]{0, 0, 0, 0},
        null);

CompositeOp innerGlowFilter
    = new CompositeOp(innerBlur,innerAlphaScale);

// Create outer blur
GaussianKernel outerBlurKernel = new GaussianKernel(neonRadius);
ConvolveOp outerBlur = new ConvolveOp(outerBlurKernel);
Dimension outerBlurMargins = new Dimension(neonRadius*2, neonRadius*2);
RescaleOp outerAlphaScale
    = new RescaleOp(
        new float[]{glowScale, glowScale, glowScale, glowScale},
        new float[]{0, 0, 0, 0},
        null);

CompositeOp outerGlowFilter
    = new CompositeOp(outerBlur, outerAlphaScale);

// Create layer for inner glow
FillRenderer innerGlowRenderer = new FillRenderer(neonInnerColor);
ShapeLayer neonInnerTextLayer
    = new ShapeLayer(cmp, textBlock, innerGlowRenderer);
neonInnerTextLayer.setImageFilter(innerGlowFilter, innerBlurMargins);
```

```
// Create layer for outer glow
FillRenderer outerGlowRenderer = new FillRenderer(neonOuterColor);
ShapeLayer neonOuterTextLayer
   = new ShapeLayer(cmp, textBlock,outerGlowRenderer);
neonOuterTextLayer.setImageFilter(outerGlowFilter, outerBlurMargins);
```

More glows could be combined for an even more sophisticated effect. However, the technique would not vary: create several glows of different colors and sizes and stack them in order of size, starting with the largest one. In our `NeonGlow-MenuComposition`, we make sure to render the outer glow, the largest one, first.

```
cmp.setLayers(new Layer[]{ backgroundLayer,
                          neonOuterTextLayer,
                          neonInnerTextLayer,
                          menuLabelsLayer,
                          neonOuterImageLayer,
                          neonInnerImageLayer,
                          imageLayer});
```

Creating a background texture with shapes

The fancy background in our neon glow composition is created by the program. It illustrates how to create a texture with shapes and fit it to a specific size.

The texture results from a string of text that is scaled to fit the width of the composition and repeated from the top of the composition to its bottom.

```
Shape textureShape
   = TextLayer.makeTextBlock(backgroundTextureText,
                             backgroundTextureFont);
Rectangle textureShapeBounds = textureShape.getBounds();

// Rescale texture Shape so that it is as wide as the composition
float textureScale = size.width/(float)textureShapeBounds.width;
AffineTransform scale
   = AffineTransform.getScaleInstance(textureScale, textureScale);
textureShape = scale.createTransformedShape(textureShape);

// Position Shape at the bottom
```

```
textureShape
  = Position.BOTTOM.createTransformedShape(textureShape,
                                     cmp.getBounds());
textureShapeBounds = textureShape.getBounds();

// Now, concatenate the Shape several times to fill the background
GeneralPath backgroundShape = new GeneralPath(textureShape);
int curY = size.height - textureShapeBounds.height;
AffineTransform textureMover = new AffineTransform();
while(curY>0){
    textureMover.translate(0, -textureShapeBounds.height);
    Shape positionedShape =
      textureMover.createTransformedShape(textureShape);
    backgroundShape.append(positionedShape, false);
    curY -= textureShapeBounds.height;
}
```

backgroundShape is then used to build a ShapeLayer.

```
FillRenderer backgroundShapePainter
  = new FillRenderer(backgroundTextureColor);

ShapeLayer backgroundLayer
  = new ShapeLayer(cmp, backgroundShape, backgroundShapePainter);
```

At this point, we have a layer that would produce an even texture. However, because it shows text, it would interfere with the menu labels. To prevent this, we create a mask to hide part of the texture.

```
BufferedImage backgroundMask
  = new BufferedImage(size.width, size.height,
BufferedImage.TYPE_BYTE_GRAY);
Graphics2D g = backgroundMask.createGraphics();
GradientPaintExt maskPaint
    = new GradientPaintExt(0, 0, 0, size.height,
                           new float[]{3, 1},
                           new Color[]{Color.black,
                                       Color.darkGray,
                                       Color.white});
g.setPaint(maskPaint);
g.fillRect(0, 0, size.width, size.height);

backgroundLayer.setLayerMask(backgroundMask);
```

Note that we use a GradientPaintExt to obtain a finer control over the midpoint in the gradient: because the mask will vary from black to dark gray on three thirds of the composition's height, we ensure that most of the texture will be almost completely invisible and only show very visibly on the bottom third.

Conclusion

We have seen how simple and sophisticated glows help make text stand out by increasing the contrast between the text and its background.

No matter how sophisticated the effects in our graphical compositions are, they will only be successful if they do not cloud the message we are trying to convey. This is why we should always make sure the text we display is easily readable and adjust our compositions accordingly, for example, by increasing contrast with the background (as we saw with `RescaleOp`) or by partially masking a background texture to make it more subtle (as we saw with the shape texture).

chapter **13**

SCULPTING WITH LIGHT

■ OBJECTIVE
Create realistic lighting effects.

■ PURPOSE
Create compelling banners.

■ TECHNIQUES
- ■ Carving effect
- ■ Embossing with spot light
- ■ Extruding effect
- ■ Color adjustment
- ■ Masking

In our everyday life, we are accustomed to all kinds of lighting conditions and the various effects they produce. For example, when we are in the sun, we can see uniformly lit surfaces all around us. And when we are at a show, we can see comedians in the spotlight.

Recreating such lighting conditions is the goal of the LightOp filter, which allows us to position lights of various types (directional or spot), color, and intensity around and above the images we filter. In addition, LightOp can be used to texturize images, as we have seen in Chapter 9 (see "LightOp" on page 341).

This chapter shows techniques that we can use to texturize images and, as a result, sculpt a surface. The composition at the top of this page illustrates three different possibilities: embossing at the top, carving in the center, and extruding at the bottom. This type of effect can be used, for example, to create appealing banners for a Web page or a user interface.

In addition to texturizing, we discuss different techniques to ensure that the text displayed is legible, for the reasons we explained in the previous chapter.

The various techniques we present are contained in the LightPaintingComposition example. We first see how to get the raw material, images, and shapes needed for the composition. Then, we focus on creating the layers that provide the desired effects.

420

The Layer Stack

Figure 13.1 shows the stack of layers in the composition and the most important parameters that control them.

All layers in the stack use a `Shape` object, `bannerShape`, built by concatenating the banner text and the banner symbol. The banner text is defined by the `text` and `textFont` parameters. The banner symbol is defined by the `glyph` parameter. The gap between the banner text and the banner symbol is controlled by the `symbolTextGap` parameter.

Furthormoro, thc ѕame SpotLlight object is used for the different `LightOp` filters used in the stack. The `lightAnchor`, `lightOffset`, `lightSize`, `lightIntensity`, and `lightColor` parameters define the position and characteristic of this light.

Finally, the three effects use the same configuration, even though they use it differently. This configuration is defined by the `heightScale` and `textureBlurRadius` parameters, which define how wide and how high or deep the 3D effects are.

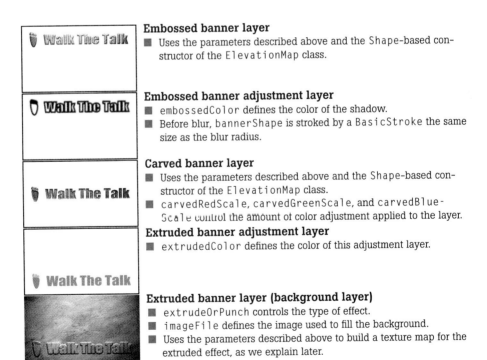

Embossed banner layer
- Uses the parameters described above and the `Shape`-based constructor of the `ElevationMap` class.

Embossed banner adjustment layer
- `embossedColor` defines the color of the shadow.
- Before blur, `bannerShape` is stroked by a `BasicStroke` the same size as the blur radius.

Carved banner layer
- Uses the parameters described above and the `Shape`-based constructor of the `ElevationMap` class.
- `carvedRedScale`, `carvedGreenScale`, and `carvedBlueScale` control the amount of color adjustment applied to the layer.

Extruded banner adjustment layer
- `extrudedColor` defines the color of this adjustment layer.

Extruded banner layer (background layer)
- `extrudeOrPunch` controls the type of effect.
- `imageFile` defines the image used to fill the background.
- Uses the parameters described above to build a texture map for the extruded effect, as we explain later.

Figure 13.1 ■
LightPaintingComposition layer stack

Getting the Raw Material

Our example uses the following raw material:

- An image, which we use for the background
- A `Shape` object that is used as a kind of bullet for each banner
- A text that is displayed in the banner

Loading the background image relies on the `Toolbox` utility.

```
BufferedImage image
    = Toolbox.loadImage(imageFile, BufferedImage.TYPE_INT_ARGB_PRE);
```

The bullet shape is built from the `Glyph` attribute.

```
Shape symbol = glyph.getShape();
```

It is then concatenated with the banner's text, so that they can be manipulated as a single `Shape` object later.

```
// Convert text to a Shape object
Shape textShape = TextLayer.makeTextBlock(text, textFont);

// Position symbol shape to the left of the text
Position symbolPosition = new Position(Anchor.LEFT, symbolTextGap, 0);
symbol = symbolPosition.createTransformedShape(symbol,
                                       textShape.getBounds());

// Concatenate symbol and text
GeneralPath bannerShape = new GeneralPath(textShape);
bannerShape.append(symbol, false);
```

Note how `Position` is used to place `symbol` to the left of `textShape` before the two are combined in a single `Shape` object (see Figure 13.2 on page 423 for an illustration of `symbolTextGap`).

Computing the Composition Size

Because we want to illustrate three different types of 3D effects in three different banners, we compute a size to give us enough space for that display, leaving some margins between the banners, as shown in Figure 13.2.

```
Rectangle bounds = bannerShape.getBounds();
int w = bounds.width + 2*margins.width;
int h = bounds.height*3 + 2*bannerGap + 2*margins.height;
Dimension size = new Dimension(w, h);
```

This is the size we use to build our `LayerComposition`.

```
LayerComposition cmp = new LayerComposition(size);
```

Now that we have all the base ingredients for the composition, we are ready to start building the different layers.

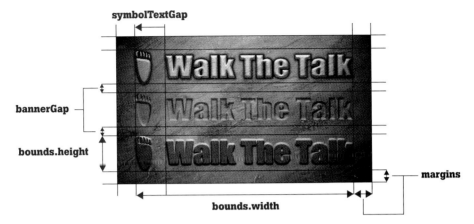

Figure 13.2 ■
LightPaintingComposition size

Embossing with SpotLight

We start with the simplest effect to implement: embossing. It is simple to implement because GLF provides default settings that create this effect. Here is what we need to do: first create a properly configured `LightOp` filter; second, attach that filter to a `ShapeLayer` object.

Using LightOp for embossing

As for all rendering operations that involve `LightOp`, we need to do the following:

1. Create the lights we need.
2. If texturizing is wanted, as for embossing, create an `Elevation-Map` object that describes the texture.
3. Create a `LitSurface` object that contains the texture description, if any, as well as the different lights.
4. Create a `LightOp` filter for the `LitSurface` object we created. `LightOp` processes light intensities according to the `LitSurface` characteristics.

Let us see how to program each of these steps.

▼ Creating a SpotLight Even though it is possible to create a SpotLight directly, it is easier to rely on the LightsStudio utility class to position and angle it correctly. We use the getSpotLight factory method to create our light.

```
Rectangle lightRect = cmp.getBounds();
lightRect.x = lightOffset.width;
lightRect.y = lightOffset.height;
SpotLight spot = LightsStudio.getSpotLight(lightRect,
                                           lightAnchor,
                                           lightSize,
                                           lightIntensity,
                                           lightColor);
```

Remember (see"LightOp" on page 341) that lightRect controls the area where the light is positioned, lightAnchor controls the position of the light within that area, and lightSize the size of the area lit by the light. Finally, lightIntensity and lightColor are self-explanatory.

▼ Creating a texture map To create an embossing effect, we create a texture map that describes the elevation on each point of the surface we filter. The ElevationMap constructor will create an appropriate texture map from a Shape for an embossing effect.

```
ElevationMap embossedMap
   = new ElevationMap(embossedBannerShape, // Shape used a base for
                                           // embossing
                      textureBlurRadius,   // Embossing width
                      true,                // Embossing (v.s. carving)
                      heightScale);        // Embossing height
```

We will see, with the extruded effect, how to create a texture map ourselves.

▼ Creating a LitSurface Once we have created the lights we need around the images we filter and the texture we want to apply, we can create a LitSurface with those characteristics.

```
LitSurface embossedBannerSurface
   = new LitSurface(ambiantLight,          // Default amount of light
                    LitSurfaceType.NORMAL, // Defines how reflective
                                           // the surface is
                    embossedMap);          // Surface texture
```

```
embossedBannerSurface.addLight(spot);// Adds a light to the surface
```

Please refer to "LightOp" on page 341 for additional details on the different parameters and their semantics.

▼ Creating a LightOp filter Once a LitSurface object has been created, we are almost done. We just need to create a LightOp instance that will use the LitSurface object characteristics. LightOp relies on LitSurface to perform all the light intensity computations.

```
LightOp embosser = new LightOp(embossedBannerSurface);
```

Attaching LightOp to a ShapeLayer

Now that we have created a `LightOp` filter for our embossing effect, we can attach it to a `ShapeLayer` object.

```
TexturePaint texturePaint = new TexturePaint(image, cmp.getBounds());
FillRenderer texturePainter = new FillRenderer(texturePaint);

ShapeLayer embossedBannerLayer
    = new ShapeLayer(cmp, embossedBannerShape, texturePainter);
embossedBannerLayer.setRasterFilter(embosser);
```

Remember to always use a `LightOp` as a RasterOp filter (that is, use the `set-RasterFilter` rather than the `setImageFilter` method), as explained in "LightOp" on page 341.

The way we have created a filter for the embossed text effect is exactly the same as the one used for the carved and extruded text effects. The only difference is the way the texture map is created. This is what the following paragraphs explain.

Carving with SpotLight

Creating an elevation map for a carved text effect is done automatically by one of the `ElevationMap` class constructors.

```
ElevationMap carvedMap
    = new ElevationMap(carvedBannerShape,  // Shape used as a base for
                                           // carving
                       textureBlurRadius,  // carving width
                       false,              // carve (v.s. emboss)
                       heightScale);       // carving depth
```

The process `ElevationMap` uses is described in "Elevation maps" on page 354. From a functional point of view, the important thing to remember about the `Shape`-based `ElevationMap` constructor is that it let us specify the following:

- The `Shape` object that should be embossed or carved
- The width of the effect
- Carving versus embossing
  If `whiteIsHigh` is false, then we get a carving effect. If `whiteIsHigh` is true, then we get an embossing effect
- The height of the effect
  The height scale controls how high or deep the embossing or carving effects are

Embossing and carving are commonly used effects, and this is why `Eleva-tionMap` provides convenience constructors for building corresponding texture maps. However, other types of texture maps can be created without the help of `ElevationMap`, and the extrusion effect is one example.

Extruding with SpotLight

The extruding effect is shown by the bottom banner on page 420. The surface seems to elevate around the edges of the extruded `Shape`. To create this effect, we do the following:

1. Paint the base `Shape` in an offscreen buffer, using white paint on a black background.
2. Blur the offscreen buffer.
3. Clean the inside of the base `Shape` by painting it again with white.

This process is illustrated in Figure 13.3.

In our example, the following method creates such a texture map.

```
private ElevationMap buildExtrudedMap(Dimension size,
                                      Shape shape,
                                      int blurRadius,
                                      int heightScale,
                                      boolean extrudeOrPunch){
// Build a BufferedImage large enough for the extrusion blur
BufferedImage buffer
    = new BufferedImage(size.width, size.height,
                    BufferedImage.TYPE_BYTE_GRAY);
Graphics2D g = buffer.createGraphics();
g.setRenderingHint(RenderingHints.KEY_ANTIALIASING,
                RenderingHints.VALUE_ANTIALIAS_ON);
```

1: Paint shape offscreen   **2: Blur**   **3: Paint shape again**

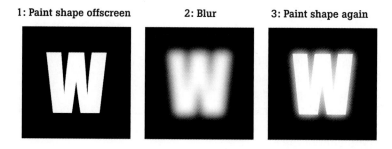

Figure 13.3 ■

Creating an elevation map for extruding shapes

Figure 13.4 ■
Punch versus extrusion

```
g.setPaint(Color.white);
g.fill(shape);
g.dispose();

// Blur
ConvolveOp blur = new ConvolveOp(new GaussianKernel(blurRadius));
buffer = blur.filter(buffer, null);

// Now, make a 'clean' shape
g = buffer.createGraphics();
g.setRenderingHint(RenderingHints.KEY_ANTIALIASING,
                   RenderingHints.VALUE_ANTIALIAS_ON);
g.setPaint(Color.white);
g.fill(shape);
g.dispose();

return new ElevationMap(buffer, extrudeOrPunch, heightScale);
}
```

Note how the `whiteIsHigh` parameter in the `ElevationMap` constructor (the second parameter), is called `extrudedOrPunch`. The reason is that when set to true, it creates an extrusion effect. When set to false, the effect is that of a punch in the surface, as illustrated in Figure 13.4.

Increasing Legibility

To make the different effects more compelling, we do the following:

- Add a dark glow under the embossed text
- Adjust the carved text's color
- Paint the top of the extruded text

Adding a dark glow under the embossed text

This is *not* done exactly as we described in the previous chapter, where we discussed different types of glows at length.

```
FillRenderer glowPainter = StrokeRenderer(embossedColor,
                                        textureBlurRadius)
ShapeLayer embossedStandOutLayer
    = new ShapeLayer(cmp, embossedBannerShape, glowPainter);

ConvolveOp blur = new ConvolveOp(new GaussianKernel(textureBlurRadius));
Dimension blurMargins = new Dimension(textureBlurRadius*2,
                                    textureBlurRadius*2);

embossedStandOutLayer.setImageFilter(blur, blurMargins);
```

Here, instead of filling the text, blurring it, and then applying a `RescaleOp` to increase the glow radius, we instead use a thick stroke (as thick as the radius we use for the blur operation) and a simple blur. When used with black, this technique yields a satisfying result and is quicker than the technique we described in Chapter 3. However, if we used a color other than black, we would not get the brightness adjustment we got with a `RescaleOp` and, therefore, the glow would not be as effective.

Adjusting the carved text's color

The dark glow under the embossed text increased the contrast between the text and its immediate background. Another way to increase contrast is to modify the text color. This is what we do for the carved text, where we use `RescaleOp`.

```
float rgbaScales[] = new float[]{carvedRedScale,
                                carvedGreenScale,
                                carvedBlueScale,
                                1};
RescaleOp scaleOp = new RescaleOp(rgbaScales,
                                new float[]{0, 0, 0, 0}, null);

CompositeRasterOp carvedFilter = new CompositeRasterOp(carver, scaleOp);

ShapeLayer carvedBannerLayer
    = new ShapeLayer(cmp, carvedBannerShape, texturePainter);

carvedBannerLayer.setRasterFilter(carvedFilter);
```

Note how we are first carving and then scaling the `carvedBannerLayer` by combining two filters into one with `CompositeRasterOp`. As we described in Chapter 9 (see "The CompositeOp and CompositeRasterOp filters" on page 370), that filter can chain two (or more) `RasterOp` filters, just like `CompositeOp` can chain two or more `BufferedImageOp`s.

In our example, we set the different scale factors to make the carved text seem more red/orange. This setting increases the color contrast against the background and increases readability. However, this contrast is not as effective as the black glow we use for the embossed text. The reason is that the black glow creates a high brightness contrast between the text and the glow, and the human eye is more sensitive to brightness variations than it is to hue variations. Therefore, increasing the difference in brightness is more effective than just increasing the hue contrast with little brightness contrast, as we have for the carving effect.

Painting the top of the extruded text

Again for the sake of readability, we use an additional layer to paint the top of the extruded text.

```
FillRenderer extrudedTextPainter = new FillRenderer(extrudedColor);
ShapeLayer extrudedAdjustmentLayer
    = new ShapeLayer(cmp, extrudedBannerShape, extrudedTextPainter);
```

Stacking Up Layers

Once we have created all the layers we want in the composition, we can stack them in the order in which they should be rendered.

```
cmp.setLayers(new Layer[]{backgroundLayer,
                          extrudedAdjustmentLayer,
                          carvedBannerLayer,
                          embossedStandOutLayer,
                          embossedBannerLayer});
```

Conclusion

The `LightOp` filter provides a rich set of features to create various rendering effects. However, just as for the glow effects, it should not be used to the detriment of the clarity of the message displayed, but rather to reinforce it.

The filter can create dramatic lighting conditions where appropriate. Where text is involved, it is often useful to combine lighting effects with others, to increase readability, as we discussed in this chapter.

Remember that `LightOp` can also be used for texturizing (we discussed several examples in Chapter 9 [see "Elevation maps" on page 354]).

chapter 14

FANCY TEXT LAYOUTS

■ OBJECTIVE

Create unusual text layouts.

■ PURPOSE

First page or instruction steps.

■ TECHNIQUES

- Circular text layout
- Triangular text layout
- Multiple stroking
- Combining layer compositions

In our discussion of the Java 2D API features in Part I and then in our presentation of the Graphic Layers Framework in Part II, we saw powerful text features that let us control text layout in many ways: line wraps, paragraph alignment, text justification, etc.

In this chapter we discuss more examples of those powerful features and explain how to create nonsquare text layouts such as the circular and triangular layouts displayed in the composition at the top of this page.

That composition (see the ShapeLayout *example) illustrates the type of graphic we might create for the purpose of a main screen or as a first instruction page of some kind. It uses three different* CompositionFactory *implementations:* CircularLayoutComposition, TriangularLayoutComposition, *and* GlyphDecorationComposition, *which displays the numbers 1, 2, 3, and 4.*

We explain how each works and briefly discuss how they are combined in a single composition.

Creating a Circular Text Layout

Layer stack

Figure 14.1 shows the two layers that make the composition and the main parameters that control them.

This is a simple stack and the `LayerComposition` is built with a predefined size.

```
Dimension size = new Dimension(blockWidth, blockWidth);
LayerComposition cmp = new LayerComposition(size);
cmp.setBackgroundPaint(backgroundColor);
```

Here is how the text border is created.

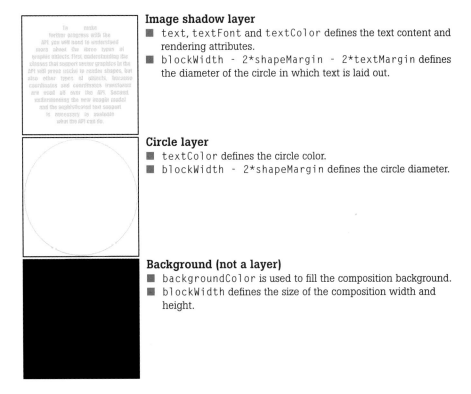

Image shadow layer
- `text`, `textFont` and `textColor` defines the text content and rendering attributes.
- `blockWidth - 2*shapeMargin - 2*textMargin` defines the diameter of the circle in which text is laid out.

Circle layer
- `textColor` defines the circle color.
- `blockWidth - 2*shapeMargin` defines the circle diameter.

Background (not a layer)
- `backgroundColor` is used to fill the composition background.
- `blockWidth` defines the size of the composition width and height.

Figure 14.1 ■
CircularLayoutComposition layer stack

```
// Create base Shape object
Shape circle
    = new Ellipse2D.Float(0, 0,
                          blockWidth-shapeMargin*2,
                          blockWidth-shapeMargin*2);

// Create Renderer to paint the border
Renderer shapeRenderer
    = new StrokeRenderer(textColor, shapeStrokeWidth);

// Create layer object to later render the border
ShapeLayer circleLayer
    = new ShapeLayer(cmp, circle, shapeRenderer, Position.CENTER);
```

Circular text layout

▼ **Laying out text**   The hard work goes into properly breaking lines into segments that fit nicely into a circle. Figure 14.2 illustrates a circular text layout.

The process is similar to the one we described in Chapter 7 (see "TextLayer" on page 253):

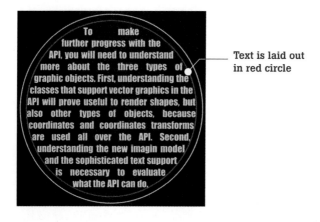

Text is laid out in red circle

Figure 14.2 ■
Circular text layout control circle

1. Create an `AttributedString` object from the text.
2. Use `LineBreakMeasurer` to break the string into lines that fit into specific width. As we will see, the desired width varies for each line.
3. Align text lines if needed.
4. Concatenate the text lines into a single text block.

The following code shows how to perform the first step and prepare for the other ones.

```
FontRenderContext frc = new FontRenderContext(null, true, true);
AttributedString styledString = new AttributedString(text);
styledString.addAttribute(TextAttribute.FONT, textFont);
AttributedCharacterIterator iter = styledString.getIterator();
LineBreakMeasurer measurer = new LineBreakMeasurer(iter, frc);
```

The last three steps all happen in a single loop: text is processed until there is no more text or until there is no more space. The following pseudocode summarizes the process.

```
float wrapWidth = 0;
GeneralPath textBlock = new GeneralPath();
Shape lineShape = null;
while(measurer.getPosition() < limit){// While there is text to process

    wrapWidth = ...; // Process wrapping width for the current line
    ....
    layout = ...;    // Get next line

    // Justify and position line. Get it as a Shape object
    lineShape = ...;

    // Concatenate lineShape into textBlock
    textBlock.append(lineShape, doNoConnect);

    // Stop if not more space to lay text out
    if(noMoreSpace)
        break;
}
```

All the effort goes into properly computing the wrap width. For a circular layout, we need to make sure that both the top of the line and its bottom fit into the circle, as shown in Figure 14.3.

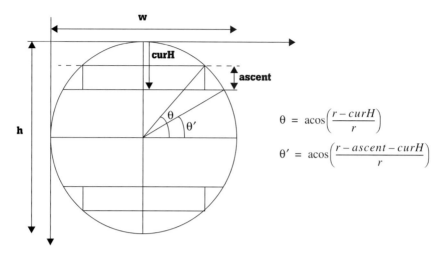

Figure 14.3 ■
Circular text layout

This explains how the following code processes the line wrapping width.

```
float w = blockWidth - 2*shapeMargin -2*textMargin;
float h = w;
float r = h/2; // radius

// Process maximum width at the bottom of the line
theta = (float)Math.acos((r-curH)/r);
wrapWidthBottom = 2*(r-curH)*(float)Math.tan(theta);

// Process maximum width at the top of the line.
// Make sure we are not going out of the circle
if(curH>ascent){
    theta = (float)Math.acos((r-curH + ascent)/r);
    wrapWidthTop = 2*(r-curH + ascent)*(float)Math.tan(theta);
}else
    wrapWidthTop = 0;

// We use the minimum of the top and bottom width to
// ensure none of the text goes out of the circle
wrapWidth = wrapWidthTop<wrapWidthBottom?wrapWidthTop:wrapWidthBottom;

layout = measurer.nextLayout(wrapWidth, iter.getEndIndex(), true);
```

The remainder of the process consist of justifying the line and moving it to the appropriate position in the bounding circle.

```
if(layout != null){
    layout = layout.getJustifiedLayout(wrapWidth);
```

```
    // Place line in bounding circle
    advance = layout.getVisibleAdvance();
    t.setToTranslation(r - advance/2, curH);

    // Convert line to Shape
    lineShape = layout.getOutline(t);// adjuster);


    // Concatenate with textBlock
    textBlock.append(lineShape, false);

    curH += layout.getAscent() + layout.getDescent() +
layout.getLeading();
}
else
    // Could not fit a single word on the line. Move down a bit
    curH += ascent/2;
```

Figure 14.4 illustrates the parameters involved in placing the lines correctly in the bounding circle.

▼ **Creating a layer**   Now that we have created a `Shape` object that contains the text block, creating the circular text layout `Layer` is a simple process.

```
Shape textCircle = new Ellipse2D.Float(0, 0, w, h);

// Build a ShapeLayer with text block
Renderer textRenderer = new FillRenderer(textColor);

ShapeLayer textLayer = new ShapeLayer(cmp, textBlock, textRenderer);
textLayer.setTransform(Position.CENTER.getTransform(textCircle,
                                              cmp.getBounds()));
```

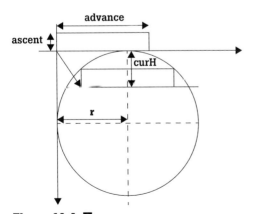

Figure 14.4 ■
Positioning lines in a text layout

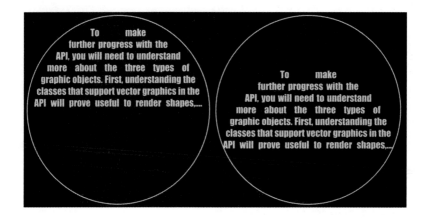

Figure 14.5 ■
Different positions for text block

Note how the text block is positioned using the transform that centers the circle in which the text block was laid out. Why not simply position the text block in the center of the composition? For example, we could do the following:

```
ShapeLayer textLayer
    = new ShapeLayer(cmp, textBlock, textRenderer, Position.CENTER);
```

When the text block fully fits into the circle, there is not much of a difference. However, if the text block is smaller and does not completely fill the circle, then there is a difference. Figure 14.5 shows the proper positioning on the left and the result obtained by centering textBlock on the right.

Using the transform that centers the circle in the composition allows us to keep the text block at the right place.

Creating a Triangular Text Layout

Creating a triangular text layout differs from creating circular text layout only in the way lines are wrapped and positioned. Otherwise, the process is similar.

In the TriangularLayoutComposition example, we lay out text in a triangle that fits into a square of a given width.

Processing the wrapping width is actually simpler for a triangle than for a circle. Because of the geometrical properties of a triangle, we know that if the tip of the triangle is on top and the top of the text line bounds fits into the triangle, then the bottom will also fit because the triangle only gets larger as we move down. Similarly, if the triangle's tip is at the bottom, we know that we should

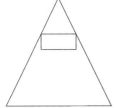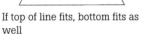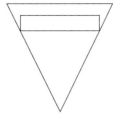

If top of line fits, bottom fits as well

If bottom of line fits, top fits as well

Figure 14.6 ■
Triangular layout with tip up or down

only worry about fitting the bottom length of the line into the triangle. This is illustrated in Figure 14.6 and is reflected in the way the wrapping width is processed (here, for the case where the tip of the triangle is on top).

```
float slope = w/h; // 1 in our example, because w=h.
float curH = 0;    // Controls the current line position (y axis)
....
// Process wrapping width at current position
wrapWidth = curH*slope;

// Get a line that fits in wrapping width
if(wrapWidth>0)
  layout = measurer.nextLayout(wrapWidth);
else
  layout = null;

if(layout != null){
  // Justify line
  layout = layout.getJustifiedLayout(wrapWidth);

  // Position line
  advance = layout.getVisibleAdvance();
  t.setToTranslation(-advance/2f, curH + layout.getAscent());

  // Position line in bounding triangle and convert to Shape
  lineShape = layout.getOutline(t); // adjuster);

  // Append line to text block
  textBlock.append(lineShape, false);

  // Move to next line
  curH += layout.getAscent() + layout.getDescent() +
          layout.getLeading();
}
```

Making Symbol Tags Legible and Attractive

The composition on page 430 uses both `CircularTextComposition` and `TriangularTextComposition` and also `GlyphDecorationComposition`, which creates the `LayerComposition` objects that render the numbers 1, 2, 3, and 4.

Layer stack

Figure 14.7 illustrates the different layers and the relevant control parameters.

Getting the raw material and computing the composition size

Two shapes are used in the composition: one for the background and one as a symbol.

```
Shape symbol = glyph.getShape();
Shape symbolBackground = glyphBackground.getShape();
```

We use the `Glyph` utility class as a convenience to extract shapes of interest from fonts. We use those shapes to compute the composition size. The composition is made big enough to contain the biggest shape and to have some extra margins around it.

```
Rectangle symbolBounds = symbol.getBounds();
Rectangle symbolBkgBounds = symbolBackground.getBounds();
```

Symbol layer
- `glyph` defines the symbol rendered by the composition. Here, the character "3," in a funky font is used.
- `symbolStrokeXXXWidth` and `symbolStrokeXXXColor`, where XXX is "One," "Two," "Three," or "Four" define the four successive strokes used to draw the symbol.
- `symbolFillColor` defines how the symbol is filled after it has been stroked.

Symbol background layer
- `glyphBackgroundGlyph` defines the symbol used as a background decoration. Here, it is a simple circle.
- `backgroundColor` fills `glyphBackgroundGlyph`.

Figure 14.7 ∎
Layers for symbol tags

```
int maxWidth = (int)Math.max(symbolBounds.width, symbolBkgBounds.width);
int maxHeight = (int)Math.max(symbolBounds.height,
                             symbolBkgBounds.height);
Dimension size = new Dimension(maxWidth + 2*margin,
                              maxHeight + 2*margin);

LayerComposition cmp = new LayerComposition(size);
```

Background glyph layer

We create a ShapeLayer to render the symbolBackground Shape in the center
of the composition.

```
FillRenderer bkgPainter = new FillRenderer(backgroundColor);
ShapeLayer symbolBkgLayer
  = new ShapeLayer(cmp, symbolBackground, bkgPainter, Position.CENTER);
```

Stroking with multiple pen width

The symbol is also rendered in a ShapeLayer, but we use a more sophisticated
Renderer.

```
FillRenderer symbolFill = new FillRenderer(symbolFillColor);
int cap = BasicStroke.CAP_ROUND;
int join = BasicStroke.JOIN_ROUND;
BasicStroke strokeOne
    = new BasicStroke(symbolStrokeOneWidth, cap, join);
BasicStroke strokeTwo
    = new BasicStroke(symbolStrokeTwoWidth, cap, join);
BasicStroke strokeThree
    = new BasicStroke(symbolStrokeThreeWidth, cap, join);
BasicStroke strokeFour
    = new BasicStroke(symbolStrokeFourWidth, cap, join);

StrokeRenderer symbolStrokeOne
    = new StrokeRenderer(symbolStrokeOneColor, strokeOne);
StrokeRenderer symbolStrokeTwo
    = new StrokeRenderer(symbolStrokeTwoColor, strokeTwo);
StrokeRenderer symbolStrokeThree
    = new StrokeRenderer(symbolStrokeThreeColor, strokeThree);
StrokeRenderer symbolStrokeFour
    = new StrokeRenderer(symbolStrokeFourColor, strokeFour);
CompositeRenderer symbolPainter
    = new CompositeRenderer(new Renderer[]{symbolStrokeFour,
                                symbolStrokeThree,
                                symbolStrokeTwo,
                                symbolStrokeOne,
                                symbolFill });


ShapeLayer symbolLayer
    = new ShapeLayer(cmp, symbol, symbolPainter, Position.CENTER);
```

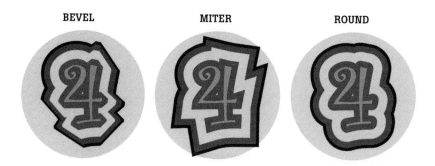

Figure 14.8 ■
Large stroke width and different join styles

Note that we are using four different strokes. This number is arbitrary—we could have used a different number. However, four is a large enough number and the result gets overly complex when that number increases.

As we explained in Part II, the `CompositeRenderer` implementation of the `Renderer` interface, one of the GLF interfaces (not a Java 2D API interface), invokes its component renderers in sequence. Here, it invokes `FillRenderer` last.

The resulting rendering is appealing if the colors of the different strokes are harmonious and if the stroke sizes are different enough. Note that the join style can dramatically affect the output when large strokes are used, as illustrated in Figure 14.8.

Putting It All Together Again

We saw in our `ShadowsComposition` example (see Chapter 11) how we can load serialized `CompositionFactory` beans and reuse them in another `CompositionFactory`. Here, we use the same technique for the decorative number elements that show in the composition. We also use the `CircularLayoutComposition` and `TriangularLayoutComposition` directly.

Reusing a `CompositionFactory` directly is actually equivalent and consists of these steps:

1. Instantiate the `CompositionFactory`.
2. Configure the `CompositionFactory`.
3. Build a `Composition` from the configured `CompositionFactory`.
4. Build a `CompositionProxyLayer` to render the `Composition` in another `LayerComposition`.

For example, here is how the top-left triangular layout is reused.

```
TriangularLayoutComposition triangleTextFactory
    = new TriangularLayoutComposition();
triangleTextFactory.setBlockWidth(blockWidth);
triangleTextFactory.setTextFont(textFont);
triangleTextFactory.setTextMargin(textMargin);
triangleTextFactory.setShapeMargin(shapeMargin);
triangleTextFactory.setBackgroundColor(colorOne);
Position topLeftBlockPos
    = new Position(Anchor.TOP_LEFT, blockAdjust, blockAdjust);
Layer topLeftLayer
    = new CompositionProxyLayer(cmp, topLeftBlock, topLeftBlockPos);
```

Other elements in the composition are created the same way. The interesting aspect is that from a high-level `CompositionFactory` (as our `ShapeLayout-Composition` example), we can propagate some or all configuration parameters to child factories and enforce some consistency in size, shapes, or colors. For example, we used two color settings, `colorOne` and `colorTwo`, for each of the different elements of the composition and created consistency between the different elements.

Conclusion

In this chapter we have seen how to lay out text in nonsquare shapes, a circle, and a triangle. The key to creating such layouts is in the calculation of the different wrapping widths needed to fit text lines into the shape. Of course, the logic depends on the type of shape into which we are trying to insert text. However, one constant concern is to make sure that the outline of each text line completely fits into the shape, not only into the base line.

The decoration elements, together with the different layout examples, have shown another example of combining simple compositions into a more complex one. This combination allows us to apply consistent parameters across several elements of the composition. This level of control is one of the things that makes the usage of an API such as GLF different from using a graphic tool, where applying different parameters in retrospect (that is, after you have drawn something) is either difficult or not possible.

chapter 15

TINTING PHOTOGRAPHS

- ■ OBJECTIVE
Use ToneAdjustmentOp creatively to tint or antique a photograph.

- ■ PURPOSE
Postcard application.

- ■ TECHNIQUES
  - ■ Tone adjustment
  - ■ Masking to create border effects
  - ■ Fast blur technique
  - ■ Using a separation layer to make text legible

The above composition illustrates the type of rendering you might want to do in a postcard application where the user provides a picture and can select borders, adjust the picture tones, and add some text. On the Web, the user might be able to print the postcard or email it to family or friends.

Our example combines several techniques. First, the original color picture and the background texture are given a different look by the ToneAdjustmentOp *filter; we will see how critical the settings of this filter are. Second, the center picture is masked to blend with the background around the edges. Third, an additional shadow is added around the image edges (on the outside), to reinforce the sense of border. That last effect uses a trick to speed up the convolution operation it uses.*

We explain each of these techniques in turn, following the order in which layers are stacked in the composition.

Layer Stack

Figure 15.1 shows the different layers that make up the composition, with the most relevant control parameters. The composition uses `ToneAdjustmentOp` to filter both the background texture and the main image displayed in the center. The `ToneAdjustmentOp` object is built with the `highlightColor`, `midtoneColor`, and `shadowColor` parameters.

Message layer
- `message` defines the text displayed in the composition.
- `messageFont`, `messageFillColor`, and `messageStrokeColor` control how the text is rendered.
- `messageAnchor` and `messageAdjustment` define the text placement in the composition.

Message separation layer
- Reuses the text block created for the message layer.
- `messageSeparationColor` defines the color used to fill the text.
- `messageSeparationOffset` defines by how much the separation text is offset under the message layer.

Image layer
- `imageFile` controls the image displayed.
- The image mask is built so that 5% of the edges are fuzzy.

Image shadow layer
- `imageShadowRadius` defines how wide the shadow is.
- `imageShadowColor` defines the shadow color.
- `imageShadowWidth` defines the amount of extra space taken by the shadow, in addition to the image size.

Background texture (not a layer)
- `textureImageFile` controls the image used for the background texture.
- The background texture is filtered with `ToneAdjustmentOp` before it is used to build a `TexturePaint`.

Figure 15.1 ■
PostcardComposition layer stack

Getting the Raw Material

The composition uses two images: one is displayed in the center and one is a background texture.

```
BufferedImage image
    = Toolbox.loadImage(imageFile, BufferedImage.TYPE_INT_ARGB);

BufferedImage textureImage
    = Toolbox.loadImage(textureImageFile, BufferedImage.TYPE_INT_RGB);
```

The two images are filtered by ToneAdjustmentOp, which is initialized with five colors. We are enforcing that black maps to black, and white to white.

```
Color tones[] = {Color.black,
                 shadowColor,
                 midtoneColor,
                 highlightColor,
                 Color.white };

float toneIntervals[] = {1, 1, 1, 1};

ToneAdjustmentOp toneAdjustment
    = new ToneAdjustmentOp(tones, // Colors used to tint image
                           toneIntervals,
                           true); // Use source ColorModel
```

Figure 15.2 shows how the input brightness is mapped to the various tone colors.

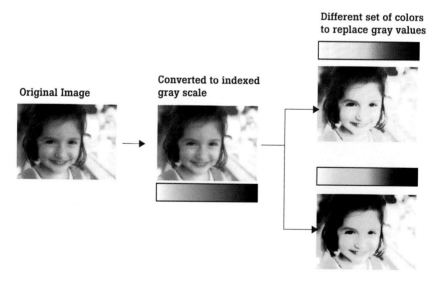

Figure 15.2 ■
Mapping brightness to tones

Remember that the last construction parameter controls the behavior when a null destination is passed to the filter. In that case and by default, the destination image uses an `IndexColorModel` instance because its internal implementation allows it to create this result very efficiently. However, this format does not support alpha compositing. The boolean constructor can force `ToneAdjustmentOp` to use the source `ColorModel` for the destination. In our example, because we have loaded our images as premultiplied ARGB, the output of the filtering will have the same format.

Computing the Composition Size

The composition size is based on center image size, leaving some margins around it.

```
int iw = image.getWidth();
int ih = image.getHeight();
Dimension size = new Dimension(iw + 2*marginSize, ih + 2*marginSize);
LayerComposition cmp = new LayerComposition(size);
```

In previous chapters, we saw different strategies for using an image in a background: trimming, scaling, etc. Here, we use yet another strategy: we build a `TexturePaint` with the `textureImage` after it has been filtered.

```
textureImage = toneAdjustment.filter(textureImage, textureImage);
TexturePaint texturePaint
    = new TexturePaint(textureImage, cmp.getBounds());
cmp.setBackgroundPaint(texturePaint);
```

Because we associate the composition bounds to the `TexturePaint`, `textureImage` will be scaled up or down to fit into that rectangle. Note that it might be shrunk along one direction and magnified along the other if the background image does not have the same aspect ratio as the composition.

Now that we have created our `LayerComposition` and defined how its background should be filled, let us create the various `Layers`.

Creating the Composition Layers

Now that we have created the raw material and that we have computed the composition size, we start creating the composition layers.

Antiquing a photograph with fuzzy edges

The `ToneAdjustmentOp` filter we used for the background texture is used again to give an antique look to the center image.

```
ImageLayer imageLayer = new ImageLayer(cmp, image, Position.CENTER);
imageLayer.setImageFilter(toneAdjustment);
```

Figure 15.3 ■
Image mask

To create the fuzzy edges, we build a mask that is transparent around the edges and that we attach to `imageLayer`.

```
BufferedImage mask = makeImageMask(iw, ih);
Rectangle imageRect = new Rectangle(marginSize, marginSize, iw, ih);
imageLayer.setLayerMask(mask, imageRect);
```

Note how we specify the `imageRect` to match the image's position in the composition. Remember that the mask is positioned in device space.

Figure 15.3 illustrates the mask built by the `makeImageMask` method.

The following code segment shows how that method is implemented.

```
private BufferedImage makeImageMask(int iw, int ih){
    BufferedImage mask
      = new BufferedImage(iw, ih, BufferedImage.TYPE_BYTE_GRAY);

    Graphics2D g = mask.createGraphics();
    g.setPaint(Color.black);
    g.fillRect(0, 0, iw, ih);

    GeneralPath triangle = new GeneralPath();
    triangle.moveTo(0, 0);
    triangle.lineTo(iw/2, ih/2);
    triangle.lineTo(0, ih);
    triangle.closePath();
    GradientPaint fuzzyEdgePaint
      = new GradientPaint(0, 0, Color.black,
                          iw*.05f, 0, Color.white);
    g.setPaint(fuzzyEdgePaint);
    g.fill(triangle);

    g.rotate(Math.PI, iw/2, ih/2);
    g.fill(triangle);

    g.setTransform(new AffineTransform());
    triangle = new GeneralPath();
    triangle.moveTo(0, 0);
    triangle.lineTo(iw/2, ih/2);
    triangle.lineTo(iw, 0);
```

```
    triangle.closePath();
    fuzzyEdgePaint = new GradientPaint(0, 0, Color.black,
                    0, ih*.05f, Color.white);
    g.setPaint(fuzzyEdgePaint);
    g.fill(triangle);
    g.rotate(Math.PI, iw/2, ih/2);
    g.fill(triangle);

    return mask;
  }
```

This is a good example both of the Graphics2D Paint context attribute being transformed. The `fuzzyEdgePaint` object is defined in user space, using the triangle Shape's metrics. When the `AffineTransform` attribute in g's graphic context (see `g.rotate(..)`) is set to a rotation, the transformation applies to the triangle shape we fill (see `g.fill(triangle)`), but the Paint is also rotated: the gradient rotates with the shape.

As we explained in Chapter 9 (see "Custom Paints" on page 304), the Paint implementer must program this behavior. We see in the next chapter that this property can be a powerful tool to create striking effects.

Fast blur to create a border effect

To reinforce the notion of border, we add another Layer to cast a shadow around the edges of the center image. Creating this effect involves the mechanisms we explained in Chapter 11: create a ShapeLayer that fills a Shape with the shadow color and attach a ConvolveOp filter to the ShapeLayer object.

Usually, the larger the convolution kernel, the better the quality of the shadow. However, the larger the kernel, the more computation intensive the filtering becomes.

What can be done to reduce the computation time?

In our example, we use a trick that consists in scaling down the image, convolving the smaller image with a smaller kernel (faster), and then scaling the image up again. Here is what the code does to create a single filter that chains those operations.

```
AffineTransform shrinkShadowTxf
  = AffineTransform.getScaleInstance(1/shadowScaleFactor,
                                     1/shadowScaleFactor);

AffineTransform blowUpShadowTxf
  = AffineTransform.getScaleInstance(shadowScaleFactor,
                                     shadowScaleFactor);

AffineTransformOp shrinkShadow
  = new AffineTransformOp(shrinkShadowTxf, null);

AffineTransformOp blowUpShadow
```

```
    = new AffineTransformOp(blowUpShadowTxf,
                          AffineTransformOp.TYPE_BILINEAR);
GaussianKernel blurKernel
    = new GaussianKernel((int)(imageShadowBlurRadius/shadowScaleFactor));

ConvolveOp shadowBlur = new ConvolveOp(blurKernel);
CompositeOp compositeOp = new CompositeOp(new BufferedImageOp[]{
        shrinkShadow, shadowBlur, blowUpShadow });
```

Notice these important points about this code.

1. The convolution applies on a smaller image and with a proportionally smaller kernel as well. That is why we divided the blur radius by the scale factor when we built the `GaussianKernel` object. Applying the convolution with a smaller kernel and on a smaller image explains the performance gain.
2. Experience shows that using a bilinear interpolation for the second `AffineTransformOp` filter provides more acceptable results than does the nearest neighbor interpolation.
3. This technique does not create an accurate result: the result is not identical to applying a larger convolution on the original image. However, for a shadow, the approximation is acceptable.
4. The technique is only worthwhile with very large kernels. It adds a bilinear interpolation to the convolution process—a costly operation. Therefore, it is only useful if the processing saved by the smaller convolution on a smaller image offsets processing added by the interpolation.

This technique also speeds up computation of large elevation maps for the `LightOp` filter and also creation of glows, as presented in Chapter 12.

Another way to speed up convolution is to apply a technique called kernel separation. This technique can be applied when the convolution kernel is the product of 2 one-dimensional kernels, as in:

$$
\begin{bmatrix}
x & x & x & x & x \\
x & x & x & x & x \\
x & x & x & x & x \\
x & x & x & x & x \\
x & x & x & x & x
\end{bmatrix}
=
\begin{bmatrix}
y \\
y \\
y \\
y \\
y
\end{bmatrix}
\otimes
\begin{bmatrix}
z & z & z & z
\end{bmatrix}
$$

The `GaussianKernel` class represents a kernel with such characteristics. The class contains a method that will return the 2 one-dimensional kernels into which it can be separated. For example, we could write:

```
GaussianKernel kernel = new GaussianKernel(kernelRadius);
Kernel seperatedKernels[] = kernel.separateKernel();
ConvolveOp convolveA = new ConvolveOp(separatedKernels[0]);
ConvolveOp convolveB = new ConvolveOp(separatedKernels[1]);
CompositeOp convolve = new CompositeOp(convolveA, convolveB);
```

At the time this book was written, a bug in the implementation prevented effective use of one-dimensional kernels, so they were not used in the book. However, by the time this book is printed, the latest version of the Java platform will have addressed this issue, and one-dimensional kernels should be a workable alternative to speed up convolution

Making text legible again

On several occasions we said that it is important to make text legible, and we discussed some techniques, such as adjusting brightness or color, to address that need. In this example, we use a simple technique to make text legible: we render it twice, with contrasting colors and at slightly different locations. This technique almost guarantees a sharp contrast on most of the text, enough to make it easily readable. Here is how we implement the technique.

```
//
// First, process the miter limit, to avoid spikes in the stroked text
//
float miterLimit = Float.MAX_VALUE;
miterLimitAngle %= 180;

if(miterLimitAngle<0)
   miterLimitAngle *= -1;
if(miterLimitAngle!=0)
   miterLimit = (float)(1/Math.sin((Math.PI*miterLimitAngle)/(360.0)));


//
// Build a BasicStroke with no spikes
//
BasicStroke messageStroke
   = new BasicStroke(messageStrokeWidth,
                     BasicStroke.CAP_ROUND,
                     BasicStroke.JOIN_MITER,
                     miterLimit);


//
// Build renderers for the text and the separation layer
//
FillRenderer textFill = new FillRenderer(messageFillColor);
StrokeRenderer textStroke
   = new StrokeRenderer( messageStrokeColor, messageStroke);
CompositeRenderer textPainter
   = new CompositeRenderer(textStroke, textFill);
```

```
FillRenderer messageSeparationPainter
   = new FillRenderer(messageSeparationColor);

//
// Compute text position
//
Position textPosition = new Position(messageAnchor,
                                     messageAdjustment.width,
                                     messageAdjustment.height);

//
// Build text layer
//
int noWrapping = -1;
TextLayer messageLayer
   = new TextLayer(cmp, message, messageFont,
                   textPainter, textPosition,
                   noWrapping, messageAlignment);

//
// Build text separation layer
//

// Extract text shape, at its final position
Shape textBlock = messageLayer.createTransformedShape();

ShapeLayer messageSeparationLayer
    = new ShapeLayer(cmp, textBlock, messageSeparationPainter);

AffineTransform messageSeparationAdjustment
   = AffineTransform.getTranslateInstance(messageSeparationOffset.width,
                        messageSeparationOffset.height);
messageSeparationLayer.setTransform(messageSeparationAdjustment);
```

Conclusion

We have seen how to mix different techniques to tint a picture, create a fancy
border effect, and to make text legible in yet another way.

The ToneAdjustmentOp filter that we used again can be used for various purposes; we used it in Chapter 2 to tint images and create buttons. There are situations where it might be important to give a common feel to a set of images,
and ToneAdjustmentOp can be used to that end. Figure 15.4 illustrates how
different settings for the filter create different moods.

Figure 15.4 ■
Different moods with the ToneAdjustmentOp filter

Note how the pictures where low saturation colors have been used seem to have an antique look (for example, lower-left and right images). Opposing those images, where more saturated colors are used, the image has a more dynamic and modern feel.

Creating a sense of unity in a design is an important aspect to achieve attractive results. `ToneAdjustmentOp` is one of the many tools that we can use along with simpler techniques such as proper font selection and consistent color usage.

chapter 16

CREATING A SENSE OF VOLUME

■ OBJECTIVE
Use gradient paints to create 3D-looking effects.

■ PURPOSE
Sophisticated graphs to represent numerical data.

■ TECHNIQUES
  ■ Creating 3D shapes
  ■ Using gradients to suggest volume and textures
  ■ Writing text along an arbitrary path
  ■ More sophisticated combinations of compositions

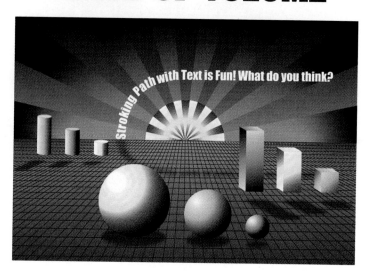

Using an API called the Java 2D API does not mean our compositions should be flat.

The above composition shows sophisticated 3D-looking graphs: spheres, cylinders, and bars. It illustrates how to create a sense of depth and volume by using gradient paints creatively: no 3D model is used—only 2D techniques.

In this chapter, we discuss how to create such 3D objects and how to combine them into a single composition where we use gradient paints again (sky and sun rays) and draw text along an arbitrary path.

The composition at the top of the page is generated by the VolumeComposition *example. It combines other simpler compositions,* SphereComposition, CylinderComposition, *and* BarComposition. *We discuss these first and then we see how to reuse and combine them in a single composition.*

Creating a Sphere

Creating a sphere consists of filling a circular shape with a circular radial gradient paint. We first explain the techniques and then look through the code that creates the effect.

Creating the proper radial gradient paint

A sphere is created by rendering a circle with a radial gradient paint. The trick consists of properly positioning the gradient paint's control circle relative to the circle and choosing the right colors for the gradient.

▼ **Positioning the radial gradient paint control circle**   Figure 16.1 illustrates how to place the radial gradient paint control circle relative to the circle shape used to represent the sphere. The idea is to position the center of the gradient circle where we want the shiniest spot of the sphere to be. In the figure, that would be in the upper-left quadrant of the sphere.

▼ **Choosing the right gradient colors**   In order for the shiniest spot to be perceived as shiniest, it should be a very bright color, such as white. Then, as we move away from this reflection spot, the color should progressively become darker and darker, giving a sense of volume to the circle and making it look like a sphere, as illustrated with different color settings in Figure 16.2.

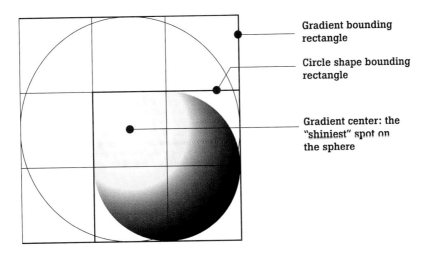

Gradient bounding
rectangle

Circle shape bounding
rectangle

Gradient center: the
"shiniest" spot on
the sphere

Figure 16.1 ■
Positioning the radial gradient control circle

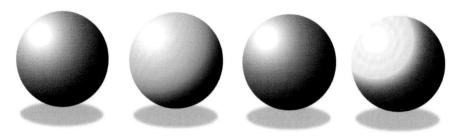

Figure 16.2 ■
Selecting proper gradient colors for a sphere

The other parameter that influences our perception of the sphere is the different color intervals in the gradient. If the gradient quickly changes from bright colors to dark ones, then the sphere will appear shiny. Conversely, if the gradient moves slowly from a bright color to darker ones, then the sphere surface will appear duller, as shown in Figure 16.3.

Now that we know how the radial gradient paint should look like and how to use it, let us see how to program it with the GLF.

Using RadialGradientPaintExt creatively

The `SphereComposition` example's layer stack contains two layers: one for the sphere and one for its shadow.

▼ **Creating the sphere**   The layer that contains the sphere fills a circular shape with `RadialGradientPaintExt`. The following code creates the circular shape and the gradient paints bouncing rectangle accordingly, as we explained earlier.

Figure 16.3 ■
Dull, normal, or reflective sphere

```
Ellipse2D sphere = new Ellipse2D.Float(0, 0, sphereSize, sphereSize);
Rectangle gradientRect = new Rectangle(-sphereSize/2, -sphereSize/2,
                                       3*sphereSize/2, 3*sphereSize/2);
```

This bouncing rectangle is then used, with the different gradient colors and intervals, to build a `RadialGradientPaintExt` instance.

```
Color gradientColors[] = {Color.white, highlightColor,
                          midtoneColor, shadowColor, Color.black};
float gradientIntervals[] = {highlightInterval, midtoneInterval,
                             shadowInterval, blackInterval};
RadialGradientPaintExt sphereFilling
       new RadialGradientPaintExt(gradientRect,
                                  gradientColors,
                                  gradientIntervals);
```

That `Paint` object can then be used by a `FillRenderer` in a simple `ShapeLayer`.

```
Renderer spherePainter = new FillRenderer(sphereFilling);
ShapeLayer sphereLayer = new ShapeLayer(cmp, sphere, spherePainter,
                                        Position.CENTER);
```

▼ **Creating the sphere shadow**   The sphere shadow is similar to a simple drop shadow, as we explained in Chapter 11. However, because we are trying to simulate the shadow of a 3D sphere, we also scale the shadow down, to further emphasize the distance from the surface. Here is how we compute the shadow's position.

```
AffineTransform shadowTxf = new AffineTransform();
// Offset shadow
shadowTxf.translate(shadowOffset.width, shadowOffset.height);

// Move back to sphere base
shadowTxf.translate(0, sphereSize/2f);

// Scale down
shadowTxf.scale(shadowScaleX, shadowScaleY);

// Move so that shape has base at elevation 0
shadowTxf.translate(0, -sphereSize/2f);

Position shadowPosition = new Position(Anchor.CENTER, 0, 0, shadowTxf);
```

Remember that by default, as in the above code, `Position` applies transforms about the center of the objects to which they are applied. This explains why moving up by half the sphere's height (`shadowTxf.translate(0, -sphereSize/2f)`) moves the bottom of the shape to elevation 0, as illustrated in Figure 16.4. Once the sphere shadow `Position` attribute has been computed, it is

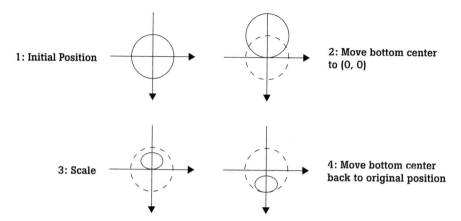

Figure 16.4 ■
Positioning the sphere's shadow

used to build a ShapeLayer. As in other shadow examples, we use a ConvolveOp filter to create the fuzzy edges that make a more realistic shadow.[1]

```
FillRenderer shadowPainter = new FillRenderer(sphereShadowColor);
ShapeLayer sphereShadowLayer
    = new ShapeLayer(cmp, sphere, shadowPainter, shadowPosition);

if(shadowBlurRadius>0){
    Kernel blurKernel = new GaussianKernel(shadowBlurRadius);
    ConvolveOp blur = new ConvolveOp(blurKernel);
    Dimension blurMargins = new Dimension(shadowBlurRadius*2,
                                          shadowBlurRadius*2);
    sphereShadowLayer.setImageFilter(blur, blurMargins);
}
```

Creating a Cylinder

Creating a 3D-looking cylinder is done with the use of a multicolor linear gradient paint to create a sense of volume instead of a radial gradient for the sphere. The CylinderComposition example creates LayerComposition objects that have three layers: one for the cylinder body, one for the top of the cylinder, and one for the cylinder shadow.

---

1. Refer to Chapter 11 for more details on shadows.

Getting the raw material: creating the cylinder shapes

Figure 16.5 illustrates the shapes used to render the cylinder. The following code creates them.

```
// Cylinder Body
Rectangle bodyBase
    = new Rectangle(0, 0, cylinderSize.width, cylinderSize.height)
Area cylinderBody = new Area(bodyBase);

float topY = cylinderSize.height -
            cylinderSize.width*cylinderTopYScale/2;
float topHeight = cylinderSize.width*cylinderTopYScale;
Shape topArc = new Arc2D.Float(0, topY,
                              cylinderSize.width, topHeight,
                              0, -180,      // Start/stop angles
                              Arc2D.CHORD);  // Type of arc
cylinderBody.add(new Area(topArc));

Shape cylinderShape = cylinderBody;

// Cylinder Top
topY = -cylinderSize.width*cylinderTopYScale/2;
Shape cylinderTop
    = new Ellipse2D.Float(0, topY,
                        cylinderSize.width, topHeight);

// Cylinder shadow
Area cylinderShadow = new Area(cylinderBody);
cylinderShadow.add(new Area(cylinderTop));
```

Building the cylinder body and top

As with the sphere, the 3D aspect comes from the gradient paint used to fill a simple shape. Here, we use a linear `RadialGradientPaintExt` instance.

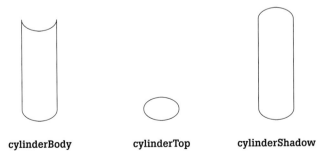

cylinderBody   **cylinderTop**   **cylinderShadow**

Figure 16.5 ■
Shapes used to render a cylinder

```
Color gradientColors[] = {Color.white, highlightColor,
                          midtoneColor, shadowColor, Color.black};

float gradientIntervals[] = {highlightInterval, midtoneInterval,
                             shadowInterval, blackInterval};
GradientPaintExt cylinderFilling
   = new GradientPaintExt(0, 0, cylinderSize.width, 0,
                          gradientIntervals, gradientColors);
Renderer cylinderPainter = new FillRenderer(cylinderFilling);

ShapeLayer cylinderLayer
   = new ShapeLayer(cmp, cylinderShape, cylinderPainter,
                    Position.CENTER);
```

Again, the result is more effective if the gradient varies between a very bright color and a very dark color. This variation gives a sense of volume and simulates reflection on a cylinder.

The top of the cylinder is filled with a `RadialGradientPaint`. Its purpose is to emphasize the edges. We reuse two of the colors used to create the body gradient.

```
RadialGradientPaint cylinderTopFilling
   = new RadialGradientPaint(cylinderTop.getBounds2D(),
                             highlightColor, midtoneColor);
Renderer cylinderTopPainter = new FillRenderer(cylinderTopFilling);
```

Then, we position the top properly relative to the body.

```
Position cylinderTopPosition
   = new Position(Anchor.TOP, 0, -topHeight/2);
AffineTransform cylinderTopTxf
   = cylinderTopPosition.getTransform(cylinderTop,
                                      cylinderBody.getBounds());
cylinderTopTxf.preConcatenate(cylinderLayer.getTransform());

ShapeLayer cylinderTopLayer
   = new ShapeLayer(cmp, cylinderTop, cylinderTopPainter);
cylinderTopLayer.setTransform(cylinderTopTxf);
```

Note that we use `Position` to process the transform that places the top relative to the body. Because the body is transformed by the `ShapeLayer` that renders it, we are careful to preconcatenate that transform to keep the relative placement correct in device space.

Creating the shadow

The cast shadow is created as we explained in Chapter 11.

Creating a Bar

To create the bars shown in the composition on page 452, we created the `Bar-Composition` factory. It uses our `RadialGradientPaintExt` to create the 3D-looking bar shape and its metallic texture. We are going to see how this example uses the fact that `RadialGradientPaintExt` control attributes are defined in user space to easily paint the different faces of the bar properly.

Our example has four layers: three for the bar itself and one for the shadow. Before we see how they are created, let's first see how to build the different shapes that make the bar.

Creating the base rectangular shapes

The composition uses two rectangles to render the bar. As Figure 16.6 illustrates, they are used as is or transformed.

The following code segment shows how we compute the relevant parameters that control the bar's geometry.

```
double angle = (float)(shearAngle*Math.PI/180f);
angle %= 2*Math.PI;
if(angle>0 && angle>Math.PI)
  angle -= Math.PI;
```

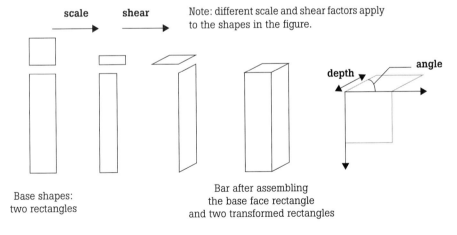

Base shapes:
two rectangles

Bar after assembling
the base face rectangle
and two transformed rectangles

Figure 16.6 ◼
Building a bar with rectangles

```
if(angle<0){
  if(angle>-Math.PI)
    angle = Math.PI + angle;
  else
    angle = 2*Math.PI + angle;
}
```

```
float cosAngle = (float)Math.cos(angle);
float sinAngle = (float)Math.sin(angle);
float sideShear = (float)Math.tan(angle);
float topShear = 1/sideShear;
```

```
float sideScale = (float)Math.abs(cosAngle*depth/barWidth);
float topScale = (depth*sinAngle)/barWidth;
```

Creating the base shapes is straightforward.

```
Rectangle baseShape = new Rectangle(0, 0, barWidth, barHeight);
Rectangle topShape = new Rectangle(0, 0, barWidth, barWidth);
```

The composition's size is based on its content.

```
Dimension size = new Dimension(barWidth + margins.width*2,
                               barHeight + margins.height*2);
LayerComposition cmp = new LayerComposition(size);
```

Rendering the bar face

To fill the bar face, we use a multicolor linear gradient paint provided by `GradientPaintExt` (one of the GLF `Paint` implementations).

```
Color gradientColors[] = {highlightColor, midtoneColor, shadowColor};
float gradientIntervals[] = {midtoneInterval, shadowInterval};
```

```
GradientPaintExt sidePaint
  = new GradientPaintExt(0, 0, barWidth, barHeight,
                         gradientIntervals, gradientColors);
```

```
FillRenderer sidePainter = new FillRenderer(sidePaint);
```

Figure 16.7 illustrates the gradient control points (upper-left and bottom-right corners of `baseShape`), and the gradient color and interval settings.

The `GradientPaintExt` object is used to build a simple `ShapeLayer`.

```
Position facePosition = Position.CENTER;
ShapeLayer faceLayer
  = new ShapeLayer(cmp, baseShape, sidePainter, facePosition);
```

It is important to understand that we have defined our gradient paint in user space. That is, the control parameters refer to the corners of `baseShape` in user space. However, rendering happens in device space. Because our `Paint` implementation operates in user space, color interpolation happens in user

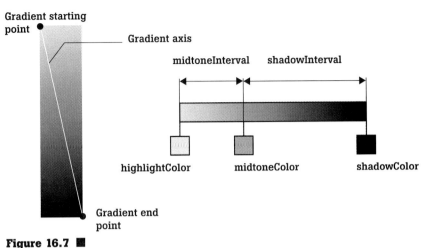

Figure 16.7 ◼
Bar GradientPaintExt control parameters

space. If a transform is applied when rendering, which we have here because we center `baseShape`, then color interpolation will appear at a different location in device space than in user space: the `Paint` follows the user space to device space transform.

Imagine we had done the following—

```
ShapeLayer faceLayer
    = new ShapeLayer(cmp, facePosition.createTransformedShape(baseShape,
                       cmp.getBounds()), sidePainter);
```

—no transform would have applied to `Graphics2D` when rendering the Shape-Layer: no `Position` or `AffineTransform` is set in the `Layer`. Therefore, user space and device space match. Our `Paint` would still perform interpolation between `(0, 0)` and `(barWidth, barHeight)` in user space. However, our invocation of `facePosition`'s `createTransformedShape` method moves base-Shape in user space, creating a mismatch between our `Paint` and the Shape object it fills.

This is a subtle point, but the key thing to remember is this: make sure the gradient paint's controlling parameters are "synchronized" with the shape or shapes with which it will be used. For example, if you define a gradient paint to fill a specific shape and you use that shape's user space coordinates, make sure the shape is not transformed in user space before rendering: such a transformation would cause the type of mismatch we just explained. As a rule of thumb and when working with gradients, it is usually best not to transform shapes in user space. This policy avoids problems and also allows the gradient to be reused with the same shape, but using different transforms, as we see next.

Creating the bar side layer

To create the bar side layer, we reuse the same Shape object and Renderer object as for the face layer. The only difference is the AffineTransform attribute.

```
AffineTransform sideTxf = ...;
ShapeLayer sideLayer = new ShapeLayer(cmp, baseShape, sidePainter);
sideLayer.setTransform(sideTxf);
```

This example further illustrates what we explained in the previous section: because the Paint attribute and the Shape object are both defined in user space, we can vary the AffineTransform attribute and get a different rendering result. Here, for example, we scale, translate, rotate, and shear not only baseShape but also the gradient used to fill it. Here is how sideTxf is built.

```
// sideShearTxf is built assuming it applies about (0, 0), as it will
// be used in conjunction with Position.

// Shear to create the perspective effect
AffineTransform sideShearTxf
    = AffineTransform.getShearInstance(0, sideShear);

// Scale down
sideShearTxf.scale(sideScale, 1);

// Rotate about center
sideShearTxf.rotate(Math.PI);

//
// Now, create a Position object to place the side relative to
// the bar's face. If the shear angle is less than Pi/2, then the
// face should appear to the left, otherwise it should appear to
// the right
//
Anchor sideAnchor = Anchor.BOTTOM_LEFT;
if(angle>Math.PI/2)
    sideAnchor = Anchor.BOTTOM_RIGHT;

Position sidePosition
    = new Position(sideAnchor,
                    -barWidth*sideScale, // Move side to right or left
                    0,                   // No vertical adjustment
                    sideShearTxf,        // Scale, shear and rotate
                    false);              // Apply sideShearTxf before
                                         // doing relative placement

// Get transform that positions the side shape (baseShape) properly
// relative to the bar's face (baseShape again).
AffineTransform sideTxf
    = sidePosition.getTransform(baseShape, baseShape);

// Remember to take the faceLayer's user space to device space transform
// into account.
sideTxf.preConcatenate(faceLayer.getTransform());
```

Figure 16.8 ■
Bar side rendered without rotate

Note how we apply a rotation to the side before it is rendered, along with a shear and scale. We do this is to increase the contrast between the bar's face and its side. The contrast emphasizes the impression of depth and volume by making the edge between the two more obvious, as illustrated in Figure 16.8.

Creating the bar top

Creating the bar's top uses the same idea:

1. Build a gradient in user space, using the top before it is sheared and positioned.
2. Compute the user space to device space transform, using the Position class.
3. Build a `ShapeLayer` object.

Our code implements those three steps.

```
// First, built gradient paint, using user space coordinates
GradientPaint topPaint
   = new GradientPaint(0, 0, midtoneColor, barWidth, 0, highlightColor);

// Compute user space to device space transform.
// Use Position to ease computation
float topScale = (depth*sinAngle)/barWidth;
AffineTransform topShearTxf
   = AffineTransform.getShearInstance(topShear, 0);
topShearTxf.scale(1, topScale);
Anchor topAnchor = angle<Math.PI/2?Anchor.TOP_RIGHT:Anchor.TOP_LEFT;

Position topPosition
   = new Position(topAnchor, 0, -barWidth*topScale, topShearTxf, false);

AffineTransform topTxf = topPosition.getTransform(topShape, baseShape);

// Remember to take the face user space to device
// space transform into account
topTxf.preConcatenate(faceLayer.getTransform());
```

```
// Build ShapeLayer
ShapeLayer topLayer = new ShapeLayer(cmp, topShape, topPainter);
topLayer.setTransform(topTxf);
```

Note that we use a `GradientPaint`. As do the GLF `Paint` implementations, `GradientPaint` operates in user space, and we can rely on it to get the behavior we described: the paint can be transformed, as well as the shapes it fills, because it operates in user space.

Creating the shadow

Again, the cast shadow is created as we explained in Chapter 11. Please refer to that section for details.

Putting It All Together Again

We have seen how to create 3D-looking forms by using different gradient paints. Let us now see how our composition on page 452 reuses them.

Layer stack

Our `VolumeComposition` contains a fairly large number of layers in its stack (see Figure 16.9), compared to the other examples we have discussed.

The composition can be seen as two parts: one creates a background with the sky, sea, sea grid, and sun and the other (see Figure 16.10) shows several 3D objects reusing the other compositions we have introduced in this chapter.

We first discuss how to create the layers that render the different background elements before we discuss how our 3D objects are reused.

Getting the raw material

The following code builds the different `Shape` objects used to render the background.

```
// skyRatio controls how much of the composition's height is taken
// by the sky. The first two lines normalize that value so that it
// is in the (0, 1) range
skyRatio = skyRatio<0?-skyRatio:skyRatio;
skyRatio %= 1;

// Sky rectangle
Rectangle skyShape = new Rectangle(0, 0, size.width,
                                   (int)(size.height*skyRatio));

// Sea rectangle
Rectangle seaShape
   = new Rectangle(0, skyShape.height,
                   size.width, size.height - skyShape.height);
```

Inside rays layer
- `sunColorOutside`, `sunColorMiddle`, and `sunColorCenter` define the radial gradient paint used to fill the sun rays (note that colors are inverted compared to previous layer).
- `sunShape` is used as a mask.

Sun layer
- `sunRadius` defines the radius of the sun.
- `sunColorCenter`, `sunColorMiddle`, and `sunColorOutside` define the radial gradient paint used to fill the sun shape.

Outside rays layer
- `rayAngle` defines the angle of the sun rays and, therefore, the number of rays.
- `skyColor` and `backgroundColor` define the center and border color of the radial gradient paint that fills the rays

Sky layer
- `skyRatio` defines how much of the composition height is taken by the sky. The remainder is filled by the sea.
- `skyColor` and `backgroundColor` define the bottom and top color of the sky gradient.

Sea grid layer
- `gridStrokeWidth` and `gridColor` control the width and color of the grid lines.
- `gridTopCellWidth` and `gridBottomCellWidth` control the width of the grid cells at the top and bottom of the grid, respectively.

Sea layer
- `seaColor` and `seaDarkColor` define the top and bottom colors of the gradient used to fill the sea area.

Figure 16.9 ■
VolumeComposition layer stack

```
// Sun
Point sunCenter = new Point(size.width/2, skyShape.height);


Rectangle sunBounds
    = new Rectangle(sunCenter.x-sunRadius, sunCenter.y-sunRadius,
                    sunRadius*2, sunRadius*2);
```

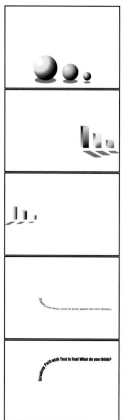

Sphere layer
- `sphereBean` defines the `SphereComposition` bean file.
- `sphereScale` defines how much the three spheres are scaled in the composition.
- `sphereAnchor` and `sphereAdjust` define where the three spheres are positioned in the composition.

Bar layer
- `barBean` defines the `BarComposition` bean file.
- `barScale` defines by how much the three bars are scaled in the composition.
- `barAnchor` and `barAdjust` define where the three bars are positioned in the composition.

Cylinder layer
- `cylinderBean` defines the `CylinderComposition` bean file.
- `cylinderScale` defines by how much the three cylinders are scaled in the composition.
- `cylinderAnchor` and `cylinderAdjust` define where the three cylinders are positioned in the composition.

Message shadow layer
- Reuses the shape built for the message layer.
- `shadowColor` defines how the shadow is rendered, and `shadowBlurRadius` controls how blurred it should be.

Message layer
- `message` defines the message content.
- `messageFont` and `messageColor` define how the message is rendered.

Figure 16.10 ■
VolumeComposition layer stack (continued)

```
Shape sunShape
    = new Arc2D.Float(sunBounds.x, sunBounds.y,
                      sunBounds.width, sunBounds.height,
                      0, 180, Arc2D.CHORD);
//
// Build one Sun Ray
//
int rayWidth = (int)Point2D.distance(sunCenter.x, sunCenter.y, 0, 0);
Point rayTopA = new Point(sunCenter.x - rayWidth, sunCenter.y);
Point rayTopB = new Point(0, 0);
float angle = (float)(rayAngle*Math.PI/180.0);
AffineTransform rayRotate
    = AffineTransform.getRotateInstance(angle, sunCenter.x, sunCenter.y);
rayRotate.transform(rayTopA, rayTopB);
GeneralPath rayShape = new GeneralPath();
rayShape.moveTo(sunCenter.x, sunCenter.y);
rayShape.lineTo(rayTopA.x, rayTopA.y);
```

```
rayShape.lineTo(rayTopB.x, rayTopB.y);
rayShape.closePath();

//
// Combine rays into a single Shape
//
rayRotate.setToIdentity();
GeneralPath sunRays = new GeneralPath();
float rayRotateAngle = angle*2;
int nRays = (int)Math.ceil(Math.PI/rayRotateAngle);
for(int i=0; i<nRays; i++){
  sunRays.append(rayRotate.createTransformedShape(rayShape), false);
  rayRotate.rotate(rayRotateAngle, sunCenter.x, sunCenter.y);
}
```

Figure 16.11 illustrates the above code.

Creating the composition layers

▼ **Sky and sea**   Creating those elements involves simple ShapeLayer objects.

```
//
// Create a layer to fade out the sky (background) color.
//
GradientPaint skyPaint
   = new GradientPaint(0, 0, skyColor,
                       0, skyShape.height, backgroundColor);
ShapeLayer skyLayer
   = new ShapeLayer(cmp, skyShape, new FillRenderer(skyPaint));


//
// Build a layer for the sea
//
```

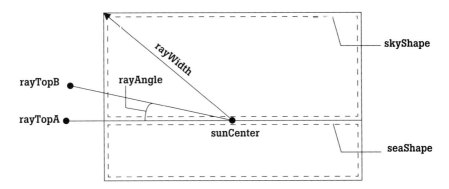

Figure 16.11 ■
Building the raw material

```
GradientPaint seaPaint
    = new GradientPaint(seaShape.x, seaShape.y, seaColor,
                          seaShape.x, seaShape.y + seaShape.height,
                          seaDarkColor);
FillRenderer seaPainter = new FillRenderer(seaPaint);
ShapeLayer seaLayer = new ShapeLayer(cmp, seaShape, seaPainter);

//
// Build a layer to render a grid on top of the sea
//
Shape grid = makeSeaGrid(seaShape);
StrokeRenderer gridPainter
    = new StrokeRenderer(gridColor, gridStrokeWidth);
ShapeLayer seaGrid = new ShapeLayer(cmp, grid, gridPainter);
```

The makeSeaGrid method simply concatenates lines into a single shape object. That grid reinforces the sense of depth in the composition by giving the viewer a sense of perspective.

▼ **Sun and sun rays**   Three different Layers render the sun: one renders the sun itself and the other two render sun rays. One of those two renders sun rays in the sky, and the other one renders sun rays inside the sun itself.

Here is how they are created.

```
//
// Create layer for rays outside the sun
//
Rectangle rayPaintRect
    = new Rectangle(0, 0, skyShape.width, skyShape.height*2);
RadialGradientPaint rayPaint
    = new RadialGradientPaint(rayPaintRect, backgroundColor, skyColor);

ShapeLayer outsideRaysLayer
    = new ShapeLayer(cmp, sunRays, new FillRenderer(rayPaint));

//
// Create layers for sun and inside rays
//
Color sunColors[]
    = {sunColorCenter, sunColorMiddle, sunColorOutside};
float sunIntervals[] = {sphereFactory.getMidtoneInterval(),
                          sphereFactory.getShadowInterval() }

RadialGradientPaintExt sunPaint
    = new RadialGradientPaintExt(sunBounds, sunColors, sunIntervals);

Color invertedSunColors[]
    = {sunColorOutside, sunColorMiddle, sunColorCenter};
float invertedSunIntervals[]
    = new float[]{sphereFactory.getMidtoneInterval(),
                    sphereFactory.getShadowInterval() };
```

```
RadialGradientPaintExt invertedSunPaint
    = new RadialGradientPaintExt(sunBounds, invertedSunColors,
                                 invertedSunIntervals);

FillRenderer sunPainter = new FillRenderer(sunPaint);
FillRenderer invertedSunPainter = new FillRenderer(invertedSunPaint);

ShapeLayer sunLayer = new ShapeLayer(cmp, sunShape, sunPainter);
ShapeLayer insideRaysLayer
   = new ShapeLayer(cmp, sunRays, invertedSunPainter);
insideRaysLayer.setLayerMask(sunShape);
```

▼ **Stroking with text**   The text that wraps around the sun is rendered by
our TextStroke implementation of the Stroke interface. One of its instances
draws the textPath shape.

```
//
// First, create the shape along which we will draw text
//
GeneralPath textPath = new GeneralPath();
textPath.moveTo(sunCenter.x - 3*sunRadius/2f, sunCenter.y);
textPath.curveTo(sunCenter.x - 3*sunRadius/2f,
                 sunCenter.y - sunRadius,
                 sunCenter.x - sunRadius,
                 sunCenter.y - 3*sunRadius/2f,
                 sunCenter.x,
                 sunCenter.y - 3*sunRadius/2f);
textPath.lineTo(size.width, sunCenter.y - 3*sunRadius/2f);

//
// Now, create a TextStroke to render textPath and use
// it in a ShapeLayer
//
TextStroke messageStroke
   = new TextStroke(message, messageFont, false, 0);

StrokeRenderer messagePainter
   = new StrokeRenderer(messageColor, messageStroke);

ShapeLayer messageLayer = new ShapeLayer(cmp, textPath, messagePainter);
```

At this point we have created all the layers that make the composition background. The remainder of the example reuses CompositionFactory beans to
render on top of this background.

Grouping compositions in a single layer

The VolumeComposition example contains three additional layers: one displays the spheres, one displays the cylinders, and one displays the bars. They
are all built and positioned using the same technique. We next look at one of
them: the sphere layer.

As we have seen in other examples (Chapter 11 and Chapter 14), we can reuse the product of `CompositionFactory` beans as follows:

1. Load the `CompositionFactory` bean.
2. Configure it.
3. Use the factory to build a `Composition`.

In our previous examples, we then rendered the `Composition` object as a layer by using a `CompositionProxyLayer`. Here, we use an additional step: we combine several `CompositionProxyLayer` instances in a single `LayerComposition` object. We then use another `CompositionProxyLayer` to include that single `LayerComposition` object as one of the composition layers.

This may sound more complicated than it is: we are simply grouping several `Composition` objects into a single one that we can manipulate and position as one single entity. Here is the pseudocode describing this process.

```
//
// First, load CompositionFactory bean
//
SphereComposition sphereFactory
  = (SphereComposition)CompositionFactoryLoader.loadBeanFile(sphereBean);

//
// Set default attributes
//
sphereFactory.setXX(..);
sphereFactory.setYY(..);

//
// Generate different Compositions
//
Composition spheres[] = new Composition[3];
spheres[0] = sphereFactory.build();

...; // Modify factory configuration
spheres[1] = sphereFactory.build();

...; // Modify factory configuration
spheres[2] = sphereFactory.build();

//
// Now, combine Compositions into a single LayerComposition
//
Dimension size = ...; // e.g. compute based on each sphere's size
LayerComposition sphereCmp = new LayerComposition(size);
Layer sphereLayers[] = new Layer[3];
sphereLayers[0]
   = new CompositionProxyLayer(sphereCmp, spheres[0], Position.LEFT);
sphereLayers[1]
   = new CompositionProxyLayer(sphereCmp, shperes[1], Position.CENTER);
```

```
sphereLayers[2]
    = new CompositionProxyLayer(sphereCmp, spheres[2], Position.RIGHT);

sphereCmp.setLayers(sphereLayers);

//
// Finally, make another CompositionProxyLayer for sphereCmp
//
Position spheresPosition = Position.BOTTOM;
Layer spheresLayer
    = new CompositionProxyLayer(cmp, sphereCmp, spheresPosition);
```

This example shows that it is possible to combine, group, and reuse `CompositionFactory` instances very much like Russian dolls: `LayerComposition` groups `Layer` instances in a single entity that can be reused in another `LayerComposition`, through a `CompositionProxyLayer`. Note that a side effect of this grouping and reuse strategy is that it becomes possible to apply attributes to a set of `Layer` instances.

Imagine, for example, that we need to apply a specific filter not to a single `Layer` object but to multiple ones. One strategy is to attach the filter to each of the `Layer` instances. However, this approach can result in unnecessary processing. Another strategy consists of grouping the relevant `Layer` objects into a separate `LayerComposition` and creating a `CompositionProxyLayer` object to render that separate `LayerComposition`. Then, we can attach our filter to the proxy `Layer`.

Conclusion

The `VolumeComposition` example shows how to use gradient paints creatively to give viewers a sense of volume, depth, and perspective. The techniques we have presented produce visually satisfying results and are used by graphic artists to approximate 3D rendering with 2D graphics tools. Note, however, that our techniques are not mathematically accurate and do not produce 3D-correct results. Our techniques are approximations that work well for purposes such as illustrations or graphs.[2] For an accurate representation of spheres or cylinders, we can turn to other resources such as the Java 3D API.

Our example has also shown how to combine and reuse our work. Usually, it is easier to create simple compositions and reuse them inside other compositions than to create a monolithic composition. The best strategy really depends on the goals of the program.

---

2. We could use our 3D object for graphs because even though they are not necessarily "3D accurate," they can be used to visualize numeric information. For example, the height of our 3D bars can represent numeric values. The same is true for cylinders and spheres.

chapter 17

This chapter presents eleven compositions created with the Graphic Layers Framework (GLF). They illustrate the diversity of graphics features provided by the Java 2D API and the programming flexibility offered by GLF. The compositions further demonstrate the wide range of styles and effects now available to the programmer.

The code for the different compositions is provided on the CD-ROM that accompanies this book: all the gallery examples are part of the com.sun.glf.demos.gallery *package.[1]*

For each composition, you will find the name of the example that produces the composition and a short description of the most interesting technical issues illustrated by the example.

Browsing through the gallery does not require that you have read the book. However, the short explanations will make more sense after you have become familiar with the Java 2D API in Part I and with GLF in Part II.

Brushed Metal

- ■ **BrushedMetal.java** on the CD-ROM
- ■ Example shown in Figure 17.1

Each of the twelve letters that make the four GLF logos are created from the BrushedMetal example, using different settings. This example creates a brushed metal texture completely by program.

An offscreen buffer is filled with a base color. Then, noise is added by randomly painting rectangles of random size and location in the offscreen buffer. Then, a horizontal blur is applied to the texture. Finally, the offscreen buffer is scaled horizontally. Both the horizontal blur and the horizontal scale contribute to create the brushed metal effect.

The resulting texture is used to fill the text (a single letter in each of our twelve examples in Figure 17.2). The background of the composition is lit with LightOp, configured with one single spotlight. This light is positioned at different locations for each row. For example, it is positioned at the top left for the first row and on the right for the last one.

Note how a white separation layer is used to increase the contrast between the text and the background.

---

1. All the examples in the gallery are in that package, except GLFWebDemoOne and GLFWebDemoTwo, which are in the com.sun.glf.demos package.

Figure 17.1 ■
Brushed metal

Recessed Shadow

- **RecessedShadow.java** on the CD-ROM
- Example shown in Figure 17.2

This example shows four different uses of `RecessedShadow`, one shown in full size and other ones scaled down to illustrate variations in text color, texture, or light positioning.

This example reuses the technique we described in Chapter 11 to create a recessed shadow effect. However, the composition is more sophisticated. An image is used as a texture. That texture is colored by `ToneAdjustmentOp`, and light is cast on it by `LightOp`. The resulting image is used to create the background. The text is drawn with the same texture, but after it is colored differently, again with `ToneAdjustmentOp`.

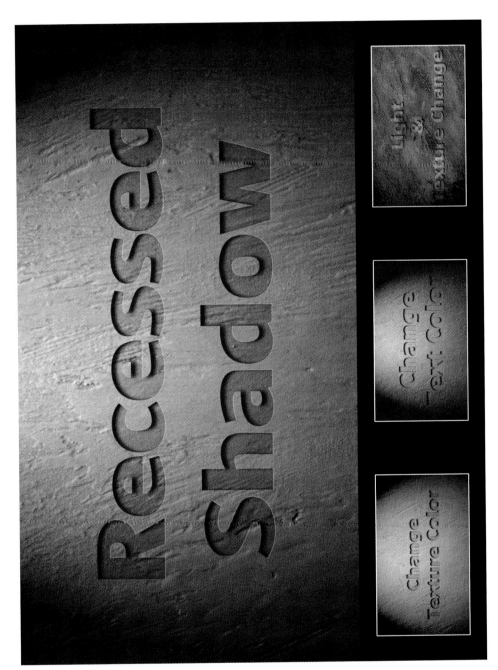

Figure 17.2 ◼
Recessed shadow

Shadow Stand-Out

- **ShadowStandOut.java** on the CD-ROM
- Example shown in Figure 17.3

The ShadowStandout example was used four times and with different settings to create the four images in the figure.

This example shows another shadow effect. It is similar to the drop shadow we introduced in Chapter 11, except that the object (the text, in our example) does not hide the background. This creates a specific visual result that we call a stand-out shadow.

To increase the contrast with the background, the "& volution" text, rendered by a ShapeLayer, is filtered by RescaleOp to increase its brightness. The bottom "&" symbol, also rendered by a ShapeLayer, is inverted by LookupOp.

The symbol shows what the ampersand symbol used to look like when it was still close to the "et" letters it represents. That symbol has evolved into the "&" symbol we now use.

GALLERY

Figure 17.3 ■
Shadow stand out

GALLERY

GLF Logo

- **GLFWebDemoTwo.java** on the CD–ROM
- Example shown in Figure 17.4

The Graphic Layers Framework logo is a case study that investigates how to utilize Java 2D's extensible design. The border is drawn by two separate layers, one using `Shape-Stroke` (an extension of the `Stroke` interface) and one using `ColorComposite` (an extension of the `Composite` interface). The circular text is built by `BumpTransform` (which provides nonlinear transforms of coordinates), filled with `RadialGradientPaintExt` (a multicolor radial paint that implements the `Paint` interface) and filtered with `LightOp` (a `BufferedImageOp` implementation).

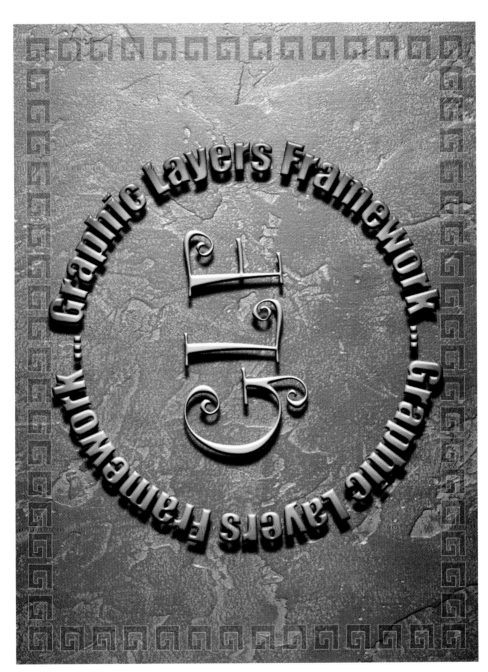

Figure 17.4 ■
GLF logo

Gradient Waves

- **GLFWebDemoOne.java** on the CD-ROM
- Example shown in Figure 17.5

This example, programmed with GLF, uses standard Java 2D features exclusively. It shows how alpha compositing can be used for creative rendering effects. For example, the "Cool" text, which seems to be partly in the water, is composited with the background waves. Similarly, the "Hot &" text's shadow fades in the background because `Gradient-Paint` is used to fill it and one of the gradient colors is fully transparent.

GALLERY

Figure 17.5 ■
Gradient waves

Text Flowers

- **TextFlowers.java** on the CD-ROM
- Example shown in Figure 17.6

The figure shows four different outputs created by the TextFlowers example, using different settings for the configuration parameters.

This example is a modest tribute to Wucius Wong [Wong1987] and his work on color design. The example shows how to achieve striking results simply. The same text ("GLF" using a fancy font) is drawn several times at different angles, rotating about the bottom-left corner of the text bounds. Each time the text is rendered, the brightness of the color used to fill it is increased. The example can be configured to cycle an arbitrary number of times between a minimum and a maximum brightness. Similarly, the example can draw the text a configurable number of times.

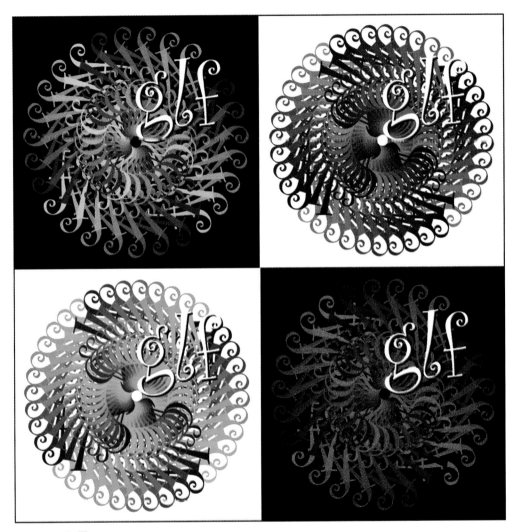

Figure 17.6 ■
Text flowers

Soft Focus

- **SoftFocus.java** on the CD-ROM
- Example shown in Figure 17.7

The soft focus effect is achieved by compositing an image with its blurred version. This example shows how photofinishing techniques can be implemented with the Java 2D API. Here, the original images are shown on the left. The image after a soft focus effect has been applied is shown at the top.

Figure 17.7 ■
Soft focus

Sunset

- **SunSet.java** on the CD-ROM
- Example shown in Figure 17.8

Each of the four sunsets in the figure was created by the `SunSet` example, using different settings.

This is another type of sky and sun rendering, different from the one we discuss in Chapter 16. Here, the sky is filled with `GradientPaintExt`, the multicolor, linear, gradient paint implementation of the `Paint` interface that is part of GLF. The sun is rendered with `RadialGradientPaintExt`, another implementation of the `Paint` interface. Note that to create a fuzzy edge on the outside of the sun, the radial paint is initialized with a fully transparent paint so that the sun appears to fade out into the sky.

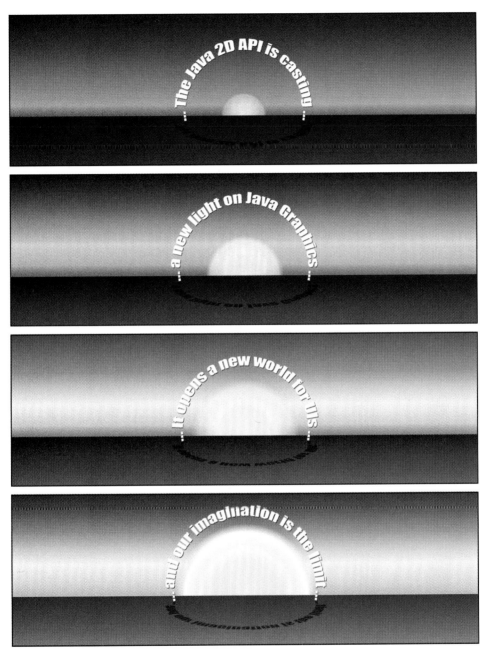

Figure 17.8 ■
Sunset

Shape Texture

- **ShapeSplatter.java** on the CD–ROM
- Example shown in Figure 17.9

This example illustrates different strategies for interpolating colors. In each example, the same text is rendered multiple times, each time scaled up and translated a little bit.

In the top example, the color varies between an initial value and a destination hue value. In-between colors use interpolated hues. In other words, this example interpolates colors in the HSV space. If you experiment with this example, you will see that it can create surprising results because hue interpolation is not very intuitive.

The bottom example uses brightness interpolation: the color varies between an initial value and a destination brightness. Again, interpolation happens in HSV space, but the result is more intuitive.

The background texture is created by painting shapes at random locations, applying random rotations and scales. It is another example of texture created with the API only (that is, without using other resources, such as images).

Figure 17.9 ■
Shape textures

Lookup Pattern

- **LookupParts.java** on the CD-ROM
- Example shown in Figure 17.10

This example shows a modest tribute to the work of Andy Warhol. The same image is reused over and over (36 times exactly), but manipulated a little differently each time. If you separate the composition into four parts—top left, top right, bottom left, and bottom right—you can see that the same image is painted nine times in each of these parts with different transparency values: fully opaque in the upper-left corner and almost fully transparent in the lower-right corner. The four images used as a base for each quarter are built from an RGB image that is processed by a `LookupOp` filter, to reduce to eight the number of colors used in the image, and by a `BandCombineOp` filter, to swap the image colors, creating different results for each quarter of the image.

Figure 17.10 ■
Lookup pattern

Lights

- **Lights.java** on the CD-ROM
- Example shown in Figure 17.11

This example illustrates most of the things you can do with the GLF `LightOp` filter: embossing (text), texturizing (background), and spotlight ramps (top of image). Combined, these features can create striking results, as in our example. Note, however, that `LightOp` is computation intensive and that the larger the filtered image size, number of lights, and texture image sizes are, the longer the processing will be.

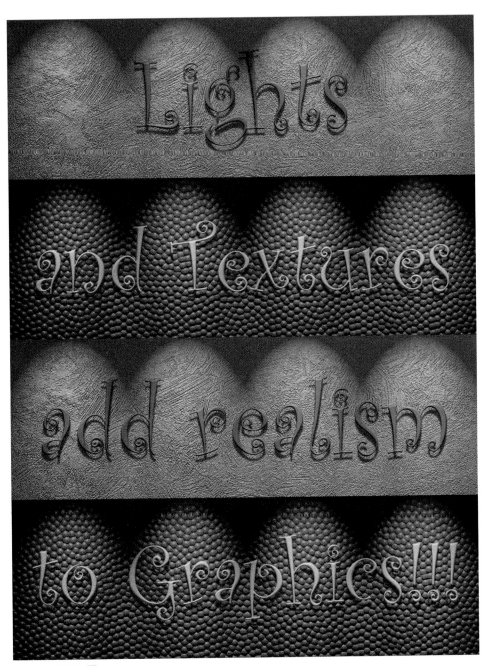

Figure 17.11 ◼
Lights

BIBLIOGRAPHY

[Adobe98] *PostScript® Language Reference Manual*, Second Edition, Adobe Systems Incorporated. Addison Wesley, ISBN 0-201-18127-4.

[Campione 1998] *The Java Tutorial*, Second Edition, Mary Campione and Kathy Walrath. Addison Wesley, ISBN 0-201-131007-4.

[Crane 1997] *A Simplified Approach to Image Processing*, Randy Crane. Prentice Hall, ISBN 0-13-226416-1.

[Englander 1997] *Developing Java Beans*, Robert Englander. O'Reilly & Associates, Inc., ISBN 1-56592-289-1.

[Flanagan 1997] *Java in a Nutshell*, Second Edition, David Flanagan. O'Reilly & Associates, Inc., ISBN 1-56592-262-X.

[Foley 1997] *Computer Graphics, Principles and Practice*, James D. Foley, Andries van Dam, Steven K. Feiner, and John F. Hughes. Addison Wesley, ISBN 0-201-84840-6.

[Giorgianni 1998] *Digital Color Management, Encoding Solutions*, Edward J. Giorgianni and Thomas E. Madden. Addison Wesley, ISBN 0-201-63426-0.

[Hearn 1997] *Computer Graphics*, Second Edition, Donald Hearn and M. Pauline Baker. Prentice Hall, ISBN 0-13-530924-7.

[Geary 1998] *Graphic Java, Mastering the JFC, Volume 1: AWT*, David M. Geary. Prentice Hall, ISBN 0-13-079666-2.

[Geary 1999] *Graphic Java, Mastering the JFC, Volume 2: Swing*, David M. Geary. Prentice Hall, ISBN 0-13-079667-0.

[Porter 1984] *Compositing Digital Images*, T. Porter and T. Duff. SIGGRAPH 84, 253–259.

[Pratt 1997] *Developing Visual Applications. XIL™: An Imaging Foundation Library*, William K Pratt. Prentice Hall, ISBN 0-13-461948.

[Smeijers 1996] *Counter punch, making type in the sixteenth century, designing typefaces now,* Fred Smeijers. Hyphen Press, ISBN 0-907259-06-5.

[UNICODE97] *The Unicode Standard,* Version 2.0, The Unicode Consortium. Addison Wesley Developers Press, ISBN 0-201-48345-9.

[Wong 1987] *Principles of Color Design,* Wucius Wong. Van Nostrand Reinhold, ISBN 0-442-29284-8.

INDEX

R

LICENSE AGREEMENT AND LIMITED WARRANTY

READ THE FOLLOWING TERMS AND CONDITIONS CAREFULLY BEFORE OPENING THIS SOFTWARE MEDIA PACKAGE. THIS LEGAL DOCUMENT IS AN AGREEMENT BETWEEN YOU AND PRENTICE-HALL, INC. (THE "COMPANY"). BY OPENING THIS SEALED SOFTWARE MEDIA PACKAGE, YOU ARE AGREEING TO BE BOUND BY THESE TERMS AND CONDITIONS. IF YOU DO NOT AGREE WITH THESE TERMS AND CONDITIONS, DO NOT OPEN THE SOFTWARE MEDIA PACKAGE. PROMPTLY RETURN THE UNOPENED SOFTWARE MEDIA PACKAGE AND ALL ACCOMPANYING ITEMS TO THE PLACE YOU OBTAINED THEM FOR A FULL REFUND OF ANY SUMS YOU HAVE PAID.

1.   **GRANT OF LICENSE:** In consideration of your payment of the license fee, which is part of the price you paid for this product, and your agreement to abide by the terms and conditions of this Agreement, the Company grants to you a nonexclusive right to use and display the copy of the enclosed software program (hereinafter the "SOFTWARE") on a single computer (i.e., with a single CPU) at a single location so long as you comply with the terms of this Agreement. The Company reserves all rights not expressly granted to you under this Agreement.

2.   **OWNERSHIP OF SOFTWARE:** You own only the magnetic or physical media (the enclosed software media) on which the SOFTWARE is recorded or fixed, but the Company retains all the rights, title, and ownership to the SOFTWARE recorded on the original software media copy(ies) and all subsequent copies of the SOFTWARE, regardless of the form or media on which the original or other copies may exist. This license is not a sale of the original SOFTWARE or any copy to you.

3.   **COPY RESTRICTIONS:** This SOFTWARE and the accompanying printed materials and user manual (the "Documentation") are the subject of copyright. You may not copy the Documentation or the SOFTWARE, except that you may make a single copy of the SOFTWARE for backup or archival purposes only. You may be held legally responsible for any copying or copyright infringement which is caused or encouraged by your failure to abide by the terms of this restriction.

4.   **USE RESTRICTIONS:** You may not network the SOFTWARE or otherwise use it on more than one computer or computer terminal at the same time. You may physically transfer the SOFTWARE from one computer to another provided that the SOFTWARE is used on only one computer at a time. You may not distribute copies of the SOFTWARE or Documentation to others. You may not reverse engineer, disassemble, decompile, modify, adapt, translate, or create derivative works based on the SOFTWARE or the Documentation without the prior written consent of the Company.

5.   **TRANSFER RESTRICTIONS:** The enclosed SOFTWARE is licensed only to you and may not be transferred to any one else without the prior written consent of the Company. Any unauthorized transfer of the SOFTWARE shall result in the immediate termination of this Agreement.

6.   **TERMINATION:** This license is effective until terminated. This license will terminate automatically without notice from the Company and become null and void if you fail to comply with any provisions or limitations of this license. Upon termination, you shall destroy the Documentation and all copies of the SOFTWARE. All provisions of this Agreement as to warranties, limitation of liability, remedies or damages, and our ownership rights shall survive termination.

7.   **MISCELLANEOUS:** This Agreement shall be construed in accordance with the laws of the United States of America and the State of New York and shall benefit the Company, its affiliates, and assignees.

8.   **LIMITED WARRANTY AND DISCLAIMER OF WARRANTY:** The Company warrants that the SOFTWARE, when properly used in accordance with the Documentation, will operate in substantial conformity with the description of the SOFTWARE set forth in the Documentation. The Company does not warrant that the SOFTWARE will meet your requirements or that the operation of the SOFTWARE will be uninterrupted or error-free. The Company warrants that the media on which the SOFTWARE is delivered shall be free from defects in materials and workmanship under normal use for a period of thirty (30) days from the date of your purchase. Your only remedy and the Company's only obligation under these limited warranties is, at the Company's option, return of the warranted item for a refund of any amounts paid by you or replacement of the item. Any replacement of SOFTWARE or media under the warranties shall not extend the original warranty period. The limited warranty set forth above shall not apply to any SOFTWARE which the Company determines in good faith has been subject to misuse, neglect, improper installation, repair, alteration, or dam-

age by you. EXCEPT FOR THE EXPRESSED WARRANTIES SET FORTH ABOVE, THE COMPANY DISCLAIMS ALL WARRANTIES, EXPRESS OR IMPLIED, INCLUDING WITHOUT LIMITATION, THE IMPLIED WARRANTIES OF MERCHANTABILITY AND FITNESS FOR A PARTICULAR PURPOSE. EXCEPT FOR THE EXPRESS WARRANTY SET FORTH ABOVE, THE COMPANY DOES NOT WARRANT, GUARANTEE, OR MAKE ANY REPRESENTATION REGARDING THE USE OR THE RESULTS OF THE USE OF THE SOFTWARE IN TERMS OF ITS CORRECTNESS, ACCURACY, RELIABILITY, CURRENTNESS, OR OTHERWISE.

IN NO EVENT, SHALL THE COMPANY OR ITS EMPLOYEES, AGENTS, SUPPLIERS, OR CONTRACTORS BE LIABLE FOR ANY INCIDENTAL, INDIRECT, SPECIAL, OR CONSEQUENTIAL DAMAGES ARISING OUT OF OR IN CONNECTION WITH THE LICENSE GRANTED UNDER THIS AGREEMENT, OR FOR LOSS OF USE, LOSS OF DATA, LOSS OF INCOME OR PROFIT, OR OTHER LOSSES, SUSTAINED AS A RESULT OF INJURY TO ANY PERSON, OR LOSS OF OR DAMAGE TO PROPERTY, OR CLAIMS OF THIRD PARTIES, EVEN IF THE COMPANY OR AN AUTHORIZED REPRESENTATIVE OF THE COMPANY HAS BEEN ADVISED OF THE POSSIBILITY OF SUCH DAMAGES. IN NO EVENT SHALL LIABILITY OF THE COMPANY FOR DAMAGES WITH RESPECT TO THE SOFTWARE EXCEED THE AMOUNTS ACTUALLY PAID BY YOU, IF ANY, FOR THE SOFTWARE.

SOME JURISDICTIONS DO NOT ALLOW THE LIMITATION OF IMPLIED WARRANTIES OR LIABILITY FOR INCIDENTAL, INDIRECT, SPECIAL, OR CONSEQUENTIAL DAMAGES, SO THE ABOVE LIMITATIONS MAY NOT ALWAYS APPLY. THE WARRANTIES IN THIS AGREEMENT GIVE YOU SPECIFIC LEGAL RIGHTS AND YOU MAY ALSO HAVE OTHER RIGHTS WHICH VARY IN ACCORDANCE WITH LOCAL LAW.

ACKNOWLEDGMENT

YOU ACKNOWLEDGE THAT YOU HAVE READ THIS AGREEMENT, UNDERSTAND IT, AND AGREE TO BE BOUND BY ITS TERMS AND CONDITIONS. YOU ALSO AGREE THAT THIS AGREEMENT IS THE COMPLETE AND EXCLUSIVE STATEMENT OF THE AGREEMENT BETWEEN YOU AND THE COMPANY AND SUPERSEDES ALL PROPOSALS OR PRIOR AGREEMENTS, ORAL, OR WRITTEN, AND ANY OTHER COMMUNICATIONS BETWEEN YOU AND THE COMPANY OR ANY REPRESENTATIVE OF THE COMPANY RELATING TO THE SUBJECT MATTER OF THIS AGREEMENT.

Should you have any questions concerning this Agreement or if you wish to contact the Company for any reason, please contact in writing at the address below.

Robin Short
Prentice Hall PTR
One Lake Street
Upper Saddle River, New Jersey 07458

ABOUT THE CD-ROM

The CD-ROM contains the Graphic Layers Framework (GLF) and all the examples included in this book. Please, refer to the preface of the book for details on how to install and run the software included on the CD-ROM.

Technical Support

Prentice Hall does not offer technical support for this software. However, if there is a problem with the media, you may obtain a replacement copy by e-mailing us with your problem at:

disc_exchange@prenhall.com